Sometimes the Blues

The Letters and Diaries of Frank Hammon,
a Lonely Frontiersman in Globe
and Phoenix, 1882–1889

Susan Clardy

By Susan Clardy

Foreword by Don Dedera

The Arizona Historical Society
Tucson

Library of Congress Cataloging-in-Publication Data

Clardy, Susan
   Sometimes the blues : the letters and diaries of Frank Hammon, a lonely
frontiersman in Globe and Phoenix, 1882-1889 / by Susan Clardy ; foreword
by Don Dedera.
      p. cm.
   Includes bibliographical references and index.
   ISBN 0-910037-47 (alk. paper)
      1. Hammon, Frank Malcolm, 1855-1906. 2. Pioneers—Arizona—Globe—
Biography. 3. Pioneers—Arizona—Phoenix—Biography. 4. Globe (Ariz.)—
Biography. 5. Phoenix (Ariz.)—Biography. 6. Frontier and pioneer life—
Arizona—Globe. 7. Frontier and pioneer life—Arizona—Phoenix. 8. Globe
(Ariz.)—History—19th century. 9. Phoenix (Ariz.)—History—19th century.
I. Hammon, Frank Malcolm, 1855-1906. II. Arizona Historical Society.
III. Title.

F819.G5C58 2007
979.1'7304092—dc22
[B]   2006043070

To Mom, Dad, and cousin Harvey.

They "crossed the river" before I realized my dream.

TABLE OF CONTENTS

Foreword

At the time, I had no clear motive for my travel to California's Central Valley. Maybe a book. Probably not. In early summer 1997, Ruth and Aaron Cohen, proprietors of the Guidon Bookstore in Scottsdale, Arizona, had urged me to go. Our forty-year friendship and Ruth's ominous illness certainly were factors. I owed them. But for making that trip neither Cohen offered a compelling reason beyond, "We've had a call from an interesting woman who possesses the original diaries kept by her great-grandfather during the 1880s on the Arizona frontier."

Of all people, the Cohens should have been leery of yet another unevaluated, unpublished personal journal. Such artifacts are about as rare as family Bibles, bane of antiquarian book dealers everywhere. (Along with old *McGuffy's Readers*, printed in warehouse lots.) The week scarcely passes but a stranger offers to sell the Guidon a handsome edition of the Good Book wherein is documented the genealogy of some branch of mostly deceased and rather ordinary humanity. Except to surviving kin, they are of little historical or literary value. The same may be said as a rule of diaries and journals—unless penciled by a trooper under fire with the command of George Armstrong Custer on the Little Bighorn in late June 1876. Not many of those!

At any rate, I took a Sunday morning flight from Phoenix to Fresno to be met by Susan Clardy, a young attractive California grandmother of abounding curiosity and sensitivity, and vast ignorance of the cold realities of researching, writing, and publishing. While that judgment may seem harsh and ungallant, in perfect hindsight she might allow the same. In fact, had she realized the extent of her naiveté, she might have abandoned, then and there, a project that soon would become her obsession.

Over lunch that Sunday, Susan unveiled a clutch of notebooks, original correspondence, and antique photographs associated with her great-grandparents, Frank Malcolm Hammon and Daisy Lee Howell, and their considerable extended and scattered clan. In a concentrated labor of three months, employing bright light and a magnifying glass, Susan had deciphered most of the handwriting, much

i

of it faded, stained, and casually spelled and punctuated. She had typed the raw data into her personal computer.

"My first goal was to put the material into a form that could be read and enjoyed by Frank and Daisy's large number of descendants," Susan said, "but now I am beginning to believe that there is greater historical significance. And I wonder if I should write a book."

Lord love her, I thought to myself, there is no book here for me. She has decided to take on this task herself, and there is nothing that I can do to dissuade her. Better prepare her for the letdown likely when she seeks a publisher for her finished manuscript. So I related the saga of Haldane (Buzz) Halstrom, a gas station attendant of Coqville, Oregon, who long ago took it into his head to challenge the boiling rapids at the bottom of the Grand Canyon. Buzz felled a cedar tree, sawed it into planks, and crafted a fifteen-foot skiff. In October 1937 he launched in Wyoming. Alarmed by sensational press coverage, readers worried when Buzz disappeared down the racing Colorado River, like a moth down a bathtub drain. The world could only wait...and wait. Seven weeks later into Lake Mead drifted Buzz and his boat, to be ambushed by film and book agents with offers of fame and fortune. But the hero of the first recorded solitary run through the gut of the Grand spurned them all, explaining, "I find that I have already had my reward, in the doing of the thing." My best advice to Susan: let her journey be her destination.

Not that the chronicles of Frank Hammon were without promise. In 1878, at age twenty-three, this educated Easterner seeking adventure had accompanied an older cousin to the mining boomtown of Globe, Arizona. Shortly the cousin moved on, leaving Frank to go partners in a tobacco-stationery-periodicals shop almost within the shade of the "hanging tree" that dominated Globe's twisting, plunging main street. Frank made entries into his diaries over most of a decade. While primarily a reminder of his money debts and debtors, Frank's thumbnail notes make reference to a roll call of Arizona characters: renegade Indians Nantia-tish and the Apache Kid, luckless sheriffs George Shute and Glenn Reynolds, eventful gunmen Black Jack Newman and Ed Tewksbury, unique politicians George W.P. Hunt and J.W. Wentworth, irresistible achievers Al Sieber and a score of fascinating women friends. By nature taciturn, Frank could cram an epic into the most succinct entry: "George felt better and we harnessed up and came to town. Found house burned. Otherwise nothing new."

Frank's penchant for brevity scarcely muted his pride in his bride, his prospering cattle ranch and town investment properties, and swiftly arriving one after the other, his three children. Then, the wrenching shock of his letter to his parents, "I have had a terrible affliction. We buried Daisy today." Somehow Frank Hammon, still in his twenties, saw to the needs of his motherless brood. He deflected his haunting loneliness, and for his offspring vowed, "I hereby resolve to play no more cards, to drink no more liquor during this year.... I need help from above to enable me to do right, and for it I do pray. I cannot afford to spend any money on these foolish things, when my little ones need it."

The man worked, oh, how he worked. He handled explosives, shoveled ore, guarded desperate criminals, delivered milk, graded roads, sold insurance, collected taxes, branded calves, and wore a badge. He played a little, too, jotting down his involvement in lawn parties, holiday celebrations, dramatic presentations, church socials and lodge activities. Before his days were done he would cultivate and sell fruit trees all over the West, and even serve as a host at the Chicago World's Fair.

Susan's odyssey as investigator and narrator rivaled that of her forebear. In five extended visits she delved into the archives and libraries of Arizona. She walked the ground, past faint foundations and unmarked graves; pored over the ink and newsprint of another age; felt the perverse wind and pitiless sun of a still-uncrowded, elementary rural Arizona; acquired a broad academic perspective and the specific photographic images that lend larger meaning to the often hasty, sketchy scribblings of Frank Hammon. She grew with his story, and gave life to it. In the "doing of the thing," Susan succeeded as the "grassroots historian" so highly regarded by the late Dr. C. L. Sonnichsen. In praising the amateur researcher, the history buff, the family tree tender, Dr. Sonnichsen reminded us, "The fact that we have a recorded past distinguishes us from the other animals and gives us something in common with the hosts in heaven, where St. Peter is said to keep careful records. With a past, we can profit from our mistakes and become civilized."

In the end, with her work in our hands, it is obvious that Susan Clardy was not only the writer who should have created this book; she was the only one who could have done it. And whatever Ruth Cohen had in mind when she was alive and offering advice almost a decade ago, today I believe she would be delighted with the result.

Don Dedera

Introduction

Feeling like intruders, we rummaged through my parents' personal items in drawers and closets. As my sisters and I moved our parents from their Midwest home to a retirement facility, the daunting task led down a familiar path. Each item jogged a remembrance from long ago: a drawer's scent, 1940s cooking utensils, Dad's WWII uniform, old photos. Transported on a nostalgic journey, we relived our childhood. What began as a job of dread became a labor of love and the beginning of my journey.

The cedar chest in the attic contained a black metal box carefully placed under mother's wedding gown. Inside, small leather books, yellowed correspondence, and faded photos lay waiting for my discovery. As I perused my obscure ancestors' faded script, my questions begged answers: Who were Frank and Daisy Hammon? Where was Globe City, Arizona? Unearthing my great-grandparent's letters and diaries inspired my search for their story. Their lives, reduced to words on paper, deserved validation.

With great care, I opened each yellowed letter and attempted to read the faded longhand. As I studied the images of stoic faces and somber expressions, I sought to perceive their essence. Their eyes reflected struggle and dignity. The black worn diaries recorded a different time, a different place, and a story.

Into the wee morning hours, I strained to read Frank's small, neat script in his leather-bound journals. His monogrammed gold stickpin tucked in a back pocket hinted at an untold tale. I perused Daisy's newsy but intermittent correspondence and Frank's heartrending letters home. In the bottom of the box lay Daisy's worn copy of Longfellow's poetry and Frank's inscribed Bible with a wildflower pressed between the Psalms.

These items suggested an intriguing story of love, death, danger, unrealized dreams, and faith. The diary entries contained the thoughts of a young Pennsylvania man in territorial Arizona, but to fully grasp their meaning required research. He chronicled names, places, and events in the Arizona territory between 1882 and 1889. How did Frank Hammon fit into these events? Who were the people casually mentioned daily in his journal? Of what significance were the events Frank referred to? How did these diaries survive over a century?

Answers to these questions required historical perspective. I launched myself in the pursuit. First, I needed to understand territorial history prior to Frank's arrival. I needed to absorb the history of the little mining camp precariously perched on a creek in Arizona's Pinal Mountains. My journey took me to Phoenix, then over to Globe.

Entering Globe, mountainous waste from smelter and mine was a grimy indication of spent wealth. Evidences of twentieth-century technology couldn't be ignored. I strained to imagine the beautiful, unblemished country as it appeared to the early settlers, and tried to reconcile its remarkable history with its present culture.

Certain aspects of the human spirit remain. Globe's descendants of the original pioneers exhibit the same resilience and hospitable manner of their ancestors. The oldtimers still enhance yarns told by their grandparents. These are legends based on fact, altered by bias, and twisted to protect future generations. Frontier newspaper reports varied from day to day. Disappearance of notable *Arizona Silver Belt* issues makes it difficult to assess the folklore. Only a few worn diaries remain to point an inquiring descendant in the right direction.

By matching diary entries with newspaper accounts, history books, and county records, I pieced together a comprehensive look at early Globe. Violent episodes enlivened Globe's struggle to become a peaceful community. An old sycamore tree in "dead man's flat" took on a new meaning. Here, two lives ended at the ends of ropes.

Frank Hammon's letters are sparse but revealing; his diaries offer a dull account of a tedious existence. Some empty pages reflect a lawman's caution. Given the eventful impulses of frontier Globe, his omissions often reveal more than his entries. In such cases, other historical sources help explain his silence. Wherever human names appear in Frank's diaries, additional biographical information should appear in an endnote or in text. This was not always possible. Many times incomplete data, missing newspaper issues, and lost documents preclude elaboration on an individual or an event.

Interpreting Frank's brief journal entries became this writer's greatest challenge. This quest often led down meandering paths that intersected upon a particular bit of information. Many times that crucial bit of information proved necessary to clarify an event that Frank failed to sufficiently describe. Sometimes his brief account led to a discovery casting light on a historically misinterpreted action. Though some statements provided the impetus for investigating well-documented Globe events, Frank Hammon's entries occasionally contradict the accounts of respected historical writers.

I have reconstructed Frank's life employing the attitudes, phrases, and terminology of that period in history. Some of his expressions are inexcusable in today's society; I do not ascribe to their use. If I have inadvertently offended anyone by including them, I apologize. To maintain the integrity of the original letters and diaries, all spelling and expressions remain as written. However, I have taken some liberties with punctuation for easier reading.

As I journeyed, Arizona's remarkable history came alive. Globe became more than a dot on the map; the handsome man in the faded pictures developed a personality. Through extensive probing, I found answers to my questions, and the nature of Frank's character emerged. With his essence exposed, I vicariously experienced Frank's disappointments, desires, and distress, establishing an emotional connection beyond my expectations. Frank's footsteps had beckoned me; his poignant words propelled me; my introspection brought a new self-understanding. Cajoled by happenstance and coincidences, I questioned if they were coincidences after all.

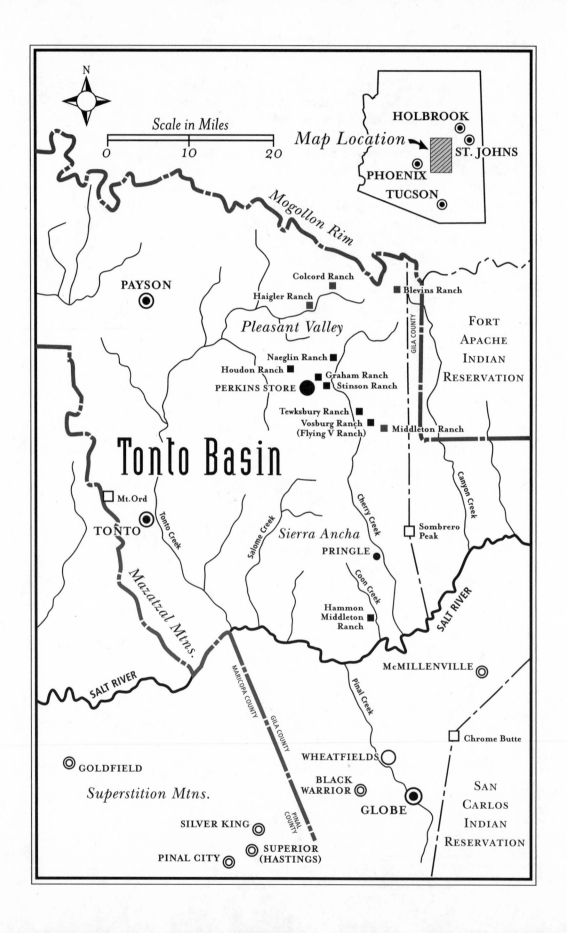

Part One

The Letters

It is a noble faculty of our nature which enables us to connect...

with what is distant in place or time... to hold communion at

once with our ancestors and our posterity...

DANIEL WEBSTER

Chapter One

PATHS UNKNOWN

My childhood home sat empty. The bare rooms that
once resonated with chatter echoed in sad silence. An eerie sensation
passed over me as I sat cross-legged on the floor sifting through the
remainders of Mom's cedar chest. Each item conjured up a remembrance. Sorting through the treasures, I noticed the black metal box
placed under mother's wedding gown. As I opened the box, a stack of
envelopes tied with a deteriorated ribbon caught my attention.
I untied the knot; the ribbon disintegrated. Selecting from the top,
I carefully removed a letter from its yellowed envelope. The postmark
read, Globe City, Arizona Territory, March 6, 1882. With only a
dim overhead light, I strained to read the faded script.

Frank Hammon's letter to his sister, Bertie,
March 6, 1882. Author's collection.

Dear Sister Bertie,

    I was married on Mch 1st to a beautiful and good young lady
here. Her name was—Daisy Howell. It was not our intention to
get married so soon but her mother who is lying at the point of
death requested it, and we got married to please her. We had been
engaged some time. I wish you could see her you could not help but
love her. She is so beautiful modest and good. I love her truly and
am satisfied I shall never regret it

    I am now old enough to settle down have a good business and
bright prospects. Now I must close for this time as I am buisy and
have several letters to write

Yours Truly
Frank M. Hammon

    A letter from my great-grandfather lay in my hand. As I picked up the next envelope,
I wondered if these letters and diaries would answer my questions. Who was Daisy Howell?
Where was Globe City, Arizona? What lured Frank into the uncivilized territory?

Frank M. Hammon in
San Francisco, ca. 1878.
AUTHOR'S COLLECTION.

Displaced, disheartened southerners drifted to Arizona from their war-torn homeland. Dedicated Mormon families advanced their caravans across the continent determined to find inexpensive farmland and religious freedom. Discouraged miners arrived from depleted California gold fields in search of riches. Texas cattlemen drove their herds to the lush, unencumbered rangeland above the Salt River. Immigrants arrived in their adopted territory armed with hope. Undesirables, escaping checkered pasts, sought refuge in Arizona's isolation. They rightfully believed the law did not extend into Arizona's unexplored expanses. Some searched for opportunities and adventure, all hoped for a new life. Cousins Frank Malcolm Hammon and Wendell Philucius Hammon joined this migration.

The two Hammons set out for Globe City, Arizona, sometime in 1878. The newly established town, located seventy-five miles east of Phoenix, must have seemed thousands of miles away to the young adventurers. The formidable Superstition Mountains rising vertically out of the desert needed to be circumvented. The amber formations ascended to form a barrier between the desert lowlands to the west and rugged Pinal range to the east.

From the west, no wagon roads existed, only a narrow mountain path. Sculpted from perpendicular rock walls, the trail via Picket Post Mountain and the Silver King Mine left no room for the careless slip of a hoof. Ancient powerful forces pushed skyward the sienna strata dotted with manzanita, cactus, and catclaw. Hundreds of feet above the canyon floor, pillar-like formations, topped by precariously balanced boulders, stood resolute against the casual intruder.

Perhaps the Hammon men arrived by wagon over the easier route, through the southern Gila River towns of Florence and Riverside. Twelve miles east of Globe City lay the San Carlos Indian Reservation, home to both peaceful and hostile Apaches. Reservation roads were avoided. The northern route, known today as the Apache Trail, followed the Salt River. Where the Pinal Creek flowed into the Salt River, the trail turned south following the waterway into Globe City. A community complaint written to the postmaster general in January 1879 gives insight into the road conditions:

> The route as now run is via Picket Post and Silver King by wagon road and then by trail for 35 miles by jackasses, over the most difficult mountain passes in the Territory of Arizona. Mail matter coming to hand broken and in pieces and wet when the weather is stormy.[1]

The town itself sprawled across the rolling foothills between the Pinal and Apache mountain ranges. Penetrating the area required motivation and determination. The promise of rich mineral deposits provided the motivation; the Hammon men had determination.

The 1873 establishment of the San Carlos Reservation had promoted a false sense of security to the mass of newcomers. The Hammons, along with hundreds of other settlers, ignored the dangers, staked their claims, and settled on the Apaches' former homeland. As the cultures clashed, Globe's citizens paid a heavy price.[2]

Surveyor A.G. Pendleton laid out the newly established town in 1876; the post office opened on December 22, 1877; Globe officially became a municipality on May 1, 1878. By that time, flimsy wooden shacks had replaced the miners' tents clustered along the east bank of Pinal Creek. A potholed mule trail and an occasional boardwalk lined with saloons and storefronts constituted the main thoroughfare. With its new growth, the rough-and-tumble town took on a permanent appearance. Pinal Creek flowed through the town, supplying water to the mills down creek. The valley widened towards the north, where a small settlement of farmers irrigated crops. It was known as Wheatfields.[3]

The *Arizona Sentinel,* in October 1877, described Globe the year before Frank and Wendell Hammon arrived:

> a group of closely built houses… merchants are carrying stocks of goods that indicate a large population scattered among the neighboring mountains. Saloons abound and flourish as they only can in a thrifty mining community. Here the town spreads out and boasts of several streets. A number of livery stables destitute of carriages denote the absence of good roads around here, and the equestrian habit of travelers.

What inspired the Hammon cousins to venture west? Had the postwar depression in northeastern Pennsylvania driven them to California? Or had San Francisco newspaper reports of Arizona opportunities captured their imaginations? Maybe Scott Bell, their Pennsylvania friend, convinced them of the opportunities in Globe City.

Twenty-one-year-old Wendell P. Hammon first ventured to San Francisco from Conneautville, Pennsylvania, in 1875 after attending Pennsylvania State Normal School at Edinboro. Following two years of college, he landed a job in San Francisco with L. Green & Sons, a large fruit importing company from Perry, Ohio.[4]

Frank Hammon remained in Pennsylvania to attend an agricultural college. About 1877, twenty-two-year-old Frank joined his cousin in San Francisco. The following year, the twosome appeared in Globe, Arizona, enticed by the promise of lucrative mining ventures and business opportunities.[5]

Frank Hammon joined Scott Bell as proprietors of one of Globe's earliest business establishments, the News Depot. They conducted their Broad Street business in a small frame building in the shade of a sycamore tree. Frank's shop specialized in the sale of newspapers from most major cities across the continent. Homesick settlers welcomed current news from home. Newspapers, tobacco, and backroom billiards offered welcome diversions to a miner's dull existence. The old sycamore in front of the News Depot produced a shady gathering place for local folks and weary mule trains. It played a significant role in early Globe history.

Farmer-miner Francis "Frank" N. Howell frequented Frank Hammon's News Depot. Francis preceded his family to Globe City in 1878 and penetrated the forbidding Pinal Mountains in search of its hidden treasures. The risks were great, but with few successes in life, he had nothing to lose. His family's well being depended upon his mining and farming ventures, so he faced the risks. Eleanor Howell and their three children remained in Sonoma County, California, with her family. They waited to join him or looked forward to his return home.[6]

Francis's lifelong search for gold began at age eighteen, when he left Missouri for El Dorado County, California, and the Gold Rush. Once again, at age forty-six, gold fever gripped him. Francis left his family on their Santa Rosa, California, farm to chase his dreams. Undeterred by the dangers or isolation of Globe, he joined the mass influx of fortune-seekers that infiltrated the area following the establishment of the San Carlos Reservation.[7]

In October 1878, Scott Bell witnessed the location of the Howell gold mine two miles south of Pinto Creek and ten miles west of Globe. Frank Howell, J. H. Eaton, Hiram Palmer, and Wm. M. Luther registered the claim. It produced enough gold for Howell to summon his family to Globe.[8]

The Hammon cousins and Scott Bell rented rooms from English butcher Joseph Redman and his wife Elizabeth. The adobe house stood on the corner of Broad and Mesquite streets near the News Depot. In April 1880, Frank Hammon took the first step toward becoming a permanent Globe resident. He purchased

Wendell P. Hammon.
JOHN HAMMON COLLECTION.

Broad Street, Globe, ca. 1882. The "hanging tree" stands across from the News Depot on left. ASLAPR #96-3569.

the adobe house from the Englishman as an investment in Globe's continued growth.[9]

In spite of the booming economy, Scott Bell sold his half of the News Depot to Charles Taylor and returned to Pennsylvania. Frank Hammon, with his new partner, expanded inventory in response to the community's growing demands. The *Arizona Silver Belt,* under Judge Aaron Hackney, provided an invaluable forum for advertising the expanding business: "A large assortment of Photograph and Autograph Albums at Hammon & Taylor."[10]

Prospectors trekked from one mining camp to another, took the most abundant and accessible gold and silver, then moved on to other "diggings." By the end of 1880, silver mining in Globe became unprofitable and the copper boom began. Within a year, the value of copper ore surpassed that of silver. San Francisco speculators who had dominated the local mining companies, and "who had gutted the Comstock lode by 1880," gave up on the sluggish earnings from extracting Arizona copper ore. Purchasers from New York and Boston moved in to take over the operations. Globe's workforce converted from transitory miners extracting valuable metal to salaried employees mining industrial ores.[11]

The slow profits combined with lovesickness probably sent "Mine Operator" Wendell P. Hammon back to California. Upon his return to San Francisco, he married Augusta "Gussie" Kenney in April 1881. In later years, Hammon became known "as a builder of electric railroads and a leader in the development of hydro-electric power projects, as well as the world's most prominent dredge-mining operator."[12]

On any frontier, once the wilderness had been conquered, civilization followed. "The fight for life against Indians and nature is the first battle, then comes the building of homes and planting of crops. These are the battles of men. Though the men have been the conquerors, women are the civilizers." Women became the sculptors of Arizona civilization.[13]

Wives said tearful goodbyes to their miner husbands, expecting a brief parting. As months turned into years, homesickness, loneliness, and monotonous domestic chores overwhelmed the miners. They yearned for their families. The wives knew they needed to join them, or terminate their marriages. Gradually, wives and children arrived in Globe, bringing with them some degree of refinement. Women polished Globe's rough edges by organizing churches, schools, voluntary organizations, and activity centers. These activities linked women to their past lives and gave them a sense of identity necessary to bear the burden of isolation.[14]

In 1877, Mrs. John Kennedy and her daughter Tonnie held the first Sunday school classes in a local saloon. Mrs. Kennedy, a resourceful woman and devout Methodist, spread sheets over the bottles and bar to make the surroundings acceptable for religious instruction. Two years later, Methodist missionary John J. Wingar walked thirty-five miles from the Picket Post settlement to provide religious services in the *Silver Belt* office. Judge Hackney generously furnished "the room, fuel, lighting, and made them welcome." For months, Reverend Wingar

St. Paul's Methodist Episcopal Church, Globe. ASLAPR #96-3657.

Reverend John J. Wingar. St. Paul's Methodist Church, Globe.

continued the long weekly trudges to save the souls of Globe.[15]

In 1880, Judge Hackney began a fund drive for a permanent church building by donating a lot on the south side of Cedar between Broad and Hill streets. General Clinton Fisk, father of Globe banker Charles T. Fisk, donated half of the $3,500 expenses for the fifty-foot by thirty-five-foot structure. Alonzo Bailey laid the cornerstone on April 21. Dedicated on November 7, St. Paul's Methodist Episcopal Church became the center of Globe's religious and social activities. The steeple bell, installed two years later, served as a call to worship and a signal for danger. Referred to as "God's Alarm Clock" by the townsfolk, the bell tolled often during Globe's early years.[16]

Married frontier women held school classes in their homes and viewed teaching children as an extension of motherhood. Besides the three "Rs," they taught religion, morals, and manners for several months a year. As the towns matured, schoolhouses opened and teachers arrived. The primitive conditions challenged the best of them. Most schools were one-room buildings with a pot-bellied stove, poor ventilation, dim lighting, and no textbooks. For idealistic young educators, teaching under these conditions was a lonely, frustrating profession.

For single women, teaching was "the road to honourable independence," even if they commanded a lower salary than men. To maintain their respectability, single women teachers usually boarded with local families. Under constant public scrutiny, they often endured bad food, poor lodgings, and the drudgery of household chores. Consequently, the turnover was great, especially when single female teachers were wooed and won by the mining camp's transient bachelors. "In Arizona, there was no choice for women but to get married."[17]

Few doctors ventured into the mining camp. Impostors and incompetents, attracted by the promise of wealth and isolation, filtered into Globe to aid the sick and make their fortunes. Some surgeons arrived under military contract and remained. Usually, families relied upon home remedies derived from local plants. The roasted pulp from the prickly pear cactus provided relief for everything from dysentery to boils. In Globe, Dr. W. E. Vail dispensed medications from his drugstore until he sold the business to concentrate on his promising mine—this was his undoing.[18]

After an outbreak of smallpox, an enterprising Jennie VanWagenen established the first hospital. By passing a hat in the local businesses and saloons, she raised enough funds to buy a four-room adobe house on the corner of Cedar and Pine streets.[19]

Some of the first women to arrive in the mining camps found economic opportunity. High-priced courtesans, dance hall girls, and self-employed prostitutes endured harassment, professional jealousies, and virtuous outrage. The public indignation often demanded confinement of "bawdy houses" to one area of town. According to the *Silver Belt,* Globe's "soiled doves" worked the saloons in the lower end of town but contributed to Globe's "civilization." As singers and dancers with questionable pasts, they sought a new life out west. Many came from respected eastern families whom they had disgraced, but to their credit they helped establish churches and schools. Some even abandoned their old lifestyle for marriage, a family, and respectability.[20]

Into this developing community, Eleanor Howell arrived with her three children. The *Silver Belt* on January 1, 1881, announced their arrival: "Frank Howell's family from California arrived on the 30th...intend making this place their permanent home. Such people are always welcome."

Brave women followed their husbands, bringing with them the rudiments of civilization. Eleanor Wilson Howell brought books, linens, and cooking utensils, establishing a link to the life she had left behind. Some women survived under the most primitive conditions, but many did not. Eleanor succumbed to illness her second year. During her mother's illness, seventeen-year-old Daisy Lee Howell assumed responsibility for her teenage brothers, Edward and Clarence, and the household.

According to historian Julie Roy Jeffrey, "Fairs and balls became vehicles for fund raising, entertainment, and the affirmation of proper behavior." Young ladies of the community participated in Globe's social activities, and Daisy joined Clara Bailey and Marien Wilson at the Masonic Ball. The *Silver Belt* described the

Daisy Lee Howell, about sixteen years old, probably taken in Santa Rosa, California. AUTHOR'S COLLECTION.

dance and the attendees, and extolled women's virtues: "The ladies were there in force, and why not? What would a ball room be without them? 'There is in woman, all that men believe of heaven, amazing brightness, purity and truth, and that angels are painted fair to look like them.'"[21]

How Daisy and Frank met is unknown. A young man certainly would notice a pretty young girl in the small mining camp. Daisy may have purchased her autograph book from Frank at the News Depot, or maybe they met at a dance or in church. Their courtship developed through a difficult period in Daisy's young life. The care of her dying mother placed an emotional burden that required support and friendships. Frank Hammon filled those needs as he courted Daisy under the stately sycamore tree in the middle of Broad Street.

> "Fair was she to behold, that maiden of seventeen summers"
>
> —LONGFELLOW.

The binding broken, Daisy's copy of Longfellow's Poetical Works automatically opened to a stained page of Evangeline. *An inscription inside the frayed cover read, "Presented to Daisy Howell for good scholarship from her teacher. [signed] Miss Nice." Did Frank and Daisy read Longfellow's* Evangeline *by the flickering firelight? I wondered what special meaning Daisy's delicate book held for Frank? For the cherished book to have survived, along with his diaries, indicates it held exceptional memories for him:*

> And, as he knocked and waited to hear
> the sound of her footsteps,
> Knew not which beat the louder, his heart
> or the knocker of iron.

The small family circled Eleanor Howell's deathbed while Reverend David W. Calfee performed the brief marriage ceremony on Daisy's nineteenth birthday, March 1, 1882.[22]

> Thus beginning their journey with morning,
> and sunshine, and gladness.

Chapter Two

UNFETTERED VENGEANCE

I remember her portrait hanging on the wall of our Illinois home. Its ornate gold frame overwhelmed her childlike face. The feather fan, unfolded in her delicate fingers, projected the deceptive appearance of sophistication. Her direct gaze revealed a self-confident teenager; her firm mouth implied resolve. Daisy Lee Howell was an enigma. Who was she? Where was her beginning? Mother could never answer my questions.

When my search for Daisy began, an obscure piece of information pointed the way. After months of disappointments and dead ends, I located records of Daisy's family in Santa Rosa, Sonoma County, California. I was euphoric with the bizarre discovery that Daisy Howell and my husband were raised in the same hometown— almost a century apart.

As a midwestern girl I had never been west of the Rockies. Following our marriage, my husband took pride in showing me his hometown. David recalled playing ball in Julliard Park during the 1940s. He remembered riding his bike past Luther Burbank's house, then peddling down Santa Rosa Avenue. This was Daisy's neighborhood in 1880. I experienced one of life's many unexplainable coincidences.

Globe City AT
May 3rd 82

Dear Sister Bertie,

Your kind letter was recd and perused with much pleasure with
Daisy my wife. It seems so very queer to be able to say my wife, yet
it is a reality, not a dream, and a happy reality. She is worth to me
a happy life time. I feel that I have done one of the best acts of my
life, toward my own happiness and I hope also toward the happiness
of her whom I have made my wife. She is a good true loving and
lovely little woman. I do wish you could meet and know her; you
could not but love her. I enclose a letter from her to you.

We are keeping house and are quite comfortable and very
happy. Our business is very good and improving, although times are
some slow on account of indian troubles. Several acquaintances of
mine have been killed in this recent outbreak as well as in the one
a year ago. Yet there is little danger around here, as the renegade
bands have left here and gone south. I suppose you will leave St.
Louis soon for home. I hope you have proffited largely from your
very good opportunity. I may not go home for a year yet, as I wish to
take Daisy with me when I go. I recd a letter from W. A. Hammon of
Conneautville [PA] yesterday said Mamie had returned from Boston
where she had been to take lessons in music. She must be a very
pretty as well as smart and inteligent girl now. Well for this time I
will say—Auve Voir. With love to all Aff your bro Frank

P.S. Daisy has no photos at present and we can get no decent ones
here. Yet I will get some tin types and send before long as they are
the only thing in which semblance of likeness can be found—which
our artist here produces.

Five hundred years before Frank's arrival in Arizona, the ancient civilization
of the Salado Indians occupied Globe's townsite. As a peaceful tribe sustained by
gathering and hunting, they were master makers of baskets, pottery, beadwork,
and weaves. The Globe area became a trading hub for their crafts—bringing
them wealth. Other cultures infiltrated the area, attracted by the year-round
availability of water and abundance of wild game.

Natural resources and a temperate climate encouraged over-population.
By the end of the 1300s, severe drought triggered fighting over scarce food and
water supplies. By AD 1450 the Salado villages had disappeared.[2]

By the late 1500s, the Western Apaches occupied the Globe area. Unlike
the Salado, the Western Apache bands were semi-nomadic farmers, hunters,
and raiders. They roamed seasonally, planting corn in the spring and returning
to harvest it in the fall. Between seasons they wandered, living off the natural
resources and confiscated stock. Their makeshift dwellings constructed of brush

and skins could easily be dismantled or left behind. No permanent structures denoting ownership existed.[3]

The various Western Apache bands, recognizing their differences from one another, maintained clearly defined territorial boundaries. Each band claimed exclusive entitlement to their hunting grounds, believing that they derived power from their land. But when crops failed and hunger hit, they raided. The Western Apache drew a sharp distinction between raiding and warfare. Initially, raiding parties of five to fifteen warriors confiscated material goods, preferably livestock, and "maintained a pacific attitude." They waged war only to avenge the deaths of kinsmen killed in earlier battles, not to expand their territory.[4]

The emergence of the Anglo miners and settlers into Arizona produced competition for the natural resources. The Apaches raided the settlers' livestock; the Anglos hunted the tribal lands. This precipitated a contest of weapons and wills—a collision of cultures. "The whites had come to exploit the land, the Indians lived as part of it." No permanent Apache homes existed; their ancestral land was their home. According to anthropologist Keith Basso, "in the Western Apache case…. The people's sense of place, their sense of their tribal past, and their vibrant sense of themselves are inseparably intertwined."[5]

The early settlers found the area "both paradise and hell on earth. It became a theater of dreams and horrors where people found themselves enacting their truest desires and deepest fears. It offered endless opportunity and relentless frustration; it was the land of adventure and boredom. Its topography was extreme, contradictory, and inconsistent." In spite of the hardships, Anglo settlers found a moral justification in the phrase "Manifest Destiny." They believed the Providential plan for the destiny of the American people was to subdue and own the continent.[6]

In 1863, the year Arizona became a territory, gold lured miners and Anglo settlers into Tonto Apache country. The military presence increased to protect them. Viewing the raiding natives as subhuman, the soldiers near Fort Whipple arbitrarily killed Apaches. Anglos who had a profound hatred of the natives went on "Indian-hunting expeditions" to exterminate them. During a peace conference Apaches were poisoned like animals. The Apaches retaliated with their own atrocities. The overwhelming military response to their depredations left the Indians vulnerable and hungry; their reliable food supplies dwindled. With few options, the Indians agreed to discontinue raiding and settle near military posts in exchange for rations and protection. These feeding stations marked the beginning of Apache pacification, but raids continued.[7]

In 1871, a Tucson "committee" led by William S. Oury took matters into its own hands. Enraged citizens massacred Western Apache women and children at Camp Grant. Following the Camp Grant Massacre, the federal government's policy changed from one of extermination to one of peace. The policy designated the placement of all Apaches on reservations. This cost-saving consolidation protected the Anglo citizens but created havoc for the Apaches. The intermingling of diverse Apache groups bred distrust, resentment, and violence among the bickering bands. Smoldering feuds ignited.[8]

That June, General George Crook assumed command of U. S. military forces in Arizona. Although responsible for the Apaches' eventual defeat, "he [Crook] developed great admiration for their knowledge and endurance, and consistently treated them with intelligence and understanding."[9]

In February 1873, the Indians from Camp Grant were placed under a temporary civilian agent at the San Carlos Reservation. The "program of removal" had begun. Twelve miles east of Globe, the San Carlos Reservation proved to be an inhospitable habitat for the accumulation of Apaches. The U. S. Cavalry herded thousands of Western Apaches to San Carlos, where warring bands competed for its limited resources. First amassed were 1,400 Tonto Apaches, followed by the White Mountain and Cibicues. After the arrival of the Chiricahua Apaches, 5,000 Indians occupied San Carlos. A tenuous coexistence reigned. Hoping to curtail the continuing raids, the U.S. government provided the Indians with land and agricultural tools to promote self-sufficiency. They worked the arid soil, surviving on meager crops and government rations. But old habits were hard to break; the skirmishes and raids continued.[10]

In August 1874, inexperienced John P. Clum was assigned as San Carlos's civilian agent to implement the Office of Indian Affairs' (OIA) "peace policy." In spite of his youth, twenty-two-year old Clum's supervisory methods reflected "integrity, energy, and civilizing purpose." But cross-cultural hostility and U. S. Army-OIA administrative rivalry fostered instability and complicated his mission.[11]

Skeptical of the "peace policy," Crook considered the civilian Indian administration "cowardly, incompetent, and corrupt." Crook's tour of San Carlos confirmed his beliefs. By 1875, Crook was reassigned to the Northern Plains. The following year Clum resigned his position.[12]

Some Apaches had adjusted to their new surroundings; others found the reservation oppressive and waited for a chance to break out. Victorio succeeded in the fall of 1879, taking with him 310 men, women, and children. His escape triggered a run of depredations that terrorized the entire Southwest.[13]

Fifty-two-year-old New Yorker John Capron Tiffany piloted the San Carlos Reservation from 1880 to 1882. A deeply religious man with boundless vigor, Tiffany was appointed to his post by the Reformed Church Missionary Board, the organization responsible for placement of civilian Indian agents. During his first year, he successfully opened an Indian school, developed a reservation irrigation system, constructed slaughterhouses, and repaired existing agency buildings.[14]

In spite of Tiffany's initial success, problems plagued his second year. A second-rate businessman of "mediocre intelligence," Tiffany's piousness offended many who distrusted his sincerity and humanitarian leanings. His unswerving advocacy of Indians' rights angered local settlers intent on confiscating Indian lands for personal use. In February 1881, the discovery of coal on the reservation created chaos. Tiffany alienated locals when he refused to restore reservation land to the public domain. Indians, alarmed by the fifty prospectors staking claims on the reservation, protested the invasion. Tiffany defended what was rightfully the Indians' property and recommended leasing the land to the miners, with the Indians sharing in the profits. The Indian Office rejected Tiffany's proposal and looked the other way while miners excavated ore.[15]

The public viewed Indian agents as corrupt; in reality, most were just incompetent. Humiliation and controversy surrounded Tiffany's management of the reservation. Criticism soon erupted on all fronts. "Self-serving" Apaches accused Tiffany of misdeeds to exonerate themselves; the *Arizona Star's* editor inflamed the public and influenced opinion by expounding unsubstantiated charges; a biased witness with a questionable past leveled corruption charges and disappeared. Tiffany resigned due to ill health, never having his day in court, and the charges of corruption remained unproven. This contemptuous commentary appeared in the October 24, 1882 issue of the *Arizona Star*: "We feel it our duty…to express our utter abhorrence of the conduct of Agent [J. C.] Tiffany and that class of reverend peculators who have cursed Arizona as Indian officials…. Fraud, peculation, conspiracy, larceny, plots and counterplots, seem to be the rule of action upon this reservation."[16]

In May 1881, Frank Hammon's friend, Charles T. Connell, took a special census of the reservation Indians. Alarmed, he reported to Tiffany that the White Mountain Apaches living near Fort Apache were starving, poorly clothed, and demoralized. Grasshoppers had eaten their crops, leaving the Indians destitute and dispirited. Tiffany sought help by asking the Indian Office to reimburse traders for seed sold to the Indians. Lieutenant Britton Davis later wrote: "Everywhere the naked, hungry, frightened little Indian children, darting behind bush or into wikiup at sight of you. Everywhere the sullen, stolid, hopeless, suspicious faces of the older Indians challenging you…to prove yourself anything else than one more liar and thief."[17]

In desperation, the superstitious Indians turned to a White Mountain mystic to achieve through religion what war parties had failed to accomplish. Ten years before, Noch-ay-del-klinne had accompanied a delegation of Apaches to Washington, D.C., and became intrigued with Christianity. Upon his return, he meditated and fasted in the wilds. When he emerged, the harmless prophet initiated revival-like "Ghost Dances." He developed his own "Messianic Movement," with a misconstrued account of Christ's resurrection. He predicted the reappearance of two dead chiefs, the whites' removal from Indian lands, and better times. The slight statured medicine man led his followers in passionate dances misinterpreted as anti-white. Indian scouts at Fort Apache requested passes to participate in a dance held forty miles away. The shaman displayed increasing influence over the discontented partiers, and the Scouts returned to the fort wildly enthusiastic, restless, and edgy.[18]

Officers at Fort Apache reported the Indians' petulant dispositions to their superiors, who became concerned. Fearful of a full-blown uprising, Col. Eugene Asa Carr received orders to arrest Noch-ay-del-klinne for inciting a riot. On the advice of veteran frontiersmen and army officers, Carr wired Washington, D.C., requesting permission to discharge disloyal scouts. A storm felled the telegraph lines before he received a reply.[19]

On August 29, 1881, Carr left for the Indian village at Cibicue Creek with five officers, seventy-nine enlisted men, and twenty-three armed scouts. They reached their destination before dusk the following day. Noch-ay-del-klinne was arrested without incident, and the troops moved four miles upriver to camp for the night. One hundred angry White Mountain Apaches followed. When Capt. Edmund C. Hentig ordered them to leave, a defiant Indian Scout named Dandy Jim raised his rifle and shot Hentig in the back.[20]

The scouts sided with their brothers as the battle at Cibicue Creek commenced. When the smoke cleared, one officer and three enlisted men lay dead, and four soldiers were wounded. The Indians suffered moderate losses. Among their casualties was the medicine man Noch-ay-del-klinne, shot by trumpeter William O. Benites. Twenty-one "hostiles," led by Nan-tia-tish, fled toward the Tonto Valley. Meanwhile, the troops headed back to prepare for an attack on Fort Apache. On September 1, 1881, over 200 renegades assaulted the post. Thwarted by Carr's men, the Indians burned outlying buildings as they withdrew. Meanwhile, Nan-tia-tish with his new band approached Cherry Creek.[21]

The incessant clicking of telegraph keys broke the early morning calm in Globe's telegraph office. A conversation was interrupted between Frank Hammon's friends George Turner and telegraph operator Mack Allison. The attention of both young men focused on the message arriving from Fort Apache. The deciphered communication told of the skirmish at Cibicue Creek, a subsequent attack on Fort Apache, and the renegades' movement toward the familiar territory of Cherry Creek and Pleasant Valley.[22]

Without a moment to spare, George Turner mounted his horse and raced north to warn families of impending trouble. Past the Salt River, he enlisted Henry Moody's help in alerting the Middleton family, twenty miles away. The next morning the pair raced towards Cherry Creek, uncertain what they would find.[23]

In 1881, William and Miriam Middleton had moved their ranch to the isolation of Cherry Creek in the Tonto Basin. To avoid the encroaching settlers near Globe, they established a promising dairy business on land still claimed by the Apaches. A "pailing" fence provided limited security to their log cabin and milk house. Living at the ranch were Mr. and Mrs. Middleton, an adult son Henry, two daughters Hattie and Della, and three small boys.

As soon as Turner and Moody reached the ranch, they relayed the telegraph message received the previous morning. Alarmed, Henry Middleton and his friends corralled forty horses grazing nearby. The family planned to drive the horses, under the safety of darkness, to Globe sixty miles away. Following lunch, Middleton finished a packsaddle at a carpenter's bench behind the house. Willis sat watching his father. In the milk house, the younger children watched their mother churn butter to sell in Globe. Henry was in the back room lying down. Hattie sat on the front porch with Henry Moody, while near Mrs. Middleton George Turner drank a glass of buttermilk.[24]

Seven Indians, claiming to be friendly Cherry Creek Apaches, emerged from the nearby woods. Professing to be hunters, and ignorant of the Cibicue and Fort

Middleton's Cherry Creek Ranch, ca. 1880. ASLAPR #96-3658.

Apache incidents, one Indian requested a cooking utensil to prepare their game. Meanwhile, his six campanions placed themselves in strategic positions around the yard. Charles T. Connell later wrote that the "Apaches, who never attack unless they think they have the advantage, kept the family under surveillance." With the command "now!" the Indians simultaneously opened fire.[25]

At first fire, Mrs. Middleton grabbed the children and ran for the cabin. A bullet entered the wall where Willis had been sitting, piercing Mr. Middleton's hat. Father and son ran for refuge. On the front steps, a bullet entered Henry Moody's eye, killing him instantly, and clipped a lock of hair from Hattie's forehead. George Turner never tasted his buttermilk as a fatal bullet felled him.

Hearing the gunfire, Henry snatched his Winchester and headed out the back door—stumbling over an Indian running for cover. An Indian fired from

Eugene Middleton, ca. 1875. SHM.

behind a boulder near Turner's body. Eugene Middleton later recounted how the bullet struck Henry in the "left breast over the heart, but being a glancing shot followed the ribs and came out under the left shoulder blade, Henry was then pulled back in the house by his mother."

According to Eugene, the terrified family barricaded themselves in the cabin, while father and son made portholes to shoot through "by knocking out punchings from between the logs." The renegades unleashed a barrage of bullets that penetrated the walls. One projectile shattered a large hanging clock and lodged behind a smaller clock hanging on the opposite wall.

The Indians left at dusk, taking all the corralled horses, plus the mounts of the two dead men. As they withdrew, the Apaches shot Henry's horse, saddled and tethered by the house. The superficial shoulder wound only stunned the animal. Fearful that their assailants would return, at dusk the family fled to Globe with wounded Henry and an injured horse. After a few miles, Middleton hid his terrified family behind brush and boulders, mounted the wounded horse, and headed for Pleasant Valley to find help. Arriving before daylight, he found the four Tewksbury boys gone. Middleton could only muster "old man Church" and one calm horse for the women and children. On their return, the twosome encountered the renegades riding their stolen stock. Despite the lame horse, the pair outran their pursuers.[26]

When Middleton hadn't returned by daybreak, the family feared the worst. Fighting panic, they remained in hiding until he and George Church appeared late in the day. The weary family then trudged toward Globe with Henry riding the wounded horse and the women and children taking turns on Church's mount.

Upon hearing of the Tonto Basin outbreak, Eugene Middleton raced north from Globe to help his family. At Cherry Creek, he joined a six-man rescue party composed of "Lowther, Eaton, Birchett, Burbridge, Martel and Clerk [Clark]." Eugene, acting as guide, found his exhausted family near Sombrero Butte at about ten o'clock that night.[27]

The Indians continued into Pleasant Valley, where they slaughtered eleven corralled horses. It was later explained that "they wanted fresh mounts and would throw a rope on a likely looking animal and if he proved to be a 'broncho' they would shoot him in order to get the rope back—one fine unbroke horse was also killed in the Middleton corral presumably for the same reason." The party escaped into the Mogollon Mountains, with the Fort Apache cavalry in pursuit.[28]

Frank Middleton, notified in Payson of the rampage, arrived with friends to find the carnage and a deserted ranch. The party buried George Turner, twenty-seven, and Henry Moody, twenty-three, under a pine tree near where they had fallen. In a matter of hours, violence had altered the lives of the Middleton family: their stock had been stolen, Henry was wounded, and two friends lay dead. The Middleton ranch experienced further violence later that year, and Frank Hammon lost other friends in Apache episodes.[29]

Rumors of a war of extermination against the Apaches resumed in late September. Fearful of reprisals following the Cibicue incident, Juh, Naiche (son of Cochise), and Geronimo led a band of Chiricahua and Coyotero men, women, and children south toward Mexico. Once again the Southwest steeled itself for raids and war. The troops and Apache scouts patrolled the mountain passes to intercept the escapees as they returned to contact their San Carlos relatives.

The next spring, Chiricahua envoys returned to San Carlos from Mexico. Near the reservation, they crossed paths with Chief of Scouts A. D. Sterling and a companion. The insurgents killed the pair, and coerced Chief Loco into leading an "exodus" of 700 followers into Mexico via the Upper Gila. Along the way, they ambushed settlers and raided farms, including that of the York family. Globe businessman Felix Knox was in the wrong place at the wrong time.[30]

Frank Hammon's amicable competitor, Felix Knox, was a popular gentleman gambler and family man. He and W. T. McNelly ran a respectable Globe establishment, the Champion Billiard Hall. Located on the corner of Broad and Push streets, the saloon served as the town meeting place before its replacement by Judge Hackney's newspaper office. The Billiard Hall had "no batwing doors, no dancing girls, but it did have poker tables in front and in the wine room in back." Adorned with an oak and mahogany bar, gilded mirrors, and lavish chandeliers, the establishment served the town's thirsty gents while they anted their earnings at the tables.[31]

In April, Knox and his family left Globe on a disastrous trip to Clifton. They ate their mid-day meal at the York ranch above the Gila River. Despite warnings of Indian raids, they proceeded with a wagonload of whiskey destined for the mining community four miles away. As the wagon started up the dry wash, Indian parties appeared on the ridges above them. Surrounded, the only escape lay back down the wash.[32]

A fusillade of bullets showered the Knox party as they dashed back toward the distant York ranch. Knox jumped from the wagon to divert fire but a bullet downed him before he could reach cover. One of the horses stumbled, wounded. The horrified women jumped from the wagon and ran toward the York house, their frantic flight assisted by the rifle fire of a young Mexican boy in the wagon. The horse recovered his footing, and the fleeing women were hoisted back into the jolting whiskey wagon.

Hours passed while warriors circled the adobe house, waiting for an opportunity to kill the occupants, pilfer supplies, and steal stock. The defenders sighted their guns through holes in the thick adobe walls, firing until the attackers retreated, leaving the shattered families to grieve.

When it was safe, the young York men and their cowhands retrieved Knox's body from the wash. The Yorks' front yard served as burial grounds for Felix and five Chiricahua warriors. The Apaches continued their rampage south but did not remain in Mexico long.[33]

Chapter Three

DANGER, TOIL, AND SNARE

*The driving rain had turned to sleet. I pulled my
hood up around my face as the February storm persisted. Carefully, I
picked my way through the overgrown weeds, stopping occasionally to
brush debris from the granite markers at my feet. Soggy candy wrap-
pers and empty beer cans lay mixed with faded plastic flowers. Slowly,
deliberately, I worked my way up the gradual incline inspecting each
monolith for a name. It was a name not to be found: Eleanor Wilson
Howell, born somewhere in Arkansas, November 10, 1844.*

*Approaching the summit, I turned to look out across
to the gray shrouded hills in the distance. The small town of Globe
was enclosed in the valley below. I tried to envision the country as it
looked over a century ago. Before me lay a town born of the struggles
of its intrepid citizens. They were courageous men and women who
had braved the dangers and isolation of those early years. Those same
pioneers now rest on this lonely hill. I turned back and gazed down
at the windswept graveyard behind me.*

*My search had been futile, and I felt sadness for the
forgotten firstcomers of Globe. Down the hill to my right, charred
wooden slabs offered a sad memorial to those who had endured the
hardships of that primitive, unforgiving land. Some pioneers buried
within those grounds have been memorialized, scrutinized, and pub-
licized— but not my great-great-grandmother. Her remains are forever
lost among the unmarked graves on a hill at the end of Hackney*

Street. Lost in thought, I shivered and walked back down the hill to
the warmth of the waiting car.

Globe
Miss Bertie Hammon

Dear Sister

Frank read your kind letter to me some time ago and gave me
a little scolding the other day because I had not written to you. I am
very sorry to have been so dilatory, but you will forgive me wont you?

No doubt you think it strange to be called sister by one whom
you have never seen but nevertheless we are sisters (in law) as much
as the laws of Arizona can make us and I truly hope we will be sisters
in love as well. A sister would be highly appreciated by myself as I
never was blessed with one. Frank has read letters to me from most
every member of his family and I begin to feel almost acquainted
with some of you already. I should like very much to see all of you,
especially your mother. They say mother in laws are always to be
dreaded but in spite of all that is said about them I would like to
see mine and would love her. My own poor mother died eleven days
after our marriage after a lingering, painful illness. I feel so lonely
sometimes. I miss her more now than at first and although a mothers love can never be replaced yet in having so kind and loving a
husband I am truly blessed. We are keeping house and my father
and two brothers stay with us and we are just as happy as any one
could be. Likely you have heard [unreadable] this of the Indian
troubles, through the papers. As Globe is too large for them to
attack we feel perfectly safe.

Hoping this worthy an answer I am with much love your Sister—
Daisy[1]

Not all "renegade bands" went south as Frank indicated in his May 3 letter
to his sister Bertie. Daisy's reassuring letter to her sister-in-law minimized the
extent of "Indian troubles" occurring around them. Daisy and Frank attempted
to ease family concerns and never hinted at Frank's pending legal problems. It
would seem that Globe's bars and saloons, just outside their Broad Street adobe,
were not conducive to tranquil married life. Whiskey bolstered the bravado of
quarrelsome cowboys. The local newspapers reported that "As a mining camp,
Globe is not infested with many of the quarrelsome cowboys…[but] a few lawless
characters here. . .have taxed the forbearance of law abiding citizens and greatly
offended the ears of families by boisterous and vulgar talk."[2]

Jacob Abraham, a twenty-seven year-old New York barber, and his family
were neighbors of Frank and Daisy on Broad Street. The cause of the altercation
between Frank and Jacob Abraham is unknown.

Jacob Abraham. AHS/TUCSON #42301.

THE TERRITORY OF ARIZONA

Against

Frank M. Hammond [*sic*]

The said Frank M. Hammond is accused by the Grand Jury of the County of Gila Territory of Arizona, by this Indictment, found this 10th day of May A.D. 1882, of the crime of Assault with a deadly weapon committed as follows: The said Frank M. Hammond on the 28th day of April A.D. 1882, at the County of Gila, Territory of Arizona, did make an assault in and upon one Jacob Abraham and…did strike, beat and bruise, with a certain deadly iron weight, the same being a deadly weapon…to inflict upon said Jacob Abraham….

"We the jury find the defendant not Guilty." [Signed] C. M. Cook, Foreman[3]

In 1904, the same Jacob "Jake" Abraham managed a Clifton-Morenci hotel owned by his brother Sam. As prominent Jewish businessmen, the brothers headed a vigilante squad that kidnapped thirteen Irish orphans placed by the Catholic Church in Mexican homes. Furious town leaders nearly lynched the nuns and the local priest. The abducted children were placed in "acceptable Anglo" homes. The Catholic Church prosecuted to regain custody of the children, but the courts, including the U.S. Supreme Court, ruled in favor of the vigilantes.[4]

Although absolved of assault, Frank had more on his mind than the fracas with Jake Abraham. Following the Cibicue incident and Felix Knox's ambush, Globe residents circulated a petition calling for the removal of all San Carlos Indians. According to historian John Bret Harte, the one hundred thirty-five signatures represented an "amalgam of apprehension and avarice…. The reservation Indians were 'generally hostile to the whites, and treacherous in peace.' " The petition accused the natives of raiding at will, fully armed with weapons and ammunition procured at the agency. When the settlers retaliated, the Indians fled into Mexico only to return to San Carlos to restock on food, clothing, and more ammunition. The petitioners requested that the government remove the Indians from San Carlos, or at least confiscate their weapons. They also demanded that Agent Tiffany be replaced with a "Westerner." Tiffany responded, refuting the petitioners' charges and insinuating that his removal would delight white men interested in obtaining Indian lands.[5]

As summer approached, more trouble surfaced. Nan-tia-tish had not fled to Mexico with Loco's band. Instead, he and Nadiski joined forces, leading sixty warriors on a rampage that included the murder of John L. Colvig (Cibicue Charley), chief of Indian police at San Carlos.[6]

Charles Connell wrote years later that Nadiski's band had lived on Cherry Creek, but moved to San Carlos to avoid the wrath of the infringing settlers who blamed his band for the depredations on Cherry, Coon, and Canyon creeks. Once on the reservation, the Indians became "insolent." They demanded more rations, and ridiculed the white man's cowardice and his inability to control the Chiricahua Apaches. Colvig's destruction of their "tiswin" supply, and the subsequent incarceration of inebriated friends, fueled their frustration. Nadiski's band took out their rage on Cibicue Charley. But John Bret Harte offers another motive for Colvig's murder—revenge for killing three members of Nadiski's band two months earlier.[7]

Every Friday the agency issued rations, and on Thursdays several men rode out to distribute ration tickets among the bands. Each Indian, no matter how old, was entitled to one ticket. Charley's territory covered twelve miles up the San Carlos River with Chief Nadiski as his last stop.

On Thursday July 6, as Charley and his scouts passed through cottonwood trees near the river on their approach to the twelve-mile post, a barrage of gunfire peppered them from the underbrush. They never knew what hit them. Cibicue Charley died clutching the ration tickets in one hand and the reins of his dead horse in the other. A cloud of dust signaling an approaching wagon dispersed the attackers.[8]

Charles T. Connell. AHS/TUCSON #22333.

Newlyweds Charles T. Connell and his wife, Chesie, returned from the Fourth of July celebration in Globe, accompanied by fellow San Carlos trader, Rube Woods. Fortunately, their late start put them at the San Carlos river bottom about eight o'clock in the morning.[9]

As they approached a narrow place in the road, an Indian stepped out of the underbrush signaling them to go back. He shouted to Connell in Apache, "Go back, everybody killed at San Carlos." Thinking it a prank, Connell wielded his whip, but the Indian drew his gun and repeated the warning more forcefully, "Go back; Apaches." Convinced, they turned their rigs around and raced back towards Globe. The lone Indian turned and ran back over Black Mountain. From a nearby hill a party of Apaches raced to head off the fleeing whites before they reached Gilson's Well—eight miles away.

Rube Wood drove the lightest rig, followed by Connell and his wife. Years later, Rube Wood described the events:

> I was ahead and had the lightest rig and Connell had his wife, who was the coolest of the bunch…. It was a race for blood, I can tell you…. Connell drew his gun and was ready for business while his wife held the reins. He held a gun in one hand and plied the whip in the other…. Mile after mile we drove with that band of yelling devils after us, until we entered the narrow canyons just before you get to the well. The brutes did not follow any further.

Mark Moore and freighter Al Rose, watering their horses at the well, took the disheveled Chesie into Rose's house and bolted the door. With his wife safely barricaded in the house with the men, Connell borrowed Rose's fastest horse and rode the twelve miles back to Globe. Inaccurate news of a massacre at San Carlos passed like wildfire. The new church bell rang, warning of impending danger. Couriers were dispatched to the outlying areas, including the Tonto Basin and Cherry Creek. The citizens of Globe gathered behind the walls of the OK Corral, anticipating an attack that never came. The marauders instead headed north toward McMillan. Meanwhile, Charles Connell and a posse of a dozen men arrived at Al Rose's house. With the frightened bride escorted safely back to Globe, the posse pressed on to San Carlos, dreading what they would find.

Along the way, they met telegraph repairman Layfayette "Fate" Grime. Grime had discovered 300 feet of severed line cut about eight o'clock that morning. As the Indians later explained, they sliced it in two places, "so it would not jump together again." Cautiously, the party entered the narrow road at the twelve-mile post, only to find a large cottonwood log blocking the way. Any wagon passing through would have to slow down, leaving it vulnerable to attack. The Indians had obviously planned to ambush the Connells and Rube Woods. Years later, Woods recalled that "Connell looked at me and I looked at him. That was all, except the lines hardened on his face and I think he was thinking more of the fate of his wife than he was of himself." Around the edge of the point, the posse found Cibicue Charley's body. They placed it in the wagon and proceeded to San Carlos, where they buried Charley Colvig next to his predecessor, Sterling. Their plot foiled, Nan-tia-tish and his fifty-four warriors headed north.[10]

News of the brutal murders quickly reached McMillan northeast of Globe. Anticipating an attack, the women and children sought safety in the Stonewall Jackson Mine tunnel, while the men defended the town from the top floor of Pat Shanley's mercantile building. The hostiles contented themselves with capturing a few head of cattle and torching outlying buildings as they departed. Once again the war party headed north toward Horseshoe Bend and the Tonto Basin—back toward the doomed Middleton ranch on Cherry Creek. Alice Curnow described the nights she spent in a tunnel on the other side of the mountain during the raid:

> The Indians always waited until after the summer rains to go on the war-path, when there would be plenty of feed for their horses and

muscal [*sic*] for themselves....Tom...carried bedding and clothing to the tunnel that ran South and a branch tunnel turned sharply East and it was in this branch tunnel the women and children had gathered.... Over the entrance a blanket had been hung.... Tom placed the mattress on the ground near the opening with the head toward the canvas for which I was thankful as the air was better there. I layed down hugging and comforting the baby...the men stood on guard with rifles ready.... Two nights were spent here before a runner came to tell us that the Indians had passed on the other side of the mountain from us and the danger was past.[11]

Enter the infamous Globe Rangers. Defenders against Indian aggression, the casual militia commanded by Daniel Boone Lacy consisted of Sheriff W. W. Lowther, Eugene Middleton, William Beard, Ferd Hatch, Winthrop House, Lindsey Lewis, Mike Whaley, Newton Clark, Lafayette Grime, Al Bechtman, and David Hunter.

With the telegraph repaired, Eugene Middleton received word in Globe that the Apache war party was once again headed north. He rounded up the Rangers for an all-night ride to the Middleton ranch. Following the previous attack, the Middleton women and children had found safety in Globe, leaving only men at the ranch. At daybreak, William Middleton and his sons fed the weary Rangers breakfast. After turning their spent horses out to pasture, Eugene and Henry took fresh mounts and set off to warn Pleasant Valley settlers. Upon their return, they heard gunfire in the canyon a half-mile away. Racing ahead at a full run, Henry's horse was wounded just as they reached the gate to the ranch. Henry dashed on foot to the safety of the house. Eugene vaulted over his horse's head and followed close behind. After dark, the Indians stole all the horses—leaving the Globe Rangers to trudge on foot the fifty miles back to town and providing comic relief to Globe's unstrung citizens.[12]

Back at San Carlos, Rube Woods reported that defiant Indians were hanging around the agency with guns hidden under long blankets. The reservation's 5,000 Indians greatly outnumbered the civilian contingent. General Orlando B. Willcox, the department commander, inundated San Carlos and the surrounding area with troops, further unnerving the edgy Indians. The friendly Apache who had warned Connell was well compensated for his bravery.[13]

From the Middleton ranch the renegade band moved through Pleasant Valley. At the Tewksbury spread, they killed stock out of "devilment"; at the Sigsby and Meadows, they left behind death and suffering. Cavalry detachments from five Arizona posts pursued the Indians into a canyon above the Tonto Rim. By July 17, the Apaches were trapped in the Big Dry Wash Canyon and overwhelmed by troops under Majors Evans and Chaffee. Nan-tia-tish was killed in the bloody battle that followed. Although minor skirmishes continued, the battle of Big Dry Wash was the last major conflict with the demoralized Apaches. Fourteen days later, Brig. Gen. George Crook resumed command of the Department of Arizona. Future skirmishes would involve the southern Chirachauas and Geronimo.[14]

Chapter Four

BENEATH THE BOUGHS

I envisioned pregnant Daisy alone while her father and husband witnessed the extinction of two men's lives. I felt certain of young Daisy's reaction—horror! On the other hand, my uncertainty lingered over whether Frank wanted to hang all three or spare Cicero's life. His friendship with Rev. David Calfee provided only a clue. Could my bias prevent my objectivity? I fought against this tendency. Frank's final action confirmed my intuition.

As promised, Frank sent tintypes of Daisy home to his family. Nearly destitute, thirty-four-year-old Cicero Grime needed their business; the artist and proprietor of the Photograph Gallery could not support his wife and four children on his meager income. Grime and his family had moved to Globe to be near his wife's aunt, Miriam Middleton, hopeful that Globe could sustain his photograph business. Cicero's younger brother, Lafayette "Fate" Grime, accompanied them.

During the summer of 1882, diminutive Fate Grime made a name for himself as a member of the Globe Rangers and as a telegraph line repairman. Following his ride with the Globe Rangers, Fate retained two of the Rangers' repeating rifles. Perhaps he already had a plan for their use.

In the drab photographic shop, Curtis Hawley provided the Grime brothers with a solution to their financial woes—a solution with tragic repercussions. Forty-three-year-old Curtis B. Hawley had moved his family from Utah to Globe—one step ahead of the law. In Globe he supplied timber to the mines and had just been hired by the Mack Morris Mill. It was general knowledge that the mill's sizable payroll was due by stage at Pioneer Pass on Sunday, August 19. Andy Hall, the Wells Fargo agent, and head packer Frank Porter would meet the stage and transfer the gold coin and mail to a waiting mule train for the twelve-mile trip to Globe.[1]

Curtis Hawley planned the robbery figuring that Fate's arsenal would give them the needed firepower. The bandits did not intend to injure Porter and Hall, only simulate an Indian attack. They figured the packers would abandon the payroll and hightail it into Globe for reinforcements. They underestimated Andy Hall.

Hall was accustomed to danger. Twelve years before, he had been the youngest member of Maj. John Wesley Powell's first exploration of the Colorado River. He was one of four men who weathered the miseries of the expedition. Afterward, he remained in Arizona and eventually landed a job as the Wells Fargo express agent between Casa Grande and Globe. Hall was no stranger to trouble. After three years, he was still awaiting trial in Globe for killing Chinese cook Gee Fan.[2]

On that fateful Sunday morning, Cicero Grime hung around the stage company at Pioneer Pass. He assisted Frank Porter in loading the heavy boxes onto the packsaddle. When he had finished, he returned to where his companions lay in wait. Cicero informed them that Porter was unarmed, Hall had only a six-shooter, and the coveted payroll was on the lead mule. With his job completed, Cicero headed back toward Globe.

Fate Grime and Curtis Hawley lay in ambush behind a boulder at a curve in the trail. Before long, Hall appeared slowly leading the train down the steep, winding route. Just as Cicero had reported, the roan mule carrying the $5000 payroll and registered mail led the train. Frank Porter followed fifty yards behind, leading the second section.[3]

The first barrage of gunfire from behind the rocks dropped the roan mule in his tracks. With war-whoops, the two robbers continued firing in the air.

*Nineteen-year-old
Daisy Hammon, from
a tintype taken shortly
after her marriage.*
AUTHOR'S COLLECTION.

Middleton pack train ascending Devil's Canyon Trail in early 1880s. ASLAPR #96-3556.

Alarmed, Hall turned and raced back up the trail, yelling at Porter to get help. Porter whirled his pony and sprinted across the switchbacks toward Globe, careful to avoid the main road. Andy crept back to the crime scene in time to witness the bandits stuffing their spoils into canvas saddlebags before retreating into the brush. They were not Indians.

       That morning, druggist Dr. W. F. Vail had bid his wife goodbye at her bakery and left Globe to prospect at El Capitan mine. As he ambled up the trail, the early morning calm was broken by the staccato of repeating rifles. Thinking there were Apaches in the area, he changed his course. By coincidence his path intersected Fate and Hawley running on foot. Vail inquired about the gunfire and commented on the pair's heavy loads. Alarmed, the thieves felled him with three shots and left him for dead. The outlaws then hid in the brush near a spring to talk over their situation.

Meanwhile, Hall began to follow the tracks of the robbers, unsure of who they were. He encountered the dying Dr. Vail on the trail. After making the doomed doctor comfortable, Hall continued on. As he approached the spring, he spied the hijackers resting with their heavy bags. They looked familiar. The startled bandits opened fire. Hall attempted to defend himself with his six-shooter but was no match for the large-caliber arsenal. He never fired a shot. He was riddled by eight bullets and died by the spring. Brutality was not limited to the Apaches.[4]

Their payroll caper had gone awry. Dismayed at the turn of events, Fate and Hawley continued on foot to Russell Gulch, where they split the loot three ways and buried it along with their rifles. They pocketed three twenty-dollar gold pieces to hold them over until they could retrieve the booty.[5]

About midday, Frank Porter burst into Globe and reported the supposed Indian attack. The Methodist Church bell once again tolled an alarm, and Globe's citizens prepared for another Indian scare. Sheriff W. W. "Tip" Lowther hurriedly deputized John Jones, Daniel B. Lacy, and Frank Porter, and rode toward Pioneer Pass.

At the crime scene, the posse found the dead mule and the looted express box. Following the trail left by Hall, they came across Dr. Vail near death. His last whispered words were: "Two men—one a tall dark complected man, and the other a small light complected man, and that they both belonged in Globe." A prospector named George E. Lockwood, who lived in a nearby shack and had been hunting in the area, agreed to stay with Vail until the sheriff could bring a wagon from Globe. The doctor died in Lockwood's arms.[6]

On his return with the wagon, Sheriff Lowther enlisted the help of Eugene Middleton and Lindsey Lewis, who were working at Breman's sawmill. The posse began a search for Hall and the missing payroll. They found Hall's bullet-ridden body by the banks of the spring a short distance from Dr. Vail.

Several men searched for evidence left by the perpetrators. In the soft mud around the spring, they found spent rifle shells and boot prints. Eugene Middleton recognized the unique casings as belonging to rifles used by the Globe Rangers. The small boot prints jogged his memory of another trail on the long walk from Cherry Creek the previous month.[7]

The bodies were returned to Globe and placed in the Wells Fargo office for viewing. Rumors ran rampant among the horrified citizens. Who among them had perpetrated this dastardly deed? Eugene Middleton thought he had the answer and confided his observations to Lowther. The sheriff offered a $5,000 reward for the capture and conviction of the murderers, and notified the Wells Fargo office in San Francisco of the robbery. The next day, Wells Fargo replied to Lowther's telegram: "Damn the money. Hang the murderers." (Signed) "Valentine, Office Manager." Globe residents petitioned Governor F. A. Tritle, requesting a reward "for the apprehension and conviction of the murderers and robbers."[8]

Reverend David W. Calfee. AHF #B-357.

The following morning, the packed Methodist Church heard Reverend David Calfee bless the souls of Globe's fallen citizens. Meanwhile, a jurisdictional question arose. Daniel Boone Lacy, distrustful of Sheriff Lowther, notified U. S. Marshal Pete Gabriel in Florence of the heinous crime. Gabriel arrived at Globe within two days. Dan Lacy and Charles Clark accompanied him to question Fate Grime.[9]

After hours of interrogation, young Fate confessed, incriminating Curtis Hawley and Fate's brother, Cicero. Fate maintained that Cicero had only served as a lookout. The lawmen then proceeded to Hawley's Pine Street house, where the elder Grime was taken into custody. Lacy and Gabriel spirited the brothers out of town after dark and sequestered them in a cabin at the Bloody Tanks Wash to wait for the stage. Their final destination was Tucson and safety.[10]

By this time the reward had risen to $6,000. Lacy and Gabriel intended to split the money, but that depended upon a conviction. Lowther intercepted the pair at the cabin and demanded custody, claiming that murder charges held precedence over U. S. mail tampering. Almost coming to blows, Gabriel countered, "They would be lynched in an hour" if they returned to Globe. He and Lowther agreed to honor Globe attorney J. D. McCabe's recommendation as to the appropriate jurisdiction. After some legal haggling, the prisoners were turned over to Lowther and placed in Globe's dilapidated jailhouse to await trial. Rivalry and greed had clouded Lowther's judgment.[11]

Once the townsfolk learned of Fate Grime's confession and the subsequent arrests, their mood darkened. Talk of lynching infiltrated the otherwise sedate community. Saloons were closed to discourage hanging by a drunken mob—all for naught. By dark, a well-controlled mob converged upon the little jailhouse and demanded that Lowther turn over his prisoners. Fearing further bloodshed, the sheriff urged the crowd of 200 to allow a hearing before Judge George Allen. The growing mob reluctantly agreed and crowded into Stallo's Dance Hall to view the judicial process. As expected, the trio was found guilty, their confessions were signed, and their affairs put in order. Hoping for a reprieve, the prisoners consented to reveal the whereabouts of the hidden payroll. Under heavy guard, Fate Grime and Curtis Hawley led a small band of men to Russell Gulch and the buried booty.

Back at the dance hall, Silvia Grime, with her four children, pleaded for her husband's life. John Wentworth issued an impassioned argument on her behalf: "Her plea is not prompted for the erring husband and father, but in response to the wildly beating hearts of the anguished wife and four helpless children, who implore the life of him who has succored them as best he could in pinching want."[12]

Reverend Calfee and members of his congregation likewise pleaded for mercy on behalf of Cicero Grime. However, the most touching appeal came from Irene Vail, widow of the murdered druggist. She implored that her neighbors find compassion for Cicero Grime's poor wife and children; his hanging would only bring more misery to the distraught family. As a result, Cicero lived.[13]

At two o'clock in the morning, the tolling church bell broke the stillness of the sultry darkness. Empty wooden beer kegs were rolled into the middle of Broad Street and set ablaze. The bonfire illuminated Frank Hammon's News Depot. Dark shadows eerily danced on the clapboard walls as the crowd approached the old sycamore tree. Ropes dangled from the tree's horizontal limb fifteen feet above the dusty ground.[14]

Jerry Vosburgh stood behind the prisoners with a coiled rope looped through his folded arms. With nooses placed around the prisoners' necks, Reverend

Calfee asked if they wanted a prayer. Fate contritely agreed, but Hawley refused. Before they placed the blindfold, Fate fell to the ground and removed his boots. With a signal, a dozen men yanked the killers up into the "leafy gallows." Grime died quietly. Hawley's gasping breaths, however, could be heard blocks away as he struggled against death.[15]

The rigid bodies remained hanging from the sycamore until the next afternoon. Sheriff Lowther claiming no part in the execution, refused to remove them. Finally the lynching party passed the hat to pay for lowering the bodies and for burial expenses. The August 28, 1882, *Arizona Gazette* condoned the hangings. "We do not, as a general rule, believe in lynch law, but this was a case that not only justified, but demanded it," the paper editorialized. "A community cannot afford to trust the punishment of such desperate and heartless criminals to the slow and uncertain methods of the law."[16]

To understand the events of August 24, we must understand the Arizona territorial justice system. First, a complaint would be brought before the justice of the peace (JP), followed by an investigation. If the JP found reasonable cause for the complaint, he would issue an arrest warrant. After locating the accused, the sheriff would bring him before the JP for examination. If strong evidence existed against the defendant, he either put up bail or sat in jail until the next court session; district court judges heard cases only twice a year. Once the court convened, the district attorney presented evidence in the case to the grand jury. If an indictment followed, the defendant stood trial.[17]

Often, ineffective courts run by incompetent judges and prosecutors found juries unable or unwilling to bring verdicts. Gila County's slow judicial system had been ineffective. The year prior to the Globe hangings, only nineteen of twenty-seven district court cases had been indicted, gaining only two convictions. Too many acquittals were the issue, not excessive crime. Citizens felt that by electing their justice officials they had created the system. When it failed, they fixed it. Richard Maxwell Brown reinforces this thought in his book *Strain of Violence*: "As a lyncher he 'no longer looks to the appointed officers of the law for protection, but becomes in his own estimation an officer of the law himself...he comes to regard lynching as one of his more sacred and inalienable rights.'"[18]

Sheriff Lowther's poor judgment, triggered in part by greed, set the stage for the lynchings. Right or wrong, when the law failed, the people assumed their roles as jurors. The brutal nature of the crime, an impotent court system, and a lawman's misguided decision created a situation ripe for "extra-legal justice."[19]

A block away in the little adobe house, Daisy Hammon undoubtedly lay awake to the sounds of the angry mob and the last strangling gasps of Curtis Hawley. How did the events of August 24 impact Frank and Daisy? Less than two months later, they moved from "Deadman's Flat" to a house on the hill behind the Methodist Church—a better place to raise their expected child.[20]

Chapter Five

Hoofbeats of Fate

*T*he house was gone! What remained was a crumbling stone wall demarking the perimeter of a weedy lot. Most of the century-old houses in the neighborhood were well maintained. What happened to Frank and Daisy's house on the hill? I continued to search for some physical evidence of my family in Globe, but I was disappointed once again.

A gentle Sunday breeze dusted the hair from my face. The wind brought with it strains of music from the church below. I felt like a child following the Pied Piper as I strolled toward the familiar sound. At the other end of the block, I paused in front of St. Paul's Methodist Church. This was not the original 1880 church that Frank and Daisy attended. That one had been replaced years ago. Nevertheless, I was drawn into the sanctuary by a familiar hymn.

As I sat in an empty pew, I was absorbed in my own thoughts. It seemed appropriate for me to be a guest of Frank and Daisy's former congregation. I felt a strange familiarity in spite of my Episcopal upbringing—a comfortable feeling. This was not the same building, minister, or time—but the music, prayers, and scriptures remained unchanged. This continuity brought me a serenity that was unexpected. Frank and Daisy had listened to these same words over a hundred years ago.

The tiny house was gone, and the old church replaced.
Now my journey extended beyond locating a house or a grave. The
parishioners of Globe greeted me warmly as "God's Alarm Clock"
tolled.

In their house on the hill, Frank and Daisy found respite from the bawdy scene unfolding below them on Broad Street. For Daisy, the January birth of Alberta Estelle helped fill the void left by her mother's death the previous year. The added responsibility of a new baby forced Frank to re-evaluate his future in Globe.[1]

Frank's joy was probably tempered by the depression that hit Globe's mining industry early in 1883. Beginning in February, copper prices began a downward spiral. By summer they had fallen from eighteen to fifteen cents per pound. High-grade coke, shipped from Cardiff, Wales, and coke of a lesser quality from the Colorado coalfields, fueled the smelters. It arrived in Willcox via the Southern Pacific Railway and was transported to Globe by wagon across the San Carlos Reservation. The exorbitant freight cost shut down the smaller mines. Only the Old Dominion Mine remained in operation. Globe miners and merchants suffered; a more cost-effective method of transportation was needed. A railroad was the solution.[2]

Frank Hammon joined ninety Globe residents who subscribed to 958 shares of Arizona Mineral Belt Railroad stock offered by Chicago speculator Colonel James W. Eddy. An original locator of the San Carlos Deer Creek coalfields, Eddy recognized that Globe's economic survival depended on a railroad. He proposed a rail line connecting with the Atlantic and Pacific Railroad 180 miles north at Flagstaff. With only the Old Dominion Mine operating in June of 1883, "The articles of incorporation capitalized the Arizona Mineral Belt Railroad at $8,000,000 for building a line between the A&P and Globe, with the provision that the line might be extended to the southern boundary of the Territory." By mid-summer, Eddy had contracted for surveys, lined up eastern investors, and convinced the A&P that the Mineral Belt would be a moneymaker.[3]

Although underfunded, Eddy proceeded with construction. In the eyes of at least one historian, "[his] plans far exceeded reality." Globe crews labored for ten shares, along with free room and board, to build a tunnel rising 2,000 feet through the sandstone face of the Mogollon Rim. In desperation, the August 18, 1883, *Silver Belt* lobbied for more workers. "Let them not hang back and say, 'I can do nothing'" the newspaper urged. "Indeed, there is not a single man in the section through which the road will pass, who is so weak physically, or so poor financially, but what they can assist."[4]

By September, the work stopped seventy-feet into the cliff. Eddy's funds were depleted and the A&P rejected his request for more money. A Wall Street panic, plus A&P negotiations with the Southern Pacific for a more lucrative route, tabled the project. The Globe railroad had received a severe setback. Then rumors of other railroads and new surveys brought false hope to the discouraged townsfolk. The Denver and Rio Grande Railroad announced plans to run a line from Denver through the Deer Park coalfields into Globe, and on to Tucson. The Globe & Willcox Narrow Gauge Railway ran a preliminary survey, but nothing happened.[5]

Anticipation of the coming railroad, and the prospect of economic stability, affected Frank's business plans. In May 1883, while Eddy incorporated his railroad, Frank sold his half of the News Depot to Ferdinand Hatch, and with Henry Middleton, became a partner in the Coon Creek Ranch in the Tonto Basin. Undeterred by the Apache episodes of the previous year, Henry had settled on Coon Creek with his new bride. Lush grasses covered the undulating range below the Sierra Ancha Mountains. The clear creek provided an abundant water source north of its confluence with the Salt River—west of Horseshoe Bend.[6]

A market for their beef lay in Globe, twenty-eight miles south, and beyond Arizona. To the new partners, this was "bovine paradise." With the rapid increase in cattle prices, the Coon Creek Ranch appeared to be a good investment. In 1880, cattle sold for fifteen dollars a head; three years later twenty-five dollars a head wasn't unusual. A cattleman could show a profit a few years after establishing his stock. Frank and Henry could not have foreseen the eventual overabundance of cattle, drought conditions, and fading hopes for a railroad.[7]

The partners spent almost a year clearing land and building cabins above the creek. By mid-March 1884, Frank moved his family to the ranch. By June 7, the Hammons and Middletons returned to Globe for safety and for the summer social whirl.[8]

In Globe, excitement ran high for the round of summer festivities. The Globe City Club held a lawn party on the spacious grounds of Dr. Stallo's home. A large platform was constructed for dancing and adorned with Chinese lanterns. A large flag draped over one end of the music stand gave the party a patriotic theme. Ladies, dressed in their finest attire, enjoyed the luxury of Dr. Stallo's handsome parlor and the comforts provided by their host.

Three weeks later, Globe residents anxiously awaited the Fourth of July celebration. Families arrived in town for a day full of amusements. Children chased slippery pigs; youths tried to climb greased poles; and oldtimers kept time to patriotic tunes as they reminisced. "Thanks to a few patriotic spirits, our national holiday is to be celebrated in a befitting manner on next Friday," the *Silver Belt* reported. "To Frank Hammon, members of the Miners Union and Globe City Club is most of the credit due. They have taken charge of the affair and have arranged an attractive programme."[9]

With Frank in charge of the event, Daisy and Alberta possibly sat in the shade of the sycamore to watch the parade with their Globe friends. Little Alberta's eyes must have been wide with wonderment at the costumes as the parade passed down Broad Street. Daisy probably listened quietly to the orations but beamed with pride at her husband's part in the successful day.

Dr. Stallo's 1884 lawn party on the banks of Pinal Creek.
J. H. McClintock Papers, PPL.

The pleasantries were short-lived. Trouble was already brewing out in the Tonto Basin as the *Silver Belt* issue of July 12, 1884, indicated: "Coroner [Francis] Frank N. Howell and Dr. N. H. Cook went out to Tonto on Monday and held an inquest on the body of Tom Moore who was shot May 28th." Moore had been shot in the back.

The serenity and solitude that Frank and Daisy sought at Coon Creek would not last. Pleasant Valley was poised for a different kind of war, one that would terrorize the territory for the next decade.

Globe A.T.
Sept 16, 1884

Dear Mother,
    I should have written several days ago, but better late than never. On the 10th we had an addition to our family. Another baby girl—nine pounds—fairly pretty they say—looks just like its father too. Daisy did not have a hard time and is getting along excellently, and also the baby. We have not decided what to name her yet. I have been working for awhile, have laid off now for a couple of weeks to go out to the ranch and look after the cattle.
    We shall probably move out again in the course of a few months. Now with much love from all to all. I remain aff. your Son.

Frank

P.S. We just received your letter and enjoyed it much.

    The summer months passed quickly. To be near a midwife, Frank and Daisy remained in their house on the hill in Globe, waiting for the birth of their second daughter, Eva Pauline. The September 13, 1884 issue of the *Silver Belt*, incorrectly, announced the event: "BORN—In Globe, Sept. 11th, to the wife of Frank Hammon, a daughter."[10]
    While Daisy was occupied with baby Eva and twenty-month-old "Bertie," Frank divided his time between Globe and the ranch. When in town, Frank found work at the Old Dominion Mine until the ranch could produce an income. By mid-November, Frank left for the Coon and Cherry Creek rodeo (roundup) as indicated in the November 15, 1884 issue of the *Silver Belt:* "Joe Redman, Patrick Shanley, Frank Hammon left on Tuesday to attend rodeo at Coon and Cherry Creek." The November 22 *Silver Belt* reported the results from the round-ups: "A large number of calves were branded, and perfect harmony prevailed among stockman interests." But harmony did not prevail for long above the Salt River. A new breed of cowboy had drifted north of the Salt River and into the Tonto Basin.
    The pristine Pleasant Valley lay at the northern end of the Tonto Basin under the towering Mogollon Rim. A million acres of grassy meadows, meandering creeks, and stately conifers graced the prime land adjacent to the Fort Apache Indian Reservation. The Sierra Ancha range to the south formed a natural barrier between the northern valley and the drier Salt River settlements. Tonto and Canyon creeks encompassed the virgin range, allowing year-round water to irrigate the stirrup-high grasses.
    In the late 1870s, subsistence farmers settled in Pleasant Valley. The Middleton family initiated the settlement, followed by the Tewksburys. James Dunning Tewksbury had supposedly sailed from Boston to California via Cape Horn during the Gold Rush. He settled in the wilds of Oregon, where marriage to a Shoshone

45

Indian produced a daughter and four spirited sons. Edwin, John, James Jr., and Frank shared their father's infatuation with pureblood horses and a penchant for racing.

Following his wife's death, J. D. Tewksbury's restless spirit carried the family to bustling San Francisco, on to ore-rich Nevada, then Prescott, and finally Globe. In Globe, he met Lydia Crigger Shultes, a widowed Englishwoman with three children. Married in 1879, the couple produced two sons of their own: Walter and Parker. That year, the Tewksbury boys moved to Pleasant Valley, on Cherry Creek, with their prized horses. Their father and Lydia followed and helped create an inviting ranch that drew visitors from throughout the valley. For the next four years peace reigned over the region.[11]

In 1881, James Stinson drove 450 head of cattle to his Cherry Creek ranch north of the Tewksburys. He became an absentee owner, leaving his volatile foreman, John Gilliland, in charge of the operation. Stinson periodically arrived from his Tempe ranch to inspect his Pleasant Valley holdings. In a November 1930 interview with the *Arizona Republican,* James Stinson disclosed that "It really was my cattle that started the Pleasant Valley feud."[12]

During the summer of 1882, a fateful meeting between Ed Tewksbury and Tom Graham set the stage for a complex feud that left Arizona reeling into the next century. In a Globe saloon the young men formed a friendship that eventually soured and ended in bloodshed. Originally from Boone County, Iowa, Tom Graham and his brother John had traversed the West from Alaska to Mexico. They became savvy miners and cowhands, as well as "proficient pistoleers," before landing in Globe.[13]

With the encouragement of Ed Tewksbury, the brothers drove a small herd they had purchased to Pleasant Valley. They appropriated a few additional head along the way. With the help of Al Rose, the brothers selected land south of the Stinson ranch. Their spread was advantageously positioned with a view of the valley and the Tewksbury place to the south. The Graham herds rapidly increased, while their neighbors' cattle mysteriously dwindled.[14]

At this point, registering a brand was optional. Advertising Stinson's unrecorded "T" probably wouldn't have deterred the "acquisition" of his cattle. His well-known brand was easily altered and inviting to rustlers. With a searing iron, the "T" was easily converted to the Graham-Tewksbury "E".[15]

On January 12, 1883, Stinson's intoxicated foreman, John Gilliland, appeared at the Tewksbury ranch with his nephew looking for missing stock—both men were armed. After an exchange of heated words, shots were fired, one of which wounded Gilliland's nephew.[16]

The Prescott grand jury brought indictments against Gilliland, and the case proceeded to trial. The Graham brothers supported the Tewksburys' claim of self-defense. Gilliland was eventually acquitted, but not before tragedy struck the Tewksbury family. Frank Tewksbury was summoned to testify, even though he had nothing to add. The long, hard ride from Pleasant Valley to Prescott was too much for the frail teenager. He died from measles contracted en route home.[17]

What caused the disintegration of the Tewksbury–Graham partnership? In March of 1884, John Graham registered the "Ⱶ" brand in Yavapai County—omitting the Tewksbury name. Was this the catalyst for the feud? For years, writers of fiction and non-fiction have expounded numerous theories. The accidental discovery of a misfiled document may have finally shed light on the mystery.[18]

Don Dedera, in *A Little War Of Our Own*, gives a logical explanation. After years of research, Dedera discovered what he believes is the last piece to the century-old puzzle. Using a misplaced document, he concludes that sometime after the Gilliland court proceedings the Grahams double-crossed the Tewksburys. They contracted as snitches for James Stinson and tattled the questionable branding practices of their former friends and cohorts the Tewksburys. On March 29, 1884, John Graham filed a felony complaint against Edwin Tewksbury. Tewksbury was charged with altering the brands of sixty-two head of cattle belonging to James Stinson and his new partner, John Graham.[19]

With this betrayal, indictments followed against the Tewksburys. Rumors raged, and the Tonto Basin polarized into opposing factions. Neutrality was nearly impossible. Soon, resentments festered, distrust surfaced, and paranoia set in. The stage was set for disaster.

Into this complicated scenario a new breed of cowman arrived. In the Tonto Valley, Texas cattlemen found open, fence-free land suitable for their massive herds. Independent, and unaccustomed to restrictive laws of civilization, they administered their own laws.[20]

In the summer of 1885, Colonel Jesse W. Ellison shipped by rail 2,000 head of cattle from Texas to Bowie, Arizona; 1,200 head survived the drive into the Tonto Basin. Among his drovers were hard-riding, tough Texas cowhands: son Perle Ellison, Glenn Reynolds, William Voris, Bob Samuel, John Jacobs, Houston Kyle, Bud Campbell (the last two eventually became sons-in-law), and William McFadden.

Already overwhelmed by cattle, the bruised land lay bare to erosion by thousands of hooves. With the plentiful grasses trampled, the forces of nature played havoc on the pristine valley, once abundant with filaree and wildlife. Adding pressure to the range land, the Aztec Land & Cattle Company settled on two million acres of railroad grants above the Mogollon Rim. Eastern railway kingpins and New York bankers became absentee owners of the prime land, which they flooded with 33,000 beeves. Range land previously occupied by game animals and pioneer settlers was raped by the "bovine population explosion."[21]

Into this equation arrived the Hashknife cowboys. Hired by the Aztec Land & Cattle Company, they worked the huge herds above the Rim—no questions asked. Some of these tough, young cowpunchers were hard-riding drifters handy with a rope or gun. They knew the intricacies of marks and brands and operated under various aliases. Some formed an alliance with the Grahams in the Pleasant Valley feud.[22]

One of these drifters was Andy Blevins (aka Cooper), wanted in Oklahoma for selling whiskey to Indians and in Texas for rustling. Looking for a haven, he bullied his way into ownership of meadows near Canyon Creek adjoining the Graham spread. From there, Andy persuaded his parents to relocate the family to Arizona from Plano, Texas. Martin and Mary Blevins's third son, Hampton, was no stranger to law enforcement. Sixteen years old, he had already served time in a Texas penitentiary for horse stealing. In 1885, the troubled family joined Andy on Canyon Creek. The area was ideally situated to control the north-south passage of herds through the valley. Andy Cooper's name became synonymous with rustling and re-branding horses from Colorado to Mexico. Before long, the Blevinses and Grahams shared grazing land and mutual enemies.[23]

Andy Cooper expressed his disregard for the law in a letter written to his sister on April 17, 1887. "You Write in your last letter Jim Was under a 75.00 doler Bond," he remarked. "You tell Jim…that he had Better jump his Bond and come to this countery for a man stands no chance in that countery."[24]

While the dispute developed in Pleasant Valley, the Salt River settlement had its own trouble brewing. The *Silver Belt* noted on May 31, 1884 that "Frank Hammon is here from Coon Creek and reports San Carlos Indians roaming in that vicinity, and on Cherry Creek. A horse and mule are missing from Hammon & Middleton's ranch, but cannot say that the Indians took them." Determining ownership of Frank's branded stock, shouldn't have been difficult. Nothing, however, indicates that he found the horse and mule or that he was involved in the developing feud.[25]

Chapter Six

Fires Consumed

Saguaros graced the undulating hills, their spiny arms silhouetted against azure. A profusion of periwinkle and gold permeated the emerald carpet in the distance. Magenta blossoms peaked from their prickly hosts. A purple haze covered distant red ramparts ascending toward a threatening sky. The treeless expanse lay before me, reminiscent of a virgin land. Soon the deserted winding road was intersected by the trickle of Dry Creek, marked by a weather-beaten sign. Within miles, the road descended into a thicket of Sycamore and Alder trees, signaling water and Coon Creek. A refreshing sense of serenity prevailed in the spring stillness. Frank and Daisy sought tranquility and contentment in this spot but it was not to be found.

Coon Creek Ranch
Jan 30th 1885

Dear Sister Alberta

I owe you numerous letters but nevertheless am only going to write a note this time. We moved out to the ranch one month ago and have none of us been to town since. Henry is going in tomorrow and I must write several letters tonight.

We are enjoying good health with the exception of bad colds which Bertie and Eva have had. Bertie is beginning to talk and is quite amusing. Eva is a very pretty baby and is better natured than she used to be although she is beginning to get teeth. We have not got settled yet and are so buisy with so much to do it seems that we cannot get it done in time for spring.

Our cattle are getting along first rate and everything looks favorable. Now excuse me this time I must say—How are you to Glenn.

Tell mother I will write to her soon. Love to all from us all

Aff your bro
Frank

The primitive life at Coon Creek made incredible demands on Daisy's delicate frame. Though accustomed to hard work while employed as a domestic in California, her chores at Coon Creek exceeded anything she had previously known. Lack of conveniences complicated her life, adding extra hours to ordinary tasks. Without a well, she carried water from the creek daily for bathing, cooking, and laundering. Washday covered two days, one day to bring up the water, another scrubbing grimy clothes over a washtub. By the evening firelight, Daisy stitched Bertie's and Eva's clothing on her treadle machine. She saved remnants for stitching quilts and curtains; rags became rugs and cut-up dresses adorned windows.[1]

Out on ranches, women wore rough and rugged clothing, but most women still longed for feminine fashion. The discussion of fashion trends, "reinforced their sense of identity and increased their feeling of control over their environment." Globe resident Alice Curnow recalled browsing through the wish book. "I was the fortunate possessor of a catalogue from 'Weinstock and Lubin' of Sacramento, the first catalogue I had ever seen," she reminisced. "I have heard that, to the early settlers of the prairie country Montgomery Ward's catalogue was called 'the Desert Bible' because it was studied so continuously."[2]

Food preservation was essential. Dried fruits and vegetables from Daisy's garden needed to last the family throughout the winter. Meat, served fresh only in the winter months, had to be dried into black jerky. The preserved meat could be chewed raw, reconstituted in a stew, or boiled into soup stock. Daisy wasted nothing. She used the excess fat for cooking; tallow mixed with ashes created soap and candles. Beans, sugar, and flour bought in Globe could be safely stored for later use. By preparing extra amounts of beans, biscuits, and gravy, Daisy could provide unannounced visitors with a hearty meal. "Hospitality was an important feature of western life, and women were expected to provide comfort and entertainment to travelers."[3]

While Frank and Henry tended their growing herd, care of the children and households rested solely on Daisy and on Ora Middleton. The women shared their garden and gossip. For Daisy, the female conversation and companionship probably became a survival tool in relieving anxieties, boredom, and loneliness. In some women, isolation created a separation anxiety; their distance from civilization, lack of transportation, and continuous danger created overpowering insecurity. Female confidences helped discouraged women vent their frustrations and share their feelings. In a society primarily catering to a man's needs, women lost their identity, and often their health, while nurturing their families. Different standards dictated men and women's lives: men typified valor, violence, and venture; women exemplified altruism, nurturing, compassion, and endurance. According to historian Christiane Fischer, "Without the society of their kind, often without the comforts of life, without the relief afforded by active adventure, and often in danger, they [women] had no choice but to endure."[4]

Frank's brief reports home omitted mention of Daisy's weakened condition, but ranch life had taken its toll.

Coon Creek Ranch

Feb 29, 1885
Dearest Mother
　　Your very welcome letter I recd some time ago which I will now answer briefly. We have got nicely settled on the ranch and are getting things fixed up as fast as possible but it is slow work. We are now building a fence around the houses, garden, orchard, and a small field where we intend planting some grain for horse feed. We have no wagon and have to drag up the poles with the horses from about half a mile down the creek. We are making it hog tight as we have quite a lot of hogs but only one sow and four pigs up. The others are out on the range and so wild that one can scarcely get a shot at them with a rifle. We intend as soon as we get time to get after them and round them all up—and gentle them. We have about thirty to forty young calves already this spring and are milking about twenty five cows. We give the calves half the milk from our share we make about twenty five lbs butter per week using milk and butter for the two familys. We get 60 cts per lb for our butter. We have a house now for each family and are very comfortable for Arizona—yet you might not think so if you were to look in upon us this evening.
　　Dirt floor, walls, bare logs—with mud between—the whole covered with newspapers for wall paper. For a roof we [have] a thatch of bean grass with a mud roof underneath. We have one window,

a door and a fire place—our room is 12-16. Ceiling is about 9 feet high. It is built on the bank of the creek or rather brook under some beautiful Alder trees and is surrounded by fig and cherry trees. Our peach trees are all blossoming out. We are enjoying most beautiful weather and have for in fact all winter. Our coldest weather will freeze ice in a vessel about ½ inch during a night. Daisy and the babys are all well and getting fat and send love. I have been riding all day and am tired so good night with love to all.

Aff your son   Frank

P.S. Dear mother—just came to town first chance to get this to office since I wrote it. All are well. I will write again soon. Aff Frank

Although their life appeared monotonous, it wasn't as uneventful as Frank indicated. Occasionally, White Mountain Apaches returned to their former hunting grounds. Intrigued by the settler's lifestyle and curious by nature, they often peered through the open window at the terrified family within. At times alone, Daisy needed self-reliance to survive. Well armed, she was prepared to defend their children. Globe friend, Alice Curnow, related her own Indian experience when "four of the squaws followed me and pressing their faces against the window, looked in. But I, pretending bravery which I didn't feel, still ignored them. Then they boldly entered the house and closing the door they sat with their backs to it on the floor and in their harsh, cacle-like voices were evidently discussing my housekeeping which was giving them much amusement, while I was trembling so I could scarcely stand."[5]

Coon Creek Ranch
June 22, 1885

Dearest Mother
    Your dear letter I recd day before yesterday while in Globe and intended answering it before I left but was so buisy that had to pospone it until my return home. I took Daisy and the children to town with me and left them to make a visit, limited only by their pleasure to return. Henry took his family in also, I expect we will have them to bring back in a few days. You see we are alive and still wear our hair notwithstanding. The indians have broken out. We are not alarmed here. There has only one band or family of the Apaches left the reservation—viz The Chiricahuas, who are the worst indians in America. They never have been whipped or conquered, but they never come in our direction always go south toward and into Mexico. This locality used to be the range of the White Mountain Apaches. They are also bad indians but have been conquered and little danger is expected from them. Again should

any trouble occur with them it is telegraphed to Globe and a messenger would be sent to us before the Indians could get here.

Do not worry about us mother for we are in no danger, yet will be careful. We always go armed. I am so used to wearing my six shooter buckled around me that I should be lonesome without it. Daisy is in good health and likes to live on the ranch better than in Globe. Bertie is a small delicate child but very healthy, much like her mother in that regard. She tries to say every thing. Eva is fat and robust and healthy. She is darker and is going to be more of a Hammon than Bertie and is almost as large.

My cattle are doing very well. Will have about 95% calves this year. Our orchard is growing finely. We have a nice garden, have had all kinds of vegitables some time ago. Had ripe strawberries about two months ago. Our Fig trees are bearing. Next year we will have considerable fruit. As long as I have to remain in Arizona I prefer this business. I should not like to think of remaining here a lifetime. I expect by the time my children are old enough to need schooling that I will be able to sell out and engage in some business in a civilized country which will suit me better. Will write again soon. Will send this to the office as soon as an opportunity offers. With love to all from all. I remain aff your son. Frank

Frank's reassuring words alleviated his mother's fears as the Chicago newspapers reported Geronimo's well-publicized departure from San Carlos. He conveniently omitted the real purpose of his trip to Globe. Summoned on June 13 to appear as a witness in a larceny dispute, Frank brought his family to town for their safety while he gave his June 20 deposition.

TERRITORY OF AZ vs **John Thomas.** Grand Larceny

On or about May 1, 1885 "That he the said John Thomas did wilfully, unlawfully, and feloniously brand a certain sorrel mare the property of Stallo and Moody with the brand of him the said John Thomas with intent to feloniously convert said mare to his own use." [signed] A. Moody, June 10th, 1885—John W. Wentworth J.P.

Witnesses called: Andy Pringle, James and Joe Hazzard, Fred Medler, Frank Hammon, Joseph Redman.

September 28, 1885—Territory vs. John Thomas—"Grand Larceny" Brand a certain sorrel mare, the same being the property of T. C. Stallo and Alexander Moody, and of the value of $50, with the brand of him the said John Thomas, with intent to feloniously convert said mare to the use of him the said John Thomas.

Case dismissed on a technicality.[6]

Similar to many early Arizona court cases, the charges were dismissed. Interestingly, prosecution witness Andrew Pringle posted Thomas's bond.

For the first time, Frank expressed the intention to remove his family from Arizona. With the developing range disputes and Indian outbreaks, Frank re-evaluated the future. Frank, Daisy, and the children were happy at Coon Creek, but were they safe?

Coon Creek Ranch
Aug 3rd '85

Dear Sister Bertie,

I have before me your kind letters of April 22nd and June 15th which I will try and answer. You must have enjoyed your visit to Chicago very much. Charley was indeed very kind, which is not unusual for him. He is the best of brothers. I feel ashamed when I think what he has done for our home folks and that I have done nothing. Not even have I given them the pleasure of seeing me in the long eight years since I bid you farewell. Well—circumstances so arranged it. If there is any one thing I would enjoy, it would be a visit home or to see my home folks, for I have my own home now and my little family to love and care for. They are all in excellent health. Bertie talks almost everything. Eva is just commencing to stand alone. Daisy is trying to wean her. She has more of the Hammon look than Bertie. Daisy is in good health but quite thin. She has so much to do just think all our washing cooking house work and attending to the two babies.

Bertie is such a good child. She helps MaMa a great deal in looking after Eva and is very little trouble herself and is only about 2 ½ years old herself. We are getting along very nicely here at the ranch—living a calm peaceable life, with nothing exciting or of very much interest to break the monotony. Our cattle are doing well considering the season which is very dry. In the latter part of June we took our families to town. They remained there about three weeks. Then we brought them back.

I am at present building an addition to our house which when finished, will be quite comfortably fixed here. We have all kinds of vegitables from our garden and in a year or so will have all varieties of fruit from our orchard which is doing finely. We have nothing more of the indians that left the reservation a couple of months ago. They have probably arrived at their old refuge in Mexico and will probably not trouble us more until they are brought back and turned loose with plenty of arms to get fat and accumulate plenty of ammunition for another bloody raid. Write soon love to all.

Aff your bro Frank

Frank's sarcastic statement mirrors the sentiments expressed in the petition circulated the previous year. He was right. The Chiricahuas were the most violent Apaches in southern Arizona. For years, they left behind death and destruction while escaping into the Sierra Madre Mountains of Mexico. On July 29, 1882, the Mexican and United States governments signed a limited "hot pursuit" agreement permitting the U.S. Army to cross the Mexican border in pursuit of fugitives. With the signing of the agreement, the elusive Chiricahuas risked entrapment.[7]

General George Crook's reassignment to Arizona the summer of 1882 had a specific purpose: to conduct an inquisition into the violent episodes involving the Apaches and correct the problem. Known as "The Gray Fox," Crook rode into Fort Apache on a large gray mule that matched his unkempt beard. Adorned with a yellow canvas coat over blue military trousers, he balanced a double-barreled shotgun across the pommel of his saddle. His non-military demeanor was deceiving.[8]

After a seven-year absence, Crook found that "no military department could well have been in a more desperate plight." Two major skirmishes had occurred in the past months, more than fifty whites had been massacred; and 600 Chiricahuas raided north and south of the border. Throughout October, Crook held council sessions with 400 Apache chiefs and military officers. He reported, "The simple story of their wrongs, as told by various representatives of their bands...satisfied me that the Apaches had not only the best of reasons for complaining, but had displayed remarkable forbearance in remaining at peace."[9]

Crook vowed that each chief would be held responsible for the behavior and discipline of his tribesmen. The military would be called upon only if the Apaches neglected to govern themselves. Indian police were restored to their former positions. Crook proposed relocating Apaches who needed better farm land. Peaceful, industrious Indians would receive assistance; hostile, lazy Indians would be shown no mercy.[10]

Depredations stopped once Crook assumed command of the reservation. His new concerns centered on the Chiricahuas in Mexico. Only a massive expedition into Mexico's Sierra Madre would rout out the hostiles. He enlisted scouts and organized mule trains, but needed a reason to cross the border. That justification came in late March, when Indian depredations resulted in the deaths of U. S. judge Hamilton McComas and his wife, and the abduction of their six-year-old son. The insurgents disappeared across the border, and Crook had his excuse.[11]

On May 1, 1883, Crook, his officers, forty-two enlisted men, and 193 Indian scouts pursued Geronimo's band into Mexico. Led by Al Sieber, the scouts worked alone. Crook's aide, Capt. John G. Bourke, admired the scouts, "with eyes keen as a hawk's, tread as stealthy as a panther's, ears that heard everything. At times, they laughed and joked.... At night they washed their hair; cut sections of cane and made pipes for smoking or flutes with which they produced a weird music; or built an air-tight hut, poured water on hot stones, and took sacred sweat baths."[12]

Penetrating the mountains was slow and treacherous work. By mid-May an advance party of scouts discovered the hostiles' camp on a mountainside. After several skirmishes, Geronimo requested a parley with Crook. In a face-to-face meeting, Crook promised a pardon for the Chiricahuas in exchange for their peaceful return to San Carlos. The short meeting marked the most nerve-racking military conference in frontier history. Forty warriors attended, with each side anticipating treachery. Crook listened to Geronimo's legitimate grievances and peaceful overtures. Over the next few days and several conferences later, they reached an agreement.[13]

More than 300 Chiricahuas trickled back to San Carlos. By February 1884, Geronimo arrived on his white pony, angry that he required a military escort. He had made peace with the white man. Why did he need protection from him? In truth, Geronimo was being shielded from inebriated ruffians anxious to settle the score. The band brought with them 350 head of stolen cattle that the military immediately confiscated and sold, distributing the proceeds to the Apaches' Mexican victims.[14]

The January 12, 1884 edition of the *Arizona Silver Belt* reprinted an exchange of articles indicating the popular mood:

> General Crook in his annual report speaks highly of the intelligence of the Chiricahua Indians, who, he says are excessively shrewd in making treaties, and very quick to understand when they get a good bargain with the government—*San Francisco Exchange*

The *Tombstone Epitaph* replied:

> No wonder he thinks the Chiricahuas are intelligent…it would be a stupid Indian indeed who would not agree to return to a reservation and live in ease and idleness, after the assurance that he should receive immunity from punishment for all the past robberies and murders by him in the section to which he was returning.

The fate of the Apaches lay in Crook's hands. He aimed to provide them with agricultural skills designed to improve their living conditions. Just the same, Geronimo remained on the San Carlos Reservation slightly more than a year.

On the morning of May 15, 1885, an intoxicated group of armed Indians congregated outside Capt. Britton Davis's quarters. Objecting to military restrictions on the disciplining of wives and the manufacturing of tiswin, the agitated Indians demanded changes. Sensing a possible revolt, Davis promised to send for Crook at Fort Whipple to hear their grievances. Davis instructed Capt. Francis C. Pierce to send the wire.

Inexperienced and new to the post, Pierce lacked understanding of the Apache character. On this fateful day, instead of telegraphing the message as instructed, he sought Al Sieber's opinion. Sieber, himself dissipated from a night of drinking and gambling, dozed while Pierce read him the message. Sieber dismissed the dissension, telling Pierce, "Oh, it's nothing but a tizwin drunk.… Davis will handle it." Unconcerned, Pierce pigeonholed the telegram, leaving General Crook unaware of the developments at San Carlos.[15]

Without word from Crook, Geronimo became uneasy as rumors of punishment surfaced. His distrust of the white man was exceeded only by his hatred of

Mexicans, who had slaughtered his wife and children in 1858. He also recalled the brutal slaying of Chief Mangas Coloradas by U. S. soldiers during a peace council in 1863. Geronimo had stated years before, "whenever I...saw anything to remind me of former happy days my heart would ache for revenge upon Mexico." Consumed by hatred and fearful for his life, Geronimo fled for Mexico on May 18, 1885, taking with him fifty Chiricahua Apaches. In the months that followed, ten officers, nearly 100 settlers, and some peaceful Indians were killed by Geronimo's band before they crossed the border.[16]

Crook pursued the Chirichauas back into the Sierra Madre. With increased manpower, he was well prepared to wait out Geronimo's starving, depleted band. Throughout the operation, the troops relied heavily on the Indian scouts. Their keen eyesight, tracking skills, and intimate knowledge of the Chiricahuas' habits made them an invaluable asset. Hardened to the punishing 100+ degree temperature that wilted the soldiers, the scouts could travel great distances without water and locate sparse water holes. After few days in the rugged country, the sharp rocks disintegrated the soldiers' boots. Barefoot troops fell back while the scouts' tough feet allowed them to continue. Without the Apache scouts, the final Apache campaign would have failed. Crook wrote years later that "During the entire campaign... every successful encounter with the hostiles was due exclusively to the exertions of Indian scouts, ...the Chiricahuas were the most subordinate, energetic, untiring and...the most efficient of their command."[17]

In a March meeting with Crook at Cañon de los Embudos, Geronimo agreed to surrender with his band the following day. That night, Geronimo went on a drunk with liquor supplied by Robert "Bob" Tribollet. Supposedly in cahoots with the corrupt contractors who supplied the military, Tribollet told the fugitive that Crook planned to kill him after crossing the border. By morning, Geronimo had vanished.

General-in-Chief Philip Sheridan and President Grover Cleveland found the terms of Geronimo's surrender unacceptable. Serious philosophical differences occurred between Crook and Sheridan over the Indian scouts' role. Sheridan mistrusted the scouts. Frustrated by Geronimo's disappearance and under extreme political pressure, Crook resigned. General Nelson Miles, an accomplished and politically aspiring officer, replaced him.[18]

Delighted with the high-profile Geronimo assignment, Miles reveled in the recognition the position brought him. In agreement with Sheridan's "no scout" policy, Miles used only white troops. He instituted a heliographic communication system manned by a Signal Corps detachment. By flashing the sun's rays from one mountain top station to another they communicated the Indians' movements. To the superstitious Apaches, the distant flashes represented ominous and powerful spirits. In the end, the mirrored messages dashed the Apaches' last ray of hope.[19]

For three months, Miles ran 5,000 soldiers ragged pursuing the dwindling Chiricahua band, to no avail. Reluctantly, he reinstated twenty scouts, a company of infantry, and thirty-five handpicked cavalrymen to pursue Geronimo's diminished band. Finally, with dwindling supplies and overwhelming odds against him, Geronimo made surrender overtures to Capt. Henry W. Lawton through an Apache woman. Lieut. Charles Gatewood's troops tracked her back to Geronimo's rocky position. Two scouts, Martine and Kayihtah, carrying a white flag, gained access to the hideaway. One of the scouts warned Geronimo, "The troops are coming after you from all directions.... You people have no chance whatever. The War Department's aim is to kill every one of you if it takes fifty years to hunt you down."[20]

Geronimo consented to a conference with Gatewood. Then, after days of negotiations, he met with Miles. The general reassured Geronimo that his life would be spared in exchange for his surrender. "Lay down your arms and come with me to Fort Bowie, and in five days you will see your families, now in Florida with Chihuahua, and no harm will be done to you." The Chiricahuas' lives were spared, but their ancestral homeland was lost forever. They endured twenty-seven years of captivity, first in Florida, then in Alabama, and finally at Fort Sill, Oklahoma.[21]

The last military campaign with the Chirichauas extended over a year. Frank's sarcastic prediction proved wrong, Geronimo never returned to San Carlos. As Arizonans pressed for Geronimo's execution, Miles recognized the necessity of relocating the Indians immediately. The *Tombstone Epitaph* focused on the authorities' dilemma over what to do with Geronimo. "Since it has been shown that there is no legal way to hang Geronimo why not stop talking about it and hang him?" the newspaper asked. "He has forfeited all right to live."[22]

Troops herded the terrified Chiricahuas like cattle onto a ten-car train for internment in Florida. The warriors were shipped to Fort Pickens, while their families were sent to Fort Marion. Among the exiles were the loyal Indian scouts who had won the Apache war. "The shadow of the shameful way they treated these faithful Indians and United States Scouts still lies over us," one of the Chiricahuas recalled. It was the ultimate punishment—to die alone in the muggy, stifling climate foreign to them. Dr. Walter Reed found the Apache death rate from tuberculosis appalling; lung problems had been non-existent among the Indians in Arizona.[23]

In a pathetic epilogue, during Geronimo's final years in detention he reinvented himself as a notorious celebrity by selling autographs, photos, and baubles at state fairs to amuse curious Easterners. He died of pneumonia after a drunken binge that left him exposed to the elements. Symbolizing Native Americans as they entered the twentieth century, he had awkwardly straddled the fence between two worlds. As C. L. Sonnichsen perceptively put it, "Unfortunately Geronimo lived too long. He should have perished in Mexico, fighting valiantly beside his men." In later years, Geronimo's nephew Daklugie said: "we knew why Geronimo was punished. He was unwilling to give up, and he offered to die fighting for what was his by right—his country.... He tried to win back his country for his people and died a prisoner." Although isolated Apache incidents continued, the violent era of an exploited and misunderstood culture had ended.[24]

Chapter Seven

CONSTANT IN MY SOUL

*Nestled carefully in the black box lay three diaries
that were not Frank's. The top one was engraved with 1865 on its
brittle flap. Inside, the scrawled handwriting was imprecise. Splotches
of splattered ink interrupted the abbreviated entries written either by
an inexperienced hand or in haste. Written inside the front cover,
"Diary of Adeline F. Hammon 1865 & 1868." This was the diary
of Frank's mother. Accounts for each date of both years were thriftily
entered on a single page. The two smaller diaries belonged to Frank's
sister Bertie and were written twenty years later. I deduced that
Adeline's offspring inherited the inclination to chronicle their lives.*

*It appeared that Adeline was uneducated, but she was
undeterred from faithfully entering her curt passages. On the surface,
her brief statements covered only the day's toil and mundane events.
Between the lines were evidences of a depressed woman. I was struck
by the absence of cheer. Unmentioned were spring flowers, happy
music, children's prattle or joyous faith. Beauty probably surrounded
her, but perhaps she was too weary or preoccupied to notice. Why did
Adeline keep the journal? It could be that the laconic statements were
her only means of self–expression.*

*There are several types of diaries or journals. Some give
insight into the soul; others provide only a peek. Adeline Hammon's
writings give a peek into a life controlled by the circumstances that
defined her generation. Her words also offer a glimpse into Frank's
development and adventurous longings.*

Coon Creek Ranch
Oct 12ᵗʰ '85

Dear Father and Mother

I have not written to you for some time—but it is not because I do not think of you. Some-how of late my thoughts have turned toward home or my home people more than has been usual. My heart has yearned for a sight of your loved and loving faces, and it sometimes seems that "I must go home." I know that the world affords no heartier or more loving welcome than awaits me. Eight long years have passed and great changes have occurred since I bid you good bye so long ago. Little idea had any of us what the hand of time would do for us, and little thought I that so long a time would pass without my seeing your dear faces again. As I said—I often think I must go home and yet I have felt that I could not think of going without taking my little family with me. Our babies are the best and dearest in the world and I have been and am so anxious for you to know Daisy my wife—I do really believe that no better woman ever lived and you would all love her so much.

We could not go because I had not the money—the other day I recd $500.00 on my mortgage—I owed $500.00 cash borrowed in Globe. I paid $400.00 on that a/c and the balance to the merchants whom I owed. My first impulse upon receiving the money was to start East, but I owed so much that I could not do it. You see I have had not a cent return from my ranch business for two years. I have had to rustle for a living. I owe now in Globe about $200.00. In three months some notes I have will bring me in $400.00. The mortgage I held was settled a few days ago—by $500.00 cash—a deed to a house and lot in Globe valued at $500.00 and 3 mos. notes well secured for $400.00.[1]

Daisy is in Globe at present, dont know when I shall fetch her out. All were well when I left home a few days ago. This is the dryest season we have had for four or five [years] and the feed is very short and dry—yet our cattle are looking quite well.

Now I wish you should write to me father. I am anxious to hear from you and you mother when you can. I know you have so much to do and it is quite an effort for you to write. I value your letters the more on that account. With much love to all. I remain affectionately your son.

Frank M. Hammon

During Frank's eight-year absence, his aging parents, Daniel and Adeline Hammon, moved from Pennsylvania to Illinois. "Home" to Frank meant family, not his childhood home in Conneautville, Pennsylvania.

Daniel Hammon.
AUTHOR'S COLLECTION.

Adeline Fisher Hammon.
AUTHOR'S COLLECTION.

Frank was born during times of tribulation. He spent his youth fishing, playing war, and dreaming with cousin Wendell. Unaware of the complicated world he lived in, he witnessed the Civil War's residue through his parents' eyes. The war affected every aspect of his mother and father's overworked lives. Almost every local family had a member fighting; some returned intact, and some returned to die. Adeline's thirty-nine-year-old younger brother, Henry H. Fisher, died in July of 1864 in Richmond, Virginia's Libby Prison, of battle wounds.[2]

Adeline faithfully wrote in her diary every evening:

<u>March 27, 1865</u>. Verry pleasant day after a coald night—Baby a little better—washed and baked—called to see poor Byrses that the rebels starved.

Two days later Adeline attended the poor man's funeral.

The Hammons fared better than most, although raising a large family during the war took its toll. Daniel Hammon, at forty-five, was either too old or exempt from serving in the Union Army. His tannery business supplied hides to the military for boots and saddles. Daniel often traveled to Cleveland to purchase stock, then continued east to sell his hides. An educated man, he encouraged education in his sons, music in his daughters, and Sunday school for all. During Daniel's absences, lonely Adeline raised her brood and ran the household.[3]

The Hammon family lived in a substantial house requiring extra maintenance. Fifteen-year-old Dell helped her mother with the backbreaking housework. Although Adeline had little time or energy to dwell on the war, infrequent references to noted historical events creep into her monotonous diary entries:

> April 5, 1865. Windy but pleasant—done a large washing and went to the Methodist nite sosiety—good news Ritchmond taken.

Two weeks later this solemn notation:

> Wednesday April 19, 1865. Verry pleasant—visited with [illegible name] all day. D. [Daniel] went to Kingsville—the funeral services held at all places and a general time of morning for our lamented president.

During those years, Adeline's worries focused on her children's health:

> August 13, 1865. Coald but pleasant—stayed to home all day and took care of Dell and Forist [Forest]—both sick called a dockter.

In her August 13 entry, Adeline neglected to mention Frank's tenth birthday. Was it because of family illness or were birthdays not acknowledged? Perhaps birthdays had become burdensome to weary Adeline.

As an accomplished homemaker and proficient seamstress, Adeline kept careful financial accounts, listing the costs of household and sewing supplies. Her lists include yards of calico, lace, muslin, and woolens. Besides her routine chores, Adeline sewed clothing daily.

The family's social life centered on neighborly visits, friends for dinner, and evening church meetings.

> May 11, 1865. iron in the forenoon—cut glenns clothes…temperence meeting in the evening.

Adeline's focus rested on the babies and ill family members; Frank and his younger brother, Glenn, received infrequent mention in her diaries. They caused their mother little anxiety. The middle boys exhibited exceptionally good health; only her brief comments on clothing construction or occasional happenings indicate their existence.

> May 8, 1865…. Frank went to Mr. Dodges and get him a little white kitten.

Omission of her middle children's names did not reflect a lack of love. A devoutly religious woman, a devoted wife, and a tender mother, long-suffering

Adeline was preoccupied with her babies' illnesses. At a time of low infant survival, forty-four-year-old Adeline delivered her seventh and last child.[4]

Adeline knew grief. She lost two ill infants prior to Frank's birth in 1855; her brother died in a Confederate prison in 1864; both parents succumbed in 1867. Perhaps this explains the anxieties that left Adeline worried, depressed, and humorless.[5]

She punctuated her entries with notations of illnesses and funerals:

<u>August 16, 1867</u>. Bad news Marcus Hammon died at 1 o'clock this morning and heard that Charles was very sick in Erie.

<u>August 17, 1867</u>. Charles fetched home and died at eight in the evening with the lockjaw—attended Marks funeral at 2 o'clock—a very sollom time. O if Daniel was home how glad I shall be.[6]

<u>January 1, 1868</u>. A very gloomy New Years day—attended a funeral of two little boys that were drowned. Not very coald—Victor worrisum getting teeth—got a leter from sister Chloe.

<u>January 4, 1868</u>. Some snow—plenty of work— made pies and made 3 dosen candles—45 years old today…bought cutlare.

<u>January 5, 1868</u>. Pleasant winter weather—thawed some—went to church and heard a good sermon—wish to profit by it I hope that I may live a better life this year than the one that has passed.

<u>March 12, 1868</u>. Warm and Cloudy—Victor got sore eyes today verry worrisome—went to Mrs. Landons to the nite society…. Daniel got home from Cleaveland today.

<u>May 17, 1868</u>. lonesome—a very long and lonesome day—staid to home all day

<u>May 28, 1868</u>. made determination to serve the Lord.

It appears that God-fearing Adeline saw suffering as punishment for failure to "serve the Lord." She sought atonement for her perceived sins.

<u>August 31, 1868</u>. Sit still all day and took care of Victor—he is verry sick.

<u>Sept.3, 1868</u>. Pleasent weather—Victor lays stuped most of the time. I have woried all day about him but the dr thinks he is better—he gave him some new medison to night—hard work to get it down.

Frank appears to have been the healthiest of Daniel and Adeline's seven children. Perhaps to ease his mother's load, Frank spent extended periods with cousin Wendell's family. In their youth, Frank and Wendell shared dreams and adventures that grew as they grew.

The gallant tales of Frank's progenitor inspired him. Thomas Hammond was admitted a "freeman" in Providence, Rhode Island, in 1760. The son of "a

*Frank Hammon (left), about ten
years old, and Glenn Hammon
(right), about eight years old.*
AUTHOR'S COLLECTION.

*Alberta "Bertie" Hammon,
about four years old.*
AUTHOR'S COLLECTION.

sea-faring" Englishman, he settled in Scituate (Foster). About 1800, he briefly relocated his family to Killingly, Connecticut, and then migrated to Dryden, New York, about 1803.[7]

It was Thomas's youngest son, Daniel Hammon, Sr., that brought his large family to Conneautville, Pennsylvania, in 1832. At that time, Frank's father was twelve years old and the youngest of ten children. A proficient brick mason, he possibly relocated his family to work on construction of the Erie Canal. It was in Conneautville that Daniel, Jr., married Adeline Fisher and raised seven offspring.[8]

About 1870, Daniel, Jr., sold his Conneautville tannery to John Landon to become a merchant with Hammon & Gillespie in Sharon, Pennsylvania. Thirteen years later, Daniel sold his interest in the store and retired on Ottawa, Illinois, property to be near his sons. Charles, Daniel and Adeline's oldest son, owned a Traveler's Insurance Agency in Chicago; Dell married and lived in Tennessee; Glenn attended Rush Medical School in Chicago; and the three youngest, Alberta, Forest, and Victor, lived at home with their parents. Adventurous Frank, the third child, drifted the farthest away. Stories of the western frontier nourished Frank's boyhood dreams as he approached manhood. Those tales motivated his pursuit of western adventure, offering an escape from the Pennsylvania post-war depression and a somber childhood.[9]

Frank Hammon (center row, second from right) and Old Dominion Mine workers, 1885. GCHS.

Homesickness and guilt permeate Frank's last letters home. Perhaps he finally related to his parent's sacrifices. What prompted his sudden need for family support? The Chiricahuas had fled to Mexico and no longer posed a threat; a developing range dispute had not reached a crisis. Frank faced new burdens. Locked into an unprofitable ranching venture on overstocked land hit by a devastating drought, he needed to look for winter work.

The situation in Globe was bleak. In August 1884, Swiss mining engineer Alexander Trippel took over as superintendent of the Old Dominion Mine. By reorganization and wage reductions, he kept the mine operating. By January 1885 the *Silver Belt* reported:

A serious disagreement between the company and their late employees would…be unfortunate for Globe… under continued high operating expenses it would be impossible to run any longer…a general reduction in expenses was decided….The company ordered wages cut to $3.00 per day, but Superintendent Trippel…held out for a rate of $3.50 for miners and surface laborers at $3.00.

Some fulltime employees of the Old Dominion held Alexander Trippel responsible. Alice Curnow offered another side to the story:

> Through mismanagement the Old Dominion did not pay… unnecessary expense was what Trippel called a 'Blow Out'…the smelter was closed once a month and a celebration was held although no one know what was being celebrated. It was very expensive to start the smelter again and was a disadvantage to close it from a business stand. Every man was asked to donate a day's pay for this celebration…. Tom had to give a day's pay which was four dollars…. Trippel posted a notice that the mine would have to cut expenses. One half the men would work the first half of the month and the other half would work the last half of the month. But he continued to hold the 'Blow Outs'…. The old Dominion was the only mine that had been operating.[10]

Operating parttime with a minimum workforce, the Old Dominion prepared to shut its doors. Merchants were urged to lower their prices in order to relieve the financial burden on Globe's citizens. Alexander Trippel received a written dismissal and the Old Dominion shut its doors in May 1885. Alice Curnow recalled that "Through mismanagement the Old Dominion did not pay. An old man named Trippel, an educated man but with no business ability was the manager."[11]

The next winter, Frank joined hundreds of seasonal miners looking for jobs. As usual, he neglected to mention his deepest concerns to his worried parents. A weakened Daisy, feeling the effects of strenuous ranch life, expected another child. Guilt-ridden Frank realized the opportunity to take his family to Illinois had vanished. Frank left Globe to find winter work in Phoenix. Little did he realize how soon he would reunite with his home folks. The January 16, 1886 issue of the *Silver Belt* announced: "Phoenix—Mr. Frank Hammon from Globe, Gila Co, has purchased Mr. Furguson's place two miles northeast of Phoenix and will move his family here."

Chapter Eight

Sweet Bye and Bye

Our youngest daughter chose to attend Arizona State University at Tempe rather than a California college. During the next four years, my husband and I often drove east to visit her and to explore her environment. While unaware of our family's historical connection, I seemed inexplicably drawn to Arizona.

When I returned to Phoenix six years after our daughter's graduation, I arrived with new historical insight and interest. I realized that gleaming skyscrapers had replaced the alfalfa fields of an agrarian culture; built over the extinct "old town ditch," the Arizona Center revitalized the deteriorated downtown; a Bank One parking lot covered land previously occupied by Frank's archaic swimming baths. Not far from the multi-million-dollar America West Coliseum, a wrought iron cemetery fence served as a backstop for the city's indigent. Progress commingled with blight.

I looked beyond the mirrored buildings, consumerism, and sports venues. Vainly, I searched for an elusive grave in the Old Pioneer Cemetery. Frank never removed Daisy's remains as he intended. Unsuccessful in my search, I felt as if Daisy had died again. A century after her death, I grieved for Daisy lying in an unmarked grave with Phoenix's downtrodden as her sentries.

Phoenix, March 11th 1886

Dear Sister Dell

Your very kind letter reached me day before yesterday, being
delayed some days at Globe. As you see we have changed our abode
once more and I sincerely hope for the last time for some time
to come. I do not wonder you thought some of us were sick. How
ungrateful you must think me for not acknowleging the receipt of
your kind letter and thoughtful presents. But I thought Frank had
written that we had received them. There has been so many things
taking place lately that I can scarcely settle myself to write and have
been postponing it from time to time untill I would be in a more
settled and composed state of mind. First I will thank you over and
over for your kind and thoughtful presents. Rest assured they were
more appreciated and gave us more pleasure than elegant ones
from the store. The pleasure in receiving a present consists not in
the value of the present but in the spirit in which it is given. Eva's
little dress fits perfectly and she does look so sweet in it. Indeed
I think it is lovely. You surely don't find so much work on all her
[Mabel's] clothes. Bertie and Eva were so proud of their little gloves.
The first they ever had. They wore them on way from Globe here.
Frank and I were equally pleased with our presents. Mine has been
very much admired, something new here. The other things were
likewise appreciated. Eva could not get her foot in the stocking but
nevertheless they can be utilized in the sweet bye and bye of which
I will tell you presently. You see Frank and I are old fashioned, we
believe in having a large family (since we can't help ourselves).

The day before New Years Frank left Globe for Pinal, Silver
King and Phoenix to see if he could not get into some kind of paying business for the winter as we could not go out to the ranch again
soon. Well he came to Phoenix and was so taken with the beauty of
the place and the advantages it had, both mineral and agricultural
over Globe, that he stayed here two weeks looking around and
investigating and trying to find a place his cattle ranch on Coon
Creek would trade for. He did not succeed but bought a place two
and one half miles from here paying $4,000.00 for it in $1,000.00
payments and…has three and one half years to make the payments.
He came back to Globe about Jan 15th and we began packing up
and selling off our furniture and getting ready to move and we have
been upset ever since. By Feb 11th we were all ready and left Globe.
It was rather a sad leave taking for me, notwithstanding it is such a
miserable place in which to live. But I came to Globe just five years
ago last January and it was there I met Frank, it was there I lost my
mother. We were married there and our first children were born

there. So it seems more like home to me than any other. My father and two brothers are there still. We had gathered quite a circle of friends around us, in fact there was very few in Globe that I was not acquainted with and some that I thought a great deal of.

Well—we came over a very rough mountain road about half the distance, but the remainder was level as the floor. Mr Chapel a man from Globe was moving over so we all came together. Mrs C. is a very nice lady and was very kind and helped me with the children else I never could have stood the journey. In fact every one in Globe said I would be sick before I reached Phoenix as I had been feeling miserable for some time. But I stood the journey much better than I expected. Frank left us at Riverside the second day to return to Globe, hence to the ranch to gather up his cattle to bring down. It took us 3½ days to come and what a tired lot we were to be sure. But such a lovely place this is going to be. One great objection is the warm and sultry weather during all summer. The town and surrounding country for miles around is supplied with water from Salt River so named on account of the salt and brackish taste the water has. That is another objection, the well water is no better the children have been troubled with their bowels ever since we arrived and Eva has catarrh of the bowels slightly. The country is laid off in sections of 640 acres or one square mile with an irrigating ditch and broad road separating and surrounding each section. Most of the ditches have cottonwood trees planted from 15 to 20 feet apart along their banks and the wire fencing is attached to those trees. Most of the farms near Phoenix are planted in alfalfa which afford pasture for the town stock. Frank's place has about 100 acres in alfalfa, he has a quarter section or 160 acres, so we have a road on two sides of our place. The Ice Works are 1½ miles from us and the territorial Insane Assylum 1½ miles from us and about two miles from town. The building is not completed yet. The laying of the corner stone takes place next Saturday. After our arrival I was very fortunate in getting a room and board with Mrs. Calfee the Methodist ministers wife. We were quite well acquainted in Globe and fortunately Mrs. Chapel rented a house adjoining theirs so we are all together and it is so much better and pleasant for me than going to the hotel among strangers. It has been storming and disagreeable ever since we came with the exception of a few bright days. I have been expecting Frank for several days but so much rain has swollen the streams so there is no telling when he will come. I am very anxious that he should come as the first payment was to have been made March 9th but it was impossible for him to get here but the young man he bought of wants to go east for his health and I am afraid will sell to some one else; however I'll not worry as it will

Daisy Howell Hammon, tintype probably taken by Cicero Grime in summer 1882. AUTHOR'S COLLECTION.

not help matters but I know Frank is troubled. I do wish he were here this minute. I have had one letter from him and he was one days drive from Coon Creek with 65 head of cattle but it was storming and they had lost their horses. The letter was dated Feb 26th and said it would take them 10 days to make the drive providing they found their horses....

If you do not hear from me anymore untill after the last of May, do not be alarmed as at times I feel so perfectly wretched that I can scarcely hold my head up and have to neglect house, children and everything at such times. My system has been too heavily taxed the last 3 years the doctor says. Hoping this will find you all well. I will bid good bye. Give my regards to your husband and my and the babies love and kisses to little Mabel. From your loving sister.

Daisy[1]

Like the mythical Egyptian bird, Phoenix rose from the ashes of an ancient culture. It rose from the desert wilderness of a vanished society to become an agrarian paradise. Resourceful entrepreneurs rebuilt the hand-dug trenches abandoned by the Hohokam in the 1400s. For centuries, the Salt River had run uncontrolled from the eastern Arizona mountains into the Salt River Valley.

Jack Swilling and John Y. T. Smith reclaimed the first desert lands in 1868. Resurrection of the ancient aqueducts converted thousands of acres of desert into an agricultural garden. With the waters of the Salt River channeled, the pioneers cultivated the valley's fertile earth. The "Garden of the Territory" soon supplied products to military posts, Indian agencies, and mining districts. By 1879, the Southern Pacific Railroad recognized the developing town, and extended their main line to Maricopa, thirty miles to the south. The business hub of Central Arizona emerged as stagecoach and freight lines connected Maricopa with Phoenix. The *Silver Belt* observed in 1881 that "Phoenix is a pretty place with wide streets laid out at right angles and fringed with tall graceful trees. It is a dreamy place, as still as if it had taken some sleeping potion and had not recovered from the effects. Phoenix is one of those towns whose future is assured (though it may never be a great one) because it has stable industries upon which to build agriculture."[2]

The first irrigation canal, the Town Ditch, directed enough water from the Salt River to irrigate 1,000 acres. The fifty farmers who settled along its banks planted wheat and barley crops. Large wooden crates floated into place and, weighted with brush and rocks, created diversion dams that controlled the water's flow. The rich soil could be cultivated with the weirs in place. The land flourished.

From the Salt River, the ditch ran northwest along the north line of the townsite, and then turned back toward the river. As the town grew, the ditch ran through it, flowing under doorways and houses along Van Buren Street. In those early days, the ditch had several uses besides irrigation: bathing, drinking, laundry, and trash disposal. There were even rumors that saloon owners secretly washed their spittoons in its brackish waters. As Daisy indicated, even the city wells became contaminated. The *Arizona Weekly Gazette* reported that "Complaints reach us of indecent exposure of boys, and even men, bathing in the town ditch, during the day time, in plain view of the surrounding houses." The Globe *Silver Belt* saw humor in the ditch's creative uses. "The boys still bathe in the ditch running along the city," the paper observed. "The style of bathing suit used last year is still in vogue. It consists of cotton in each ear." Finally, in December 1882 the Tucson *Arizona Citizen* announced the construction of a 100-square-foot rock-sided swimming bath for decently attired swimmers. Meanwhile, construction on other canals began.[3]

Financed by outside capital, the Arizona Canal relied upon the ingenuity of William J. Murphy. A former Santa Fe Railroad contractor and Illinois Civil War officer, Murphy guided the troubled project to completion. Adequate funding challenged the project, built on speculation. Murphy traveled to major cities throughout the United States selling bonds to complete the canal. By organizing the Valley Bank of Phoenix, Murphy secured liberal loans to keep the project alive.

When completed June 1885, the canal connected to the Salt River thirty miles northeast of Phoenix. Based on the same principle as the existing system, it traversed the north valley, connecting to the New River forty-one miles away. The Arizona Canal, wider and longer than the other aqueducts, provided cultivation to 80,000 acres of desert.[4]

Subcontractor J. T. Simms worked on section four and took his salary in bonds totaling $75,000. Though other subcontractors quit the struggling project, Simms stayed on until the spring of 1884. W. J. Murphy, quoted in the *Weekly Phoenix Herald,* April 10, 1884, complained that "Simms has abandoned his contract. He had been trying to get me to pay to him the final 10% of what work he has already done. He is not entitled to…bonds." By the summer of 1885, Simms advertised the sale of his discounted bonds in a Chicago newspaper for $33,000.[5]

Phoenix Apl 9th '86

Dear Bro Glenn

I recd your kind letter yesterday, and will answer it immediately and then wont forget it. I am very tired and so my letter may be, if so, you have my excuse. I am very buisy all the time, work hard, and am glad to see night arrive and am so tired then that it is difficult to persuade myself to use a pen. You have perhaps seen my letter home ere this. I am located at Phoenix on a farm, which has been neglected for a longtime, and needs lots of work. We will get it into shape as soon as possible and all into alfalfa. We shall make a speciality of cattle and dairying. My partner Mr. Ferguson can get money from the East and we shall probably put a lot of cattle on our range near Globe. We can drive the steers down here and fatten them on the ranch and have a good market for them here.

We have 160 acres of as fine land as ever lay out of doors—I own only ½ interest in ½ of it. It is only two miles from Phoenix, and has as good water privledges as any place in the valley—Every foot is as level as a floor and will grow anything from semi tropical fruits to fruits and crops raised in the East. We cut alfalfa here five times every summer and get an average of 1½ tons per acre per cutting, making 12½ tons of hay per acre and it will then furnish good pasture all winter. We are sure of a crop, because we depend upon irrigation we are proof against drouth.

We dont suffer near as much from the heat as you—and we never have cold enough to make one uncomfortable—The country here is perfectly level for probably hundreds of miles it is all desert beyond the limits of the water. This was all a desert before the canals were dug which reclaimed this beautiful section. Now it is a genuine paridise. You could not wish to see a nicer country. It will, before many years be a great fruit country. It is as good and will be as noted as California.

We like it very much and are much pleased with our change. Are all in good health. Will try and write home oftener—Write often. Love to all from your brother and sister.

Frank and Daisy

A year earlier, the May 1885 *Phoenix Herald* had reported that "The Phoenix Swimming Baths now in preparation by Mr. J. R. Simms just at the head of Center street will be a great convenience to the city. They will be very available being but a little over three blocks from the line Washington street. They will be ready for business in the next twelve or fifteen days." Was sub-contractor Simms the same gentleman who ran the swimming baths and returned east for his health? Probably. During the summer of 1886, in addition to his dairy business, Frank Hammon assumed management of the swimming baths on the corner of Van Buren and Center (Central) Street.[6]

Phoenix A Ter.
April 26th '86

Dear Sister Alberta

Before me are two letters from you, one written in Jan and the other on April 16th. I dont remember if I have answered the former or not, I know I have not the latter. You are my best correspondent. You have so much patience and perserverance in writing—I dont deserve it—for I am so irregular in writing, myself. I value your letters more that I can tell. We are getting along very well— are starting a dairy and will start a milk wagon in town in a few days.

I am working hard every day and am very tired when night comes. Daisy likes it much better than in Globe and so I am contented. I am so anxious to get every thing comfortable and pleasant for her and the children. I tell you Bertie she is the best little wife and mother in the world. I believe I admire and love her more and more as we grow older. Our babies are the best and sweetest. How much I wish you could see them. Bertie is a regular little chatterbox and so is Eva. Bertie has such a good disposition—taking after her mother—Eva has lots of temper—taking it I suppose from her Dad—All are well.

I was greived for our cousins over Aunt Harriets death—Dear Aunt Harriet. She always seemed the dearest Aunt to me—I was always there so much and she was always so kind to me—May she rest in peace. Daisy sends love to all and also your affectionate brother.

Frank[7]

Although Frank never mentioned the swimming baths in his letters home, he wrote enthusiastically of his new dairy business. By early summer he and his partner, Wilson B. Ferguson, had established commercial and individual milk accounts with "Assylum, G. A. Chapel, Frank Luke, Smith, G. Hop, Meyers (Baker), Garside, Percy Fulton, P. Smith, St. Cloud Restaurant, Cabinet Restaurant, Capitol Saloon, [and] Mr. George Slushinger."[8]

Phoenix A Ter
June 12th '86

Dear Mother,

I suppose I have not written home for a long time and you are anxious to hear from us, I am so very buisy that I get no time to write scarcely—I get up at 3 OC in the morning and help milk the cows and then start immediately for town with the milk. I come back about 8 OC AM and work until two OC PM when we milk again and start again for town. I get back about 6 PM in the evening and when I get the cans washed and scalded and the chores done it is about 8 or 9 OC and bed time. I get only about 6 hours sleep.

About one week ago tomorrow night Daisy was sick and gave birth to a young <u>Hammon</u> a boy and both are doing well. I have intended every day to write but have neglected it. He weighed about 6½ lbs and is very thin, probably on a/c of Daisys working up to the time of her confinement. He is strong and healthy and is getting fat. Daisy has reminded me every day that I ought to write but have neglected it until now.

Bertie and Eva are well and fat. Now must go to bed but will write again soon. Love to all. Aff your son

Frank[9]

Daisy and Frank's letters exuded hope and happiness. They found serenity, but fate interceded.

Phoenix Arizona
Aug 18th '86

Dear Father and Mother

I have had a terrible affliction. We buried Daisy today. She died yesterday about two o'clock in the afternoon—The doctor said from child birth fever. Oh how lonesome I am I can scarcely realize my loss, and the poor little babies how fearfully sad for them. They do not know their loss and it is better so. I dont know what to do now, and may bring them on to you. I know they would be welcome. Without their mother I dare not try to raise them in this demoralizing country.

Daisy was sick a long time with her breast which pulled her down considerable and then with a kind of fever and ended as stated above. I am so very very lonesome. I feel as if it were all a dream—she bid me good bye yesterday morning as I left for the ranch and said she felt better, I came back about noon and found her delerious. I brought the doctor immediately, but we only came to see her die. Before this reaches you I may be on my road for home. The children are well now. Love to all. Affectionately your son.

Frank

Her father's anguished cries bewildered and frightened three-year-old Bertie. "Oh, Daisy! Oh, Daisy!" Frank cried as he paced the floor of the tiny house. Bertie followed him, back and forth, trying to comprehend her father's suffering and her mother's absence. Frank's confused daughters filled his arms, and he wept uncontrollably into their tousled hair.[10]

With spent emotions, Frank passed through the rituals of death remembered so well from his childhood. Dazed, he found the strength to write his parents. The children's welfare was foremost on his mind. The thought of raising his motherless babies alone was incomprehensible. Daisy had raised the children and handled the household; Frank provided for his family. The Coon Creek ranch, Globe properties, and the Phoenix enterprises tied up his funds. Abandoning his holdings was unthinkable. They were his children's future. As an honorable man, he had debts to pay. In his grief, Frank could think of only one answer to his dilemma: take the children to his parents in Illinois and return to Arizona to settle his business affairs.

The August 20, 1886, *Arizona Gazette* carried Daisy's obituary:

The wife of Frank Hammond, who is conducting the swimming baths in this city, died in this city yesterday. She was a most estimable lady, and was pledged in marriage to Mr. Hammond at Globe. Her illness was a protracted one, nevertheless the death was unexpected. Mrs. Hammond was about 21 years of age and leaves several children to mourn her early death. The funeral took place this afternoon. We extend our condolences.[11]

In the same issue, the newspaper noted: "Twenty-five milk cows for sale on pasture within three miles of Phoenix. Enquire of Frank M. Hammond at Phoenix swimming baths, Phoenix, A.T."

The August 28, 1886 *Silver Belt* reported that "The news of the death of Mrs. Frank Hammon, in Phoenix, on the 18th, was received in Globe her former home, with profound sorrow. She was a woman of exemplary domestic and christian virtues, and in her demise society has lost one of its brightest ornaments."

No records exist indicating that Frank actually sold his cows. Daisy's sudden death added new debts: Dr. Wharton's bill, expenses to Henry Ryder for Daisy's burial, $600 that Frank had borrowed from his brother, Charles. With the money from home, he purchased train tickets for his family and for baby Milton's wet

Alberta (left) and Eva (right) Hammon, Frank and Daisy's daughters, taken after their arrival in Ottawa, Illinois, following their mother's death.
AUTHOR'S COLLECTION.

nurse. The logistics of taking the children to Illinois had to be staggering. But perhaps the trip was a blessing for desolate Frank. It distracted him from his internalized grief and guilt.[12]

The dusty, jolting stagecoach ride to the train depot in Maricopa took six hours. Exhausting as that trip was, it paled in comparison to the two-week trip that lay ahead. Frank and his brood traveled on the Southern Pacific from Maricopa to Oakland, California. They rested at Wendell Hammon's home before continuing. From Oakland, the Atlantic & Pacific Express carried them to Ogden, Utah, where they transferred to the Union Pacific destined for Chicago. No dining cars, or disposable diapers, existed to ease their journey. The train stopped periodically so that passengers could get off and purchase food and drinks.[13]

At one of the stops, Frank disembarked to buy food, leaving the children with Milton's nurse. While the baby nursed, Bertie and Eva entertained themselves in the car. Frank returned to find two-year-old Eva missing. A frantic search ensued as the train slowly pulled away from the station. To the relief of all, a passenger found little Eva curled up under his seat, asleep.[14]

A week later, as the train pulled into Chicago's Union Station, Frank searched for the "loved and loving faces" that he longed to see. He and his little ones needed their love more than ever. Daniel and Adeline Hammon, familiar with Frank's pain, welcomed the heartsick, bedraggled family with open arms.

Part Two

THE DIARIES

Each young and ardent person writes a diary

which when the hours of prayer and penitence arrive,

he inscribes his soul.

EMERSON

Chapter Nine

RESOLVE

*T*he disparity struck me! Frank's emotional letter to
Bertie contrasted sharply with his impersonal journal entries. Daisy
and the children were unmentioned. It was as if the children did not
exist. How could Frank have suffered such loss without mentioning
them? What was the purpose of the journals?

I finally understood. Frank experienced such raw,
intense grief that he suppressed it. Struggling against paralyzing
remorse, his life's purpose centered on providing for his babies. He
could not afford the luxury of melancholy.

My mind filled with questions. Was the Phoenix move
premature in light of Daisy's condition? Had Frank's ambitions
outweighed his better judgment? Why had Frank returned to Globe,
a place offering few opportunities? I assumed that his old friendships drew him back. These were intriguing questions that begged for
answers.

I struggled to resolve in my own mind how Frank could
leave his babies. A century later, I found it easy to second-guess
Frank's decisions. Certainly he weighed his options and considered
his family's best interests. Sadly, these same concerns probably filtered
through Frank's mind as he stoically drove his cattle to the Tonto
Basin.

As for his journal, what began as an impersonal financial accounting gradually became something more.

Phoenix Ariz
Oct 1st '86

Dear sister Bertie

Your very welcome letter I recd last evening, and I assure you
it did me good. I could almost imagine that I was back there talking to you and not that two thousand miles seperates us who were
together only a few days ago. I feel very lonely here now. The only
thing I have to love is the lonely grave in the cemetery at Phoenix.
Oh how I dread to leave it. I wish I could take it with me where ever
I go. Some day if I ever get able I shall remove the remains to some
beautiful spot in some beautiful place back East. It does me good to
think that if I live an upright religious life that I shall meet Daisy in
a happier land where there will be no more seperation and I have
determined that come what may, I will trust in the lord to give me
strength to be a christian even in this country, and to live a better
life than I have that I may be worthy of joining her in that happier
land. I feel I need much help for I think there is more temptation
here to the square inch than in a whole county back home. I am
trying to get things straightened out as much as possible but it is
discouraging work.

We will start back with the cattle for the range inside of a week
so direct all communications for me to Globe—until further notice.
Give my kindest regards to Mr and Mrs Fletcher, and ask their pardon for my neglect in not calling upon them.

Now I am anxious to hear often even if your letters are short
or even a postal. Tell mother I expect to sell my RR ticket [any] day
when I will send some money. With love to all I remain your affectionate bro.

Frank

P.S. I want you to make efforts to get a good girl and one that will
stay—I dont want mother to attempt to try to get along without
one even for a short time, if she does I shall be offended, for if she
should get sick I should think I was the cause. I will find some way to
get the money to pay the expenses.

To conserve on money, Frank probably returned to Arizona by overland
stagecoach, a tedious and difficult journey. Fourteen days and nights of continuous dusty travel must have tried his patience. Frank either rode backward in the
stage's front seat or in a middle seat, interlocking knees with passengers facing
him. With heavy mail in the boot, the rear-end weight forced front- seat passengers
awkwardly forward. The coach's swaying caused queasiness in many unseasoned
travelers, dismaying other passengers. Respite came when the travelers disembarked to lessen the uphill load or to push a mired stage from sand.

Riding for days with unwashed, ill-mannered, cigar-smoking, inebriated gents might curb any traveler's appetite. If not, cowboy cuisine at the stage station would: leathery beef, greasy pork, soggy cornbread, mesquite beans, and coffee. Frank's return trip with nine or more jostled passengers in a cramped coach could not have been restful. Lost in reverie, Frank probably was unaware of his surroundings and discomfort. The miles passed before his unseeing gaze as he contemplated the direction of his life.[1]

There were no allowances for frail human emotions in that callused country. Death, violence, and survival were part of frontier life. The early settlers didn't have the luxury of dealing with their grief; they just endured it. In Frank's case, coping with work and impersonal business dealings probably diminished his pain. Impassively, Frank went through the preparations of returning to Coon Creek.

> Oct 3 [1886]. Paid Mr. Lount one months rent making three mos paid to Oct 9th on swimming baths.

> Oct 4. Sold to second hand store a lot of old goods for $34.00 Excepting the sewing machine—sent $30.00 home.

On October 7, Frank, Mr. Ferguson, and hired hand "Boody" began their cattle drive to Coon Creek. By the third day Ferguson became ill and returned to Phoenix. Boody and Frank soldiered on, following the Salt River route with the cattle.[2]

> Oct 8. Linebacks calf went back last night—Drove to three miles this side of McDowell. Fergusons...feeling bad and about played.

> Oct 9. Ferguson afraid he cant get through and went back. Boody and I drove to Ateros [Oteros]—all OK.

> Oct 10. Drove to Sam Flowers and found good feed.

> Oct 11. Drove to Tobe Kleins and correled cattle. Bought hay for horses for 3.00.

> Oct 12. Drove to Salt River near Kenton's.

> Oct 13. Drove home to Coon Creek with everything all OK.

> Oct 14. Went up on range found horses and our colt all OK. He looks well.

> Oct 15. Went down creek found cattle. We drove in all OK.

What a lonely homecoming it must have been. Silently, Frank entered the empty house, repaired the broken corral and persevered.

> Oct 18. Went over to Rogginstroghs [Rogginstroh, Rockinstraw]—Not at home shot a duck. Caught some nice fish and had a boil supper.[3]

With the cattle settled on the range for the winter, Frank wrote to Mr. Ferguson dissolving their partnership. His dream deserted, Frank decided to concentrate on the Coon Creek ranch.[4]

Oct 19. Boody drove down horses. Kept up Katy and Black mule which he will start with to Phoenix tomorrow. Wrote to Ferguson to close partnership.

Frank needed to keep busy, but more importantly he needed an income. He left for Globe and stopped to visit friends along the way.

Oct 21. Left Moodys for town, stopped at Pringles Camp, went on and stopped at Geo. Shutes overnight.

Oct 23. Stayed with Geo Shutes over last night, and went down to Bob Pringles with Henry [Middleton] and Bob whom I met coming from town.

Sun. Oct 24. Stayed last night at Bob Pringles. Went to work this morning for the Pringle Estate. Am to ride my own horses and help the boys at the cattle ranch at Cherry Creek. Henry and I went over to ranch today.

The *Silver Belt* on October 28, 1886, reported that "Frank Hammon, who has resided in Phoenix for sometime will give his whole attention to his cattle, which have been placed on his Cherry Creek range."

Frank's temporary employment with the Pringle Estate resulted from an unfortunate incident the previous spring that left Bob Pringle shorthanded. For years, Andy and Bob Pringle had owned two ranches: one on Pinal Creek below the Salt River and the Flying H north of the confluence of the Salt River and Cherry Creek. The Cherry Creek range was adjacent to the Flying V (old Middleton ranch) owned by George Newton and Jeremiah J. (Jerry) Vosburgh.[5]

Springtime arrived early on Pringle's Cherry Creek range. By late May desert-like conditions prevailed, offering dried, mature grasses. The higher elevation brought a late spring to the Flying V and provided an abundance of lush spring grasses well into June.

For years, Andy Pringle had shifted his herd north as the grasses withered in the lower basin. Over the years, friction evolved between Jerry Vosburgh and the Pringles. Andy claimed a legal right to the unfenced range. Vosburgh suggested constructing a drift fence between the two ranges. Being a frugal Scotsman, Andy refused to share expenses. Animosity festered until, in the spring of 1886, Andy Pringle's life came to an inauspicious end.

Twice a year, local cattlemen cooperated in round-ups. When Andy Pringle joined his neighbors at the Flying V ranch for the spring rodeo, his distrust of John Thomas and the dismissed court charges the previous fall were still on his mind. On the morning of May 28, Andy and John argued over ownership of a saddle blanket. Pringle's temper flared, and he challenged Thomas with a knife. Thomas grabbed the blanket and ran, with Pringle in pursuit. Overtaken, Thomas turned and fired his six-shooter, fatally wounding the startled Pringle. Was Andy set-up to be killed?[6]

Rumors circulated suggesting the Flying V ranch had offered a $500 bounty on Andy Pringle's life. In spite of Thomas's claim of self-defense, Robert Pringle pressed for the arrest of his brother's killer. An indictment for second-degree murder was brought against John Thomas. His defense hinged on Jerry Vosburgh's testimony and character witnesses from Globe. Vosburgh never appeared. With a weak defense, John Thomas was convicted.[7]

Thomas's supporters thought Pringle's money had influenced the verdict. Why did witnesses fail to show for the Prescott trial? Did Vosburgh keep a low profile to avoid implication? John Thomas spent five and a half years of a fifteen-year sentence in Yuma Territorial Prison for Andy Pringle's murder.[8]

Shorthanded in the fall of 1886, Robert Pringle offered Frank a temporary solution to his financial worries. By the end of the rodeo in mid-November, Frank once again looked for work.

Nov 19. Moved our duds over to Coon Creek—Bob Samuels went down to the river took my pack saddle and wants to buy one. Henry and I went up and changed horses. I got the bay colt Charley and he my mule Jack. I have worked for Pringle 26 days. Wrote to Ferguson.[9]

Nov 20. Rode around on Dry Creek. Drove up and branded Blabs steer calf. Lamed my horse Charley badly.

Nov 22. Started for Globe—Henry and I arrived at dark, rode Jack in.

Nov 23. Loafed around town and was subpoenaed as trial juror to appear on 25th.

Nov 24. Pringle paid me $39.00 for labor in full. Deposited with Sultan. Drew $40.00 from Van Wegenen and 5.00 yesterday. Sent $30.00 home.

Nov 25. Thanksgiving Day—Very dull—sent order by Wm Brookner for suit of clothes to N.Y. to cost about $21.50 to 25.00—Shall go on jury duty tomorrow.

Nov 26. Court opened—Sat on case of Robinson vs Pascoe—We could not agree— discharged about 8 pm.

Nov 28. Saw McCabe about renting house—Very quiet and hard to pass the time.

Nov 29. Appeared in court and was put on jury to try Geo Frazier, alias Tuttle for forging. Could not agree.

Nov 30. Was on no jury today—Thompson was tried for perjury, but not convicted.

Dec 1. Got excused from jury for term. Got order from clerk Mileage $6.00—four days @ $2.00=$8.00—Paid to Bailey on a/c $14.00. Went to tanks [Bloody Tanks Wash] to get Henry to go out to ranch and help me drive in some beef steers.[10]

Dec 2. Went to ranch arrived at dark. Charley Tebbs [Tibbs] arrived—found a steer on river and corraled there.

Dec 4. Cy and Floyd Blivens [Blevins] arrived last evening, went out and drove in two steers and 4 cows and calves for Henry.

Dec 5. Found my other steer and Henry found what he wanted and turned them over to Cy Blivens for his ranch on river. Went to Geo Shutes, namely 6 cows with calves. Drove my steers to Wheat Fields. Henry and Chas Tebbs accompanying me.

Dec 6. Drove steers to Globe and corraled at Redmans. Arrived about one o'clock. Paid my taxes at $47.37. Withdrew of Sultans $39.00. Withdrew from VanWagenens 8.50. Went to the tanks on the road to Phoenix.

On December 7 Frank left for Phoenix to dissolve his partnership with Wilson Ferguson.

Dec 13. Ferguson and I disolved our partnership. He taking the ranch at Phoenix with the water right, tools and the black mule. He to pay the taxes. I to take for my share the brand of cattle and horses and all horse stock belonging to the firm but the black mule, also the spring wagon and harness. Found date of note at bank—Oct 23, 1886. Talked with Ryder about bill and Joe Chinaman. Left sewing machine in charge of Ferguson for Sears if he wants it for $25.00 payable in mo. payments of $5.00 each. Mr. C. H. Burie left RR ticket with. Got Herald office bill. Mrs. Melton will send bill to Globe. Sent $10.00 to father telling to get Christmas presents for my babies. Will start for Globe tomorrow around road in wagon.

Dec 14. Went to town, saw Dr. Horton [Wharton]. He will give me time on my bill. Left sewing machine at Sears office perhaps he will buy it. Left for Globe with spring wagon.

Dec 19. Drove to Globe arrived all OK at 4 pm.

Dec 20. Moved my things into house on the hill until I rent it. Recd photos of Eva and Bertie. Took up my note of Mrs. Welch of $200.00 and gave a new note for $500.00 securing it by a chattel mortgage on my brand of cattle. She paying me $300.00 cash. Paid Mrs Welch the interest on note $200.00 up to date and destroyed it. Paid Wm. Brookner for my clothes ordered through him $23.50. Paid ½ acknowledging mortgage $.50. Sent to Henry Ryder to apply on a/c funeral $50.00. Received from Van Wegenen to apply on house rent to me $25.00. Sent Alonzo Baileys check for $205.00 on the Wells Fargo & Co Bank

Globe skating rink, ca. 1885. C. S. FLY PHOTO, AHS/TUCSON #13,774.

of San Francisco to the Valley Bank of Phoenix in payment of my note of $200.00 due Dec 23, 1886.

Dec 21. Started a raffle for Dick the sorrell colt I drove from Phoenix—20 chances @ $5.00 each.

Dec 22. Worked up raffle around town.

Dec 23. Arrived town. Henry arrived from Salt River. Went to Athletic Exibition and Dance.

The reconstructed rink became the social center for the town's respectable activities. It served the town as a theater, dance hall, and skating rink in the winter. On this Wednesday night, the Globe Athletic Club gave a fencing and weightlifting exhibition at the decorated rink. Refreshments and dancing followed the demonstrations.

Frank Hammon (front row, left center) with Globe athletes, ca. 1885.
AHS/TUCSON #61-145.

<u>Dec 24</u>. The day before Christmas witnessed the Christmas exhibition and tree.

The Methodist church was resplendent with boughs and wreaths of evergreens. A representation of a pipe organ stood behind the pulpit, and musicians accompanied the enthusiastic caroling of young and old. On a platform, left of the pulpit, stood a Christmas tree glittering with crystal ornaments that "scintillated under the radiance of the wax tapers interspersed among the branches, and which twinkled like diminutive stars."[11]

Perhaps the joyful Christmas carols, messages of hope, and good friends helped fill Frank's emptiness. On the other hand, the joyous celebration without

Daisy may have accentuated his loneliness. Certainly, his thoughts were of his babies and of past Christmases.

> Dec 25. Raffled of[f] my sorrel colt and got $80.00 for him. He was won by Wm. Zimmerman. Paid Charles Taylor my bill to date of $20.90.

What a sad and lonely Christmas for Frank. As his fractured family spent the holiday 2,000 miles away, he auctioned off his horse. With quiet dignity and no mention of his distress, he found comfort in his friendship with Reverend Calfee.

> Dec 27. Gave Calfee present of $10.00—Am looking for work, but poor prospect.

> Dec 28. Around town with little to do.

> Dec 30. Helped Mr. Calfee fix curbing for well and broke dinner with him.

> Dec 31. Was around town found nothing to do.

It was the sad conclusion to a tragic year. Frank's spirits were down but not broken.

Chapter Ten

NECESSITY AND HONORABLE

I chuckled to myself, envisioning the reaction that several discoveries would have on my conservative elders. They had claimed Francis Howell was a displaced teacher from Georgia who had migrated west after the Civil War. In reality, he was an uneducated 49er from Missouri suffering from "gold fever." At age sixty-seven, Francis Howell married a twenty-three-year-old unwed mother!

I later discovered poor Francis had sold his Globe holdings and moved his bride and baby to bustling Bisbee, where a few years later he died alone in a rented room. No family member attended his funeral. A century later, I placed wildflowers on the headstone donated by Bisbee's Masons. Unlike Eleanor and Daisy, he lies in a marked grave.

For Frank it was a new year with renewed hope, and a new job sorting ore for Jack Eaton in the Howard Mine at Pioneer, ten miles south of Globe.

Jan 4. Moved trunk to Mr. Calfees house. Will go over to the Pioneer tomorrow to work. Sat on jury today. Durea vs Copeland.

Jan 5. Jury case continued until today. Left my note for $100.00 against J. W. Ellison in Julius Sultans safe....

Jan 7. I find sorting ore not hard nor heavy work, but tedious.

Jan 8. Am getting used to my task.

Over at the Howard Mine, Frank found the miners' morale low with wages at $2.50 per day and a pay increase denied.

Jan 9. Scotty quit today so I think my job secure.

Jan 16. Looks like a storm. Weather has moderated. Recd postal from Calfee.

Jan 17. Went out and got Jacks horses. Have not seen Kitty for several days. Globe Mine and Smelting have closed down. Only 18 men left in mine. Channcy Gunn came over today.

Jan 18. Windy and chilly–Calfee wrote that he would be along on way to Tuson tomorrow. Will look for Kitty in morning.

Jan 19. Got up Kitty for Mr. Calfee, and sent her to him by the buck board.

It would appear that a man of the cloth was not immune from being robbed. The *Silver Belt* had this snappy little comment under the heading of local news: "The horse of Reverend D. W. Calfee, which disappeared from his view, bare-footed, about the 1st of January has reappeared a few days since, shod and having the appearance of hard usage. The gentleman who had him spotted and will doubtless be called upon to account."[1]

Jan 23. Sent Mrs. Anna Welch an order on Van Wagenen for $10.00 for interest on note for one mo. from or to Jan 20, 1887. Sent to Brookner by Charley the stage driver $3.00 to make out P. O. order and enclosed in letter sent him and directed to D. N. Hunsaker, Wilcox, A. T. to pay for 1 mo. advertising in Stockman.

Jan 26. Clouding up some rain. Prospect of a raise of wages.

Jan 28. Calfee sent Kitty back. Wrote to Brookner to enclose in letter enclosed to him a P. O. money order for $50.00 which amount Redman deposited with him for me. Enclosed letter directed to D. Hammon, Ottawa, Ill.

Jan 31. Asked for increase in wages. Didn't get it.

Francis "Frank" N. Howell.
AUTHOR'S COLLECTION.

<u>Feb 1</u>. Dan came back from town and said miners came with him. Wind blowing from the South, some like a storm.

<u>Feb 2</u>. Will stay for the present. The boys are dissatisfied.

While Frank Hammon sorted ore in the Howard Mine, his father-in-law, Francis Howell, sold merchandise in Alonzo Bailey's store in Globe. Daisy's father also expressed his loneliness in correspondence with Frank's sister. In four short years, Francis had lost a wife, a daughter, and three grandchildren.

Miss Alberta E. Hammon
Globe, A. T. Jan 26, 1887

Miss Hammon
    No doubt you think me naughty in not answering sooner, but miss, allow me to beg pardon. I wrote on Sunday evening after receiving your letter and stuck it in my pocket and forgot to mail it and the other evening I happened to find it which gave me surprise to think I had been so negligent, but shall be more punctual in the future. Was glad to hear from the children and hope someday to see them. Oh, how bad I want to see Bertie and Eva. Tell them I am

at the store and have nice crackers, and wish it was so I could give them some. Tell Bertie I often times think of her and always will. I feel quite lonely. If she were here I could enjoy her little prattle very much. Eva does not remember me I suppose. Tell them their Pa is quite well and at work in the mines. I will look for this photo soon. I think they are so pretty. Tell Bertie, Susie Van Wagenen is well and Aunty White also.

Globe is quite dull at present, but we hope for a better future. I will enclose a program for next Friday. You can see that we are not dead out here, but enjoy ourselves sometimes. Hoping to hear from you soon. I remain yours. Love to the children.

[Francis] Frank Howell

Francis Howell must have found comfort in Globe's social activities and the camaraderie of the Freemasons. As promised, Francis enclosed a program for the Globe Athletic Club's Masquerade Ball.

The masked ball was the first social event of 1887 and well attended. The partygoers dressed in every conceivable disguise, some artistic, others humorous. Among the costumed guests were Francis Howell camouflaged as a domino; Cy Blevins and Ed Howell disguised as defeated football players; Charles Connell draped as Liberty; G. W. P. Hunt masked as a Monk. Who would have predicted that G. W. P. Hunt, the cloaked monk, was destined to become Globe's famous adopted-son.[2]

George Wiley Paul Hunt trudged into Globe during the fall of 1881, leading a mule loaded with his earthly possessions. The overalled, mustached youth found work at Pascoe's Hotel, "walloping pots" and hurling hash while studying political science and business on the side. He toiled as a "mucker" in the Old Dominion Mine and tried his hand at ranching. His break came in 1890 when Alonzo Bailey hired him as a delivery boy, eventually promoting him to clerk and then to manager. Within a few years the balding businessman rose to become president of the Old Dominion Commercial Company. He entered politics and served seven two-year terms as Arizona governor. The state rose with G. W. P. Hunt from obscurity to self-respect. Helen "Duette" Ellison, daughter of J. W. and Susan Ellison, became Arizona's First Lady.[3]

Feb 3. Teams left with five tons of ore. Tom Curry came today.

Feb 4. Beautiful day. Three men came today; one miner, one engineer, one ore sorter.

Feb 5. Cloudy and looks like a storm. May go to town tomorrow. Letter from Mother tonight.

Feb 10. Presented my time check to Durea. He paid me $5.00 on it. Left it on deposit with him until returns come in bal due on it $52.67. Witness quite a mess at McNallys [McNellys]. One man nearly killed.

The February 19, 1887 *Silver Belt* gave this account of the altercation: "J. M. [Cap] Adams bound over for assault on Cornelius Crowley bond of $2,500. Charge of assault with intent to kill Cap Adams who feloniously assaulted Cornelius Crowley with intent to kill ran raving mad during preliminary hearing."

Feb 11. Put Kitty in Frakes's stable. Paid Joe Hollender $3.00 leaving bal. due him $1.00.

Feb 12. Notified Frank Blackledge to vacate my house inside of four days. Went to Salt River.

Feb 13. Slept at Mr. Kenton's. Henrys hand is very bad with a fever. Went over to the ranch. Some person has robbed house of flour, yeast powder, chaps, my ring too. Saw several young calves.

Feb 14. Went up to look for the horses. Found Katy & Bessie with 3 colts. Could not find others. Must be at Oak Springs. Cattle look thin.

Feb 15. Went to town. F. Blackledge came to me and I will let him stay in the house for present. He owes for rent from Aug 1, 1886 at $10.00 per mo.

Feb 16. Around town waiting developments. Returns not in yet. Don't think I shall go back to the Pioneer [mine].

Feb 19. Henry returned home. Went out to the Fame Mine today and got employment. Will go out next Tuesday. Blankets arrived from Pioneer today.

Feb 20. Attended farewell party given at Dr. Treppels [mine superintendent] for Ed Lynes and Gene Aschelman.

Feb 21. I feel rather mixed this morning. Peeped in to Misses Ogdens [teacher] birthday party this evening.

Feb 22. Went to work at the Fame Mine @ $3.00 per day. Am batching with Harry Hancock.

Meanwhile, Frank Hammon still tried to collect wages from the Howard Mine.

Feb 27. Went out and found Kitty and went to town. Jack Eaton has not read the returns yet, so I could not get my pay yet....

Mar 2-3-4-5. Worked full time.

Mar 6. Went to town–will go out to ranch for a few days–collected from my work at Pioneer $57.67. Paid C. E. Taylor $5.00 which I borrowed of him. Paid Durea $6.50 in full. Sent home to Father $40.00.

Mar 7. Clare Howell and I went out to the ranch–arrived at dark. Met Mr Middleton at Wheat Fields coming home from Flagstaff.

<u>Mar 8</u>. Went up and drove down the horses. Branded Kate, Jack and Charley. Also Kates mule colt and Bessies colt. Also branded Henrys two year old colt and two calves, 1 heifer and 1 Steer.

<u>Mar 9</u>. Bessie got away last eve I had to hunt for her this AM. Branded for Clare today 2 steer calves and for Henry 2 steer and 5 heifers.

<u>Mar 10</u>. Drove down from dry creek and left [cattle] in corral.

Frank drove his cattle from Dry Creek to the corral, unaware of the tragedy unfolding at San Carlos that day. Tranquility had reigned over the reservation following Geronimo's deportation to Florida. The San Carlos Apaches made progress assimilating into the Anglo world, but the transition was easier for some than others. For Nah-deiz-az the adjustment appeared smooth.

Nah-deiz-az easily acclimated himself to his environs after his family's relocation in 1875. His mother wasn't as fortunate, dying shortly after their arrival at San Carlos. The bright Apache youth attended Carlisle Indian School near Harrisburg, Pennsylvania. As a promising student, Nah-deiz-az studied general academic courses. He learned to speak English and excelled in agricultural classes that were most applicable to reservation life.[4]

When he returned to San Carlos, Nah-deiz-az settled with his father on a small plot of fertile land. Dubbed the "Carlisle Kid," he became self-supporting and abided by "white man's" rules. Unfortunately, the rules kept changing. His land now fell within the right-of-way of a proposed road, and the industrious Indian was ordered to vacate his farm. Feeling an injustice, Nah-deiz-az refused.[5]

On Thursday, March 10, twenty-two-year-old Nah-deiz-az was plowing his patch of land when farm boss Frank Porter approached the fence. Porter repeated his order to vacate the property. In broken English, the young farmer defiantly reiterated his position, pleading for Porter's reconsideration. His plea fell on deaf ears. Frustrated by his failure to remove the Indian, Porter returned to the agency and reported the incident. Captain Francis Pierce rationalized that an authoritarian figure would be more effective in achieving the assignment. He sent Lieut. Stewart Mott with Porter to evict the farmer.[6]

Following his 1886 West Point graduation, Mott's benign duties included instructing farm and irrigation methods at San Carlos. As a soft-spoken, diplomatic officer from Mechanicsville, New York, twenty-four-year-old Mott had earned the respect of officers and subordinates alike. Pierce felt confident that the young lieutenant could persuade the reluctant youth to move.[7]

There are conflicting accounts as to what happened next. One version relates that when Nah-deiz-az saw the two unarmed men approach, he disappeared into his wikiup and emerged with a Colt revolver. Unaware of the danger, the officer and the farm boss dismounted. The troubled Indian fired his weapon in their direction. Mott fell to the ground gravely wounded. A slightly wounded Frank Porter tore off to the agency headquarters for help. It was a ride reminiscent of another frantic dash he had made five years before. Constance Altshuler's version of Mott's killing in her book *Cavalry Yellow and Infantry Blue*, differs from the *Silver*

Belt account. Altshuler states that "A young Apache, whose father was confined to the guardhouse, began an altercation with Mott, stabbing him several times."[8]

The March 12, 1887, *Silver Belt* reported:

> An Indian on the San Carlos reservation, becoming dissatisfied with the allotment of land, constituted himself arbiter and with murderous intent drew a Colt's revolver and commenced shooting at Lieut. Mott and Frank Porter (neither of whom were armed) and wounded both of them—Mott seriously. Ten shots were fired.…[A]lthough groups of Indians were present and fire arms within sight, it is reported that Porter was refused a gun with which to defend himself.

Despite Dr. T. B. Davis's valiant efforts, Mott succumbed the following day, a promising career cut short. A remorseful Nah-deiz-az was tried before federal judge W. W. Porter in the Second Judicial District in Globe. In spite of testimony that his errant shots were meant for Frank Porter, Nah-deiz-az was found guilty and received a life sentence in Yuma Territorial Prison. He was later transferred to the federal penitentiary at Menard, Illinois, but his saga wasn't over. Nan-deiz-az would eventually see the end of a rope.[9]

<u>Mar 14</u>. Went to work again for the Fame Co. The weather hazy…hope for rain.

<u>Mar 15</u>. Am tired. Worked shoveling all day.

<u>Mar 20</u>. Am thankful for Sun. Washed my clothes, did some cooking and rested. I read a bit today….

<u>Mar 21</u>. Went at my work this morning feeling quite cheerful. Ogden [teacher] remained in town…. Treppel [Trippel] indisposed all day. Letter from McCabe regarding Dr. Hortons [Wharton] bill sent him for collection.

<u>Mar 22</u>. Very windy and looks like rain.

<u>Mar 23</u>. Cleared off no rain, a letter from Father today.

<u>Mar 24-25-26</u>. Worked running car and shoveling.

<u>Mar 27</u>. Went to Globe last evening. Saw McCabe [attorney] and arranged to pay Dr. Hortons [Wharton] bill in two or three weeks. Returned to the Fame.

<u>Mar 28-29-30-31-Apr 1-2</u>. Worked everyday steadily although hard work and I don't agree very well yet it is a necessity and honorable.

While Frank and the men piled up ore at the Fame mine, methods of transporting it remained crude and costly. Rumors indicating resumption of work on the Mineral Belt brought optimism to Globe miners and businessmen. The *Phoenix Weekly Herald* reported:

Alex G. Pendleton [surveyor] writes from Flagstaff as of February 23d that track laying on the Mineral Belt is progressing at the rate of a half-mile a day, and that ten miles will be done by the 15th inst. He and his brother Will were to start the following day for Strawberry Valley…with a view to locating a more favorable route over the rim-rock, and avoid the business of tunnelling [*sic*].[10]

Persistent Eddy had not given up his dream and the Mineral Belt saga continued. Once again the Atlantic and Pacific Railroad agreed to subscribe to Mineral Belt stock. This time the contract stated the A&P would pay $25,000 for every five miles of track in return for controlling interest in the Mineral Belt Railroad. Still lacking capital to begin construction, and unbeknown to the A&P, Eddy enticed Chicago railroad tycoon Francis E. Hinkley to invest cash in exchange for $345,000 in Mineral Belt bonds. Construction began in January 1887, and within two months nearly forty miles of track had been laid to Mormon Lake. By summer, confident of a solid agreement with A&P, Eddy announced plans to extend the line from Globe to Tucson. He had almost exhausted Hinkley's capital.[11]

In October, construction on the ill-fated railway halted. A&P refused to pay the $175,000 due, claiming breach of contract. Discovery of bondholder Hinkley's strong position to control the company probably cooled the deal. Hinckley and other investors refused to advance more capital. Eddy scrambled for the next year, determined to keep his dream alive. Finally, on December 4, 1888, the Mineral Belt was sold at a sheriff's sale to satisfy labor liens and taxes. Hinckley and lumberman Dennis Riordan purchased the discounted railroad for $40,440. Thousands of dollars remained unpaid to creditors. Again the railroad and prosperity evaded Globe.[12]

Apr 3. Went to town. Heard that Henry had gone to Flagstaff. Notified Frank Blackledge to vacate my house. He is 3 mos. in arerrs on rent. Amounting to $30.00.

Apr 4-5-6-7-8-9. Worked all the week and quit tonight and will go to the ranch & then to Phoenix.

Sunday Apr 10. Settled with Harry and went to town. Have worked 34 days for the Fame Co. @ $3.00 per day amounting to 102.00…. Due S. Klein Co. $3.80–due Mrs. Ramsdell order $24.50–my ½ provisions bid $16.22–H. Hancock order $2.50–My credit Joe Redman $17.42. Sold Kitty to Harry Hancock for $65.00. He to pay me when he can get the $ from the Fame Co. I will ride her to the ranch and get another horse. Blackledge vacated my house owing me $30.00–raining steadily today.

Apr 11. Started for Salt River in the rain and arrived at Henry's all OK and pretty well soaked.

Apr 12. Talked with Hazard about trading town property for his station on the river. Henry and I went over to Coon Creek.

The *Silver Belt* faithfully monitored the effect of weather on the cattle industry: "Mr. Middleton says that his cattle on Coon Creek are doing reasonably well, although low in flesh and that the increase this season will be very large."[13]

Apr 13. Henry hired a Mr. Lee to stay at the ranch at Coon Creek for $12.50 per month and board commencing on the 4th. Weather has cleared off nicely this AM. Henry took Jack and went after his mules. Will start branding calves when he returns. Got up a couple of cows to milk.

Apr 22. Went to Salt River can not trade with Hazard....

Did Frank see a business opportunity in Hazard's Way Station on the Salt River?

Apr 23. To the Fame and delivered to Harry Hancock my mare Kitty which sold to him for $65.00. Will stay here tonight and go to Globe tomorrow.

Sunday Apr 24. Went to Globe collected Mrs. Pendleton $30.00 to apply on $50.00 due from Dick Barclay for 2 Bulls. Bal. due $20.00. Harry Hancock paid me check on Bank Cal no 604 drawn by Klein Co. for Kitty–amt. $65.00 Collect from Fame Co. amt in full for my work in two chks one for $26.00 and one for $42.45 and cash $4.00. Ordered from Sultan paper .25 and stamps .10. Bot [bought] ink, beans 1.50, salt .50, soda, 10 lbs corn, tea 1.00, flour 1.00. Paid A. Bailey my bill in full of $5.70. He giving me the balance of $42.45 check in cash amting to $36.75.

Apr 25. Paid Dr. Whartons bill of $26.50. Frank Blackledge accepted an order on him for board in full of my account against him in amt. $30.00. Sent to Father a P.O. order for $60.00. Sent provisions ordered of Sultan yesterday for the ranch down by Henrys by Hoyle Higdon. John Murphy took order on Frank Blackledge and accepted by him amt 30.00 and will board it out and pay the amt to Tom Lonergan. Gave my assessment to sheriff as follows: house [adobe] lot 3.50, House [above church] lot 3.00, Ranch on Coon Creek 1.00, 83 head cattle @ 11.00 = 9.13, horses and mules 1.50, poll tax 1.00 = $18.44.

Apr 26. ...Left my deed of adobe house and my note against J. W. Ellison for $100.00 and my note against Henry Middleton for $70.00 with Tom Lonergan [Frank's business manager] and also left my house in his charge.

Apr 27. Left Globe for Phoenix rode to Whitlows ten miles below Pinal and camped on the desert, distance 42 mi.

Frank meticulously put his financial affairs in order before returning to operate his Phoenix swimming baths for the summer. While Frank tended to his baths, another noteworthy episode occurred at San Carlos. What began as an unfortunate incident, evolved into a series of abstruse events that ended tragically and mysteriously.

There are so many versions of the Apache Kid legend that it is difficult to separate reality from myth. Born about 1857, Has-kay-bay-nay-ntayl witnessed the white man's world and adapted to it. Off the reservation, he picked up English by associating with Globe's saloonkeepers, miners, cowboys, and merchants. Butcher Joseph Redman hired the young Apache to work his cattle, and taught him Anglo ways. The youth emulated Globe's gentlemen by wearing stylish blue jeans, jackets, and hats. Soon, local businessmen labeled him "Apache Kid." It is likely Frank Hammon knew Kid during his early association with Joseph Redman.[14]

Kid became a skilled horseman and proficient roper as a cowboy with Pat Shanley's Cross S outfit near San Carlos. His fascination with military pageantry ultimately lured him to enlist as a U.S. Army scout. At San Carlos, Kid became Al Sieber's prodigy. In July 1882, 1st Sergeant Kid accompanied Sieber at the Battle of Big Dry Wash above the Mogollon Rim. In November 1885, he reenlisted as a scout, probably under either Capt. Wirt Davis or Capt. Emmet Crawford. According to interpreter Tom Horn, Kid became Sieber's "pet Indian." Sieber recognized Kid's intellect, ingenuity, and physical attributes, especially his distant vision. His unique abilities made him a valuable asset in planning strategy. Ironically, these same attributes enabled him to avoid military capture in later years.[15]

Following Geronimo's surrender in 1886, Kid's duties undoubtedly involved policing the reservation. It is uncertain whether he viewed alignment with the military as betrayal of his Apache brothers. Possibly those feelings influenced his behavior. In May 1887, Al Sieber and San Carlos commanding officer Capt. Francis Pierce departed on an inspection tour of Fort Apache and the White River Reservation subagency. They left Lieut. F. B. Fowler in command of the reservation and the reliable Sergeant Kid as interim chief-of-scouts.[16]

With Sieber and Pierce away, Kid's family band of Apaches held a party lasting over several days. When Kid and his four army scouts arrived at the dance, instead of breaking up the party, they joined it. Despondent and ignited by tiswin, Kid avenged his grandfather's tragic murder by killing the Indian he held responsible. Then Kid fled. A clerk later recorded Kid's deposition: "Rip is the man who put up a job to kill my grandfather and Rip said (to me) 'I shall kill you.'"[17]

Kid and his scouts were absent from the post for five days. Meanwhile, Sieber and Pierce returned from Fort Apache amid circulating rumors of the tiswin affair. They sent Chief Gonshayee to bring in the delinquent scouts. At dusk on June 1, the absentee Indians straggled single file to Sieber's tent. Interested bystanders watched as the sulky scouts dismounted. San Carlos blacksmith Ed Arhelger said to Frank Porter, "Frank, that looks like old times, I believe we're going to have some fun here tonight." Many written versions and even more speculation surround what occurred next.[18]

Sieber started for his tent followed by Pierce. A large contingent of scouts and Indians had congregated, some armed. When the captain arrived at the tent, he ordered the five absent scouts to step forward and surrender their arms. They obeyed. He motioned toward the guardhouse shouting, "calaboose!" Then, chaos erupted.

Sieber's later testimony indicates that he recognized trouble brewing. The congregated bystanders were "cross and grum looking...with arms which is against orders here." An unpopular interpreter named Antonio Diaz purposely misinterpreted Pierce's order. By making a circle in the palm of his hand, he indicated imprisonment on the "island." Did this mean Alcatraz, or Florida with the exiled Chirichauas? Whatever the signal, the alarmed scouts grabbed for their confiscated weapons. Scuffles ensued and shots rang out from the crowd. Arhelger vividly recalled the scuffle: "Kid grabbed for his gun but Sieber kicked it out of his hands and Kid had to run without a gun. Sieber came out of the tent with his own gun to get some of the Indians. Curly [sic], an Indian, lying in an adobe hole to the left shot Sieber's leg."[19]

During the melee, Kid and the five unarmed scouts caught horses and rode for the hills, accompanied by eleven sympathizers. Lieut. Charles Elliott and his mounted troops pursued the fugitives until dark, without luck. The next morning, they found a trail leading back toward Aravaipa Canyon and the San Pedro River valley. Within days, Lieut. Carter Johnson and scouts from Camp Thomas joined Elliot.[20]

The evening of the outbreak, scout/interpreter Tom Horn turned his horse loose to graze near his mine. At dusk, he went to fetch the horse and it was gone. Horn noticed moccasin tracks covering the horse's trail. The insurgents and his horse were headed south. Horn returned to the mine for another mount and rode twenty miles to the agency. At two o'clock in the morning, he reported his loss and learned of the outbreak. But a stolen horse was the least offensive crime attributed to the fugitives. Cowpuncher William Diehl was killed at Crowley's ranch on the San Pedro River and Mike Grace was murdered at Sonorita Creek.[21]

Arizonans had felt secure following Geronimo's surrender eight months before. With the fresh outbreak came renewed outrage and fear. The Indians became angered and agitated following Kid's escape. General Miles, the ultimate politician, journeyed from the San Francisco Presidio to oversee pursuit of the escapees and calm the discontented Apaches. He issued this comment for the press: "The Indians have been well treated, and the affair is the result of the innate deviltry of the Indian character, excited by very bad liquor."[22]

On June 11, Lieutenant Johnson surprised the dissidents in the Rincon Mountains east of Tucson, but they escaped capture. Instead of fleeing into Mexico, Kid opted to remain in Arizona. He reasoned that he had not shot Sieber. He felt bound by tribal custom to avenge his grandfather's murder, so he didn't perceive himself as an outlaw. As he saw it, a five-day absence from the post was his only crime. The term AWOL was meaningless to the nomadic Apaches. Miguel, a Yaqui Indian running with Kid's band, independently had killed William Diehl and Mike Grace. Kid, with this mindset, negotiated with Miles through a mediator.[23]

By June 22, Miles sent a messenger to Kid requesting his surrender. Kid consented if Miles would call off his troops. Miles accepted Kid's terms. The troops were withdrawn, and the badgered band gave itself up. Kid's mother mediated his surrender.[24]

Opinions differed over who had shot Sieber. Telegrapher Dan Williamson said Pas-lau-tau fired the shot into Sieber's leg. Paul Patton, ex-scout and full brother of Pas-lau-tau, agreed with Ed Arhelger that Curley was the culprit. Witnesses were unanimous in stating that Kid was unarmed when Sieber was shot. Miles believed that Miguel had fired the first shots that started the whole affair. Miles might have excused Kid's behavior as ignorance of U.S. military regulations if outraged newspaper editorials had not applied pressure.[25]

On June 25, 1887, a general court-martial found all five scouts guilty of mutiny and desertion. They were sentenced to death. After reviewing the findings, Miles reduced the sentences to ten years imprisonment, reasoning that Diaz's translation was inaccurate and there were no indications the "mutiny" was premeditated. By special order, Miles changed their place of incarceration from Fort Leavenworth Military Prison in Kansas to Alcatraz Island, California. Early in 1888, the five heavily guarded prisoners left to serve ten years on the dreaded "Rock."[26]

Dr. Davis saved Sieber's leg, but the scout never fully regained its use. By spring of 1888, he ambled around San Carlos on crutches as he attempted to work. Opinions varied on Sieber's feelings toward Kid. Some said he was extremely bitter, holding Kid responsible for the uprising that crippled him for life. Others maintained that Sieber "never bore a grudge." Within a year, political forces and a legal loophole returned Kid and other Indian prisoners to San Carlos.[27]

Kid's saga would continue. Eventually, he would cross paths with Frank Hammon.

Chapter Eleven

SWIMMING BATHS

With my family's blessing, I left on a whim, chasing an obscure tale gleaned from fragmented thoughts written a century ago. I had read Frank's guilt-ridden letter home telling of his swimming bath venture, his fervent efforts to send funds for his children's care, his articulate apology for placing such a burden on his aging parents. His moving letter reduced me to tears. I wondered if our email will evoke the same emotion a hundred years hence. Will our stories be deleted from our hard drives? Without Frank's written word, his story could never be told.

Apr 28. Rode to Tempe distance 48 mi. Saw Webster. Tempe's prospects are improving. The new RR from Maricopa will be here soon.

Yes, Tempe's prospects had improved by April 1887. By the time Frank returned to Phoenix, Charles Trumbull Hayden and investors had spearheaded legislation designed to bring higher education to central Arizona. On February 8, the Arizona Territorial Normal School began educating thirty-one students in a one-room brick classroom. Twenty-three of the pupils were women. Anticipating growth, the Tempe Land and Improvement Company purchased 705 acres to develop a townsite constructed of brick houses and buildings, instead of the usual adobe. Tempe initiated the "business boom that extended across the Salt River Valley."[1]

Phoenix and Tempe citizens anticipated the arrival of the Phoenix-Maricopa spur line linking the Salt River Valley to the Southern Pacific transcontinental railroad at Maricopa. Besides providing farmers access to eastern and western markets for their produce and livestock, it would carry merchandise on the incoming trains. The railroad carried Arizona into the industrial age by transporting its natural resources elsewhere for conversion into viable by-products.[2]

On November 1, 1886, M&P railroad construction began at Phoenix Junction five miles east of Maricopa. Contractor W. J. Murphy, noted for the Arizona Canal project, hit a snag just short of the Gila River. The shortest route for the proposed rail line ran through the Pima Indian Reservation. Federal law required a signed contract before grading crews could encroach on the reservation. By February, twelve Indians had received reimbursement for their farmland, and an agreement was signed clearing the bureaucratic red tape for the right-of-way. Construction, running months behind schedule, resumed a month later. As Frank ferried across the river to Phoenix, he must have admired Tempe's new red brick buildings and the first two Salt River Bridge spans. Within two years, Phoenix lawmakers would use the M&P railroad to promote relocation of the territorial capital from Prescott to Phoenix in 1889.[3]

Apr 29. Came over from Tempe this morning 10 mi. Went out and saw my cows. Old spot has a nice black & white calf. The others are looking well. Saw Orin about the Ferguson note. I think it will be all right. My baths are in very bad condition. Benches, lamps & towels are all stolen.

Apr 30. Arranged to have the water taken from the baths by the steam pump early next week & will then clean them out.

May 1. Was around the baths all day and went to church in evening.

May 2. Worked at the baths—pump will come tomorrow.

May 3. Steam pump arrived and went to work pumped the water half out.

May 4. Finished pumping out the water and went to work cleaning out the bottom

May 5. Contracted with the Mexicans to clean the bottom for $4.00— They got about ½ through today. Put in a new spring board.

May 6. Mexicans finished cleaning out the bath. I put in a new swing and run the water in the evening.

May 7. Did odd jobs of repairing and got about ready to open up. Took in cash of .55—Left my sewing machine at the auction store for sale.

The *Phoenix Gazette* for Sunday, May 8, 1887 announced: "The Baths are open for this season. Go and cool off!" The Van Buren and Center streets (today Central Avenue) baths provided welcome relief from the stifling triple-digit temperatures. But the baths' success depended on favorable weather and an abundance of water.

May 8. I open the baths to the public. Not a very heavy day. Took in cash of $7.10.

May 9. A quiet day, but grandly pleasant. Cash receipt $4.40.

May 10. Days are getting quite warm. A fair day $6.00.

May 11. Rainy, cool and windy. A slow day, amt. $3.65. A man committed suicide by shooting himself with a pistol today. Met and made the acquaintance of young Mr. Fulton, a cousin of Daisys last Friday.[4]

Albert Fulton, Daisy's cousin and childhood playmate, grew up in the farming community of Fulton Crossroads, five miles north of Santa Rosa, California. His mother, Melissa, died prematurely, leaving a husband and six children. Eleanor Howell served as a surrogate to her sister's motherless brood that included ten-year-old Albert.[5]

James and Melissa Fulton had arrived in Sonoma County in 1855, accompanied by James's brother Thomas and their father, Richard. The family pitched a tent under a tree north of Santa Rosa until they could afford redwood lumber for a house. As the Fultons prospered, a farming community – the township of Fulton – developed around them. The Fulton brothers, devout fundamentalists, established the Disciples of Christ Church and became the church's first elders. Prominent in community affairs, James moved his family to Santa Rosa's prestigious McDonald Avenue following Melissa's death.[6]

Albert's appearance in Phoenix during the summer of 1887 raises several questions. What brought twenty-year-old Albert to Arizona? Was he looking for work, adventure, or possibly escape from a rigid religious upbringing?

May 15. A very fair day for so early in the season—$8.60. Ordered from J J Pfister & Co. of San Francisco a bill of swimming suits amounting to $26.37. Sent with order P.O. order for $5.00 per Ex COD. Bal. $21.37.

May 18. Windy and disagreeable—very dead $2.85. Will go down to Gila Bend tomorrow.

May 19. Started for the Gila Bend. Alan Hall, Rev. McMullen & Mr. Lancaster Arrived about 7 pm.

May 20. Went up and saw the head of the Hall ditch. Then arrived through the valley and around through the lower valley. Well pleased with it throughout and may locate.

Frank considered another venture while his babies remained with his family. This caused considerable consternation in Illinois.

May 21. Left for Phoenix at half past five arrived at about half past six in the evening—found the baths running in good shape.

May 22. A moderate day at the baths.

May 23. Wrote to father and sent $10.00 for the children…. Enquired about the $30.00 due from John Murphy. Went out to see the cows, Spot, Tiny and Broad have calves. Jim not yet. Brought in Jack the mule for Albert Fulton to ride to Globe.

May 24. Went out and showed the cows to Mrs. Murphy. She will take Spot and try her and if satisfied will pay me $70.00 for her.

May 25. Went in and drove in Spot and Calf for Mrs. Murphy to try. Albert Fulton started for Globe with Jack.

Jack, the trusted mule, carried Albert over the treacherous trail to Globe. Was Albert visiting his uncle Francis Howell or looking for work? On June 9, Frank Hammon received a letter from Albert's older brother, Somers B. Fulton. Was Albert's family concerned about his whereabouts and safety? Frank's meticulous records include no other correspondence with Albert's family—including his father.[7]

May 26. Cool and showery—nothing doing at the baths.

May 27. Cool and windy—no business

Rain cooled the air, as well as the bathers' desire to swim. Frank's frustration with the unpredictable weather surfaced.

May 28. Warmed today, yet very light day at the baths, it is quite discouraging.

May 29. A warm day and very lively at the baths. Best day by far this season. $14.50.

May 30. A fair day at the baths. Today has been strictly observed as decoration day here.

Jun 1. Collected from Mrs. Murphy for Old Spot $70.00. Sent $45.00 to Father.

Jun 2. Beautiful day. Cool, breeze blowing. fair business.

Jun 3. Wrote to mother. Sent $20.00 for childrens clothes.

Phoenix Arizona
June 3rd '87

My very dear Mother

Your good but anxious letter of May 22nd I recd yesterday. I was very glad to get it and perused it with pleasure yet my pleasure was mingled with sadness. Your letter indicates and I am satisfied that you and Father allow events and prospects to worry you very much. Which you should not do. God takes care of the birds of the air and the cattle on the hills and has promised to look after his children, should you not have faith. Again you have five big boys, to aid you, not one of whom would hesitate to sell his coat even were it necessary to save you from suffering or privation.

If you should get a little behind dont allow it to worry you, for we will make it up to you. It dont cost me much to live, I have bought one suit of clothes in the last three years. That cost me about $30.00. My occupation dont require much dress. My board costs now about $4.50 per week. So you see after my debts are paid my money can be almost wholely applied with you where all my love and interest centers. You may be sure it has been and is my one aim to try and be punctual in sending money home.

While I had sickness and death in my family I ran behind some. I owed probably $450.00 in merchants, druggists—and doctors bills and the money I borrowed to take the babies home. I have paid the larger part of it. Those bills which I was forced to pay at the same time I had to send money to the home for the babies, pay my own expenses—look after my cattle and other business and pay the expenses thereof. Pay my taxes—and interest on the money I had borrowed. I had one trip to make horse back from Globe to Phoenix and back. I had my cattle to drive from Phoenix to the ranch—I had two trips to make to the ranch to look after my cattle and horses there. So you see the time I could work and earn money was all broken up.

I tell you all this only to show you that I have been rustling hard all the time, and although I have been short in my remitances home, it has not been through carelessness or idleness, I dont think I have had one idle day since I left you last fall, except Sundays while I was mining. I am bound to overcome the obsticles in my path. I have my children to provide for. My debts to pay and some property to accummulate with which to educate them when they get old enough.

My own comfort or pleasure shall not be considered until all other claims are provided for. I am bound to accomplish these things and with Gods help I shall—How to best do so in the quickest and best way is the question, whether I can accomplish more here or in the East.

Nothing would make me happier then to be with or near my children in their happy childhood. I have thought the matter over a great deal. I want to do that which will be for the best. I cannot decide yet and not until my interests are disposed of. I am negotiating with parties for the sale of my cattle, may and may not make a sale. The Rail Road is being pushed through to Globe. When it gets through I will be able to dispose of my property there. My swimming baths are doing quite well and also my cattle. All things considered I feel encouraged.

Regarding the investing in more land which I wrote about, and which seems to worry you some, I only thought of locating some government land under the desert filings. It would cost me $1.25 per acre and I would have three years to pay for it in, but I have not located it and may not.

Dear mother I appreciate your great goodness and unselfishness in taking my babies in your charge after your hard life of care and anxiety in raising so large a family. When approaching the shady groves of the eventide of life, after the labor and heat of the day have been passed and the work more than well done. When rest and calm reflection should have been the portion of your remaining days here below. Then to take upon your poor tired shoulders the care and anxiety of rearing three little babes. Oh mother, I can never reward you. Not one single demand had you and father ever made upon the huge debt of filing gratitude which I owed you and then you took upon you the care of my little motherless babes, thereby adding to my obligations to you beyond my power to compute them. In my despair and sorrow I did not realize the extent of the demand which I was imposing upon you when I took my babies to you. My heart was full of anguish and my thoughts of other things. Yet without a murmur you opened your warm mothers breast and received your grief stricken boy and his poor little ones in your kind loving arms. Oh mother, can all that I have and all that I can do repay one small fraction of the debt due you. It is all yours I assure you. I simply manage it for you to the best of my ability.

After your labors here are over, after the severe strain on your great loving unselfish nature is ended and your poor weary body is laid away to rest, when you have crossed the dark flowing waters—which will take from you all earthly cares and sorrows, and you have landed upon the golden sands of endless bliss, there with loving arms Daisy will meet you and give you her blessings for what you have done for her little ones. There will your reward begin and it will surely be great.

I enclose a P.O. order for $20.00 with which to procure necessities for the children. Give them my love—with love to all I remain. Aff your son

Frank

<u>Jun 8</u>. Bought sign and put up at corner of Center and Washington Sts. Cost $6.00.

<u>Jun 9</u>. Albert Fulton returned from Globe this morning. Carl Frakes and Jim Woods came with him. Tom Lonergan sent me $15.00 paid by John Murphy on Frank Blackledge a/c bal. due $15.00. business still slack.

<u>Jun 10</u>. Dr. Stallo arrived from Globe. I sent $20.00 to Mrs. Welch at Globe to pay the interest on my note from Feb 20 to April 20 87.

<u>Jun 11</u>. Weather getting hot. Business ought to be better at the baths.

<u>Jun 12</u>. Not a very good day of business at baths for Sunday. Went out and showed the cows to a man. May sell him out. Paid Smith $10.00 and pasture bill.

<u>Jun 13</u>. Paid Mr. Lount $10.00 on rent of baths which pays to Dec 9th '86.

Frank rented his Center Street baths from Samuel D. Lount, an innovative Canadian renowned as the inventor of Arizona's first ice-making machine. Lount fabricated a small compressor by combining a steam engine and pump that manufactured ice by circulating ammonia through pipes submerged in water tanks. Arizona, with its sweltering summers and mild winters, became a logical market for the product of his invention.

Samuel Lount moved his family from Michigan and opened Arizona's first ice plant in a little wooden shed in Phoenix. His brother, a Prescott pioneer, recognized Phoenix's potential market and financed the venture. Shipping ammonia from San Francisco and across the Mojave Desert posed a major challenge. The journey took several weeks, causing the "aqua-ammonia" to lose strength in the heat. Inventive Samuel devised a solution. He constructed a still and concentrated the mixture several times, producing a solution strong enough to freeze water.[8]

In spite of sweltering heat, ice received a chilly reception that first year. Saloons became Lount's primary customers. His daily orders amounted to only sixty pounds, far below his capacity of half a ton per day. Then as demands for ice increased, Samuel distributed his product door to door in an old wooden wheelbarrow. Toward the end of the second year, the factory increased daily sales by several hundred pounds. By the time Frank moved to Phoenix, Samuel Lount sold his ice machines throughout the Southwest and was one of the territory's most affluent citizens.[9]

Jun 14. Started for the Castle Creek hot springs. Camped Aqua Frea with Mr. [unreadable] and family.

Jun 15. Arrived at springs at noon. Very nice springs, but the turns are too steep for me.

Jun 16. Left for Phoenix. Camped ten miles north of Desert Wells 12 oclock at night.

Jun 17. Pushed on into Phoenix arrived at noon. The baths have been running very slowly.

Jun 18. A little better today but not satisfactory, especially for Saturday.

Jun 19. A fair day. Today weather getting pretty hot. Albert Fulton left for Cal. today. Via Tempe.

A month later, Frank received a letter from Albert Fulton. Frank never indicated whether it was written from California or from the Rim country, nor what happened to Albert Fulton. Don Dedera suggests one possibility in his book, *A Little War of Our Own.* "Al Fulton was a cowboy, just passing through, in September, 1888, and up on the Rim at Lake Number One he was shot and killed for no known reason," Dedera explains. "Folks buried him decent, and put up a marker at Al Fulton Point. At least they remembered that he lived, and that he died.[10]

Another interesting account notes that Al Fulton drove a herd of sheep through cattle country, where a cowman stampeded Al and his herd into a sinkhole. His headstone read, "Murdered in 1888," but the inscription on a replacement indicated, "Shot in 1901." Such confusion raises the question: Could Daisy's cousin Albert be the same Al Fulton entombed atop the Rim at Al Fulton Point? Albert Fulton's name is not found in Sonoma County records after 1887. In 1895, James Fulton deeded property to his son, Somers B. Fulton. Albert remains a riddle.[11]

Jun 20. Took charge of my pasture. Will get some one to run it during the Fiesta.

Jun 21. Sold Jim and calf to Jas McCarty for $65.00.

Jun 22-23. Water out of canal and nothing doin. Will be out several days. Very damaging to me.

Jun 24. Fiesta commenced today—Hot-Hotter-Hottest.

Jun 25-26. Very, hot—No business. Hamilton not doing much. Did pretty well today after all 12.00. A scratch at Fiesta.

The Fiesta occurred annually in an alfalfa field adjoining the city. Ramadas (brush sheds), canvas tents, gambling booths, entertainment, dancing, and food provided a carnival atmosphere. The festivities ran day and night from San Juan Day (June 24) until July 4. In early years, bullfights drew many spectators into the newly constructed bleachers. One ferocious bull chased a Mexican bullfighter through the stands and into a field. With the expensive grandstand destroyed and spectators terrified, the Fiesta bullfights became a memory.[12]

The railroad's progress slowed in the unbearable summer heat. Frazzled tracklayers, encumbered by buckskin gloves, worked day and night handling the sizzling rails. The Fiesta provided the crews with a welcome diversion. Many railroad workers disappeared into the large crowd, never to be heard of again. Once again, work stopped as inexperienced labor replaced the absent tracklayers for the last push into Tempe.[13]

Jun 27. Very hot. Water turned in yesterday. A good day $10.00—up nearly all night.

Jun 28. A fire Alarm. Paid Mr. Lount on rent of bath ground which pays to June 9, 1887.

Jun 29. Weather very hot, business pretty good.

Jun 30. Showering around the mountains, baths running pretty well.

Jul 1. Water again turned out of the canal. Bad luck to it. Sent father $50.00.

Jul 2. Paid Henry Ryder on a/c $50.00. Sold to Mr. Fields for $16.00 Lynys yearling heifer.

Jul 3. Very warm today. Baths did well considering the circumstances $6.50.

Jul 4. Quite lively time today, but my business at a standstill on account of no water but it cannot be helped. Will hope for the best.

On July 3, while Frank's baths dried up from lack of water in the town ditch, a small crowd assembled to witness surveyor William A. Hancock drive the last spike. The swimming baths could not compete with the celebration east of town. The arrival of the Maricopa & Phoenix Railroad signaled the beginning of an era for Phoenix. Loaded freight wagons would no longer lumber listlessly across the desert to supply the Salt River Valley. The valley's produce could be safely shipped abroad, packed in locally produced ice.

An enthusiastic crowd cheered as the first scheduled train slowly pulled into the station at 7:00 A.M. on July 4, 1887. The increased comfort and decreased travel time to Maricopa pleased passengers who paid the $2.50 fare. In a blustering sandstorm, Phoenicians celebrated the national holiday with a picturesque parade and patriotic oratory. Without a turntable to switch ends, the celebrated train chugged the thirty-five miles back to Maricopa in reverse.[14]

Jul 5. No water in the canal yet. Went out and helped drive in old Broad and let Mr. [unreadable] use her until I can sell her. Old Jim I still left with Smith. Sandstorm today.

Jul 6. No water yet but it will be turned in tomorrow. Wish I could sell out. Have not heard from home for over two weeks am awaiting anxiously for a letter.

Jul 7. Water turned in today and had a good day. River is raising. Started mexican to irrigating pasture.

Jul 8. A moderate days receipts.

Jul 9-10. Fair or rather good business. Weather hot—plenty of water.

Frank's frustration increased over the next few weeks. Water flowed into other canals during the hottest weather. When the "town ditch" filled, turbid, unswimmable water flooded into the baths. Discouragement crept into Frank's journal entries.[15]

Jul 11. Very poor day at baths and no news from home. It makes me nervous. Oh that I could fly to my dear ones. Cannot get water to irrigate. Gave up pasture today.

Jul 12. Dull, cloudy and looks like rain.

Jul 13-14. Nothing doing whatever at Baths. Weather cool and pleasant

Jul 15. No business. River has raised and is not fordable. Hamilton Hollands Saloon was attached today and I was appointed as keeper.

Jul 16. Water very muddy and no business. Sold old Broads calf to Smith for $5.50 amount to be credited on my account.

Jul 17. A fair days business, but poor for Sunday. Oh how I wish I could sell out. Recd a letter from Mother and Bertie today and a photo of Charles Milton. Oh how glad I was to get it.

Jul 18-19-20. Very dull at baths. Water continues so muddy. Started a mexican out with a card and bill yesterday.

Jul 21. Let Mr. D. S. Bewley take my cow Old Broad to milk until I sell him. Pat Hollands ½ interest was sold by auction today to Mr. Murphy for $35.00. I received my keepers fee of $7.50. Paid Mr. Lount $5.00 rent to July 9th—Good business today.

Jul 22. Water getting clearer in canal. Business good.

Jul 23-31. Nothing of consequence occurred, variety theater across the street opened and it helps me considerably.

Frank referred to the Garden City Theatre at the head of Center Street. "The place is purely variety in character," the *Phoenix Herald* explained, "but anything offensive to eye or ear is strictly prohibited."[16]

Aug <u>1</u>. Good day for Monday. Paid Henry Ryder $100.00 on acc't. Herald bill $2.80 and Arizonian bill of $3.30. Sent Father P.O. order of $50.00.

Aug <u>2-3-4</u>. Quite a good business. Weather very hot and sultry.

Aug <u>5</u>. Paid Smith in full for pasture.

Aug <u>6-7-8-9-10</u>. Nothing of importance occurred. On 10th paid $5.00 bill at Gazette office. Business fair until 10th.

Aug <u>11</u>. Nothing doing at all. Am surprised as the day is hot. Rec'd good letter from Bertie today.

Aug <u>12</u>. Very hot. Sand clouds hanging around the horizon. A fair day at the baths. Am trying to trade off Bessie for a pony.

Aug <u>13</u>. Wrote to Tom Lonergan to notify J. W. Ellison to pay my note of $100.00 when due. Paid Lount for mos. rent til Aug. 9th.

Aug <u>15</u>. Bought a bay horse of Joe Lombry for $25.00. Branded on left shoulder. Nearly blind in right eye.

Aug <u>16-17-18-19-20</u>. Nothing exciting has occurred. Baths very slow. Water out of canal. Weather hot, Harry down with rhumatism.

Feeling a financial pinch from his unpredictable income, Frank prepared to take legal action against Colonel Ellison.

Aug <u>21</u>. Wrote to J. W. Ellison that I expected my note paid when due. Wrote to my agent Tom Lonergan to place my note for $100.00 against J. W. Ellison in hands of attorney for collection. If not paid when due legally.

Frank wasn't the only person with financial difficulties. Cattleman "Colonel" Jesse W. Ellison by all accounts was a hard-driven, slight-statured, tough-talking Texan with an unwavering belief in his own principles. In his youth he saw action with the Texas Rangers, fought in the Kiowa and Comanche wars, and served with the Sixth Texas Cavalry during the Civil War. Following the Confederate surrender, he established his cattle ranch and Q brand in Texas. After his barbed-wire fences were repeatedly cut, Ellison pulled up stakes and headed for Arizona's expanses stating, "If I stay longer I'll have to fight my neighbors."[17]

In the summer of 1885, Jesse Ellison's wife, Susan, drove into the Tonto Basin a wagon loaded with half her brood, her household goods, and a grand piano. Her husband, sons, and neighbors shipped their combined cattle herds by rail to Bowie. Once unloaded, the thirst-crazed cattle stampeded for water, even knocking houses from their foundations. Twelve hundred beeves survived the fiasco. The remaining herd was driven two hundred miles north to the Tonto Basin. The Ellison family eventually settled on land between Payson and Pleasant Valley. Once at their destination, they lived out of wagons until their cabin was completed. They called their place the Apple ranch.[18]

Life in Arizona wasn't easy. In the first years, the Ellisons' cattle starved for lack of salt. The harsh winter claimed beeves unaccustomed to scraping through snow for feed. Texas farming methods had destroyed frail Arizona grasses. Ellison's Texas herd, purchased for seven and eight dollars a head, sold the first year in Arizona for twenty dollars each. But by 1887, cattle prices had dropped to six dollars a head. J. W. Ellison was broke. He later explained: "I was not only clean broke, but I owed $10,000, and I not only had to face it, but I had to make my family realize it, my wife and daughters who had everything that money could buy."[19]

Ellison's over-indulged daughters were of hardy stock and worked along-side their father driving cattle, roping, and hunting. They forfeited the fineries claiming, "We helped you spend it when you had it, and we'll stay with you until you have it again." Son Perle found his place among the rough-talking, roping Texans that rode the Rim country. During the summer of 1887, Jesse and Perle Ellison became members of a self-appointed committee of enforcers.[20]

Aug 23-27. Nothing of importance occurred. Very dull at baths. Think I shall close up soon.

Sep 5. Sold my yearling steer to Mr. Murray for $11.00. Paid for Joe Guns, the chinaman, my bill due him with my sewing machine.

Sep 6. Had my tooth filled and am getting ready to leave....

Sep 7. Will leave for ranch in morning. Will leave baths with Harry Hamilton to close and leave suits and moveables at Ryders.

Frank returned to Coon Creek without mentioning the escalating feud involving his Tonto Basin neighbors. Was he unaware or unconcerned?

I paused on the hilltop marveling at the northern panorama before me. The Salt River listlessly flowed, winding west toward the desert, its energy spent in the canyons. Lake Roosevelt harnesses the waters reclaimed from the restless river. Destined for wasteland a century ago, today the bridled reserves advance to irrigate a desert oasis—"The Valley of the Sun." I applauded Frank's forward vision—a man ahead of his time. A dependable water source for Frank's swimming baths and alfalfa fields might have altered his future.

Chapter Twelve

MAN'S INHUMANITY TO MAN

The deafening roar resounded above my head. Rumbling like surf battering against craggy cliffs, the gale reverberated through the treetops. The southern wind accelerated up the sandstone face, gaining velocity as it rose against the resistant Mogollon Rim at Al Fulton Point. Stunted ponderosa pines swayed and tossed in the blustering gusts. On the precipice, I gazed over the verdant valley below. In the distance, the violet hue of the Mazatzal Mountains ascended to interrupt a hazy western horizon. I stood 1,500 feet above Pleasant Valley, windblown and in awe of the panorama before me.

Pine needles crunched under my feet, releasing a pungent scent that jarred nostalgic memories from my youth. Rosy stones covered with lichen lay at my feet. They were not the rocks of my quest. A rocky embankment surrounding extinguished embers gave me false hope. I scoured the fringes of Crook's trail looking for a mound with a marker. I searched in vain for an identifying headstone. Instead, I found inspiration.

The horrified herdsmen watched as the bleating, woolly bodies toppled 1,500 feet onto the conifers below the Rim. Buck sheep plunged to their deaths driven by cattlemen determined to eliminate the scourge upon the land. The rest of the herd lay bludgeoned and bloody at the precipice. The message was clearly stated: keep your sheep out of Pleasant Valley.

The Daggs brothers of Flagstaff owned the largest sheep outfit in northern Arizona. For years their huge flocks grazed on the open range above the Rim. Trouble began in 1885, when the Aztec Land and Cattle Company placed their massive cattle herds in traditional sheep country. Lawsuits over water and property rights filled the courts. Violence replaced sadistic, intimidating practical jokes.[1]

Former Daggs employee John Paine aligned himself with the Hashknife outfit to drive sheep from cattle lands. Noted as a fearless fighter, excessive drinker, and master intimidator, he pistol-whipped shepherds and shot up stockmen's campsites to monopolize grazing lands. His camp served as headquarters for horse thieves, drawing undesirables to the area.

The Daggs brothers hired the Tewksburys to work on shares driving several herds into Pleasant Valley. By moving sheep into the valley, the Tewksburys hoped to force out the Grahams. The scheme backfired. The Grahams found support within the ranks of the Hashknife outfit.[2]

In February of 1887, the Daggs brothers broke an unwritten law. They hired two Indians and Tewksbury friend William Jacobs to move two herds into the mild valley below the imaginary demarcation line along the snowy Mollogon Rim. The body of one of the Indian sheepherders was found near his Pleasant Valley camp. Several newspapers reported that the assailant's trail led to the Graham ranch. Rumors implicated a Hashknife cowboy in the decapitation of the herdsman. The Tewksburys held the Grahams responsible. Sensationalized reports and unsubstantiated facts circulated in territorial newspapers that labeled the Graham-Tewksbury conflict a sheep vs. cattle vendetta. In reality, the smoldering discord was rooted in rustling, deceit, and betrayal. The sheep only added fuel to the fire.[3]

Graham's errand boy Andy Cooper circulated a contract among Pleasant Valley stockmen by which the signers agreed to pay Cooper a bounty of fifty dollars for any Tewksbury scalp. In a Holbrook bar, the liquored-up Grahams reportedly bragged of hiring a hitman to eradicate their enemies. Years later, George W. Shute wrote, "strange, tough characters began coming into the valley who were friends of Andy Cooper. Many of them were Hashknife cowboys…and for some unknown reason becoming more and more friendly with the Grahams."[4]

The Blevins family's involvement in thievery is uncertain. Only Andy's participation has been indisputably established. In July, old man Blevins's suspicious disappearance while looking for horses sparked violence that extended for the next year. By August, Hamp Blevins suspected foul play. He enlisted Robert Carrington and Hashknife cowboys John Paine, Tom Tucker, and Bob Glaspie to help locate his father. Instead of taking supplies, they went armed for battle. As the search party headed south through Graham country, their number increased. By the time they reached Cherry Creek, their faction numbered eight.[5]

On August 9, 1887, the ill-fated Middleton cabin (Flying V ranch) once again experienced violence. The Tewksburys, part-time Newton employees, were in the house. Other occupants in the well-defended cabin probably included Jim Roberts, Joseph Boyer, A. E. Edmonson, and Jake Lauffer. Ranch manager George Wilson, George Newton's teenage brother-in-law, was reportedly away.[6]

Andy Cooper and company arrived at the Flying V ranch pretending to be hungry. The Tewksburys were prepared. Who fired first became clouded in the subsequent accusations and denials. Jim Roberts stated Hamp Blevins fired the first shot. Tom Tucker pointed his finger at the men in the cabin. Jim Tewksbury claimed that Paine instigated the shootout.

In the end, Hamp Blevins, John Paine, and three horses lay dead in the clearing. Tucker, Glaspie, and Carrington were wounded. Overpowered by the superior Tewksbury arsenal, the combatants retreated. Badly wounded Tucker survived a thunderstorm and a bear attack before finding refuge. Three days later, Glaspie reached the Blevins ranch with his leg wound. The humbled gladiators hobbled homeward.[7]

Later, Jim Roberts told his son a comical anecdote. While the cabin-bound defenders were on the alert, a large party on horseback appeared on a hill behind the house. The Tewksburys, with their Winchesters trained on the approaching horsemen, prepared for another assault. As the group approached, the occupants realized that war-painted Apaches were descending upon them. The unsuspecting warriors rounded the cabin, viewed the scattered carnage of dead humans and horses, and saw the arsenal trained on them. They yelped and ran for their lives. Laughing, Roberts said, "All you could see were G-strings and horsetails." At dark, the Tewksbury allies withdrew to a canyon hideaway. Before morning, flames had consumed the old Middleton place.[8]

On August 14, Louis Parker brought criminal charges in Yavapai County against young George Wilson for the murders of Hamp Blevins and John Paine. At the trial, defense witness Robert H. Schell testified that he and James V. Vale had spent the night of August 9 with George Wilson in Kenton's corral. His testimony corroborated that of Gila County deputy sheriff George Shute. Shute swore he saw Wilson forty miles away at Kenton's ranch on the Salt River on August 8 and 9. After hearing the testimony, Tewksbury friend, Justice of the Peace J. V. Meadows, dismissed the charges against George Newton's brother-in-law.[9]

Had George Shute and Robert Schell perjured themselves to protect the youth? Years later, George Wilson's son verified his father's account of the shootout. "According to the story often repeated to friends," he recalled. "He could not even move a muscle. His feet seemed glued to the floor and his gun never left its rigid hold in his hands until relaxation came after the murderous reality was over."[10]

Eight days after the Newton ranch gunplay and three days after Louis Parker filed criminal charges, Billy Graham was ambushed. The youngest Graham brother was searching for missing horses on August 17, when he crossed paths with Apache County deputy sheriff James D. Houck, brother-in-law of the slain shepherd. Deputy Houck, a Tewksbury partisan and sheepman, supposedly held

Yavapai County Sheriff William "Bill" Mulvenon. AHS/TUCSON #60613.

an arrest warrant for John Graham. Houck later explained, "We both drew at sight of one another, but I shot first and got him."[11]

Young Billy couldn't compete against the seasoned executioner. Well trained in combat during the Civil War, Houck blew open Billy's belly, spilling his intestines. Left for dead, young Graham pushed his entrails back inside, tied his shirt around himself, and somehow remounted for the ride home. Along the way the shirt untied, and Billy arrived home with his innards dragging. With the nearest doctor a hundred miles away, his family sewed him together with a needle and thread. Billy died an excruciating death. The Grahams vowed vengeance. Three witnesses testified that Billy had uttered a deathbed statement: "I saw Ed Tewksbury shoot me." The war turned up a notch![12]

By this time, another lawman happened on the scene. Sheriff William Mulvenon and his posse from Yavapai County found the Graham faction at Charley Perkins's store in the Tonto Basin. The lawmen held no warrants for the Grahams' arrest, only for the Tewksburys.

At the Flying V ranch, the posse discovered freshly dug mounds and ashes of a torched house, but no Tewksburys. Without evidence pointing to the arsonists, Mulvenon returned to Prescott with ten unserved murder warrants against the Tewksburys. If Mulvenon had remained in Pleasant Valley longer, the next tragic episode might not have occurred. Instead pitiless barbarism commenced between the Grahams and the Tewksburys.[13]

The Graham alliance closed ranks after Billy's death. With three of their number dead, one missing, and five wounded, they planned a brazen reprisal on the Tewksbury compound on Cherry Creek. Early on September 2, 1887, John Tewksbury and William Jacobs rounded up several horses after a night of standing guard. The Graham faction, including Andy Cooper, lay in ambush behind boulders. As Tewksbury and Jacobs led horses toward the house, the bushwhackers blasted them from behind. Jacobs stumbled a few feet and fell. A shot to the back of the neck, three point-blank shots in the chest, and a crushed skull ended John Tewksbury's life. Classic overkill by a vengeful family.[14]

Inside the cabin were John's parents, his pregnant wife Mary Ann, daughter Bertha, John Rhodes, and a houseguest. Ed Tewksbury and Jim Roberts remained ensconced in the mountain hideaway. The romanticized tale that survived for a century asserts that Mary Ann Tewksbury hovered over her dead husband's body for days to keep wild hogs from devouring him. In reality, Mary Ann, pinned down by gunfire, was unable to reach her husband's half-eaten corpse. For days she pleaded for a pause in gunfire to bury the bodies. The snipers refused. In darkness, the expectant mother crawled out to cover her dead husband's body with a blanket. Quoted later, Jim Tewksbury threatened, "No damned man can kill a brother of mine and stand guard over him for the hogs to eat him and live within a mile and a half of me."[15]

Andy Cooper left the protracted assault at the Tewksbury's ranch early and headed back to Holbrook, a two-day ride. Following Old Mart's disappearance and her son Hamp's death, Mary Blevins had rented a small house across from the railroad depot. Full of bravado, Cooper boasted of the Tewksbury killings at the local saloon.

A few hours after Andy's arrival, Sheriff Commodore Perry Owens rode into town armed with a longstanding warrant for Andy Cooper's arrest on horse stealing charges. At thirty-five, Owens presented a colorful picture as a longhaired eccentric with grit. Claiming ignorance of the Tewksbury ambush, he went to Mary Blevins's house to arrest Cooper. Spectators positioned themselves at the railroad depot across the street to witness the event. They got more than they bargained for.[16]

A conglomeration of Blevins family and friends had gathered in Mary Blevins's house on the afternoon of September 4. Witnesses agreed that Owens strolled to the Blevins home, Winchester across his arm and six-shooter on his hip. Andy Cooper answered the door. Owens told Andy he had a warrant for his arrest. Cooper stalled and then refused to go. With that, Owens shot him point blank in the chest.[17]

From another doorway, John Blevins fired at the sheriff. The errant shot killed Andy's horse tied outside. Owens returned fire. As John Blevins lay wounded, Mote (Mose) Roberts, dived from a side window toward a wagon. A blast from Owens's Winchester halted Roberts's escape. Sporting Andy Cooper's six-shooter, fifteen-year-old Sam Houston Blevins ran out the front door with his frail mother desperately restraining him. The sheriff killed the youngster before he could shoot. Poor Mary Blevins mourned two more dead sons that evening. Within a minute, sharpshooter Owens, single-handedly, had maimed one opponent and killed three, including a boy.[18]

A coroner's jury exonerated the sheriff in Andy Cooper's death. They found that Cooper had resisted arrest, and that Owens had acted in "the official discharge of his duty." During the melee, only one slug was fired from three guns in the Blevins house. The element of surprise had worked in the sheriff's favor. To some, Commodore Perry Owens became a legendary hero; others assumed that county officials had hired an assassin to eliminate the desperadoes. Few disputed Owens's courage.[19]

Although Owens acted within the scope of the law, he probably underestimated how many occupants were in the Holbrook house. When faced with danger, he overreacted. If Owens had accepted assistance to arrest Cooper, or brought in a posse, the outcome might have been different. Political pressure and his campaign promise to clean-up rustling may have influenced Owens's overzealous performance.[20]

John Black Blevins, the only male survivor of the Blevins family, was tried and convicted of "assault with intent to commit murder" and sentenced to five years in Yuma Territorial Prison. While en route to Yuma, the crippled prisoner received a pardon from Governor Conrad Zulick. Old Mart Blevins's fate remains a mystery. Dan Thrapp, in his *Encyclopedia of Frontier Biography,* suggests that Tewksbury sympathizer Tom Horn knew the answer. Before his execution, embellisher Horn confessed to committing a murder during the feud. U.S. Deputy Marshall Joe LeFors recalled Horn's confession that "at twenty-six he killed his first man…a coarse S.O.B." Old Mart's disappearance coincides with Horn's age at the time. Tom Horn, hanged in 1903, took his victim's name to the grave.[21]

The month's convoluted events became gory fodder for every national publication. The Pleasant Valley War embarrassed a territory bent on achieving respect and statehood. Its tribulations presented federal lawmakers with ample ammunition to oppose beleaguered Arizona's statehood. General William T. Sherman's sarcastic statement echoed national sentiments: "We fought one war with Mexico to win Arizona; we ought to fight another war to make her take it back." Statehood seemed a long way off for a society still settling its squabbles with a six-shooter. Laws were unenforceable in the expanses of Apache and Yavapai counties. A "committee of fifty" exercised their own laws in Pleasant Valley.[22]

Chapter Thirteen

THE ENFORCERS

*O*n a Monday morning, I waited in line with Gila County fine-payers. The Clerk of Court office seemed unusually busy. I didn't help matters. The harried clerks graciously searched for an obscure film containing obsolete court cases. While waiting, I perused the district court record books, researching the feud. As usual, I began with the H's, not expecting to see Hammon. I did a double take. The name "Frank Hammond" flew off the page. My heart pounded as I absorbed the meaning of the handwritten entry in 1882, "Arrested— not guilty." Inadvertently, I had stumbled on a story. Not the one I expected, but a personal one.

Late in August 1887, while Frank Hammon prepared to return to Coon Creek, Governor C. Meyer Zulick, District Attorney John C. Herndon, and Sheriff William Mulvenon of Yavapai County held a conference in Prescott designed to end the range war. Their strategy called for Mulvenon's posse to sweep through Pleasant Valley, arresting all feud participants. To ensure secrecy, they planned to detain anyone they encountered along the way. Ultimately, they hoped for speedy, effective trials. The lawmen left Prescott, merged in Payson with a Flagstaff posse, and headed for Pleasant Valley, where Deputy Joe T. McKinney's posse joined them. They totaled twenty-five well-armed men.[1]

While Mulvenon's expanded posse headed toward Pleasant Valley, the Graham party once again assaulted the Tewksburys. Returning from Holbrook, Jim Roberts and the Tewksbury brothers set up camp at Rock Springs. In the pre-dawn hours, Jim Roberts climbed a hill to collect horses and noticed men approaching through the meadow grasses. Roberts hollered down to his friends, "Look out below boys!" Jim and Ed Tewksbury, dressed only in underwear, grabbed their guns and ran for cover. The Graham party charged through the camp, firearms blazing.[2]

Graham supporter Harry Middleton (unrelated to Globe's Middleton family) was critically wounded in the skirmish. Pitched from his horse, Joe Ellenwood found shelter behind a narrow tree. With Ellenwood's ample backside exposed, Ed Tewksbury couldn't resist a well-placed posterior shot. A friend of Ed's later confided, "Ellenwood patted his rump in a derisive gesture, and Ed obliged him by shooting him there. 'He jumped ten feet'." The attackers retreated to bury their dead. Hashknife cowboy Harry Middleton died days later and was buried next to Billy Graham. Ellenwood rode sidesaddle back to the Graham ranch and, to avoid the law, eventually sought medical treatment at San Carlos—120 miles away. Joe Ellenwood and Frank Hammon would become well acquainted a few months later.[3]

Meanwhile, Frank left Phoenix for Globe.

<u>Sep 10</u>. Rode to Kentons on Salt River.

<u>Sep 11</u>. Started raining last night and rained all day. Traded Bessie off for a pony....

<u>Sep 12</u>. Rode up to Globe. Good feed all about Globe. Picketed horses on hill. Met Mike Welsh on his way to Salt River.

<u>Sep 13</u>. Put trunk in room back of Chas Taylors saloon with rifle and shotgun.

<u>Sep 14</u>. Jimmie Patton paid me $10.00 on house rent, bal. due from him $10.00 to be paid Oct 1st. Will start for ranch tomorrow.

<u>Sep 15</u>. Started with Dr. Stallo and Johnie Delarge for ranch arrived about dark.

<u>Sep 16</u>. Got water out and irrigated orchard. The fruit trees are about ruined but may save a part of them.

Sep 17. Rode up and found the horses. All but my sorrell colt, which is over on Cherry Creek. Went up to Oak and Mud springs. There are a lot of **W** and **V** cattle up there. Saw two of my calves which Lee marked in Henrys mark.

Sep 18. Went up Cherry Creek met Bob Pringle at Stallos and came down with him, drove several of our cattle back to Coon Creek. Bob came over and stayed with me over night. Saw two more of my calves marked to Henry.

Sep 19. Bob and I rode up Dry Creek by the Salt River divide over high mesa and up home.

Sep 20. I went over to Cherry Creek and Bob and I went up nearly to Gleasons Flat found horses. Found there my sorrel colt was with them.

Sep 21. Fixed up the fences and will go to Globe tomorrow. My new pony Dandy got killed today accidently. All my fault. I feel so bad about it. Got up Kate and Mary and dragged him down creek.

Sep 22. Came to Globe today.

Sep 23. My amount of tax for 1887—$79.27. It will be tight rustling for tax money this year. Taxes become delinquent the third Monday in Dec.

Sep 24. Globe is duller than ever have seen it before. I shall have to go elsewhere to get employment for this winter.

Sep 25. With no church, but a Sunday School, but cannot have the impudence to attend. They have had fine feed here for some time, better that I ever saw it in the past. Received news of the killing of Al Rose and John (Tewksbury) [crossed out] Graham and Middleton and Inglewoods [Ellenwood] getting fatally shot. Jim Anderson fell down the shaft of his mine and was instantly killed.[4]

Frank Hammon's confused diary entry reflects the rampant rumors that added fuel to the already volatile feud. The September 23, 1887, *Phoenix Herald* published an erroneous article in which it reported that "Under Sheriff Waddell has received word from Tonto Basin that a fight occurred on the 18th instant in which Thos. Graham, Joseph Ellingwood and a man named Middleton were killed on the Graham side and George Newton and James Tewksbury on the Tewksbury side."[5]

After days of riding, Mulvenon's posse reached Haigler's ranch and formulated their game plan. Before dawn the next morning, the contingent hid behind an extended rock wall at Charley Perkins's store. A decoy rode slowly past the Graham complex, hoping to draw the Grahams' attention. The lone rider repeated the exercise before he was noticed. From his house down the road, Al

Rose fired a signal. A single shot responded from the Graham quarters. With that, John Graham and Charley Blevins emerged, mounted horses, and followed the decoy to Perkins's store.

The concealed posse waited until the riders were within fifteen feet of the wall. Mulvenon stepped from behind the barrier and ordered, "Put up your hands boys, I want you." Instead of complying, Graham and Blevins wheeled their horses and drew weapons. Sheriff Mulvenon discharged his shotgun, killing Graham's horse. The posse then opened fire on the overmatched twosome, leaving both men mortally wounded.[6]

The maneuvers extended up the road to the Graham complex. As the posse approached, Louis Parker and William Bonner hightailed it from the barn and vanished. The lawmen next focused on the occupants of Tom Graham's house. Instead of Graham, they found the wounded Ellenwood, with his wife and children. The posse continued down the road to Al Rose's place, where they arrested Miguel Apodaca.[7]

Assured of the Tewksburys' peaceful surrender, Sheriff Mulvenon proceeded to the family compound. Ed and Jim Tewksbury calmly acquiesced, along with George Newton, Jim Roberts, Jake Lauffer, George Wagner, and Joe Boyer. Without further incident, the contingent of lawmen, witnesses, and warriors rode to Payson for a preliminary hearing.

Justice of the Peace John Meadows, uneducated and disabled in an Indian raid, ran his court simply. He appointed unlicensed John W. Wentworth to defend Rose and Apodaca. At that time, a license to practice law was unnecessary. Wentworth's legal fees consisted of a $150 saddle horse and $600 in gold. Wentworth later confided that the defense of Apodaca and Rose was his "biggest shyster case." District Attorney J. C. Herndon arrived from Prescott to represent the territory. Wentworth coached his clients to "deny the charge and don't let Herndon confuse you on cross-examination." Before the hearing began, Justice Meadows indicated to Wentworth that a dismissal of charges would be worth sixty dollars in gold.[8]

George Newton brought charges of arson against Al Rose, Billy Bonner, Louis Parker, Miguel Apodaca, John Doe, and Richard Roe. As a member of the August 10 burial party, William Voris's testimony confirmed Al Rose's part in burning Newton's cabin. Al Rose testified, in a carefully worded statement, of naiveté. The charges were dropped.[9]

Al Rose's taunts and tart tongue would be his demise. Wentworth wisely advised his clients to leave the country. Apodaca left, but Rose returned to Pleasant Valley. Tom Graham escaped the dragnet but surrendered to Mulvenon in Phoenix, following his October 8 marriage to mother-to-be Anne Melton.

> Sep 29. Globe as quiet as ever. No mail. Geo. Newton came in today from Pleasant Valley.

Although Frank Hammon never revealed it, George Newton probably expressed frustration with the corrupt and crippled legal system. Delayed justice, arduous proceedings, and consideration of old friendships paralyzed the courts. Cowardice, indifference, and graft had produced an impotent legal system. Complaints, true bills, and arrests were dismissed for lack of witnesses or evidence. Dangerous travel to distant district courts resulted in absentee witnesses, jurors, and defendants. The questionable quality of judges, liberal changes of venue, and high incarceration costs bred resentment that outweighed the repugnant offenses. Distrust of the justice system united good, law-abiding men for their mutual preservation. Texas cowmen in the Tonto Basin countered with their own modus operandi—a vigilance committee. In the fall of 1887, under a veil of secrecy, Jesse W. Ellison commanded the "Committee of Fifty."[10]

If Frank Hammon had knowledge of the committee, he did not indicate it. He hired on with Bob Pringle for the fall roundup.

Sep 30. Hired out to Bob Pringle to work on Cherry Creek for $40.00 for month and board & ride my own horse.

Oct 1. Went to the Wheat Fields with Bob and Tom Burns and will go over to Cherry Creek tomorrow.

Oct 2. Went over to Cherry Creek and will gather horses tomorrow.

Oct 3. Went up creek and brought down a yearling which we killed and partially jerked.

Oct 4. Finished jerking the beef and went up and got two colts which we shod.

Oct 5. Went over to Coon Creek and got my colt Charley and one of Bobs colts and brought them home and shod them.

Oct 6. Packed up and went to the Salt River. Found that the rodeo had gone to the Wheatfields.

Oct 7. Went up Pinto's Creek and found several head of cattle.

Oct 8. Went up to Blevins spring. Bob and Tom went to campagne. Got no cattle today.

Oct 9. Rodeo party came in last night from the wheat fields and we all moved up to George Shultzes range today.

Oct 10. Rounded up Georges range today. Branded and drove to the river.

Oct 11. Rounded up back of Wm. Ganns and camped at Pete Ganns.

Oct 12. Drove around into Campagne and camped below Narrows.

Oct 13. Rounded up Campagne and to Tule Springs and camped same place as last night.

Oct 14. Drove down to Pembertons and camped there or will tonight.

Oct 15. Worked the county back of Robinsons and Danforths and will camp at Beards.

Oct 16. Worked back of Mrs. Medlers. Did not move camp today.

Oct 17. Worked country down to Hazards Gulch.

Oct 18. Moved camp and worked up to Walnut Springs and camped.

Oct 19. Worked over to the Celler gulch and camped at Old man Cottonwoods.

Oct 20. Worked down cottonwoods and up river to Hazards and broke up the round-up until after court.

Oct 21. Drove over to Cherry Creek 24 head of ℋ cattle; 1 ♏ Heifer—two years old; 1 cow and calf ℰ of Pendletons. Branded with ℋ while on river; 2 ⌀ cows and calves—1 heiffer & st.; 1 ℋ cow, Heiffer, Calf.

Oct 22. Tom [Burns] and Bob [Pringle] drove the bunch over on to the river and I went to Coon Creek and got my colt, and Rattler and the buckskin horse.

Oct 23. Went over to Horse [Horseshoe] Bend to help Rogginstroh round-up his range & branded two calves for Geo.

Oct 24. Drove around down to the corral and branded. Got two 2 yr. old ℋ heifers.

Oct 25. Three boys from M. Smith came over and we drove again to the river. The boys wern't home again this evening.

Where and who were the boys Frank referred to?

Oct 26. Moved down to the river and camp and gathered up our cattle on the river. Burns left and went to Cherry Creek. We branded 2 ℋ steer calves.

Oct 27. Moved down to Redmans Flat and gathered between here and there and branded 5 heifers, calves and steer calves, and for Bohse. Bob Pringle went to town.

Oct 28. Traded Geo Rogginstragh my sorrel stud colt, which is running on Cherry Creek, for his brown horse Kit. Drove down Big Sand Wash to corral and branded one heiffer calf ℋ for Pringle and two bull calves for Bohse and one two year old stud for English George ⊙ . Found more. Found none of Henrys nor my cattle on south side of the river.

Oct 29. Moved back to Horseshoe Bend and stayed overnight.

Al Rose should have taken Wentworth's advice. Instead, during the first week in November, Rose collected his stray cattle at the Houdon ranch. While Louis Naeglin cooked breakfast, Al collected firewood. Naeglin later claimed that masked men abducted him from the kitchen, placed a noose around his neck, and told him never to divulge what happened there. If he recognized his abductors, he carried their identities to his grave.[11]

Initial reports indicated Rose had been shot. Ed Tewksbury told Joe McKinney that Glenn Reynolds was the shootist. Reynolds's family vehemently denied the report. William Colcord, before his death, gave Robert Voris a firsthand account of Rose's murder. Voris said, "Al Rose was NOT shot but was hung…hanging was cheaper, shells cost money." Rose's hanging launched lynchings up and down the valley.[12]

In later years, Robert Voris tried to establish his father William Voris's participation. Robert met with eighty-eight-year-old Jesse Ellison in Ellison's Phoenix home. At first, the old man was reluctant to identify members of the vigilance committee. Finally, he said, "Don't you ever repeat anything I have ever told you or the names of anyone I tell you until everyone that is implicated is dead." Ellison then confirmed that William Voris had been a member. He also mentioned John Rhodes, William Colcord, Harvey Colcord, "ole man" McFadden, Bud Campbell, and Houston Kyle. Colonel Ellison implicated himself, but did not implicate his good friend Glenn Reynolds. "Colonel Ellison told me they hung Al Rose, he told me himself he hung him," Robert Voris alleged. His statement represents the only confirmation that Jesse Ellison was involved with the Committee of Fifty.[13]

The Pleasant Valley vigilantes represented conservative community leaders and ranchers frustrated by a justice system they viewed as ineffective in deterring the mayhem energized by the feud. Jesse Ellison and his "Lone Star" cowmen secretly set out to quench the chaos in a "violent sanctification of the deeply cherished values of life and property." While burgeoning vigilantism perpetrated quiet assassinations, Frank Hammon searched for winter work.[14]

Chapter Fourteen

BIRD IN THE CAGE

*W*hy did George Shute appoint Frank deputy sheriff? Was he selected for his capabilities as a marksman, administrator, negotiator, or neutralist? Was Frank aware of the "committee's" membership, and if so, did he support their law enforcement methods?

I scrutinized Frank's words, probing for clues to his character. My perception of him vacillated between fact and fiction. I searched for evidence of Frank as a tough, larger-than-life lawman. After all, didn't all frontier lawmen possess a swaggering attitude? I scoured each diary page for indications of arrogance and audacity. They weren't there. During my formative years, I had watched too many Westerns depicting frontier lawmen as gritty hombres.

As a descendent, I longed to romanticize Frank's role. I knew better. My intuition transcended imaginative yearnings. I finally conceded Frank was just a principled deputy determined to run an efficient office. Conscientious Frank needed a job, and George Shute needed a trusted deputy. It was as simple as that.

George E. Shute,
ca. 1880.
SHM #PC1538P.

Although the townsfolk showed sympathy toward the Tewksburys, Globe remained relatively unscathed by the feud. Compared to other mining towns, Globe was a docile community. That was fortunate because misfortune struck Sheriff E. E. Hodgson in the fall of 1887. While Deputy John Benbrook was in California caring for his sick wife, Hodgson died from complications following a horse accident. When a sheriff became incapacitated or died in office, the county board of supervisors generally recommended an interim sheriff to the governor, who made the appointment. Deputy George E. Shute was appointed to fill the vacant position.[1]

Twenty-one-year-old George had married into William Middleton's family in Maricopa County on December 14, 1874. Shortly thereafter, George and Ella Shute moved with the Middletons to the Wheatfields community near Globe. Like many settlers, George pursued a mining venture while raising a large family and herding cattle. A friendship developed between Frank Hammon and George Shute through mutual association with the Middleton family. That fall, Deputy Shute had arrested Tom Burns on assault charges. Frank Hammon was a prosecution witness.[2]

<u>Oct 31</u>. Was at work at the sorghum when a deputy came for me with a subpoena as a witness in the trial of Tom Burns for an assault with a deadly weopon upon [Carl] Smith. Went to Globe immediately.

<u>Nov 1</u>. Trial is called today at 10 AM. Am sorry to have anything to do with it. Jury brought in a verdict of guilty of assault, sentence to be passed in the morning.

<u>Nov 2</u>. Burns was sentenced this morning to 90 days confinement. Pringle gave me a verbal order on Joe Redman for $37.75 and he paid me $30.00 leaving $7.75 still due. I sent the $30.00 to Father....

As a prosecution witness, Frank testified he had seen Tom Burns pistol-whip Carl Smith. It is clear Frank dreaded possible repercussions from offering testimony that conflicted with Robert Pringle's testimony on Burns's behalf. No wonder Frank wanted little part in the matter. His job and personal safety were in jeopardy. Frank's encounters with Tom Burns were just beginning. Before returning to the roundup, Frank wrote his father but did not mention the trial.

Globe Arizona Nov 2nd '87

Dear Father

Your kind letter of Sept 6th I recd in due time. One of my chief sources of pleasure are my letters from home without which I would not know what to do.

They are next to seeing you all and my dear little ones. It is a great satisfaction to me to know of the loving care and attention which they receive and the good influence under which they live. Yet I realize now more fully than before the responsibility which I was so selfish as to remove from my shoulders to yours.

My gratitude which before was unlimited for all you had done for me, was or is enhanced if such could or can be, and for the full and heartfelt blessing of my angel wife and the future gratitude of my children I fully speak, in return for what you are doing for them and me.

I have been attending the fall round up for the last month and was fortunate in getting employment during the time for which I receive $40.00 which I enclose. I was looking after my own interests at the same time. I leave for the ranch in the morning for another weeks riding which will finish my work with my cattle for this fall.

I was pained to learn of mothers illness and was much relieved to know from another letter that she was better. My health is of the best I weigh now 170 lbs. With love to all I remain Aff your son.

Frank

P.S. The man who owes me the $40.00 could only pay me thirty dollars today, and will pay me the other $10.00 when I return in about a week from the ranch and I will then send it to you. So I enclose a P.O. order for $30.00. FR

Tom Burns spent one night in jail, paid a $100 fine, and returned to the fall roundup. If Frank sensed animosity from Burns and Pringle, it went unmentioned.[3]

Nov 4. Went over to Coon Creek branded Blacks heiffer calf, Holeys steer calf and Beauty's steer calf, and 3 of Pringles. Found Pringle and Tom Burns at Coon Creek Ranch.

Nov 5. Got Charley my gelding down. Tom & Bob came over, we branded two of his.

Nov 6. Went around Dry Creek drove in and branded: White Heads heifer calf, Kate, One Horn Spots heifer calf, Henrys White Spot cows, St. [steer] Calf for Pringle.

Nov 7. Drove around by the Salt River divide and the high mesa, branded only hef. [heifer] calf for Henry—Big Red Cow.

Nov 8. Went up to Oak Springs and worked down Coon Creek, branded three heifer calves for Henry and one heifer calf for myself. Will go to Globe in the morning.

Nov 9. Bob and Burns went to Cherry Creek this morning. I left for Globe and arrived about 4 PM. Geo Shute was appointed sheriff and he has agreed to appoint me under him. I think it will be better than anything else I can get to do.

Frank's financial concerns dictated his decision to accept the deputy position. He could earn fees generated from tax collecting, property assessment, and serving summonses, subpoenas, and writs. There is no question why Frank accepted the position, but why did George Shute appoint Frank? Occasionally, rogues were deputized to "fight fire with fire." Frank did not fit in that category. Sheriff Shute needed an educated, ethical, and efficient administrator to run his office, leaving him free to conduct other official duties. Finding these qualities in a horseman skilled with firearms, and familiar with the terrain, was difficult in a small community. Frank probably rationalized that earning a steady income offset the risks associated with the office. George Shute had observed Frank's testimony at the Tom Burns trial the previous week, contradicting Bob Pringle and Tom Burns's testimony and placing his job and his life at risk. This may have influenced Shute's selection of Frank as his deputy. After all, bravery was the primary requisite for a lawman.[4]

Nov 10. Stayed around town which is duller than I have ever seen it before. Mr. Ellison arranged to pay my note of $100. in a few days. Which will just come in good time to pay my taxes....

Nov 11. Started for Salt River this morning with Mr. Redman. Met Geo Shute below town and returned with him. He arranged about his sheriff's bond and we started for the river with Fox [Clerk of Court] and Spense. Made up bond as went down.[5]

Following George Shute's appointment, he and Frank rode north toward the Salt River to solicit sureties for the sheriff's bond. The bond would cover any liabilities the sheriff might incur in the process of collecting taxes or enforcing the law. The amount "was tied to the value of assessed, taxable property in a county." Gaining commitments from three bondmen whose total assets exceeded $10,000 could be dicey if the sheriff were a man of questionable character. As a well-respected family man and rancher, George Shute had no trouble finding bondsmen.[6]

Nov 12. Went down the river with Geo, and drove back some H steers which Geo turned over to Vosberg. Will go to Globe tomorrow.

Nov 14. Geo Shute filed his sheriffs bond and was sworn into office and I was sworn in as his chief deputy. We received the keys and took charge of the office and sheriffs duties.

Nov 15. Straightened up the papers in the sheriffs office. Got our stable fixed back of Taylors and will feed our own horses and [supply] nails for $.60 cts. Geo left for Salt River and Tonto with several subpeonas sent from Prescott for witnesses to appear at court III. Gave Charlie the restaurant Chinaman, an order on Joe Redman for $7.65 and Joe paid me .10 bal, thereby squaring the Chinaman and Joes accts. Bot [bought] on account of Fatty the Chinaman $5.00 worth of meal tickets.

Nov 17. Bot for county from Westmeyer: 1 feather duster $1.25; from Chas Taylor—stationery $3.50.

Nov 18. Got my tooth filled. borrowed $4.00 of Chas Taylor with which to pay for it. Geo returned from Tonto, served 4 subpeonas.

Nov 19. Rec'd from J. W. Ransom chk No 9647 B drawn by the Santa Rosa Bank of Cal, on the London San Francisco Bank of San Francisco Cal. for $100. in payment of J. W. Ellison's note due me dated April 1st and due Sept 1st 1887—Which I endorsed and turned over in return for the check.

Nov 20. Stayed around office. Carl Smith left town with Mr. Armor.

The *Silver Belt* gave Frank an estimable endorsement. "Geo. E. Shute completed his bond [$10,000.] and was installed as sheriff of Gila County on Monday," the Globe newspaper reported. "His first official act was to appoint as deputy Frank M. Hammon…we may expect the business of the office to be discharged in a manner satisfactory to the community—that is the law abiding portion of it." Frank's principles would be tested in the coming year.[7]

Nov 21. Board met. Allowed us another office. Turned over poll Tax receipts and license blanks to us. Raining this evening and looks very stormy.

Nov 22. Geo went to Salt River this morning. Moved our office to O. M. Andersons building across street south from the court house [and jail]. A storm is gathering and rain is falling now.

The American justice system required incarceration of lawbreakers, but few counties could afford adequate lockups. Deteriorated adobe houses and decrepit abandoned buildings served as primitive jails. Usually dirty, bug-ridden, cramped, and unsupervised, the jails held primarily the drunks and drifters. Overcrowded cells filled with ingenious prisoners led to escapes through crumbling adobe walls, especially in rainy weather. Insecure jails invited vigilantes to bestow their own sentences. Vigilante break-ins and prisoner breakouts plagued frontier sheriffs. A jailbreak represented the fundamental breakdown of the judicial system. The court system was helpless unless the perpetrator of a crime was in custody. [8]

Globe citizens endorsed prison reform by contracting for a new courthouse. The proposed edifice was scheduled for completion in September 1888. Andre Maurel's blueprints outlined a sheriff's office, with the jail cell in the sunken lower level. The courtroom and county offices would occupy the main floor. The sketches also called for a tall wooden fence to encompass a large exercise yard capable of housing temporary gallows. Until the new jail was ready, Frank settled into a six dollar-a-month rented room across the street. Not surprisingly, one of Globe's troublemakers soon broke out of the crumbling jail.[9]

Nov 23. Still storming quite hard. Nothing doing. Niebes Merville, one of our prisoners escaped this evening.

Nov 24. Storm still raining, an extraordinary rain for this season of the year. A very quiet Thanksgiving Day. Got my $100 check cashed. Bot shoes for $4.00. Paid Chas Taylor cash borrowed $4.25. Paid bill at McNelly's – 90 cts. Bal $2.00. Had a very pleasant time at the party.

Nov 25. Still storming. Geo. Shutes arrived from the river. Arrested a squaw and mexican woman for fighting.

Nov 26. Telegraphed Capt. Pierce to send for some indians who are making trouble.

Nov 27. Scouts arrived and turned over two bucks and a squaw to them. Arrested Cy Burns for disturbing the peace. Weather clear and beautiful but cold.

Nov 30. Geo returned to the river and will not return for several days.

By the end of November, the Pleasant Valley Feud had been defused. The grand jury returned an indictment against Tom Graham in the shepherd's death.

Gila County courthouse and sheriff's office.
ASLAPR #96-3652.

Ed and James Tewksbury were charged with the murder of Hampton Blevins. All parties had been released on bond until the June court session, although some of the Graham partisans remained fugitives. Conspicuous among notations written inside the back cover of Frank's diary were the names "Thos Carrington, Wm. Bonner, Louis Parker." Almost as an afterthought, Frank jotted a misspelled name upside down beneath a list of his cattle: "Joe Mkenna Constable, Winslow, AT." Frank was on the lookout for the elusive Graham supporters.

<u>Dec 1</u>. Paid Mrs Moore for ½ mos. rent and will sleep now at the office.

Frank's sleeping arrangements served two purposes: security and economy. Often a deputized jailer also worked as a night watchman, and his salary came out of the sheriff's pocket. To cut corners, Frank and George eliminated the jailer's position. Frank kept his eye on the jail.

Dec 2. Storming again, quite cold. Wrote to Bertie and sent Father $40.00.

Dec 3. Nothing doing. Two shifts were put on the mine Globe yesterday.

By year's end, mining operations resumed following the sudden rise in copper prices. Baltimore tycoons William and R. Brent Keyser bought the defunct Old Dominion Mine Company at a sheriff's sale in February 1886. Superintendent A. L. Walker took control of the company and gave the community hope for a prosperous new year. Unfortunately, poor weather would stymie the coke wagons and halt the smelters. As 1887 drew to a close, Frank struggled with his own issues.[10]

Dec 4. Have firmly resolved to play no more cards this month.

Dec 5. I sat down into a game today before I thought, but have resolved to play no more. Constable office declared vacant today by Supervisors.

Dec 6. Came down to serve a summons on Hoyle Higdan to appear at Justice court in Globe on Dec 10th. Served this evening about half after 6:00 PM.

Dec 7. Returned to Globe today. Expect George in today. Railroad meeting today.

Dec 8. Geo returned from the river this evening.

Dec 9. Geo went to the river to move his family up.

Dec 10. Attended Justice court judgement rendered in favor of J. R. Hazard.

Dec 11. News today of a military post to be established near Globe.

Dec 12. Geo arrived today with his family—Officers arrived today to locate a site for the post.

Enthusiasm for a new military post near Globe provided a temporary boost to the town's struggling economy. The proposed fort never materialized, nor did another projected railroad. During the fall of 1887, an East Coast syndicate designed a Phoenix-Globe railroad route to connect with the Arizona Mineral Belt under construction south of Flagstaff. By spring 1888, the Arizona Mineral Belt Railroad ran into financial difficulties and faltered. The concept, however, expanded into a larger proposal as several Phoenix attorneys and businessmen incorporated the Arizona Central Railway Company. Their plan called for three railroad lines branching out from Phoenix and connecting with Yuma, Prescott, and Globe. Unfortunately, the scheme died. Globe's railway woes continued.[11]

<u>Dec 13</u>. Received from McCabe a summons to serve on Jack Eaton. Made a copy of same, also a warrant of arrest for Jack Eaton. Also copy of Summons $1.00… Served summons Holmes vs Eaton.

<u>Dec 15</u>. Returned two Writs Possession. Served two summons.

What was Frank's frame of mind as Christmas approached? Although there are no diary entries to verify his sentiments, Frank's work and personal business probably alleviated his Christmas melancholy. On Christmas Day, Frank conducted business as usual. Family and celebrations went unmentioned—another bleak Christmas without his children.

<u>Dec 25</u>. Gave Fatty [a Chinese man] an order on W. H. Duryea for $40.00 in merchandise to go to my credit on my board account. Rented my house above the church to Mack Wilmans for $7.50 per month to commence Jan 1, 1888.

The New Year seemed to bolster Frank's spirits and transformed the tone of his journal entries from curt comments to hopeful, upbeat passages. Frank found fulfillment, purpose, and a steady income with his new job. Encouraged, he applied for the open constable position.

<u>Jan 1, 1888</u>. We now have three 8's to write in a row—which will occur again in a thousand years. I begin this new year as Deputy Sheriff of Gila County, Arizona Territory. A statement of my finances I enter in a memorandum page near the back of this book. With the advent of 1888 prospects brighten for us at Globe and I begin this New Year with the intent to get out of debt ere its close—and soon after to remove east.

<u>Jan 2</u>. Today is the legal New Year holliday—The board of Supervisors met and adjourned until tomorrow. Then they will commence the yearly and quarterly sentiment. My home above the M E [Methodist Episcopal] Church I have rented to M. Wilmans for $7.50 per month dating from the 1st day of January 1888 inclusive.

<u>Jan 3</u>. Met before the board of Supervisors and presented our bill for sheriff work from Nov. 3 to Dec. 31, 1887 of $226.60 which was allowed—Asked for a safe for the office—considered favorably but laid over—Was approved Constable for Globe per Gila County, Arizona. Let with bonds placed at $1,000. Chas Taylor and F. W. Westmeyer went on my bond for $300.00 each.

<u>Jan 4</u>. Received from the clerk of the board the warrant in payment of one bill $226.60.…Wrote home and enclosed order for $50.00.…We have done quite well since we took the Sheriffs office—considering the very dull times

<u>Jan 5</u>. Henry Middleton returned from California—Miners are arriving but get no work as the weather is so bad that the smelter won't

start—Roads are so bad teaming is at a standstill—Our courthouse goes on slowly on a/c of this stormy weather—Henry Middleton paid for my 1/2 of our bill for provisions at Julius Sultans for ranch and I promised to credit him with it on his note due me— Credit amt $17.05

Jan 6. Everything is very dull in this office—in fact nothing doing at all. Our bird in the cage is all alone and lonesome. Mrs. Ramsdell commenced feeding the paupers and prisoners yesterday with commitment for this year at 25 cts per meal.

Arizona territorial law required adequate food, bedding, and clothing for each inmate. Frank contracted with a local boarding house to provide meals financed from the sheriff's budget. The county allowed a daily rate per prisoner. That rate covered jail upkeep, firewood, candles, shackles, and food. Some sheriffs in poorer districts resented spending money on reprobates, and cut corners. Frank provided his inmates with the best food in town. He contracted with Mrs. Ramsdell to feed the prisoners, indigents, and himself.[12]

Providing jail sanitation and fresh drinking water added a special challenge. "Slop jars" needed to be emptied and well water supplied daily. In some counties, fulltime jailers handled these duties, but Frank managed both the sheriff's office and the jail during slow times. Frank complained of boredom, but his lonesome "bird in the cage" soon had company.[13]

Jan 7. Not a bit of work since the first of the year I am sure it is getting very monotonous and uncomfortable—A heavy storm last night and lots of snow in the mountains—I commenced boarding with Mrs. Ramsdel this morning. It may cost me considerably on a/c of must be regular at meals—but the cooking is superior which is much more satisfactory. Shute went to Wheat Fields today—and returned.

Jan 8. Recd papers today to serve tomorrow on W. H. Duryea in case of E. A. Price vs W. H. Duryea brought in Pinal County at Tuson—to secure possession of certain ore and damage of $300.00....

Jan 9. Geo served papers on W. H. Druyea case of E. A. Price vs. W. H. Druyea. Recd letter from Mulvenon of Yavapai County—with pay for last quarter—and notice that the board would not allow a guard for Ellenwood.

Frank had received a message from Yavapai County sheriff William Mulvenon requesting the arrest of Joe Ellenwood at San Carlos. Lack of funding for a jailer to guard the high profile prisoner meant Frank would be jailer and nursemaid.

Jan 10. Paid Mrs. Welch one month interest to June 20—1887. Paid Bailey for hat and shoes $10.00. Got combination of safe from Vosberg [Vosburgh] to use until his return—80 then right 4— 40 then left 3— 60 right 2—then back to 100—Put in safe money due Ben Fox $12.30. Arrested Wm Davis for fighting.

Jan 11. Wm. Davis asked for a jury—was tried and was acquitted. Collected five licenses amting to 150.00. Treas fees—1.25, Sheriffs—6.25. Went to party at Miss Benbrooks this evening and had a very nice time.

Jan 12. Went to San Carlos after Joe Ellingwood under arrest for murder in the Pleasant Valley feud. He is suffering from a wound from a bullet in the hip—and is not improving much—will take him to Globe tomorrow to give bonds or go to Prescott. Mr. [Reverend] Downs went with me to see the officials issue provisions to the indians.

On January 12 Frank and Reverend Downes left for San Carlos to transport the ailing Joe Ellenwood to Globe. Little is known of Ellenwood's background. Some said he rode the chuck line, traveling from ranch to ranch earning his keep. That seems doubtful, with a wife and family living with him in Tom Graham's cabin. Historians also differ on Joe Ellenwood's fate. Some report that he recovered from his wounds at the Graham ranch. Earle Forrest, in his book *Arizona's Dark and Bloody Ground,* reports that Ellenwood was successfully treated by Dr. Davis at San Carlos, arrived in Globe, and subsequently disappeared. Forrest goes on to say that "The *Silver Belt,* in the issue of January 14, 1888, notes Underwood's [Ellenwood] return from San Carlos and states that he was under arrest on a bench warrant. This must be a mistake, for I can find no record of a warrant issued for this man." In a footnote, Forrest adds that "His complete recovery and arrival at Globe is noted in the *Silver Belt* of Jan. 14, 1888." In reality, that issue of the *Silver Belt* reported "Joseph Ellenwood was brought yesterday from San Carlos, where Dr. Davis had been treating him for a gunshot wound received in the Pleasant Valley trouble."[14]

Jan 13. Remained around the post until eleven oclock AM and started back to Globe with Mr. Downs and Ellingwood—got through to Globe in good shape about half past four PM. Gave Ellingwood a cot in the office. Attended a party of surprise at Mrs. Van Wagenens for Sadie Ramsdel. Had a very pleasant time Made out Yav [Yavapai] Co bill and posted it

Interestingly, Frank settled Ellenwood in his office instead of the jail cell. Maybe Frank felt compassion for the prisoner, recognizing that he required special attention. The possibility that vigilantes might abduct his captive concerned Frank more than the likelihood that Ellenwood might escape. In his weakened condition, the prisoner would not go far.

Jan 15. ...Everything quiet and dull—Weather very cool and continues so. Attended church in the evening—Ellenwood continues just about the same.

Jan 16. ...Followed a peddler up on the Pinal mountains and collected his license and legal mileage for my trip—He said that he had left the money in town to pay his license which upon my return I found true and had it forwarded to him to Florence by PO money order

Jan 17. …Nothing new today—Geo went out to look for some wood. I helped around to fix up about O. O. H. hall for our meeting tonight— Six new members we balloted for and admitted only two—W. A. Horton & Hyens Aschleman were initiated—Deputy Sheriff Thomas of Pinal County came in with McNeal, the man who broke jail at Phoenix and shot Kelners [Kellner] horse—We put him in a cage—He will go on with him to Florence tomorrow.

Jan 18. …James Thomas deputy from Pinal County left for Florence with McNeal—I loaned him 15.00 which he agreed to send back immediately. Also a pair of Hand Cuffs and a pair of shackles.

Slippery W. C. McNeil, the red-headed Bostonian, would prove hard to contain. A noted horse thief and poet, McNeil escaped from the Florence jail still wearing shackles. By September 1888, Apache County sheriff Commodore Perry Owens was in hot pursuit. He stopped at a Holbrook cow camp for the night where a charming young cowpoke offered to share his bedroll. Owens awoke the next morning to find a poem pinned to his blanket:

Pardon me, Sheriff
I'm in a hurry
You'll never catch me,
But don't you worry. – Red McNeil[15]

Frank managed the sheriff's office and handled the constable's duties while Globe's civil disobeyers cooled their heels in the jail cell. The constable position paralleled that of the sheriff. As a ranking precinct peace officer, Frank was the "enforcement arm" of the justice court. For meager fees, Frank attended court, served writs, executed judgments, and issued licenses for businesses, entertainments, and travel.[16]

Jan 19. …Collected two commercial travelers licenses from Adolph Soloman and Jacob Loeb of 50.00 each. Recd three Executions from Geo G. Berry of Tombstone against the Old Dominion Copper Company for total amt of over $20.00. Geo went out and got a load of wood.[17]

Jan 20. …Got counsel on the service of the executions recd yesterday and wrote out the sheriffs sale Notices—Will levy on the Old Globe Mine and the Globe Ledge Mine and the Red Jacket Mill tomorrow—Recd warrants for Ellenwood today. Wrote Geo G Berry informing him of what we have done and of the discrepancy of $100.00 in the notation of the amt of interest in the execution's #876 and #877 and that we should levy tomorrow—making interest at $1893.75.

Jan 21. …Levied the executions of Adolf Lauenburg Et All vs Old Dominion Copper M Co on the Globe Mine and Globe Ledge Mine and the Red Jacket Mill site—Informed A. L. Walker [mine superintendent] of the fact and of the property levied upon—Advertised for sale [unreadable] under one execution as ordered—Wrote to G. Berry informing him of what we have done. Asked if we should advertise under the other two executions, If we should put on a keeper—and if we should shut down the works.[18]

Jan 22. …Attended funeral of Probate Judge Kingsbery who died yesterday. Wrote to Attorney General Briggs Goodrich regarding license for commercial drivers or Travelers and which we should collect license fee in addition to the amt of license. Attended church in evening subscribed for the pastor $1.00 per month.

Jan 23. … Wrote to Mulvenon to come for Ellenwood as we were in bad condition to accomodate him in his present condition—or if he prefered we would deliver him to him at Prescott—if he would guarantee us a reasonable compensation for the trip.

Jan 24. …Sent in order to Noland & sons of San Francisco for a pair of $3.00 shoes with extra heavy soles. Enclosed a PO money order for $4.60. Attended meeting for O. O. H. Jimmy Patton and Frank Porter were admitted and initiated.[19]

Jan 25. …Wrote to Henry to sell my pack mule Jack to Baker for $50.00 if he wanted him. Wrote to Ryder to sell my swimming baths if he could for enough to pay for my note due him….

Obviously Frank no longer viewed the swimming baths in Phoenix as a good investment. He committed himself to his deputy position.

Jan 26. …Wrote again to Geo G. Berry regarding the discrepancy in notice. The amt of interest due to date of judgement in nos 876 and 877 executions, which he sent us and which we levied contesting the said amt of int at $1,893.75 in notice of sale— (registered the letter) George returned from river tonight.

Jan 27. …Very quiet—Our O. O. H. lodge changed nights for regular meeting from Tuesday to Friday. Should like to see things get lively.

Jan 28. …Geo went to the river with Joe Redman will be back next Wednesday.

Jan 29. …Nothing doing— went to church in evening.

Contrary to popular belief, lawmen experienced mind-numbing boredom more often than shoot-outs and lynchings. Frank's longing for more "lively" times indicates that his fees were not covering his expenses. Levying the executions of *Adolf Lauenburg Et All vs Old Dominion Copper Mine Co.* paid only $1.00 in fees. The same fee was charged for executing a warrant or incarcerating prisoners. Summoning witnesses and a jury earned Frank fifty cents each. The fee schedule also authorized equitable reimbursement for travel (five cents per mile) and allowed payment for unstipulated services. No wonder Globe's tranquility disturbed Frank—crime paid. Broke, he dipped into the county kitty to send money home.[20]

Jan 30. ...Very dull, must rustle up money to send home tomorrow. Rec'd at 9 oclock P M telegram from W. J. Mulvenon to meet his deputy at Casa Grande on Wednesday night. Will leave tomorrow.

Jan 31. ...Sent $50.00 home took it from the county money and will return it soon—Paid to Treas. Lonergan license money $240.00. Deputized B. J. [Mack] McGinnis to look after things until Geo or my return. Hired the team from Frakes for the trip to Casa Grand for $25.00 and left Globe today at eleven AM and arrived at Riverside about 6 PM. Joe feeling pretty tired.

Feb 1. ...Left this morning at six oclock arrived at Florence about 11 AM. fed horses and got dinner and pulled out at one for Casa Grande, arrived at 6 PM. Joe very tired and sore. Saw Chas Holborn and Chas Starr [bartender]. Old Soda Smith came to me and wanted to go up to Globe with me.

Feb 2. ...Deputy did not arrive in last night so I deputized Mr. C. M. Marshall—Justice of the Peace at Casa Grande to take charge of Ellenwood and deliver him to deputy from Prescott when he arrived. Settled bill to this morning including breakfast and pulled out for Florence. arrived about two PM. Fryer paid me the 15.00 Thomas borrowed and I got the hand cuffs and shackles....

Feb 3. ...Left Florence at about ten oclock AM and arrived at Riverside about 3 PM. Mr. Smith, I intended bringing him with me but my carriage would not carry us including a big dog he had—and so he decided to come up on the stage. Wrote to Mr. Marshall to write to Globe as soon as he got Ellenwood off for Prescot.

Feb 4. Showery....Started for Globe at 6 AM arrived at about 3 PM. Attended meeting of the Globe Stock Growers Association of Gila Co. and was elected Secty [Secretary] for the ensuing year. Mr P Shanley retiring secretary turned over to me the record book of minutes and cash $10.00 which I paid to the Treasurer J. R. Redman taking his receipt therefor.

The code of the West was a shared belief in an unspoken, unwritten axiom of social etiquette: stay out of other people's affairs; keep your mouth shut; don't ask where a man is from; endure pain quietly; "a man's word was binding"; be hospitable to a stranger's need; do not deny a man the requisites for "survival or livelihood." The code was simple, pessimistically crude, and peculiar to the West. Frank's abbreviated journal entries for the spring of 1888 appear to reflect the code. For that reason, the backgrounds of Tom Burns and Henry Blevins are unknown.[21]

Three unrelated Blevins families living in the area gained notoriety during the 1880s: first, Mary Blevins, lived a quiet life in Holbrook following her family's annihilation; then, Henry Blevins, an uncivil fellow from the Tonto Basin who readily attracted lawmen; and finally, a separate Blevins family that settled in the Globe area in May 1885. [22]

The Hugh Blevins family, accompanied by a large contingent of relatives, homesteaded a piece of land, later known as the McFadden place, in the Sierra Ancha Mountains. It may have been a water dispute in the spring of 1888 that ignited a fracas in a Globe saloon between troublesome Henry Blevins and (unrelated) Cy Blevins.[23]

> Sun Feb 5. Warm—Wrote up minutes of our Stock Association. Wrote up our accounts. Blevins [Henry] and his crowd were in today and made considerable talk—near to having serious trouble.

Henry Blevins's visit to the sheriff's office indicated pending trouble. Frank, alerted to the potential problem but true to the code, declines further elaboration. Perhaps threats were made against Sheriff George Shute. It was just a matter of time before tough talk turned to action.

> Feb 6. …Wrote to Mulvenon and sent bench warrants for Ellenwood with our returns endorsed thereon. Wrote out three notices of sale of execution 877—with the approval of McCabe attorney for Lacy we sold at private sale to James Evans for $30.00 the ore we levied upon at the Howard mine, under execution in case D. B. Lacy vs J. H. Eaton.

What happened to Joe Ellenwood? Earle Forrest implies he recovered from his wounds, escaped legal proceedings, and disappeared. He was partially right. Frank's entries somewhat clarify the picture. They verify that an arrest warrant existed for Ellenwood and that Frank transported Joe to Casa Grande, where he transferred custody to a Yavapai County deputy. Once in Prescott, a grand jury indicted Ellenwood for murder. A year and several continuances later, legal proceedings in Yavapai District Court against Joe Ellenwood and his sidekicks were "dismissed." Lack of witnesses made a trial impossible.[24]

Chapter Fifteen

THE LAWMEN

I sat spellbound as my octogenarian relatives recalled stories passed down for three generations. I had never heard these tales before. As they retold the legends, their blurred memories sharpened and they expounded the precise details of incredible feats. By afternoon's end, Frank had evolved into a hero.

Oh, how I wanted to believe the tales. How I longed for Frank to have pistol-whipped the brazen Indian, saved lives spilled from a capsized boat, been a deputy trusted by the Apaches. Captivated, I searched Frank's writings for a hint of the tales so easily remembered. Could Frank have embellished his accomplishments to impress his home folks? Or might there be an element of truth to the adventurous yarns? I'll never know. Frank never embroidered his private thoughts. Only his reflective writings reveal him.

O. O. H. Lodge meetings and the Dramatic Society filled Frank's lonely hours. By February, notations of happiness began appearing in his diary entries. As Frank reconnected socially, he expressed increasing enthusiasm and enjoyment of life.

Feb 7. …Made sheriffs sale as advertised. Recd from Mr. Girard $50.00 to his credit on a/c of property he bid on. Employed McCabe to make out deeds at $2.50 each. Attended party at Miss Brookners—A delightful time.

Feb 8. …Delivered deed of property to F. W. Westmeyer and recd pay as per acct. Arrested a man by name of Fred Gregory alias Painter—He broke jail at Wilcox. Have telegraphed to see if they want him. Recd a letter from James dep sheriff of Graham Co to arrest James Stokes which we did and locked him up.[1]

Feb 9. …Settled up the sale with Redman, Piper & Bessig. Wrote up the accts, Posted notices under executions no 877-878 as per order. Got onto a fellow whom I think is Dan Bogan, will investigate in the morning. Attended a rehearsal at Mrs. Hazards. Got files, 2 pads of letter paper and a 6 qr [quarter] book for journal day book of Chas Taylor on county a/c through an order from Chas Martin Clerk of Board of Supervisors.

Feb 10. We arrested a man for Dan Bogan. After examining him found he was the wrong man and let him go, Made returns of order of sale in Mrs Isabell Sharp vs. W. H. Duryea, also order of sale in Jos Redman Et Al vs J. H. Eaton—Collected of Crris [Chris] for Jere Fryer and sent to him $10.00. Sent notice to members of Globe Stock Growers Association to send in their numbers of cattle and horses to the secty—F. M. Hammon.

Feb 11. …Served Replevin papers in case Robt Pringle vs John Doe and took possession of a horse, case has been settled, our costs of 7.00 paid in cash. Deputy Sheriff of Wilcox arrived this morning after McGregor—Will start with him on Monday morning. Commenced transfer of our record of business done from the old to the new books where our accts will be kept in double entry form.

Feb 12. …Worked all day at the transfer of accounts from old to new books. Was up at rink this afternoon and had a drill. Went to church this evening—a good sermon. No answer to dispatch from H K Mead.

Feb 13. …David Johnson Deputy from Wilcox left this morning with Fred McGregor for Wilcox and Tombstone. Took Pistol which belonged to McGregor, but not his horse.

Feb 14. …Finished transfer of accounts found that we have done quite well considering the times since we took the office. Attended rehersal of dramatic society at Mrs Hazards did much better than the last evening.

Feb 15. …Looks much like a storm. Recd dispatch from [Jere] Fryer of Pinal to come for Rafael Alveso and will leave tomorrow for Florence after him.

Jere Fryer replaced Pete Gabriel as Pinal County sheriff following the fall 1886 election. Gabriel's support of Fryer's candidacy helped elect him, but it was Fryer's illustrious wife, Pauline Cushman, who assured his victory. Before the Civil War, Pauline dazzled audiences throughout the South with her gifted acting. The southern beauty, known for her charm and talent, severed allegiance to the Secessionists and became a Union spy. Pauline's espionage was short-lived. Arrested by the Confederacy and sentenced to hang, Pauline's pretty neck escaped the noose when Union forces seized the town and freed Pauline.

Following the war, Pauline traveled with a theatrical troupe and settled on the West Coast. As a California hotel manager and actress, she met and married the younger Jere Fryer. In time, they moved to Casa Grande, Arizona, and invested in a hotel and livery stable.

The personable Fryer took over Pinal County's sheriff duties on January 1, 1887. Hinson Thomas became his chief deputy. According to a possibly apocryphal story, shortly after Fryer's election, a small circus with a well-trained monkey came to Casa Grande. To pay outstanding Tucson debts, the circus sold the primate to an old Mexican woman named Gusano, who was known for her celebrated tamales.[2]

The monkey soon became a fixture at the local saloons and developed an affinity for bartender Charley Starr's liquor. Excessive horseplay, teasing, and drink turned the animal into a hazard. In an irritable moment, the contentious monkey attacked a child and Sheriff Fryer was forced to destroy the pet. Gusano was bitter. Following the U. S. District Court term, Sheriff Fryer engaged Gusano to prepare a banquet. The guests included District Judge Joseph H. Kibby, District Attorney Richard E. Sloan, Granville H. Oury, A. J. Doran, Postmaster John Miller, Hon. Peter R. Brady Sr., Hinson Thomas, Dan Stephens, Charley Starr, and Mike Rice. While the distinguished company enjoyed after-dinner cigars and discussed Gusano's culinary talents, Sheriff Fryer asked the cook about her tamales. Without a word, Gusano left the room and returned, depositing the contents of her apron on the table. In front of the astonished dignitaries lay the head, feet, and hands of her beloved monkey.[3]

During the following year, Fryer arrested Rafael Arviso on an outstanding Gila County warrant. Arviso, wanted for stealing a bay mule in June 1887, required transportation to Globe for trial. On February 16, Frank left for Florence to take possession of the prisoner.[4]

Feb 16. …Left Globe for Florence after Raphel Arveso arrived at Pinal at about 5 PM. Saw Wenthouse and several acquaintances. Paid amount of $2.50 I owed him for meals and two nights lodging when at the King [mine] three or four months ago.[5]

<u>Feb 17.</u> …Left Pinal for Florence at 8 AM arrived at about 3 PM Saw Holborn, [Charley] Starr, Geo. Morse, [Pete] Gabriel at a dance at the hotel in evening.

Frank's early association with legendary Pete Gabriel possibly began in 1881 during the arrest of the Grime brothers and Curtis Hawley. Although Gabriel often pursued the lawless into Gila County, Frank's relationship with him was probably social. An obsessive card player, Gabriel often patronized the tables where Charley Starr tended bar. Although Frank periodically vowed to abstain from drinks and cards, it is reasonable to assume that he experienced random relapses.

Pete Gabriel's legendary career as a lawman began as a deputy sheriff in Idaho, continued in California during the 1870s, and ended in Florence, Arizona, where he was elected sheriff of Pinal County for six nonconsecutive terms. Over the years, Gabriel earned the reputation as a tenacious pursuer of criminals. His reckless abandon in the face of danger, combined with his physical and mental toughness, made him a formidable force to be reckoned with.[6]

During his second term, Gabriel appointed Tucson acquaintance Josephus "Joe" Phy as his chief deputy. With assurances of Gabriel's support in the 1886 election, Joe moved into a room over the sheriff's office. Friendship and respect developed between the two lawmen. Phy's aptitude for the job equaled Gabriel's, but more impressive was Phy's reputation for honesty, courage, and impulsive behavior.[7]

Before the election, Gabriel arrested and dismissed Deputy Phy for pistol-whipping Globe faro dealer Tom Montgomery. To aggravate the situation, the county board of supervisors ordered Gabriel to physically evict Phy from his living quarters. Because of Phy's heavy-handed tactics, Gabriel withdrew his election support from his deputy and backed Jere Fryer for sheriff. From that time on, Joe Phy harbored an intense hatred for Pete Gabriel.

Gabriel's hatred of Phy, on the other hand, may have stemmed from the continuing attention the deputy paid to Gabriel's beautiful estranged wife. Gabriel's May-December marriage had already faltered, but Phy's attentiveness to Pete's spouse incited his jealousy. After the 1886 election, Gabriel retreated to his mine in Dripping Springs, removing himself from a potential confrontation. When he appeared in town for supplies, Phy seized every opportunity to force a showdown, but Gabriel avoided him.[8]

In February of 1888, Frank Hammon ran into Gabriel at a hotel dance. Undoubtedly Gabriel watched his back. Less than two months later, Phy and Gabriel dueled in a "six-gun classic" in Florence's Tunnel Saloon.[9]

As the tale goes, Phy had repeatedly threatened Gabriel but never acted upon his threats. On Thursday, May 31, 1888, Gabriel shopped for supplies and imbibed with friends in Florence. As Gabriel drank inside the Tunnel Saloon, he spotted Phy stalking the bar outside. Pacing back and forth, Phy became increasingly impatient, waiting for Gabriel to exit. Finally, an armed Phy approached the saloon's swinging doors. As the doors flew open, Gabriel drew his gun. Three bullets struck his chest before he could shoot. In spite of his wounds, Gabriel returned fire with shots that ripped into his opponent's vital organs. Phy's good friend, Dr. William Harvey, unsuccessfully tended his wounds. Phy died hours later believing that he had killed Gabriel. Dr. Harvey refused to treat the stricken ex-sheriff, but Gabriel recovered anyway. A coroner's jury ruled self-defense, but Phy's death haunted Gabriel until his demise ten years later.[10]

Feb 18. …Will leave with stage and prisoner today at one oclock PM. Mrs Sharp paid me 9.35 bal sheriffs fees in case Isabell Sharp vs W. H. Duryea also clerks fees $3.50 also for recording $3.50. She gave me the deed to have recorded with letter to McCabe and Cook—Left with stage and prisoner at one oclock P.M. arrived at Riverside at 9 oclock P.M.

Feb 19. …Chained prisoner up to post but was awake with him most of the night. Left with stage early and arrived at Globe at about 5 oclock PM. George had gone to the river to subpoena some witnesses this afternoon.

Feb 20. …straightened up the books in the office. George returned having served all the subpoenas. Case is set for tomorrow at 10 oclock AM. Attended rehersal at Mrs Hazards All did quite well.

Feb 21. …Straightened up the old Sheriffs office for use as Justice of the Peace office—Case of Territory VS Rafael Arviso was postponed until Feb 28 '88. Special meeting of lodge tonight, big attendance and lots of fun.

Feb 22. …Nothing doing today—are lying by for the party this evening. Geo and I both attended. Had quite an attendence over 50 tickets sold and had a delightful time.

Feb 23. …Geo started for Dudleyville with a subpoena for Dan Carrol and Geo Blair. He rode Kit, I summoned a jury in the case of Cap Adams guarding of Jun H vs. Robt Shell. Case decided in favor of Adams. My fees were $17.00 which were paid by Adams. Paid Mrs. Ramsdell on a/c $20.00.

Feb 24. …Started for Pinto Creek to look for a Mexican wanted at Phoenix. John Kountz not at home. Arrived at Marion and stayed on with [unreadable] over night. No trail of the man for whom I am looking—No work being done in the Placer Mines at present.

Feb 25. …Went through the diggings below—all deserted, went back to Globe via Lost Gulch but heard nothing. Arrived at Globe about 4:30 PM. Geo just returned from the San Pedro. Two Mexicans from one Antonio Soto, a deputy Sheriff from Reddington from Pima Co AT arrived following a murderer, but think he went to the King or Pinal.

Feb 26. ...Soto and man left for the King, lent him $10.00. until he gets home—Attended Sunday school for the first time in Arizona.

Feb 27. ...One of my prisoners escaped last night with the help of friends, they unlocked the cage and helped him off.

Feb 28. ...Very quiet—Case of Ter vs Rafael Arviso called but was postponed again—to allow us time to go to Dripping Springs after Geo Blair. Arrested Adolph Arano for drunkeness and disturbing the peace. At the earnest request of Judge Hackney, we released him. Put a watch on the jail.

Judge Aaron Harrison Hackney obviously exercised considerable authority for Frank to release his drunken prisoner. The judge's flowery soliloquies were read weekly in the *Silver Belt,* and since his arrival in 1878, he wielded much influence. Frank obviously valued his opinion. One editor described the legendary Hackney's newspaper: "Its columns scintillated with the bright and epigrammatic writing of the Judge."[11]

Judge Hackney had arrived in Globe at age sixty-four, leading a burro that carried his hand-operated printing press. He began publishing Globe's weekly news from his Broad Street office, offering advertising space for legitimate mining ventures only. This prevented shysters from taking advantage of gullible citizens. Designated the "conscience of Globe," Hackney was instrumental in establishing the Fourth of July celebrations, the first church, and the telegraph company.[12]

Even in the face of repeated disappointments, Hackney remained optimistic that Globe's railroad would materialize. The elusive rails became his favorite editorial topic. His dream came true in 1898, a year before his death.[13]

Feb 29. ...Geo. started over to Dripping Springs to subpoena Geo Blair in case Ter vs Ralph Arveso. Sent E C Meacham Arms Co. for pistol and to Geo Barnard & Sons for pistol case, Police nippers and club or billy. Case Ter v. Rafael Arveso was postponed until next Sat.

On February 28, 1888, the grand jury indicted Rafael Arviso for stealing a bay mule from D. W. O'Carroll in Pinal County.[14]

Mar 1. ...Geo returned without getting service on Geo Blair [defense witness for Arviso]. He not having returned home. Tom Burns came in from Cherry Creek. Attended a rehersal at the rink of the Charade Company.

Mar 2. ...Sent $50.00 home—borrowed it from the county sack. Burns still in town. Attended regular meeting of O. O. H. four initiations and lots of fun.

Frank must have had a premonition that he would clash with Tom Burns. His instincts were correct. Tom Burns was looking for trouble.

<u>Mar 3.</u> ...Case Ter vs Rafael Arvisu came up and he was bound over under 500.00 bonds to appear before the Dis Court. Meeting of Stock Growers Ass, adjourned until first Sat. in Apl—Recd injunction papers at 5 oclock PM to serve on Geo E. Shute—Sheriff—to restrain him from sale under executions in case Ladenburg Thalman Co. vs Old Dominion Copper M [Mine] Co—Served them as constable at 5:40 PM.

<u>Mar 4</u>. ...Considerable writing today. Attended Sunday School and church in the evening. Recd order on Old Dominion Co for Criss for Jere Fryer amt 20.00 making 30.00 recd.

<u>Mar 5</u>. Regular monthly meeting of Board of Supervisors, attended it. Put in bill for two months jailers fees—and 6 days guard for jail at $3.25. Total amt $169.50 which was allowed—Sent assessment notices to members of the Globe Stock Growers Ass. Applied to Board for a safe—considered—Was appointed Road overseer for Globe Road District, bonds $1,000.00. Will guard the jail at night myself after this.

Frank guarded the jail in response to either a threat against a prisoner or in anticipation of an escape.

<u>Mar 6</u>. ...Mr. English, attorney for Ladenberg Thalman Co. arrived to look after sale of Old Dominion property. Gave him my bill.

<u>Mar 7</u>. ...Work on the court house going along slow. Bad weather tonight. Attended rehersal at the rink it went off quite well.

<u>Mar 8</u>. ...Gave bonds as Road Overseer of Globe dis, amt $1,000. Bob Anderson for $500.00, Geo. E. Shute $500 and recd $100 blanks @ $4.00 each $400. Was sworn in as Deputy Assessor. Cleaned out the jail and hung out the blankets out to air. Rafael says he is sick. Think he is giving us game. Collected 6 poll taxes and three road taxes. Rented my house on the street to Tom Kernew [Curnow] for $7.00 pr month.

<u>Mar 9</u>. ...Recd a warrant of arrest against Chas. Miller and arrested him. Also a subpoena for Mr. and Mrs. J. H. Eaton of Pioneer which I have served on them at 11:30 PM. Rented my house on hill to Wm Murphy for $7.50 per month.

By mid-March, Frank had gratefully immersed himself in work by accepting two more positions, Gila County deputy assessor and road overseer. That spring, he was also elected secretary of the Gila County Stock Growers' Association. Frank's voracious approach to work and community projects assuaged his numbing loneliness.

Chapter Sixteen

UNDISGUISED DERISION

Entered only as "McNeal," Frank's inmate had a history. The slippery fugitive occupying the "cage," whom Frank casually mentions in his journal, would become legendary.

Imaginative western writers have fashioned these delinquents into celebrities. Through the years, these bad guys have intrigued us, entertained us, and generated cheers or boos. Unconcerned with truth or fact, the audience clamored for more, and we got more. Nothing has changed. Scoundrels still fascinate us; writers romanticize them, facts remain obscure, but we still devour them as truths.

In a bar room brawl, a man's survival often meant disabling his foe. The losers nursed gunshot wounds, gouged eyes, broken limbs, or bitten ears. Such an altercation placed W. R. McDonald in Globe's crowded, inadequate jail cell with Rafael Arviso. A month later, ear-biter W. R. McDonald's sworn testimony describing a notable jailhouse incident won his release.

> Sat. Mar 10. [1888] …Returned from the Pioneer at noon—Eaton and wife arrived at 2:00 PM. Rev Adacus was in Pioneer last night and arrived in Globe today. Arrested Tom Mulvenon [Mulheran] and another man for fighting. The man Arkansaw, bit Toms ear off. Tom out on bail. Will have a hearing Monday. Collected $20.00 from Chriss for Fryer. Recd from Wilmans $9 in full for rent.

According to the March 7 *Silver Belt*: "The hearing of W. R. McDonald, charged with mayhem in biting off a portion of Tommy Mulheren's right ear resulted in the accused being held to await the action of the grand jury. The punishment…is incarceration in the Territorial prison for a term not exceeding fourteen years."[1]

> Sun. Mar 11. …Recd from Old Dominion check for 5.40 amt of their bill and sent 20.00 collected from Cris to Jere Fryer. Paid Chas Taylor on a/c $7.50.

> Mon. Mar 12. …Subpoenied witnesses for McDonalds hearing Geo summoned jury for Millers trial. Tom Mulheran appeared and plead guilty. Fined 1.00 and costs. Miller tried and acquited. McDonald was bound over under $500.00 bond to appear before the Grand Jury. Attended rehersal this evening at church. All did quite well.

"Justice Court Criminal Complaint against W. R. Mc Donald," signed by Justice of the Peace Job Atkins, states that the accused committed the "Crime of mayhem upon the person of said Thomas Mulheran by biting off a portion of ear of said Thomas Mulheran, thereby disfiguring the said complainant."[2]

> Tues. Mar 13. …Wrote out returns on Executions Ladenberg Thalman Co. vs Old Dominion Copper Co. Posted up books. Our entertainment came off this evening and was thourough success. Had a very good time, Recd letter from Henry Ryder.

> Wed. Mar 14. …Wrote to Henry Ryder. Wrote to Mr. Lount. Sent a local notice to the Phoenix Arizonan for sale or rent of swimming baths. Returned the executions upon which I made returns yesterday to Geo. G. Berry Tombstone by reg. mail. Paid Fatty Restaurant Chinaman in full with road and poll tax receipts.

> Thurs. Mar 15. …Got Swaseys safe and moved it to the Sheriffs office— rent $2.00 per mo… Sent bill to Mulvernon against Yav Co, Recd pistol, nippers, pistol case, club omitted. Sent case back to have changed and reordered the club.

> Fri. Mar 16. …Helped decorate hall for our ball this eve. Expect a large
> crowd, Henry Middleton came in day before yesterday and returned
> Early this morning to the river. I would like to go over to the ranch
> and will try to do so Sunday morning.

> Sat. Mar 17. …Attended the party last night and had a very nice time.
> An immense crowd filled the large house. Some boys from the river
> came up today and told George [Shute] that [Henry] Blevins and
> [Tom] Burns had put up a job to come up and kill him and Mr Frakes.
> We will watch out for them. Sold a few articles at sale today but bids
> were too low and I stopped the sale.

> Sun. Mar 18. …Sold Dr. Trippel some of the articles belonging to Frank
> Burk amting to about 20.00. Started for the ranch but met Rogginstroh
> who informed me of a row on the river and I returned thinking some-
> one would come up for a warrant and I would be needed.[3]

On Thursday, March 15, Henry Blevins and Tom Burns ignited events that
dictated the course of Frank's life for the next eight months. It is unknown what
triggered the plot to kill Shute and Frakes, or what occurred at the Salt River on
that Thursday. Incomplete court records and Frank's abbreviated diary entries
are the only evidence a conspiracy existed. Frank's matter-of-fact reference to
the plot revealed little emotion.

The scheme's success depended upon discretion, but the conniving conspira-
tors had loose tongues. News traveled like wildfire, and within a day word of the
complicity spread to Globe. Sheriff Shute and Undersheriff Hammon prepared
for trouble. At the river the following night, Burns took an errant shot at Hugh
Blevins—unrelated to Henry Blevins. Perhaps Hugh Blevins confronted Burns
about the nefarious plot. The doomed conspiracy against Sheriff Shute and Mr.
Frakes incited a furor.[4]

> Mon. Mar 19. very stormy Heavy wind last night—wind and heavy rain
> this morning…Sold Old Dominion Co a lot of Burks tools—a mes-
> senger came up from the river, for an officer.

> Tues. Mar 20. … George left for the river. Cleaned up the guns and
> tried some of them. A beautiful day. Had Zimmerman fix my house on
> the hill. Arrested a Mexican on suspicion of stealing from and robbing
> a camp out at Lost Gulch. Served a search warrant on Old Polorias
> house found none of the stolen articles.

It appears that Frank, anticipating an assault, had prepared the office arsenal. Most lawmen diligently maintained their cache of armaments. Handguns,
shotguns, and rifles provided ample firepower for any circumstances, but poor
planning could result in a regrettable situation. An outlaw's six-shooter, with its
limited range, was ineffective against the powerful 30-30 Winchester rifles carried by lawmen. Today's media presents a distorted image of frontier gunfights.
Historian Richard Prassel cautions that "…the classic duel decided by the speed

of the draw leaped from the imaginations of later writers. Lawmen and outlaws alike knew the dangers and limitations of the revolvers they sometimes carried but rarely displayed. Shooting would be avoided whenever possible, and when demanded it would often be done from cover or concealment."[5]

> Wed. Mar 21. ...Called on Old John McComb who was brought in from the Wheat Fields sick and is in the hospital. He was dying and expired about 15 minutes after. I acted as one of the pallbearers. He was a good man. No news from George yet. Went out and looked at the road to the summit.

> Thurs. Mar 22. ... Wm. Murphy is moving into my house on the hill today. Put to work on the road today to work out their tax, Frank Jordan, Fransisco Maise, Juan D. Maise, Dave Freeman.

> Fri. Mar 23. ... Geo and posse arrived with Burns. Recd citation from Shaw of Tucson to serve John Nicholson which we did. Recd summons, served it on A. Arascco, Chas Taylor Pltff [plaintiff]. Warrant issued for Blevins, went with Geo and posse to arrest him.

In District Court records in the case of Territory vs Thos. Burns, J. P. Atkins states: "Personally appeared before me, this 23rd day of March 1888, Joe Bull of Salt River...says: that one Thos Byrnes [Burns] of Cherry Creek on the 15th day of March, 1888 at Catalpi, in the County of Gila did unlawfully and Feloniously conspire with one Henry Blevins to kill and murder one J. W. Frakes and one George Shute."[6]

On March 23, the posse arrested Burns. The following day they seized Henry Blevins. Once the pair were in custody, the grand jury handed down indictments followed by a second indictment of aggregated assault against Burns for his potshot at Hugh Blevins. According to the indictment, "The said Thomas Burns on or about the 16th day of March, A. D. 1888...did...commit an assault upon Hugh Blevins with a certain Pistol...held in his right hand... did...discharge at...Hugh Blevins with...a premeditated design...calculated to inflict great bodily injury."[7]

Reasons for the conspiracy can only be conjectured. While serving as a deputy the previous fall, Shute had arrested Burns for an assault against Carl Smith. Was the conspiracy revenge, or more complicated? Regardless, at this point Hugh Blevins's son, Cyrus, entered the conflict.[8]

Thirty-one-year-old Cy Blevins, the oldest son of H. T. V. and Melissa Blevins of Tennessee, settled in Gila County in 1885. His parents and six siblings migrated as part of a large wagon train of extended family to homestead government land above the Salt River. Tempers often short-circuited when ownership of water rights were disputed. In the spring of 1888, the two unrelated Blevins families quarreled. Their neighbor, George Shute, may have participated in the dispute. For whatever reasons, Burns and Blevins became partners in crime. Years later, unsavory Henry Blevins would be known as "King of the outlaws."[9]

Sat. Mar 24. ...Returned this morning from Centenial left party at trail of Blevins. Must go on send deputy to the river with subpoenas today in case of Ter vs Burns Issued license to a Mexican for a show tonight. Left for Salt River with subpoenas, at 6 Oclock.

Sun. Mar 25. ...Arrived at [Cy] Blevins house at about 12 o'clock at night and stayed over night. Went on to Henrys [Middleton], and got breakfast. Went and summoned as witness Wm Beard. Then down to Robinsons and summoned John Parron. Then over to Hazards and secured Mr. Ingalls. Cost of trip $1.50— left for Globe at 3:30 PM arrived at 8 PM. Mr. Marshall and two other men went out on the San Carlos Road to work.

Frank stayed with Hugh and Cy Blevins's family. Was he aware of the proposed retaliation against the collaborators?

Mon. Mar 26. ...Burns hearing resulted in his being bound over in each case to appear before Grand Jury. Amt of bonds 2,000. [Henry] Blevins was also bound over amt of bonds 1,000. I am much relieved and hope they may get it at court.

The indictment handed down at the April term of the Gila County Second District Court alleged that "Thomas Burns and Henry Blevins did enter into a conspiracy...to kill and murder the said George E. Shute and John W. Frakes."[10]

Frank expressed relief following the grand jury indictment. Burns and Blevins joined McDonald and Arviso in the crowded, makeshift cell. If the new courthouse and jail had been completed, Frank might have been able to rest comfortably. Unfortunately, as the *Silver Belt* reported, "The stone work of the court house for the present is about completed, and it will soon be roofed and finished for occupancy, but not in time for the spring term of court in April."[11]

Tues. Mar 27. ...Mr. Baker and several Salt River people arrived today. Said Jno Nelson and Mrs. Blevins were on their way down to the river probably after bondsman.

Wed. Mar 28. ...Case of Taylor vs Arano was postponed until next Monday. Returned subpoena from Pinals on Horn and Graham today. Rock work on the Court House was finished today.

Could Frank be referring to Tom Horn and Tom Graham? Were they witnesses to the conspiracy, or to the botched shooting of Hugh Blevins? No court documents exist that clarify Frank's statement or reveal the contents of the subpoena.

Thurs. Mar 29. ...Paid money to Treas and turned money receipts to Clerk of Board of Supervisors. Posted notices at Mine and office of Old Dominion Company. Wm. Malory—Steve and Johnson went to work on the road to Fame. Jack and Tom Cline came up today to go on Blevins bond but for some reason did not do so.

Blevins represented a poor risk and the Cline brothers knew it.

Fri. Mar 30. …Went down to San Carlos River to see the work being done on the road there with which I was well satisfied.

Sat. Mar 31. … Made out some bill for work against county for quarter ending today. This is Easter Sunday. The season recognizes it for the country is covered with flowers. Left book of road tax blanks with Mr. White at Old Dominion office and list of names to collect [road taxes] from.

Sun. Apr 1. …What I wrote yesterday applies today. Went to Sunday school and church this evening. Commenced boarding with Fatty the Chinaman this morning. Mrs Ramsdell let us all go.

Mon. Apr 2. … Collected poll and road tax and paid them the bal. Attended meeting of Board, presented our bill which was allowed after deducting about 17.00.

Tues. Apr 3. …Recd warrant from county for 546.10—knocked off 17.80 [total] 563.90. Cashed the same. Paid George $225.30. Drew myself $200.00. Paid my taxes for 1887—Thankful am I—$84.62. Pd Van Wagenen for suit of clothes $42.00. Sent home $50.00. Paid board for Mch 30.00.

Wed. Apr 4. …Paid Mrs Welsh 10.00 interest on my note—from June 20 87 to July 20 87. Order was made this morning to draw the Grand Jury.

Thurs. Apr 5. Grand Jury drawn this morning and order issued. Started out after a man we supposed the mexican who escaped from Tusan recently, arrived at Pinal Ranch. Baker accompanied me.

Fri. Apr 6. …Left Pinal Ranch where we stayed last night, satisfied mexican has not passed this way, met him about three miles out and arrested him and took him to Globe where he was turned loose he not answering the description fully.

Sat. Apr 7. …Left for Salt River with subpoenas and summons for Grand Jurors, arrived Early and served most of the subpoenas stayed over night with the…. [illegible]

At 2 o'clock that afternoon, Frank, as secretary, convened the monthly meeting of the Globe Live Stock Association at the *Silver Belt* office.[12]

Sun. Apr 8. storming Left for Jake Lauffers on the mountains Passed Conners Glenn Reynolds and McFadden none of them at home—arrived at Redmans before sundown—found Lacy, George Hancock and another man there.

Mon. Apr 9. …Went with Mr Lacy over to Jake Lauffers. I shot off gun and hollowed and after a while he came down off a point. I summoned him for grand jury and assessed him of below: Possession right to ranch in Sierra Anches $2.00, 35 head cattle 420.00, 6 head horses $180.00, 1 burro $10.00. Returned to Redmans Ranch.

Was Jake Lauffer hiding on the "point" to avoid the county assessor, the law, or danger? The month before, Lauffer had filed charges against James Stott for stealing his iron-gray horse. Stott and his Hashknife sidekick Tom Tucker claimed that a man named "Workman" sold them the horse but Lauffer presented a receipt proving ownership.[13]

Although Justice of the Peace Atkins determined that Lauffer was the horse's rightful owner, he nonetheless dismissed the case against Stott, citing "lack of evidence to convict." Lauffer suffered permanent disability when he was ambushed five months later. In August 1888, his irate friends retaliated.[14]

Tues. Apr 10. …Mr Lacy showed me the direction to Pendletons Ranch where I arrived at 10:00 oclock. Pendleton not at home. Continued on down Cherry Creek, saw Dr. Stallo at his ranch. Arrived at Coon Crk about 6 oclock in evening.

Wed. Apr 11. …Went to Globe. Near Medlers met Bob Pringle and his men at Cherry Creek. Arrived at Globe early. All OK. Recd from Wm Murphy $7.50 for rent of house to Apl 10th '88.

Thurs. Apr 12. …Returns on order for grand jury Recd from Col White chk from Criss to Jere Fryer of 10.00. Wrote out returns on subpoenas served for term of court opening Apl 16. Sent Jere Fryer PO Order for 27.00—less order fee Amt of bill pd by county and bal of 6.00 from Criss. Paid my bill at Mrs Gills of $5.50. Recd for T. Burk from Mex Ore Co. chk for $34.26. Mr. White collected from Employees Road Tax $148.00.

Fri. Apr 13. Windy. An attempt was made last night to lynch the prisoners but was foiled. No arrests yet, Dep Belnap left yesterday for Salt River with two subpoenas. Will go in to watch jail tonight ourselves. Recd warrants for Reynolds Ellison and Cy Blevins for attempt to break jail.[15]

Where was Frank at two A.M. on windy Friday the thirteenth? Had muted voices, muffled steps, and shouts from the makeshift jail awakened him in the sheriff's office? Frank's entry that day suggests someone else guarded the prisoners. Who watched the jail?[16]

There are no indications Frank anticipated the lynch mob. If he had heard rumors circulating, he chose to ignore them. The next night, Frank and Sheriff Shute guarded the jail, anticipating another break-in attempt. Certainly, both men would have appreciated historian Larry Ball's observation: "Since the lawmen were oath-bound to protect their prisoners and uphold due process, some inner struggle must have taken place as they faced the prospect of confronting friends, relatives, and other voters among the vigilantes."[17]

Lawmen seldom recorded attempts by vigilantes to break into their jails. Perhaps they wished to forget the embarrassment. Frank never indicated who "foiled" the lynching, but later testimony revealed that the prisoners' pleas for help scared off the mob. Had Frank slept in the office and recognized the hangmen, in spite of their masks? The jailbirds had no problem identifying their self-appointed executioners when they filed complaints against Glenn Reynolds, Perle Ellison, and Cy Blevins.[18]

No stranger to law enforcement, Glenn Reynolds had served as sheriff of Throckmorton County, Texas, as a young man. Only two years older than Frank, he defended his town from Comanches while his neighbors fought for the Confederacy. In his youth, Reynolds drove cattle to the Kansas railheads. He entered into an unsuccessful sheep enterprise that soured with removal of the wool tariff. Shortly after, his prominent Texas family financed his cattle herd. In 1885, he and Colonel Ellison transported their herds to Arizona. Reynolds and his wife, Gustie, settled in the Sierra Ancha Mountains near Pleasant Valley to raise their children.[19]

Within a few years, the lawless element encroached into the valley, undermining Reynolds's attempt to protect his family and property. How far did he go to restore peace to Pleasant Valley? Reynolds reportedly took an active role in apprehending mischievous malcontents. Osmer Flake claimed Reynolds accompanied the posse to Perkin's store the day of John Graham and Charley Blevins's killing. One of the Tewksbury brothers alleged Reynolds blasted Al Rose with a shotgun; some said Reynolds hanged him.[20]

The Reynolds family denied Glenn's involvement in any vigilante pastimes. In 1936, his sister wrote, "Our people kept on the outside [of the feud] as much as possible and tried to steer clear of trouble, but even so, one was almost forced to side with one faction or the other. The Government took no hand in trying to settle this trouble, as I remember; it just let them alone until they killed each other out 'to the last man'." Reynolds's pro-active stand brought him respect, admiration, and political backing from influential friends.[21]

Also arrested was Jesse Ellison's spoiled son Perle, who had a penchant for violence and a disdain for responsibility. In 1965, Perle's son "Slim" wrote of his father's temper and sadistic sense of humor:

> Dad [Perle] grabbed me and turned me over his knee and pulled my gown up and spanked my naked little butt in a playful mood, but ruff. It hurt and I was skeered. I whimpered and he slapped me and said, 'What's the matter, you little cowardly Californy s.o.b.? Can't I play with you without you bawlin?' He pick up a stick of pitch pine kindlin about 1" x 18" and went to work on my rump and small of my back. I screamed and Maw put the baby down, grabbed up Dad's 44-40 rifle,

Lula and Perle Ellison with their sons. Glenn "Slim" Ellison on left. AHS/Tucson #53782.

levered a load into the barrel, and said, 'Stop abusing that boy now or so help me, God, I'll blow your head off!' Dad stopped and said that he only wanted to play with me and that I cried and he got mad because I was so cowardly. Ma said, 'You're the coward! You take it out on us, the dogs, and gentle horses.'

Slim Ellison added that his father "left Maw, Baby, and me alone a lot—and it was five or six mile to a neighbor. Dad couldn't stay put, didn't like responsibility."[22]

Frank also arrested his rabble-rousing friend Cy Blevins. Faced with an obvious dilemma, Frank chose his oath of office over friendship. He could easily have ignored the prisoners' pleas and surrendered them to the mob. Instead, he sent a clear message: no tolerance for threats against lawmen. All the evidence indicates that Frank honored his oath by remaining neutral to all parties.

Sat. Apr 14. windy, cldy [cloudy] Ordered from Wm. Barr Dry Goods Co, St Louis, Mo—2 woolen shirts, 1 doz linen collars, 2 neck ties, 1 silk scarf, 4 pr. socks, 6 white shirts—sent $15.00. Arrested Reynolds and Ellison, watched jail last night. Attended hearing, Reynolds and Ellison both bound over under $500.00 bonds....

Sun. Apr 15. ...Judge Berry and Anderson and Mr. Edwards arrived. Judge Porter will come in tomorrow morning. We have the Grand Jury all summoned and subpoenas served and are now ready for court.

Mon. Apr 16. ...Court commenced and commenced business on part of Grand Jury. Nothing much doing yet in court. Old Dominion suit was argued on a demand for disolution of injunction. Decision will be rendered tomorrow.

Tues. Apr 17. ...Decission in Old Dominion suit against disolution of injunction, G Jury brought in a bill or indictment against Rafael Alvezu and Tom Burns. Grand Jury found no bill against McDonald action he was released a happy man.

McDonald witnessed the entire affair while he was sharing the jail with Burns and Blevins. He never disclosed the lynchmen's names to the grand jury, which set him free. A stranger to the area, McDonald may not have known the vigilantes' identities. On the other hand, perhaps his silence was a condition for dismissing the charges. In his diary, Frank notes McDonald's release but never refers to the dropping of charges against Reynolds, Ellison, and Cy Blevins.

TERRITORY VS THOMAS BURNS

[Change of Venue affidavit given by W. R. Mc Donald]

...That about 2 o'clock on the morning of the 13th day of April 1888 an armed body of men...overpowered the jailer and attempted to break open the jail and threatened to kill the defendant and one Henry Blevins. That it is the belief of affiant that the said armed body of men were a riot who came to said jail for the purpose of breaking open the same and taking the defendant Burns and the said Blevins therefrom, and hanging them. That only for the alarm given by the parties confined in said jail the said Burns and Blevins would have been kill [*sic*] by said armed body of men. [Signed] W. R. McDonald

Subscribed and sworn to before me this 18th day of April A. D. 1888 B. G. Fox, Clerk by Charles Martin, Deputy.[23]

Before the riot, the April 7 issue of the *Silver Belt* had announced the grand jurors for the April court term. Selected were: Chas. H. Kenyon, Chas. A. Fisk, Niles S. Berry, Jacob B. Lauffer, Alfred Hanstein, J. H. Pascoe, Robert Anderson, Jeremiah Hyndmen, Chas. Banker, Marion L. Horrel, J. J. Marshall, S. E. Epley, Alex Graydon, John W. Frakes, and Alec. Pendleton. Although announced the week before, they were not seated until three days after the attempted lynching. It is understandable why the jurors never indicted Reynolds and company: Burns and Blevins had conspired against grand juror John Frakes, and Lauffer was a Tewksbury partisan. The "good ole boy" network remained intact. As Larry Ball points out: "Efforts to take court action against suspected vigilantes were usually futile. Not only was the sheriff reluctant to investigate his fellow citizens, but these lawless bands were often oath-bound and maintained a conspiracy of silence…. When cases against alleged vigilantes reached the grand jury, the results were generally unsatisfactory."[24]

Most second-hand information could not be verified—no one would talk. For years, hearsay and innuendoes surfaced privately, but fear prevented public discourse. Like other critical court documents, transcripts disappeared or never existed. All we have today is a warrant and a scribbled notation of dismissal in the record book. On the morning of April 13, Glenn Reynolds knew the identities of the grand jurors; he must have known his friends would never indict him. Four months later, unknown assailants crippled grand juror Jake Lauffer for life.

Wed. Apr 18. …Rafael Alvizu was tried this morning and convicted. Burns tried for a change of venue but failed. George sick again. Ordered to summon panel of 18 special jurors to appear Apl 19th 1888. Served Papers in claim and delivery suit on Cap Adams. Summoned the 18 jurors as ordered.

Frank's workload increased with Sheriff Shute's illness. Although convicted, and with their change of venue pleas denied, Burns and Blevins found questionable witnesses who were willing to present new evidence. Mose Wertman and W. T. Gann testified that "there exists a wide-spread excitement and bitter feeling of prejudice and animosity against the defendants."[25]

Thurs. Apr 19. …Burns tried today found guilty of the assault. Will be sentenced on next Saturday.

That same day, Henry Blevins, pleading for a change of venue, signed the following deposition in Gila County District Court:

That threats…of breaking open the County jail thereof and of lynching affiant have frequently been made by the friends of the said George E. Shute. That at about 2 o'clock on the morning of the 13th day of April 1888…an armed body of men made an attack on said jail, over-powered the jailer and attempted to break open the same and take this affiant and the said Thomas Burns therefrom for the purpose of hanging them. That said persons were armed with pistols and guns and exhibited a rope which they declared they had procured for the purpose of hanging…. That said body of armed men were masked and disguised and declared that they had come for the purpose…to kill this affiant and said Thomas Burns and that they would have done so had it not been for the alarm given and the call for assistance made by affiant and those confined in the jail which frightened and caused said unlawful body of masked and armed men to disolve [sic] before they had time to break open the cells…the parties who attempted to break open said jail…are well known residents of Gila County and are busily engaged in circulating false reports concerning this defendant for the purpose of securing his conviction and that said reports are calculated to [sic] to further predjudice the people of said Gila County….

[Signed] Henry Blevins
Subscribed and sworn before me this 19th day of April 1888
[Signed] B G Fox, Clerk[26]

Fri. Apr 20. …Grand Jury brought in indictments for the supervisors and we placed them under arrest. Grand Jury discharged. Burns and Blevins were granted a change of venue to Maricopa County, and will be taken there for trial on May 21st '88.[27]

This raises another possibility. The vigilantes may have attempted to circumvent the law in anticipation of the prisoners' removal from Gila County's jurisdiction.

Sat. Apr 21. …Rafael Arviso was sentenced this morning to three years in Yuma. Eaton tried on one indictment today, but was acquited. Howard Mining Co. against Duryea—thrown out of court without predjudice. Paid Mrs. Welch $20.00 interest on note from July 20 to Sept 20th '88.

Sun. Apr 22. … A beautiful day Court will close tomorrow. Attended church and Sunday school.

Mon. Apr 23. … Sent Mother $9.75 Sent Frank Burk returns from El Paso also money recd from tools sold – 10% retained….Court closed tonight Mr Ramsdell quite sick. I sat up with him last night.

Tues. Apr 24. ...Nice rain last night. Tom Kirnew [Curnow] paid me on rent of house $5.00. Supervisors filed bonds today. Getting ready to start with prisoners for Yuma and Phoenix. How glad I will be to get rid of them.

Wed. Apr 25. Clear pleasant Geo left with prisoners last night. Sam Bullock went as guard and Ed Cook [probate judge] to drive. Am having jail cleaned out tonight.

Thurs. Apr 26. Cloudy Rainy Board met today and advanced us $200.00 to take prisoners away with. Authorized me to advertise for bids to put up bridge below town. Sent to San F [Francisco] for pair of shoes 3.50. Henry came up today.

Twelve days after the attempted lynching, Sheriff Shute, Deputy Sam Bullock, and Probate Judge E. H. Cook departed for Phoenix with the prisoners. The convicted trio included Raphael Arviso, sentenced to three years in Yuma Territorial Prison for horse stealing, as well as Blevins and Burns scheduled for a second trial in Maricopa County. They left behind a community filled with mixed emotions. Removal of these tough characters relieved many Globe residents, but a feeling of unfinished business persisted for some.

At Riverside, Arviso felt the call of nature. While the sheriff fed the horses, Arviso complained of discomfort and convinced the deputy to remove his restraints. Unshackled, he retired to the brush near the station and vanished. A man near the river shouted as he observed the prisoner crossing the restless waters. The lawmen ignored the holler, thinking the man was scolding his unruly mule.[28]

Fri. Apr 27. Sam Bullock returned today. He got no trail on prisoner who escaped.[29]

Arviso was soon recaptured. His short-lived freedom resulted in extended jail time. A Maricopa County jury found Burns and Blevins "not guilty of conspiracy." Henry Blevins, released from the Phoenix jail, reappeared in Gila County. Consumed by a grudge, Cy Blevins returned to Gila County court on October 24, 1888 for attempting to murder Henry Blevins. Six years later, Henry Blevins was incarcerated in Yuma Territorial Prison for stealing his attorney's cattle. As an octogenarian, Henry recalled, " I did cut the corners, but the very crime I was accused of and sent up for happened to be the act which I did not do."[30]

No further record of Tom Burns exists in Gila County. On June 28, 1888 the *Silver Belt* ran an article that verified Tom Burns's confinement in the Maricopa County jail. Quoting the *Arizonan*, the Globe newspaper noted that "Burns, a prisoner... found that the Indian had spliced a couple of small pieces of rope together, and tying one end about his neck and the other to a bar of the cage, was suspended by the neck, and would have soon died but for the timely interference of Burns."

Frank's firsthand corroboration of the committee's covert activities and the subsequent arrests of Reynolds, Perle Ellison, and Cy Blevins verify events and identities protected for over a century. Sixty-six years after Glenn Reynolds's death, his family successfully censored an unflattering book by Ivan Lee Kuykendall entitled, *Ghost Riders of the Mogollon*. A Texas judgment, which stands to this day, found that Kuykendall had libeled a "brave, honorable, and Christian gentleman."[31]

By June 5, Frank stopped writing in his diary. The blank pages speak volumes.

Chapter Seventeen

SWIFT RETRIBUTION

*M*issing Silver Belt *issues stymied me. Micro-
filmed news accounts of the attempted lynching were nonexistent.
My frustration increased. Conspicuous by their absence were transcripts from notable criminal actions. To make matters worse, Frank
abruptly stopped writing. I was baffled. My disappointment grew
along with my curiosity. Was this a cover-up, clerical carelessness, or
coincidence?*[1]

*From the beginning of June until after the November
election, Frank entered only a few inconsequential notations in his
diary. Before the attempted lynching, Frank's entries had been routine. Since 1886, empty pages occurred only when Frank was despondent. Was he depressed? I doubted it. I dug deeper, gleaning bits and
pieces of information confirming Frank's absorption with work. All
my instincts told me that his silence indicated more than overwork.
Frank's revealing September entry reinforced my intuition. The blank
pages resonated! Frank knew too much!*

During the summer of 1888, secrecy and silence engulfed Pleasant Valley as the regulators eliminated rustlers, horse thieves, and interlopers unable to state their business. With swift and terrible retribution, the committee went about purging perceived predators. Strangers disappeared and horse thieves dangled from tree limbs, while families huddled together in community tents safe from unknown assailants. Years later, Judge George W. Shute referred to the committee but omitted names: "Its operation consisted principally of aiding law enforcement officers…direct actionists. Fast, grim and deadly, they soon became feared in Pleasant Valley as no other body was feared."[2]

> Sun. Apr 29. …Recd a good letter from Father. Went to Sunday school and church.

> Mon. Apr 30. …Paid county money into treasury. Mr. Cook recd a letter from Ed. They will be back tomorrow.

> Tues. May 1. …Made out the county bill. Locked up Lee Middleton, Alex Greydon and Walt Shute for disturbing Mrs. Ogden's school. George returned from Phoenix this afternoon.

> Wed. May 2. …Put up notice of col [collection] of poll tax at ODCC [Old Dominion Copper Co.] works. Left 99 blank receipts with Col White. Wrote up books on trip to Phoenix.

> Fri. May 4. …Assessed about all day and George also who is quite unwell.

Aware of the uneasy atmosphere to the north, Frank and an ailing George Shute continued assessing property and collecting taxes. They spent long days on horseback visiting frontiersmen reluctant to divulge their homestead upgrades, fearing increased taxes. Along the way, the assessors inspected mines, ranches, and businesses. Some property owners were evasive, and others were openly hostile. Settlers viewed the twosome as adversaries indifferent to their hardship. Their inability to inspect scattered herds forced the assessors to rely solely upon the rancher's word. Knowing it was impossible for Frank and George to count all the range stock, cattlemen often underestimated their herds.

Once the tax list was compiled, the newspapers published the tax rolls and delinquencies. Assessments could be appealed to the Board of Equalization. As *ex-officio* tax collectors, George and Frank handled all the county's tax monies, retaining a percentage for their fees. Irregular accounting practices would invite public criticism, so Frank meticulously tallied the tax rolls.[3]

> Sat. May 5. Storming Hard. Arranged assessments all day. Attended a meeting of Executive committy of G. S. G. Association. Think we will disband. Attended O. O. H. last evening—getting ready for the ball on the 11th. Sat up with Mr. Ramsdel last night. He was not as well as before.

The cattlemen organized as an association to provide posses, press territorial lawmakers for stricter laws, and confront rustlers. Why was the Globe

Stock Grower's Association disbanding amid all the rustling? Perhaps the vigilantes' crude tactics caused dissension, polarizing the cattlemen. However, with the regulators expunging thieves, perhaps the association's role was redundant.[4]

On Saturday, May 5, Dave Freeman hurried to Globe from the Salt River. A serious ruckus in William Beard's saloon required a lawman. Bob Pringle, Cap Adams, and John Rhodes, the husband of John Tewksbury's widow, were wounded, two of them seriously.

The *Silver Belt* reported the incident:

> … Adams was the most seriously hurt of the three, being shot through the right lung, the ball coming out at the back below the shoulder blade, and the same shot is supposed to have been the one that struck Pringle just below the left corner of the mouth…. Rhodes…is said to be wounded in the hand from a shot fired by Adams. The two shots must have been fired simultaneously, as persons present…were under the impression that only one shot had been fired. Ed Tewksbury…and Frank Montgomery [bartender]…did not witness the row.[5]

In fact, no one in the crowded saloon could state what happened or the cause. How convenient. Rhodes gave his pistol to his brother-in-law and started for Globe to surrender, only to change his mind at Wheatfields and disappear.

Frank tended to Ramsdell's undisclosed ailment and left for the Salt River twenty-four hours after the fracas. An unidentified newspaper reported that "Frank Hammon went as far as the scene of the shooting, in quest of Rhodes but failed to find him." Did Frank really expect to find Rhodes at the scene of the crime? In Frank's defense, at that time the Salt River formed Gila County's northern boundary. Further pursuit would have been out of his jurisdiction. Frank returned to Globe without Rhodes and never wrote about his unsuccessful search. The injured parties never filed charges.[6]

John Rhodes's statement to Joe T. McKinney is noteworthy. Years later, Rhodes recalled, "I moved down to the Salt River valley and went to work taking care of some cattle and I wanted to live in peace. I left off my pistol and didn't carry any gun at all." Did Rhodes hang-up his pistol before or after the encounter with Pringle and Adams? In 1892 Rhodes would again use his retired firearm.[7]

> Mon. May 7. Attended meeting of the board our bill was cut down some. Recd and accepted bid for constructing the foot bridge below town of Henry Shoap for $47.50.

> Tues. May 8. Left for Coon Creek this morning. Looked for my horse Charley at Shutes Spring but could not find him. Arrived at Ranch about 3 o'clock. Went up and caught my blind horse.

> Wed. May 9. …Went out with the boys. Vosberg and I went through by Horse Shoe Bend. Vosberg got washed down the river with his mule. I threw a rope to him and pulled him out.

The swollen Salt River, turbulent and unpredictable after the spring rains, nearly took J. J. Vosburgh's life. Dave Freeman was not as lucky. A few weeks later he drowned while bathing in the Salt River near Pinto Creek.[8]

Thurs. May 10. …Went up Cherry Creek with roundup and worked hard all day. Found the big Z steer, two cows and calves of mine and three year old bull of Henry's. On returning to camp found a message from George to come in immediately. Will ride in tonight although am very tired. A terrible and cold blooded murder has been committed. The victim being old man Wahlan.

Fri. May 11. …Arrived in Globe from Coon Creek at 7 o'clock AM. George went out last night on Wortman's [Wertman] trail with two indian trailers and Wm. Beard. Sent Baker out up the Salt River and into assessing. Gave him $20.00 to pay expenses and blank poll tax receipts.

Mose Wertman had testified on behalf of Burns and Blevins at their change of venue hearing the previous month. Sheriff Shute offered a $300 reward for his apprehension and conviction for the murder of Michael Wahlen.[9]

Sat. May 12. …Paid C. E. Taylor in full to date. Paid Julius Sultan for ½ of ranch bill to date $8.68. Recd a telegram from Holbert [in] Phoenix that he had Mose Wertman under arrest, also letter from George by indian trailer. He had trailed him to Pinal where he was notified that Wertman was arrested at Phoenix and would leave at once. Paid Fatty Restaurant Chinaman in full to May 1st '88.

Sun. May 13. Tom Curnow paid me for house rent to May 8th, 1888—$10.00. Wm Murphy paid for house rent up to May 22nd '88— $7.50.

Mon. May 14. …Paid the Belt office for my subscription for the Belt up to June 1, 1888. Mr. White settled for collecting 81 poll taxes from employees of Old Dominion Co. Two of which I must pay back as they have paid before. We have paid him $10.00 for his aid in collecting them. Went out and met Geo, Wm. Beard and Mose Wertman. Arrested Jerry Hazard—drunk and disorderly.

Tues. May 15. …George went down and arrested Mrs. Wertman last night and Wash Jacobs brought her up today, for accomplicity in murder of old man Walling [Wahlan]. Wertman had a hearing today but it was continued until next Monday.

Thurs. May 17. …Geo left for Phoenix this morning with Joe Buel and Frakes [for Burns and Blevins trial]. Belknap came in this morning and settled up. I paid Mrs. Welch interest this morning $80.00 in full up to May 20 '88 on my note due her of $500.00.

Fri. May 18. Wrote to George about rifle discovered in Wertman case in alfalfa. Discovered tracks where Walling was first shot at and found them to correspond exactly in length with the measure taken of the foot mark in the trail.

Some criminal investigations required extensive detective work. At other times, clumsy outlaws left obvious clues. Intelligence from local criminals and informers sometimes led to arrests. Often hunches netted rich results. With little training, but combining common sense and creative thinking, frontier lawmen applied many of the basic investigative techniques used today.[10]

> Sat. May 19. ...Wrote to Chas Martin at Pioneer to assess parties there if possible. Wrote to Mother and sent her 10.00. Rented my house on Mesquite St. to Ed Lynes for $7.50 per month.

> Sun. May 20. Learned of death by drowning of Dave Freeman in Salt River. Went to Wheat Fields with Mrs. Van Wagenen and husband, Mrs McNelly, Miss McClintock and Mrs. Walker and Sadie Ramsdel on a kind of picnic. Had a delightful time.

> Mon. May 21. Mose Wertman had hearing today and bound over also his wife. Quit watching jail yesterday. McCabe [attorney] thought it not necessary longer.

With Burns and Blevins's friend Mose Wertman in the jail, Frank's concern over another lynching appeared well founded.

> Tues. May 22. Mrs. Wertman allowed to go home on her own recognisance. I took her home returned about 5 o'clock PM.

> Wed. May 23. Baker returned today from assessing. Letter from George today. Very buisy—Pd. Van Wagenen for boots, pants, about $13.50 in full.

> Sat. May 26. ...Left with Ed Cook for San Carlos on an assessing trip and to look after the road which has been so bad there.

> Sun. May 27. Returned from San Carlos, was quite successful assessing and had a very pleasant visit and made some very pleasant acquaintances.

> Tues. May 30. Left for Coon Creek to brand up our calves. Got my horse at Shutes Spring. Found the boys Henry and Thomp with a lot of cattle in the corral. Branded several for myself.

> Mon. June 4. ...Commenced boarding at Mrs. Ramsdels again. Paid Fatty, Chinaman for last months board $17.35.

> Tues. June 5 to August 1. [No entries]

Frank covered the county assessing. By mid-July page after page of revised assessments appeared in the *Silver Belt*. The Board of Equalization held hearings for property owners to challenge the increased valuations. Then Frank's brief taciturn diary statements cease. No doubt assessing kept Frank busy, but could other reasons account for his silence?[11]

As Jake Lauffer stepped outside his Cherry Creek cabin during the first week in August, a bullet fired from close range by an unknown assailant shattered his arm. Earlier that day, bushwackers shot at innocent men uninvolved in the feud. The ambushers moved on to rifle Ed Rose's unoccupied house.

The two assaults may not have been related. Will C. Barnes suggests that Lauffer was targeted because "he talked too damn much." Deputy James Houck felt differently. He recalled the controversial horse-stealing case the previous spring and believed James Stott and company had exacted revenge.[12]

Frightened families who associated the two incidents sought protection by camping together. Thieves had infiltrated the Tonto Basin, confiscating stock, stealing property, and inflicting injury. Legitimate travelers avoided trails by daylight, fearful of chance encounters with adversaries. The feud's residue left innocent people unclear as to who was friend or foe. People afraid of an unknown enemy huddled together in tents in full view of their houses.[13]

Above the Rim, the Mormon communities of Heber and Wilmot were nearly deserted of families terrorized by pistol-whipping thugs who ruthlessly robbed their small farms. A sophisticated band of horse thieves took advantage of the abandoned, isolated area. Herds of horses driven from the north were swapped for herds stolen from the south. The exchange point was James Stott's isolated ranch.

Osmer D. Flake monitored the skullduggery. In later years he chronicled James Stott's connection to the Grahams, the Blevins brothers, and the Hashknife outfit. "Stott, and others… soon ran most of the respectable people out of the country," he related. Flake further maintained that Stott and company continued their established horse exchange after Andy Cooper's death. Flake estimated that "hundreds of cattle and horses were driven from the north side of the mountain and sold in the Globe and Phoenix country."[14]

An unlikely horse thief, James (Jamie) W. Stott was the twenty-five-year-old son of James and Hannah Stott of North Billerica, Massachusetts. His crippled father, mangled by machinery in his younger years, managed the Talbot Woolen Mills for neighbor Thomas Talbot. Politically powerful Talbot owned stock in the Aztec Land and Cattle Company and had been a two-term governor of Massachusetts.

An excellent student, young Stott graduated from prestigious Wilmot Academy in New Hampshire and then attended Harvard University. After an impropriety during his third year, the reckless youth headed for Texas. Talbot's brother employed him to run broncos on his Castroville ranch. Jamie's letters kept his anxious parents informed of his western escapades.[15]

In the spring of 1885, Stott left for Arizona with a string of horses he had received in lieu of pay. Anticipating a job with the Hashknife outfit, he was disappointed to learn that the Aztec Land and Cattle Company was no longer hiring "eastern dudes." Stott's father rallied behind his son, staking him to prime land forty miles south of Holbrook. Jamie's Hashknife chums helped him build the Circle Dot ranch near Bear Springs. Stott increased his stock and carefully entered his inventory into a ledger.[16]

In letters home, Stott routinely included financial records, and just as routinely he received an allowance. By some accounts, Jamie was an honest, industrious rancher. But one questionable episode marred his reputation. He possessed Jake Lauffer's iron-gray horse that he claimed "Workman" [Wertman?] had sold to him. Could this be the same individual Frank had investigated in the May murder of Michael Wahlen?[17]

A stock association detective monitored Stott's activities and confirmed that his Circle Dot ranch was the rendezvous point of the horse-swapping enterprise. Stott was warned, but the brand altering and stock exchanges continued. Stott told his friend F. A. Ames that sheepman Jim Houck coveted his ranch for a sheep station.[18]

To this day, controversy and confusion clouds Stott's guilt or innocence. Could the well-subsidized, mannerly Stott from a prominent eastern family have been involved in horse thievery? On the surface it seems unlikely, but the facts indicate some entanglement, if only by association. To the regulators, there was no question about his involvement.

On August 9, James Scott, a "drifting cowpuncher" from a prominent Texas family, was retrieving a horse he had loaned to Louis Naeglin. As Scott returned from Pleasant Valley, Houck's posse arrested him for the attempted murder of Jake Lauffer. After spending the night at Perkin's store, the posse and its prisoner rode toward Jamie Stott's ranch.[19]

When the posse arrived at dawn on August 11, three men resided at the Circle Dot ranch: Jamie Stott; Jeff "Billy" Wilson, a former Hashknife chuck-wagon cook; and Motte Clymer, a recovering consumptive who managed Stott's ranch in his absence. On that fateful day, Clymer witnessed the posse arrest Jamie Stott and Wilson. True to his gracious upbringing, the mannerly Stott invited his guests for breakfast. After eating, the posse placed Stott, Wilson, and Scott on horseback, securing their ankles with cuffs chained beneath the animals' bellies. As the three captives were led away, a posse member strongly suggested that Clymer catch the first stage for Holbrook. Clymer was the last person to see Stott, Wilson, and Scott alive.

A few days later, James Shelley was scouring the trail for the hoofprints of his missing cows when a displaced boot removed his hat. Startled, he looked up and saw three objects hanging from a ponderosa pine. Shelley was unprepared for the grisly sight of three putrefied bodies swinging silently in the blustery wind; their contorted features unmistakable. From a horizontal limb dangled the rigid remains of Stott, Wilson, and Scott. Rattled with fear, Shelley high-tailed it home leaving the gruesome trio for the next unsuspecting cowpoke.

On August 23, 1888, the Prescott *Journal-Miner* ran a biased article reporting "The general impression is that the lynching party were not composed of outlaws....Stott, although arrested several times, had always managed to secure an acquittal to the disgust and annoyance of the better class of citizens, who were cognizant of his place being a rendezvous for horse thieves and bad characters." A variety of stories with assorted points of view enhanced the tale. They all concurred on one point: the committee had systematically and deliberately strung-up their prisoners along the Verde road.[20]

It is unknown if Houck had prearranged the rendezvous with the regulators or if he stayed for the neck-tie party. Historian Joseph Fish implicated Tewksbury supporter Houck in the arrest and, possibly, the hangings. He further maintained Scott and Houck were well acquainted, claiming Scott had challenged Houck's pretentious claims in a Holbrook saloon. A humiliated Houck backed down but carried a grudge. Fish went even further and named a conglomerate of Tewksbury supporters: "Glenn Reynolds, J. W. Boyle, W. McFadden, P. Ellison, N. H. Coleman, Tom Horn, J. Tewksbury, H. A. Larson, [Harvey] Colcord, Varis [Voris], and others."[21]

Stott's grieving parents arrived in Arizona after they were notified of their son's violent death. On the advice of authorities who feared reprisal, they took no action against the executioners. W. J. Flake, the new owner of the Circle Dot ranch, found young Stott's ledgers among his possessions. According to Flake's son, his father presented the tally books to Mr. Stott for inspection. "I will never again say that my boy was innocent," the grieving father stated.[22]

Would a horse thief keep meticulous records of his crime? The reputed ledgers have never surfaced, leaving historians to question their existence. However, a letter written to Stott's family by Justice D. G. Harvey on October 10, 1888, suggests the books did exist and that horse thieves used young Stott's isolated property for their operation. To Robert Voris's probing questions, Colonel Jesse W. Ellison defended the vigilantes' actions. "We didn't hang no innocent men," he proclaimed. To the vigilantes, it was irrelevant whether their victims actually had committed the specific crime. Shiftless, chronic offenders who preyed on other people's successes were expendable.[23]

The hanging of Stott, Wilson, and Scott achieved the intended result. It was what historian Richard Maxwell Brown describes as a "graphic warning to all potentially disruptive elements that community values and structure were to be upheld." The unbridled chaos in Pleasant Valley ended. Vigilantism had proven more effective than "contentious" court proceedings. Fortunately, the vigilante movement passed as quickly as it had started.[24]

Territorial newspapers often provided "titillating" details of crimes and their repercussions. Captivated by the sensationalism, later authors have liberally written about Arizona's gunfights, feuds, lawmen, and lynchings, creating a misperception of the justice system. As an anomaly, the Pleasant Valley Feud presented Arizona at its worst. Frank's routine diary entries form a more accurate portrayal of a lawman's existence.[25]

While the regulators purged Apache County, Frank kept Globe's offenders in check. Though the incident was noted in the *Silver Belt*, Frank never mentioned arresting an Indian and his "squaw" for pursuing the Henderson children with knives. Nonetheless, the Indians caused Frank sleepless nights while the new courthouse received its final touches. On August 11, 1888, the *Silver Belt* reported: "The jail is being renovated and painted, necessitating the temporary removal of the prisoners, whom are kept underguard in one of the upper rooms of the court house building, Sheriff Shute doing duty during the day and Deputy Frank Hammon at night."[26]

Frank remained in town long enough to move the sheriff's office and prisoners into the basement jail facilities. He then left for an Illinois respite with his "dear ones." He never mentioned his trip home in his diary. His only notation, after months of virtual silence, suggests fear for his children's welfare and for his own safety.[27]

> <u>Sun. Sept 30</u>. Applied for Life insurance policy and accident policy. 3000.00 life and 3,000.00 accident in the Travelers of Hartford Conn. to C. N. Hammon, Ill State Agt. in favor of my three children Chas Milton—Alberta E. and Eva P. Hammon.

Chapter Eighteen

I Do Pray

Frank's probable route across the San Carlos reservation lay ahead of me. A paved highway bisecting the reservation has replaced the rutted, dusty road Frank labored over. As I retraced Frank's route, a new yellow school bus filled with exuberant children stopped in front of me. The red lights flashed as a tiny passenger disembarked onto a dirt-filled yard. With his backpack secured, the small Indian boy ran toward a dilapidated trailer topped by a satellite dish. Adjacent to a graveyard of gutted autos, a shiny new boat designated newfound wealth. The young Apache greeted his dog; his smiling face radiated hope.

Along the roadside, ditches filled with shards of broken bottles indicated years of shattered dreams. Discarded paper and plastic littered the parched land that a century ago carried the warriors of a struggling society. Abruptly, the debris vanished and viable enterprises appeared. A productive lumberyard and airport suggested progress.

The Apache Gold Casino and Hotel indicated prosperity. Retirees in motor homes, anxious to part with their hard-earned dollars, poured onto the casino's landscaped grounds. Across the highway, earth-moving equipment leveled acres of barren land. A well-maintained golf course transformed the desolate terrain into an oasis populated by well-clad yuppies.

I felt ambivalent. Sadly, the strewn discards suggested
that the San Carlos Apache no longer "lived as one with nature." The
trash indicated a disregard for the fragile land. On the other hand,
I was delighted with improvements to the scorched surroundings.
Today, through education and technology, pride is evolving and with
it—political power. Political clout provides Apache youth with hope.
As I exited the reservation, I wondered what Frank
would think of San Carlos today.

The timely trip home helped Frank sort through the sordid events of the spring and summer. Had he confided the concerns for his safety to his anxious family? Probably not. Perhaps he filled them with adventurous stories, omitting the gory events of the past year. Undoubtedly, he quietly explored job opportunities in Illinois.

Frank must have felt ambivalence as he contemplated moving to Illinois. Although he longed for his children, Frank found city life distasteful. Chicago's congestion and bustling energy held little attraction for him. He preferred the open spaces and rugged western lifestyle. Job prospects in Ottawa, ninety miles west of the city discouraged him. The encroachment of Chicago's booming industries had inflated Ottawa's land prices, making western real estate seem a bargain.

The health and welfare of his parents and children remained Frank's main concern. He had questioned how his middle-aged parents handled the burden of childrearing. What he saw reassured him. Five-year-old Alberta had blossomed under the care of his mother and sister. Eva, who favored the Hammon family, traipsed after her grandpa with questions and adoration. Milton, a frail two-year-old, thrived on the female attention. Frank recognized his children's need for family, especially a woman's tender touch. Sadly, without a wife, he was unable to fill those needs. Frank resigned himself. The children belonged with family until permanence entered his life.

Before leaving Illinois, Frank probably decided to remain in Globe. Seeing his children happy and his parents well, he accepted the cards fate had dealt him. His county jobs provided adequate income and he had built equity in the Coon Creek ranch and its increasing cattle herd. Globe's economic future looked brighter. Frank's writings implied satisfaction with his increased stature in Gila County. Above all, idle time no longer fed his loneliness. In late September, Frank bade his family good-bye and returned to Gila County, where an election determined his future.

By the time Frank returned, local attention focused on the campaign for sheriff. Republican candidate George Shute opposed ex-sheriff Ben Pascoe and Democratic candidate Glenn Reynolds. Reynolds garnered support from the cattlemen, who saw him as a decisive leader and defender of their cause. Worried voters tended to elect "law and order" sheriffs when disorder reigned. George Shute's continued ill heath prevented him from projecting the hardy lawman image required for re-election. Renewed animosity between the Blevins men reminded voter fears of a brewing feud.[1]

At the height of the campaign, Frank rearrested and brought charges against Cy Blevins for assault. Cy's smoldering resentment and frustration erupted on October 24, 1888, following Henry Blevins's acquittal in Maricopa County. His release by the unpredictable Arizona court system angered Gila County residents. Globe citizens saw advantages to the vigilantes' swift, sure action. One feud had cooled and the electorate wanted no part of another. Gila County voters elected Glenn Reynolds sheriff.[2]

Reynolds had used the vigilante movement to propel himself into the political arena. His commanding presence suggested a man of authority, righteousness, and power, a man willing to bring law and order to the county by any means. Alice Curnow expressed the sentiments of Globe's citizens: "At last, we had an officer who would make people obey the law. Reynolds was a big, broad shouldered man from Texas, and while he was a heavy drinker, he made everyone a law abiding citizen."[3]

After six months of silence following Reynolds's victory, Frank resumed writing with this pithy entry:

> Nov 13. Henry still in town. We hope to get away tomorrow. I hereby resolve to play no more cards, to drink no more licquor and to smoke no more cigars during this year 1888—I mean by no more cards to play no more for drinks or cigars. I need help from above to enable me to do right, and for it I do pray. I cannot afford to spend any money for these foolish things, when my little ones need it.

Without employment, Frank no longer could justify his penchant for cards and drink. Old anxieties surfaced as he contemplated his future.

No matter what emotion the election loss produced, Frank must have felt frustration and moral confusion. Due process, which he remembered from his Pennsylvania days, had proven useless in the West. Vigilantes repudiated Frank's eastern values, viewing them as unmanly and prudish. The regulators considered formal eastern laws as morally neutral and no better than bureaucratic red tape that pampered dangerous criminals. Perhaps Frank understood the vigilantes' reasons for circumventing the law, but he aspired to higher principles. Knowing what he knew, how would Frank fit in to the new political system? With the election over, and no longer in a perilous position, Frank resumed writing his daily entries.[4]

> Nov 14. We left town for the river after noon. Arrived OK in evening. Before I left I paid Mrs. Ramsdel for board up to date amounting to $29.00. Found Old Man Veach at Henrys.

> Nov 15. Packed up one of Henrys mares and started for Coon Creek where we arrived about 1 o'clock. Henry quite sick with a cold. Cleaned

up dishes, pots—about the house during the afternoon. We found plenty of hay and feed for our horses, and the fruit trees looking first rate.

Nov 16. Went up after horses and found all but my bay two year old stud colt, drove them down and branded Kates little mare colt. Charley did some tail pitching with me and almost got me off and then fell over backwards with me but for a wonder I came out unhurt. We repaired the corral and Henry kept up Charley and Jack and let the rest go.

Nov 17. Started in storming last night and still continues and looks as if it might continue for a week. Shod some of the horses, and as the rain slacked up about noon, we started out for an afternoon drive. Henry agreed to brand me fifteen calves for his note due me of 70.00 with interest and one half of the 50.00 cash which he borrowed from the sheriffs office. He branded me today 2 steer calves and 2 heiffers and I branded of my own 3 steer calves.

Nov 22. Went over to Medlers divide and drove in branded of Henrys for me one steer clf and one heff clf and of my own one heff clf. Turned out my horse Charley and Jack my mule. Will leave for Salt River with a milk cow and calf and a yearling steer. Henry is taking down home. Recd from Henry to apply on the fifteen which he agreed to brand in payment of note and 4 heff clvs and 4 steer calves—due yet 7 calves.

Nov 24. Very stormy this morning and appears to have settled down for a good rain. Will try and go to Globe today. Left for town about 8:30 AM and arrived about two or half past. It rained on me every step of the way and oh, how wet and cold I was, my boots were full of water and I was soaked to the skin. Commenced boarding at Fies the Chinamans.

Nov 25. Stormed part of today yet seems some like clearing up. The past storm has been a God send for the county. I attended church this evening. Recd my watch by mail today. Took down my election bet today.

Nov 26. Very cloudy and has turned colder and seems like snowing. Squared up the books at the office today. Henry came in last evening from the river and brt [brought] my blankets and six shooter which I left when there the other day…Henry and I bot for Veach shirts—socks and hat.

Nov 27. Paid Westmeyer for the hat and socks which I bot yesterday for Veach. Showering occassionally during the day—Attended rehersal for the entertainment at the rink tomorrow evening.

Nov 28. Henry started home this morning with his family—seems to be breaking away some. Attended the Thanksgiving Eve entertainment at the Rink with Miss Annie Pascoe and for town of Globe it was very excellent. We had to go home in a heavy storm. Attended Turkey shooting and killed a turkey at the 4th shot 200 yds off hands.

Nov 29. Thanksgiving Day and ushered in with a heavy rain which looks bad for the ball tonight. The barbeque passed off quietly and with much merriment. Weather broke toward evening and cleared off nicely. The dance well attended and passed off very nicely. I went home at 4 AM this morning.

Nov 30. Weather cloudy and stormy on the mountains—feel pretty well played from last nights disipation. Arrested a mexican for commiting a nuisance on the street. Paid Mrs. Welsch for interest on note one month to Nov. 22nd '88.

Dec 1. Mexican fined $5 and costs and paid. Weather clear and cold. Sent home $50.00 and Chas Taylor in full to date.

Dec 2. Weather cold and clear. Very quiet. Attended Sunday school and Thanksgiving entertainment and church in the evening.

Dec 3. Clear and cool. Most beautiful weather—A band of thieves are in town robbing houses. We are on the watch for them.

Dec 4. Beautiful, clear, cool morning. Will sell today Centenial Mill and Eatons corral at sheriffs sale. Board of examiners are in session.

Dec 5. Weather still clear and cool. Harley Hitchcock was married last night. Geo went to the Wheat Fields after his horses this morning. Rink opens this evening for skating. Glenn Reynolds arrived today and moved into my house.

In spite of the previous spring's events, Frank's relationship with the new sheriff had developed into mutual respect. Although Frank remained outside the Texan's intimate group of friends, he knew Reynolds to be a man of his word. Reynolds's term as sheriff would begin on January 1, 1889. Until then, George Shute and Frank remained in office. Glenn Reynolds would depend on Frank in the coming year.[5]

Dec 6. Geo returned last eve and went to the river today, storming again this evening.

Dec 8. Arrested L. Robinson last night for carrying concealed weapons. Had his trial today and was found not guilty.

Dec 9. Clear and most beautiful weather. Attended Sunday school and church. Geo returned from river last night.

Dec 10. Clear beautiful days with frosty nights. Served summons on Mr R. Gill in case vs. Mrs R Gill. Issued license for a show tonight. This is pay day at the mine and smelter.

<u>Dec 11</u>. Recd a writ of Habias Corpus to serve on Capt Bullis of San Carlos. Will go down tonight. The show a complete failure.

Captain John L. Bullis had replaced Captain Pierce as San Carlos Indian agent. Under Bullis, an ambitious building effort began on the only north-south wagon road in the eastern territory. At San Carlos, the road crossed the northeast thoroughfare leading to Utah and Colorado, connecting San Carlos with Fort Apache on the White River. Military personnel from Forts Huachuca, Bowie, Grant, and Thomas traveled the road en route to the northern post. Maintenance required extensive manpower. Bullis made liberal use of Apache prisoners as inexpensive laborers on the roads.[6]

Rumors of arrests of Apaches on unsubstantiated charges and complaints of unfair incarceration of Indians brought an investigation of Bullis's methods. Al Sieber alleged that prisoners were forced to do unpaid roadwork. He further maintained that Bullis encouraged snooping, spying, and squealing among Indians in order to load the jail with workers. It is probable that the writ of habeas corpus Frank served on Bullis required him to show cause for illegal detention of untried Apaches. Frank's official duties as road overseer for Gila County afforded insight into Bullis's tactics.[7]

<u>Dec 12</u>. Arrived this morning at San Carlos at 9 oclock. Very tired. Will not start back until tomorrow morning. Served the writ on Capt. Bullis. Some of the darkies belonging to the post are giving a minstral show here tonight I shall attend.

<u>Dec 13</u>. Attended the show last night which was excellent. Left for Globe at 10 oclock and arrived at 3 oclock P.M. Robt Holt also arrived in evening.

<u>Dec 14</u>. Sent home for Christmas $10.00 for my little ones. Commenced storming again this or rather last night. Geo is sick again.

<u>Dec 16</u>. Beautiful day. Attended Sunday school and church in evening sang in choir a very interesting sermon.

<u>Dec 17</u>. Clear and beautiful days. Nights sharp and frosty. Wrote to Charley about getting an appointment from government as I. T. [Indian Trader] and asked him if he could help me—I hope for a favorable reply. Paid Chinaman for my board to date 17.00. Paid Mrs. Welch interest on note to Dec 22 '88.

Frank focused his job search on the San Carlos reservation. With his previous experience as a merchant, Frank viewed the Indian tradership as a position that could support his family. Frank apparently intended to remain in Globe permanently; perhaps the trader job was a temporary solution to unemployment.

<u>Dec 18</u>. A minstral troop from 10 Cavalry stationed at San Carlos are coming to give an entertainment at Globe on next Thursday evening—I have secured seats. I have engaged to act as usher.

<u>Dec 19</u>. Wrote another letter to Jere Fryre. Engaged Miss Mamie Kennedy for the minstral show Thursday evening.

<u>Dec 20</u>. Clouding up some and think it will storm. Was some disappointed in the entertainment last evening. A good crowd out. They will open again this evening.

<u>Dec 21</u>. Commenced boarding at Mrs Ramsdels this morning. Show not very well attended last evening. I was given comp tickets and took Miss Sadie Ramsdel.

More than two years had passed since Daisy's death. Without his family nearby, Frank's grieving had been protracted and lonely. Work had been his salvation. But, since the election, time lay heavy on his hands. To occupy the lonely hours, Frank sought the company of Globe's young ladies.

Indeed, they were young! Frank's friends viewed him as a trustworthy escort for their young daughters, still in their teens and living at home with their families. The arrangement possibly kept Frank from risky entanglements. Daisy's memory remained in his heart.

<u>Dec 22</u>. Weather very stormy. The coons [black soldiers] are going to give a benefit for the Christmas tree this Evening.

<u>Dec 23</u>. Still very stormy. The creek up very high and almost drownded several persons this evening.

<u>Dec 24</u>. Still storming. Ladies are dressing Christmas tree today. Rev. Downs returned today.

<u>Dec 25</u>. Christmas day and lonely for me. Cloudy and sunshine mingles. Attended Christmas tree last eve, and enjoyed it much. Paid license money to Trea. Today – Amt $465.00.

<u>Jan 1, 1889</u>. New Years Day – Attended the New Years Eve ball last night, had a delightful time. Left at 12 A M. Moved into Mrs. Andersons house behind the O. O. H hall for which I have agreed to pay her $3.00 per month. Am repairing my house on the hill above the church with hopes of renting same. Glenn Reynolds moved into my house on Misquite St., Globe on December 5 '88. He to pay for first month $7.50 and afterward $10.00 per month. Commenced boarding at Mrs. Ramsdells Dec 21 '88.

Glenn Reynolds moved with his pregnant wife and four children into Globe to assume the sheriff's duties.

<u>Jan 2</u>. We turned over the sheriffs office today to Glenn Reynolds and closed up the business. Spense and the dutch-butcher Charley were arrested today for fighting. Worked at track above Turners with Fransisco Maise today. I am still Constable as – Clark – Constable elect has not and will not qualify. I remain Road Assessor until March '89.

Jan 3. Continued work on trail above Turners with Fransisco. Continued the painting my house. Had Mr. Middleton get Robinson to make me a shut iron stove for my room for which I paid him $5.00 I have also a new carpet which I bought on Dec 29 '88 from Bailey for $20.00 which with the stove makes me a comfortable little room.

Jan 4. Fransisco and I worked at grading a trail from the north end of bridge, north of town, to the road today. Had painting on my house commence today.

Jan 5. Finished painting my house today. Fransisco worked on streets today in front of Court House. Sent to A. L. Bancroft for a diary for 1889 Collected from Republican Central Committee for ½ of meals for Elections officers at last November election and pd. to Mrs. Ramsdel amounting to $2.50.

Jan 6. Arranged with Marshall to go and work roads at Pioneer and Dripping Springs. I to allow him $2.50 per day. Cashed county warrants for Holbert of Phoenix amounting to $610.76 and remitted to him by G. S. Van Wagenens check for $300. on S. F. and E. F. Kelners Co. check on S. F. for $308.25. Exchange $2.50. Made out Road Tax statement to Jan 1st '89 leaving me a credit of $22.65.

Jan 7. …Recd a letter from Connell. Wrote to Charley and sent him credentials—Connels letter. Wrote also to Commissioner of Indian Affairs at Washington for blank applications.

Jan 8. Am making arrangements to go over to Pioneer with Marshall tomorrow to work the road.

In the higher elevations, portions of narrow roads gave away under the weight of wagons. Boulders, stones, and grimy snow hurtled down the mountainsides, closing the soggy roads below. The advent of winter rains further disintegrated the wagon roads, reducing them to rocky mud holes. Helpless teams of oxen and mules destined for the Globe smelter became bogged down in quagmires of axle-high sludge near the Gila River. Wagons laden with coke were abandoned as teamsters desperately labored to free their frightened animals from the mire. The coke deliveries stopped. For the next two months, Frank and his small band of men equipped with picks, shovels, and dynamite repaired the impassable roads.

Jan 9. A. L. Walker Supt Old Dominion Copper Co. asked me to go to San Carlos and look after road on San Carlos reservation as teams cannot get through with coke for smelter. I agreed to go and will let Mr. Marshall go to repairing.

Jan 10. Jimmy Woods and I came to San Carlos today. I rode Frenchys mare. Found that Capt Bullis had fixed partially the bad place under the bluff. But has run short of powder. Will help myself now.

Crew repairing Globe road. AHS/TUCSON #47670.

<u>Jan 11</u>. Went out on the road with Elesh Laurence and five soldiers and four Indians and finished for present under the bluff. Capt Bullis paid me the bal. of money sent him by Walker... amounting to $19.50.

<u>Jan 12</u>. Went up to Bentons Camp and secured some indians to go to work in the morning and fix the point of rocks, which is in bad condition. Will stop with Jack [Capt. Jack Benton] tonight.[8]

<u>Jan 13</u>. Went up to Point of Rocks at 12 mile point with Benton and some indians and found a big wagon loaded with Coke turned over at place where we wished to repair. So I gave Jack $5.00 to pay the indians for fixing the place under his direction when the wagon was out of the way, and I came on to Globe.

Captain Bullis may have worked the untried prisoners as Al Sieber charged, but clearly Frank compensated the Indians under his direction. Whether Jack Benton ever paid them is another matter. A year later, Bullis would become embroiled in controversy resulting in more serious charges. While Frank worked the San Carlos road, he observed the job opportunities on the reservation and used his connections and friendships to pursue them.

Jan 14. Paid Mr. Walker $44.00. The $30.00 he gave me and bal. of money recd from Capt Bullis after deducting the $5.00 paid Benton. Stormed hard last night and continues today. Mr. [Reverend] Downs said he would recommend me to Capt. Bullis as Principal of School at San Carlos, and in evening showed me the letter written by him to Capt Bullis.

Jan 15. Wrote to Capt Bullis making application for Principalship of School at San Carlos. Read letter from Charley and answered same. Still storming—heavy snow in the mountains.

Jan 16. Recd a letter from C. T. Connel from Tusan [Tucson], acknowledged same, and will seek the information asked and wrote further. Storm still continues. Attended rehersal for the entertainment on 18th.

Jan 17. Weather cleared off last night and is delightful today. Find time heavy on my hands. Don't know yet what I shall do. Attended dress rehersal for entertainment of tomorrow night.

Jan 18. Weather bright and beautiful. Marshall returned from Pioneer last night. From two to three feet of snow on mountain. Weather so bad he could not work. Helped at the rink getting ready for the entertainment tonight.

Jan 19. Took Sadie to the entertainment last night. Show passed off well and had a nice dance after which was kept up until four o'clock in the morning. Some kicking away the boys as usual....Have not taken a drink or smoked a cigar today.

Jan 20. Coldest night so far this winter, bright and clear this morning. Saw Ed, the stage line man from San Carlos this morning. He says the Principal for school at San Carlos has not arrived yet. Wrote to Herman Sulton at San Carlos about employment at San Carlos. Attended church and S.S. [Sunday school] Walked home with Annie Pasco and Florence [Pascoe].

Jan 21. Beautiful, clear, cool day. Brought my blankets and saddle down to my room. Went out hunting with Rev. Downs. I got eight quail and two road runners. Mr. Howet, Ed Berry and Dick Trevarthan came to my room and we had five games of Whist. Ed and I won four of the five.

Jan 22. Weather cool and slightly cloudy. Geo Shute came up from the river last night to remove his family down. McNelly, Fox, Lynes and H. Sultan went to the river this morning for a duck hunt. Recd a letter this morning from Capt Bullis informing me that he had engaged a man from the east to fill the position of Superintendant of Indian School at agency. I have not taken a drink or a smoke for three days and feel much better for it. Am still unoccupied—am very uneasy doing nothing, am anxious to get into some business and get permenantly settled.

With abundant time on his hands, Frank spent his empty hours in Globe's saloons. Once again he imbibed and once again he proudly reinstated abstinence.

Resolute, Frank sought more acceptable amusement by assembling card parties in his rented room at Mrs. Anderson's. Just the same, he could not earn a living playing cards. In desperation, as he watched job opportunities slip away, Frank once again considered mine work.

Jan 23. Weather windy, and cold but clear. Played cribbage with Chas Banker until 1 o'clock. He quit five games ahead. Am getting up a small party of folks to go up to the Globe Mine tomorrow. Have never been through the Globe Mine and am anxious to see it. No employment in sight yet. Am getting tired of it. Called on Annie Pascoe and Mamie Kennedy.

Jan 24. Clear, bright and cool weather. Went up and through the Globe mine with Mr. and Mrs. Brookner, Miss Mamie Kennedy and Sadie Ramsdell and Mr. Berry the foreman. Attended surprise party given to Dr. Trippel this evening about thirty attended and all had a delightful time. Dancing cards, conversation and a bounteous lunch enabled all to pass the evening away and few left until after midnight.

Jan 25. Clear, bright beautiful day. Pd Mrs. Welsh interest on note to Jan 22nd '89—$10.00. Sold to Mrs. Welsh county warrants amounting to $72.40 for $69.40. Geo, Henry Middleton, George Shute and myself have employed James Head to work for us collectively, each to pay him $15.00 per month and he to board himself—said amount to be paid either in money or beef-cattle, and either one not to be responsible for the others share. Head to live at Hammon-Middleton rch [ranch] on Coon Creek. Said Hammon & Middleton and Shute to each furnish Head a saddle horse. Paid Mrs. Ramsdell on a/c of board $20.00. Paid Tom Carnow in full of a/c for work on my house $15.50.

Jan 26. Bright, beautiful morning. Attended dance at the rink (or rather Stallo's Hall) last evening. Just enough attended to have a nice time. I took no company and arrived home at 3 o'clock this morning. Have invitation out to Mrs. McNellys this evening for a game of Whist. Think I shall go out to the ranch shortly.

On January 23, 1889, the first of two tragedies struck the Reynolds household. Glenn Reynolds's youngest child died of complications from scarletina.[9]

Jess Hayes, in his book *Apache Vengeance*, presents a folktale ascribing Glenn's two-year-old son's untimely death to the Pleasant Valley feud. According to Hayes, the Reynoldses' baby grew seriously ill during the height of the Tewksbury-Graham vendetta and needed medication. A rider supposedly left the Sierra Ancha ranch, headed for Globe to buy an elixir. As the tale goes, the rider padded his horse's hooves and tied down his jingling spurs to avoid detection on the treacherous trails. Despite his stealth, the rider was shot, the medicine never arrived, and little Georgie died. Hayes implied that the Reynolds baby was another feud casualty.

Several historians suggest that this incident prompted the Reynoldses' move to Globe. According to Frank's diary, however, the Reynolds family resided in Frank's adobe house on Mesquite Street at the time of the baby's death. In reality, little Georgie died from inadequate medical treatment, not the feud.[10]

Jan 27. Bright, beautiful morning, but quite cool. Slept late. Had a pleasant evening at Mrs. McNellys. Attended Sunday School in afternoon and church in evening. Ben Pasco, Mrs. Reynolds and Mr. Cook went forward for prayers. A large attendance.

Accompanied by Ben Pascoe and Mr. Cook, Gustie Reynolds knelt to pray for her departed child. Before year's end, she and her children would receive an outpouring of prayers.

Jan 28. Very nice day. Board of Supervisors in session today. I am still unemployed and am so anxious to get to work. I can not afford to be idle. Wrote home and sent $40.00 to them—all I have. I do hope I can get something to do so I can earn money to send home for next month. Mr. Berry, Mr. Hamill, and Dick Trevarthan played Whist with me at my room this evening. Mr. Hamill and I got beaten. Posted up notice at Old Dominion works of collection of Road Tax coming pay day but the men kicked so I will postpone it to next month.

Jan 29. Beautiful clear day. Mr. Marshall left on foot for Pioneer to go to work on the county roads. I also went over on a mule borrowed from Mr. Middleton. Expect to return the day after tomorrow. I wish to go over the road and see what needs to be done. We stopped at Mr. Siddows. Found about two feet of snow on the top of Pinals.

As the snow melted, coke teams made little headway through mud up to their wheel hubs. Until Frank and his crew could fix the roads, teamsters dumped their loads to lighten the mules' burden.

Jan 30. The weather is clear and has moderated considerably. Mr. Marshall, Dutch-Charley and myself went to work on the road working toward Dripping Springs. I find the road in very bad shape and it will require considerable work and expense to fix it up as it needs. I decided to remain and manage the work myself and so I sent the mule back to Globe today by Tompson.[11]

<u>Jan 31</u>. Mr. Marshall, Dutch Chas and myself went out and worked again. Continuing on towards D [Dripping] Springs. We are doing good work and lots of it. Both of my men are good workers and we get along fast. I ordered some provisions from Bailey to be brought over by stage tomorrow. Bert Young passed on the way with Tompson today.

<u>Feb 1</u>. Weather continues fine. I went out with some men and worked to about half way to D Springs. We passed the rocky hill for future consideration. Thompson and Middleton express themselves as well pleased with our work. I hired Herman Siddow to join our crowd and he started in today.

<u>Feb 2</u>. Clear this morning but with high wind. Went out with the boys and started them to work at noon. I got on the stage and came to Globe. Found a letter from home and one from Commission of Indian Affairs awaiting me which contained blanks which I sent for a few days ago. Recd also a letter from bro Charley today. Geo Shute called in to see me this evening. He came up from the river today.

<u>Feb 3</u>. Beautiful, clear morning. Sent pair of shoes over by stage to Dutch Charley. Got them at Baileys and had them charged to John Newman. Sent two picks and another shovel over also. Bought from J. C. Lundy 5 picks for $8.75—3 handles from F. W. Westmeyer, and one pick and handle from Bailey for county roads. Attended Sunday School and church in evening. Have arranged to send things by Frenchy in morning and may go with him myself.

<u>Feb 4</u>. Put tools, bedding and grub on Frenchys wagon and left myself by stage for Pioneer, arrived at noon. Found the boys out on the road working. Got Frenchy to lay over and moove our camp down to the cottonwoods in the morning.

<u>Feb 5</u>. Got everything on Frenchys wagon and we all walked down to the grade and went to work. Frenchy arrived about noon and we made camp. Got down into the canyon today. Herman Siddow went to Pioneer tonight. Wm. Sutherland came from Pioneer yesterday with a load of ore for S. D. Meyers and left his wagons above the cottonwoods, came this day and mooved on.

Whose ore was Sutherland transporting? Herman deserted Frank's road crew to handle other pressing matters. A month later, these matters would result in legal action followed by violence.

<u>Feb 6</u>. Clear and beautiful—Herman did not return this morning. Marshall, Chas and I alone today. We did a big days work.

<u>Feb 7</u>. Most delightful day. Nothing new. Still on the grade, but getting along very well—mail and grub from Globe today.

Feb 8. Clear and beautiful day Mr. Frakes passed on way to Globe.

Feb 9. Nice clear day Lee Middleton drove stage from Globe brought news of man being killed near Gilsons by indians.

Not only did the teamsters' wagons maneuver over rough and rutted roads, but they also contended with Indians who coveted weapons. In early February, five freighters left Willcox destined for Globe with cargos of coke, wood, and hay. Freighter H. H. Cosper's two sons accompanied him, along with two men named Davidson. A twelve-horse team pulled each wagon, with the freighter riding the right wheel horse. Each man carried his rifle in a scabbard secured behind him.

On the evening of February 8, the Cosper wagon train stopped for dinner just short of the San Carlos reservation's western boundary. Two hungry Apaches, one on foot and the other armed and mounted, joined the freighters. After eating, one of the Indians noticed Freeman Cosper's fancy inlaid rifle with gold-plated bands on its stock. The armed Indian offered to trade his fat sorrel mare for the distinctive weapon. Young Cosper declined his offer.

At sundown, the freighters continued their journey toward Globe, with the Apaches trailing behind. Four miles west of Gilson Wells, before the caravan left the reservation, the Indians made their move. The mounted and armed Indian positioned himself in the rear, near Freeman Cosper, and again attempted to negotiate a trade. Thinking him harmless, Cosper refused. The Indian, however, raised his gun and shot the unsuspecting Cosper in the back. Simultaneously, the Indian afoot grabbed the rifle from its scabbard, handed it off to his mounted friend, and the two headed for the hills.[12]

Following the coroner's inquest, soldiers pursued the murderers up Timber Camp Mountain, where they captured Blue Stone (Bi-the-ja-be-tish-to-ce-an). Blue Stone cooled his heels in the Globe jail until the October 1889 court session. His accomplice, wounded in the exchange with the freighters, presumably died in the wild.[13]

Meanwhile, the *Silver Belt* used the Cosper incident to once again lobby for dissolution of the San Carlos reservation stating, "There is nothing so prejudicial to the civilization of the Indian, and provocative of discord as the reservation system."[14]

Feb 16. Recd from Clerk of Board of Supervisors 150 blank Road Tax receipts for 1889.... Notified 47 employees of the Old Dominion Co. to appear on Feb. 19th at Court House to do their road work for 1889 by written notices through Post Office....[15]

Feb 17. Sky clear this morning, air crisp. Sent notices to balance of Old Dominion employees to appear on the 20th to work out Road Tax. Wrote to Charley. Attended Sunday School in afternoon and church in evening....

<u>Feb 18</u>. ...Mr. Westmeyer made out a statement concerning me as an applicant for Indian Trader at San Carlos and agreed to go on my bond of $10,000. Berties letter I answered today. Mr. A. Bailey made a statement as above noted on Mr. Westmeyer and also agreed to go on my bond. Mr. Van Wagenen is also making a statement. I have not asked any one for a third bondsman. I feel much encouraged to receive support from such substantial men. The best and most prominent in Gila Co.

Frank had every reason to feel encouraged by the local support. The men endorsing him were respected merchants with political connections. Frank may have felt his recent association with Bullis and Benton gave him an added advantage. As an experienced merchant, Frank felt well qualified for the Indian tradership. Naively, he proceeded with the application process, unaware that his impressive recommendations held little weight in Washington D. C. Political decision makers had their own agenda.

<u>Feb 19</u>. Clear sharp morning and has been a warm delightful day. Recd from Mr. Van Wagenen statement to Government regarding me as applicant for an Indian Tradership at San Carlos. Accomplished very little today. Called on Miss Mamie Kennedy this morning.

<u>Feb 20</u>. clear, cool morning and has been a nice warm day. I had made out my application for tradership and got my bond of $10,000 with three sureties: T. W. Westmeyer, Alonzo Bailey and C. E. Taylor. Witnesses C. T. Martin and C. A. Fisk. My bondsmen are the best in this county. I have written to Charley and will send the papers in the mornings mail. Have secured Miss Mamie Kennedys company for ball on the 22nd....

<u>Feb 21</u>. Clear nice morning and warm beautiful day. U. S. Marshall Breckenridge is here after jurymen—summoned me, but I am still constable and he could not take me as I am constable yet. I put up notices today at mine and smelter informing the public that Mr. White and C. E. Taylor were authorized to contract Road Tax for 1889. Mr. Berry told me to come on in the morning to work.... Gave Chas Fisk a blank to fill for me as applicant for Indian Trader. Bot lunch bucket and will go to work at mine in morning.

Legendary U. S. Marshal Billy Breckenridge appeared in Globe to round-up men for the U. S. grand and petit juries in Phoenix. Frank was relieved to be disqualified as a juror. With the extensive federal court docket, he would have lost a month's wages at the Old Globe Copper Company. He went to work temporarily for Mr. Berry, still hoping for the appointment as Indian trader.[16]

At first I ignored Frank's omitted capitalization of "indians" and "mexicans." As I read further, subtle undercurrents of prejudice surfaced. I identified another motive for Frank's altercation with Jewish barber Jacob Abraham. His off-handed references to the "darkies" and "coons" made me uncomfortable. Unfortunately, Frank's casual idioms for African-Americans were the accepted lingo of his time. Perhaps I had judged Frank too harshly.

The settlers brought to the frontier their intolerances. Sometimes their bigotry was subtle, but most often it was blatant. They suppressed cultures that threatened their security and abused minorities they thought inferior. Our diverse nation's struggle for tolerance has been lengthy; the roots of racism run deep.

Chapter Nineteen

TOO MUCH POWDER SMOKE

Cold air blasted us as we entered the blackness. Only the laughing, raucous voices ahead indicated I wasn't alone. The clanking rail car carried us a quarter mile into the hill where it stopped briefly in a cavernous hole. The great stope etched by the "jacks" (hammers) of another generation had been stripped of mineral. The dripping limestone walls no longer echoed the single-jack taps, the boom of powder charges, or the voices of long ago.

As we moved forward, lights from our hard hats played across the massive timbers supporting the tapering tunnels. Scarcely able to stand, I realized a claustrophobic miner would not fare well. A light illuminated the youthful faces of my fellow sightseers. Laughing and joking, we found humor in a two-hole latrine on wheels. I formed a mental picture of some poor bloke scrubbing the privy for pittance; terrifying dynamite explosions in close confinement; and Frank, with boils on his arm, loading charges. The eight-dollar tour fee equaled three days' wages for Frank. Recalling his doleful diary entries, my attitude adjusted.

<u>Feb 22</u>. Cloudy and looks much like a storm. Attended ball this night with Miss M. [Mamie] Kennedy. Came home at 3AM this morning of 23rd. Went to work for Old Globe Copper Co in the mine. Worked today on the six hundred [level] helping fill cars. I have a very large boil on my wrist and it pains and annoys me very much.

Working the night shift, Frank joined the other miners descending into the bowels of the earth to earn $3.25 a day. Secured only by rope or cable, the metal cage creaked and rattled as it lowered the crew to the 600-foot level. The dreaded forty-five second descent allowed brief glimpses of timber, gushes of air, and smells of ignited powder. In the blackness, distant tapping sounds were the only indications of humanity. Once the skip reached 600 feet, the hoist operator clanged the bell six times signaling Frank's level. Undoubtedly, he and the other miners headed for the drift blasted by the previous crew. For ten hours, they shoveled ore or waste rock into cars waiting to be hoisted to the surface. When Frank's shift ended, he ascended into the fresh air and inky darkness.[1]

<u>Feb 23.</u> Cloudy, got to bed at 3 AM this morning. Nearly played out. Worked today on the first level with Clarence West had an easy day. My wrist is very bad today. Bot a doz. of underwear and hat from Kelner for cash $7.60. Chas Fisk made a statement for me on my application for Indian Tradership and I will forward it to Charley tonight.

Frank probably dressed in the customary miner's clothing: a battered wide-brimmed felt hat treated with resin to divert falling rocks; baggy trousers; heavy woven shirt; and, in wet weather, an oilskin. He possibly kept a fleece jacket in the level station to wear home during the cold February nights. His newly purchased long johns provided extra warmth.

Often during the winter months, miners set fires in the tunnels to thaw the frozen rock before drilling. Water trickling from stony walls formed knee-high pools mixed with dust. The miners wallowed in the mud to chisel dynamite holes. As the water dripped, the acidic liquid burned any bare skin, leaving open sores. These abhorrent conditions paled in comparison to the dangers miners faced.[2]

<u>Feb 24.</u> Clear morning. Have to work on Sunday at the G [Globe] mine. I worked in same place as yesterday. Last night I put a leaf of Prickly Pear Cactus on my boil and this morning it had bursted and is getting along fine now. I fear that there is another one coming. Attended church in evening, subject dancing. Last night as shift was going on, ten lbs of powder exploded at station on first level and at the side of the powder room where 700 lbs of powder was stored. It shattered the room and tore the station some, but fortunately for the men the stored powder did not explode.

The stations on each level provided a miners' lounge of sorts, which also stored explosives. The detonation of 700 pounds of powder would have destroyed

Shoring up dangerous ground in the Old Dominion Mine.
AHS/Tucson #3224.

the first level, killing any miners in the vicinity. Furthermore, a blast of that mag-
nitude would have suffocated any miners inhaling the noxious fumes and smoke.
Accidents were common occurrences. Explosions, cave-ins, rock falls, rotten
timbers, and lethal gases were among the life-threatening hazards underground.
Fume-induced vertigo caused many fatal falls from the cage, down shafts, or into
"steaming sumps."[3]

Frank, however, was afflicted by another occupational hazard. Boils were
common in crowded living quarters plagued by relatively poor hygiene. Most
men nursed the painful, highly contagious, festering sores as best they could.
Old wives' tales attributed abscesses to lack of iodized salt, excesses of sugar

and starch, or nutritional deficiencies. Today, a regimen of antibiotics and hot compresses would have cleared up Frank's bacterial staph infection. Instead, his abscesses, possibly developed while working on the Pioneer road, were acerbated by the dripping water and the rock dust. The old Indian panacea of a Prickly Pear poultice proved to be the proper antidote.[4]

> Feb 25. A beautiful day clear and warm. I am getting hardened to my work and don't mind it much in fact I feel much more contented then when not occupied. Am still working on [unreadable] in drift south of station on first level. Had a very dusty day this....

> Feb 26. Showery day. Was raining when I got up at 5:30 in the morning. Gave Chas A. Fisk my brother Charleys address. He said he might be east in about March. Worked today in old place in winge. Ordered a candle stick from blacksmith. No mail for three days. Am well and getting into good working condition now. Robt Schell is in town with baby his boy. Wrote to Charley to let me know when he would place my application before the Commission of Indian Affairs.

> Feb 27. Clear beautiful day. Got the windlan [sic, windlass] up today and it is much better now. Bot of E. T. Kelner for cash pair of pants for $2.60 and a pair of shoes for 2.70. Have an engagement to play Whist at Mrs. Foxes this evening made for me by Chas Fisk.

The windlass, a hand-operated wheel and axle attached by rope (whim) to a basket (kibble), hoisted ore or water to the surface. Eliminating the pools of water from the mine floor obviously improved Frank's conditions.[5]

> Feb 28. A warm rain falling this morning. My partner did not work today. Mr. Jackson took his place. A contract is to be let this day by the company for a one hundred foot drift—I shall not bid on it. Tomorrow we change shifts I go on night shift. Had a pleasant evening at B G Foxes last evening playing Whist.

Small groups of miners occasionally banded together to bid on a specific task the mining company deemed too difficult or too expensive to assume. Winning a contract was usually a losing proposition, with miners absorbing the loss. Contracts encouraged speed, shortcuts, and careless disregard for safety. Obviously aware of the drawbacks, Frank declined to bid on removal of the drift from the stope.[6]

> Mar 1. Pleasant day again. I worked until noon and will go on again this evening at 5:30. Changing into night shift which is one hour shorter than day shift.

Customarily, two ten-hour shifts worked around the clock. In the case of the Globe Company, night workers were probably allowed an extra hour to travel to and from work. Once underground, the crew mucked out the ore left by the blast of the preceding crew. Then, working in teams, the men hand-drilled the blasting holes. One man held the steel drilling rod while the other rammed it with an eight-pound double jack. After drilling holes in the rock's face, the men cleared the tunnel allowing the blaster room to work.[7]

First, the blaster checked the tunnel for any obstructions that might impede his hasty exit. He then loaded the drill holes with powder-filled paper cartridges, yelled "fire in the hole," lit the fuses, and hurriedly departed. Inserting different lengths of fuse staggered the explosions. The blaster counted the number of blasts from a safe distance and reported the misfired holes to the next shift. The incoming crew repeated the process. A missed hole, which was not easily detected, could contain enough powder to kill six men.[8]

> Mar 2. Clear and pleasant except windy. Called on Mrs. White and daughter. Worked last night and got to bed at 4 AM this morning and slept until 11 AM. Got my hair cut today. Gave Col White book of blank Road Receipts and a list of exceptions or exemptions.

> Mar 3. Clear and most beautiful—Had an easy night of work last night. Rose this morning at 10:30 AM. Recd a letter from Chris Connell. Blacksmith got my candlestick finished and I used it last night cost 1.00.

Frank was probably issued three candles, whose combined burn time would last his ten-hour shift. Two candles were customarily placed in the miner's boot, while the other was inserted in a lantern. Once at his station, Frank would have removed the lighted candle from the lantern and placed it in his wrought-iron holder. With the spiked holder hammered into a crack in the rock, the candle lit the wall to be drilled.[9]

> Mar 4. Windy and threatening storm. Worked last night on the six hundred level and had a tough shift. Recd from Chas. Denhart $10.00 due me for assay furnace. Sent home $50.00. Wrote to Geo Shute to send Head after my colt on river. Paid Mrs. Welsch 10.00 int on note to Feb 22nd '89. Bot a lantern from Kelner for 1.10 cash.

> Mar 5. Windy and cloudy threatening rain—Got very tired last night and the four boils on my arm were very painful, but got through all OK.

> Mar 6. Clear and beautiful this morning. Worked last night in six level shaft. I got some powder smoke and have a bad headache this morning. Called at Mr. White and arranged to go for walk tomorrow after wild flowers.

Diminished concentration due to fumes and fatigue caused many accidents, especially among old timers. Cautious greenhorns fared better than complacent experienced miners. As a part-timer, Frank held a healthy respect for danger as he descended into the mine. Historian Richard Lingenfelter describes how a miner "could be blown to bits in an explosion, drowned in a sump, suffocated and incinerated in a fire, scalded by hot water, crushed by falling rocks or cave-ins, wound up in the machinery, ground under the wheels of an ore car."[10]

Aside from major catastrophes, the mining environment lent itself to other equally dangerous conditions. Extreme temperatures, dust inhalation, and dangerous gases plagued the miners' health. Frank's inhalation of powder smoke would have long term consequences.

<u>Mar 7</u>. Another beautiful morning, clear quiet & warm. Last night Black Jack shot Jas Evans three times and then tried to commit suicide by shooting himself through the head, but only gave himself a bad wound. Evans was shot in left arm which the doctor has amputated and through both legs. He is in a dangerous condition. Was out after flowers today with Mrs. and Miss Ella White and Sadie Ramsdel. Found worlds of flowers and a pleasant time.

John "Black Jack" Newman and Herman Sidow had been partners with businessmen James C. Evans, J. H. Eaton, and W. H. [Idaho Bill] Sutherland in successful mining and milling operations at Pioneer. Newman and Sidow leased their mines to several Mexicans, agreeing to split the mined ore. While the bagged and loaded ore sat overnight ready for shipment, Newman substituted sand-filled bags for the ore bags. Newman received hefty checks for his ore, while the hardworking Mexicans earned nothing. His discouraged employees left, only to be replaced by other unsuspecting workers. Newman's partners quietly witnessed the shady dealings.[11]

Born in Prussia to a Polish mother and a Turkish father, John "Black Jack" Newman immigrated to the United States at age fourteen. Working his way to New York on a steamship, he financed his way to the Pennsylvania coal mines by borrowing five dollars from an uncle. After working a few years as a tram boy, he ventured to the northern Michigan mines.[12]

With a "nose for ore," Newman arrived in Globe in 1883 and hired on with the Old Dominion Mine as a mucker. Unable to spell his difficult Polish name, the timekeeper entered him in the ledger simply as "Jack, the New Man." Due to his dark complexion, he became known as Black Jack, differentiating him from the blond Cornish Jacks. Eventually, he officially changed his name to John B. Newman. Alice Curnow recalled that "Black Jack came to our house and offered Tom three dollars a day for his labor, which Tom refused. I had been watching Black Jack's face which took on the most villainous look and I...begged him to accept anything Black Jack offered as I was afraid of him."[13]

Evans, Eaton, and Sutherland's mines proved worthless and they prepared to abandon them. To exact revenge on behalf of their Mexican employees, they secretly poured sand into bags that, after dark, they loaded onto Sutherland's freight wagon. They knew Newman watched his assets closely and had observed them loading the sand bags. Convinced his partners were siphoning off ore, he contacted Sheriff Reynolds. Reynolds investigated and found only sand. Newman, positive he had been "defrauded out of his share of the community property and the proceeds of the work," filed suit. Justice Atkins found in favor of the defendants saying, "If Evans and Eaton wanted to ship sacks of sand and were

E. F. Kellner (left) and John "Black Jack" Newman. GCHS.

willing to pay for it, it was nobody's business." With that, he ordered Newman to pay court costs. The courtroom erupted in laughter and jeers.[14]

Newman next took matters into his own hands. Frustration at his inability to read legal documents possibly ignited his paranoia and fueled his anger over perceived injustice. The facts gleaned from deposed eyewitnesses present a clear picture of Newman's rampage. About 6:00 P.M. on March 6, James Evans entered A. E. Love's Saloon with several acquaintances and ordered a drink. Shortly after, Newman entered the saloon and walked to the other end of the bar where he ordered wine, never taking his eyes off Evans. Meanwhile, Evans's group moved toward the open doorway. Within minutes, Newman drew a .44-caliber Colt revolver and approached James Evans's backside. Unaware and unarmed, Evans faced the street, joking with friends. The incensed Newman fired his pistol, shattering Evans's arm near the shoulder. The wounded man, holding his mangled arm, ran for his life.

Newman took off in pursuit, firing an errant shot that lodged in a tree on Broad Street. Evans ducked into Hitchcock's Drugstore followed by Newman. Both men emerged seconds later. As Evans stopped to pick up a rock, Newman fired again, this time striking him inside the right thigh. The bullet passed through both limbs, inflicting only flesh wounds, but sending Evans crashing to the ground.

Newman brought his pistol to within a foot of his prone victim's head and fired. Fortunately, Evans jerked his head, resulting in only a grazed scalp.

Alerted by the commotion down the street, Deputy Jerry Ryan pursued the assassin and overtook Newman near Pascoe's corral. The cornered assailant raised his gun to his head and prepared to take his own life. Ryan grabbed Newman's shoulder, deflecting the shot and causing a superficial wound to Newman's left jaw. Newman offered no further resistance and was jailed. Later that evening, Dr. Largent amputated Evans's shattered arm and stitched Newman's lacerated face. Examination of Newman's pistol revealed five empty shells and one unexploded cartridge. Jerry Ryan testified that Newman "fired another shot at himself and I arrested him, took his pistol away."[15]

The day of the deputy's deposition, Frank met with Ryan to arrange transfer of Globe's road business.

Mar 8. Was appointed today or notified of appointment of Jerry Ryan as Road Overseer to succeed myself. Jerry Ryan arranged with me to finish all unfinished business which I will do and then turn everything over to him.

Mar 9. Clear bright and warm. I slept until 12 o'clock AM and am greatly rested. Went to office of Old G Co. and drew my check for 7 ds [days] work amounting to 22.75, less 1.50 doctor dues. I paid same to Mrs. Ramsdel for board with $4.15 cash. Total $25.45 which pays my board to March 1st '89. I drew check for road collections from Co—for employees amounting to 168.00 less 4.00 which must pay back to W. Wenthoff he being under age.

Mar 10. Cloudy and looks as if we might get some showers. Paid Fransisco Maise for 7½ ds labor on roads 15.00. Paid Herman Siddow for 5 ds [days] on Pioneer Road. 32 picks sharpened 20.50. Paid Chas Shintler 16½ days on Pioneer Road—41.25.

Mar 11. Clear and warm. I feel rather bad this morning. Got too much powder smoke last night. Paid Chinaman Charley for washing to date $3.65. Sent brother Charley my April installment on Ins Premium amt 15.57 in P. O. money order. Pd Mrs Anderson for room rent months Jan-Feb 89—6.00. Collected bill against the Stanton School Trustees due Geo E. Shute (one half of which belongs to me) amounting to $10.80.

Mar 12. Cool and a little cloudy— left 4.00 with Wm. Brookner for W. Wenthoff. I figured up Road accts and find I have not enough money to pay up bills to about $12. Geo Hunt arrived in town yesterday. John Newman [Black Jack] had hearing today bound over to appear before grand jury....

The *Silver Belt* also noted that "George W. P. Hunt and W. H. Fisher came in from Wild Rye on Monday. George returns to Globe after a protracted absence at San Diego, Cal."[16]

Frank's off-handed reference to Hunt indicates he viewed the future Arizona governor simply as one of the boys. Was Frank surprised to see Hunt after a two year absence? Leland Hanchett, in his book *Arizona's Graham-Tewksbury Feud*, raises the possibility that Hunt was involved in the killings of Tewksbury and Jacobs by Graham supporters. He bases his assumption on Hunt's undocumented verbal tales and incomplete diary entries at the height of the feud.

Despondent over the decline in Globe mining in 1887, Hunt joined his partner, W. H. Fisher, at their Wild Rye cattle ranch. According to Hanchett, Hunt's diary indicates that in September 1887 he was only twenty-miles away from Tewksbury's ranch, thus allowing him opportunity. Based on Hunt's blank diary pages during mid-September, Hanchett correlates Hunt's sudden departure for Southern California with possible involvement in the Tewksbury and Jacobs killings. Hanchett further surmises that Hunt may have left Gila County to distance himself from suspicion in the killings. Interesting speculation but unsubstantiated.[17]

Upon his return to Globe in the spring of 1889, Hunt resumed his old job as a food hasher at Pascoe's restaurant. A year later his break came. Alonzo Bailey hired Hunt as a sixty-dollar-a-month clerk/delivery boy. Within eleven years, his political gifts surfaced. Hunt managed Bailey's business as president of the Old Dominion Commercial Company. He went on to became mayor of Globe, chairman of Arizona's constitutional convention, ambassador to Siam appointed by Woodrow Wilson, and a friend of the working man. "The poker-faced Hunt was to prove one of the most capable and enduring public men in Arizona history," according to historian Howard Lamar. Hunt championed progressive causes that improved conditions for the disadvantaged and won seven terms as governor.[18]

Mar 13. Beautiful day. Am very sore between my shoulders from shoveling so much.

Mar 14. Raining and the creek is high. Am afraid the river Gila will become unfordable necessitating the closing down of the mine and smelter. Paid Mr. White 5.00 [unreadable] on collection of Road Tax and 2.00 for two tickets in lottery. Bot umbrella for 1.50 cash of A. Bailey. Made out statements of Road business.

Mar 15. Cloudy and rainy—slept until noon. Presented statements of road business to Martin, Clerk of Board of Supervisors. My bill amounting to $165.90. I paid myself from funds in my hands.

Mar 16. cloudy and rainy—I attended St. Patricks ball last night. Had a very pleasant time. Misses Hughs [Hughes], Guild [Gould] and Ghieslin [Giesling] from San Carlos were attending with Mr. [Dan]

*Dan Williamson photographed in his
later years as Arizona State Historian.*
AHS/TUCSON #98259.

Williamson and I took Miss Sadie Ramsdel. Handed Jack Bentons letter to Chas. Martin to present to the board. Turned over to Jerry Ryan
tools belonging to the Road Dist.

Dan Williamson, quartermaster and telegraph operator at San Carlos,
arrived at the St. Patrick's ball accompanied by the young teachers from the
reservation. Both Harry Temple, superintendent at the San Carlos school, and
well-connected Charles Connell had recommended Frank as principal. With
the possibility that the mine would close and potential unemployment looming,
Frank felt uneasy.[19]

Mar 17. Very heavy rain last night and still raining. Worked last night
and expect to have to lay off tonight and probably for some time soon,

as the rivers are up and coke teams cannot cross. Wrote to C. T. Connel today.

Mar 18—cleared off beautifully. Rented one room of my house on hill to Harry Hancock for 2.50 per month. Provided keys for the doors. Attended church last night. Think shall go to work tonight. Capt Bullis is in town. He has bot Old Pioneer Saw Mill in the Pinals and is going to move it above San Carlos.

Mar 19. clear and delightful. Recd letter from Father. Worked last night. Provided keys for house downtown. Some of U. S. Grand and Petty jurors returned from Phoenix last evening.

Mar 20. Clear and warm. No Cal mail last night. Gene Aschleman leaves soon for Phoenix. The hills are getting green and are covered with flowers. I am afraid the mine and smelter will close down for want of coake.

Mar 21. Clear this morning, some rain fell last night. Telegrams last evening report that the Copper Syndicate has collapsed. I fear it will seriously affect us. No Cal papers for two days now. Wrote to Harry Temple, San Carlos.

The *Silver Belt* ominously observed on April 6, "The future of copper seems to solely depend on the pending negotiations between producers and the holders of the enormous stocks of copper accumulated by the syndicate."[20]

Mar 22. Cloudy, windy and threatening today. We expect to get laid off soon on acct of no coake. I rose this day at 12:30 am

Mar 23. Clear and pleasant—Jim Head came in with Bob Anderson with beef for Pringle. Everthing all OK at ranch. One smelter closed down last night. Henry in last night from river left today.

Mar 24. Clear and bright—Ordered of [off] shift last night at ten and on this morning at 7 oclock on day shift now. Worked today at grading for hoisting works. About ten or twelve men laid off today.

Mar 25. Clear and pleasant. Worked same place as yesterday. Am very tired. Letters from Harry Temple, Charley and Bertie.

Mar 26. Clear and pleasant—Same work as yesterday. Wrote to Dr. Goodrich, Wm. Whipley, Geo. Tautan and Henry Ryder. Am very tired again tonight. Was too tired to sleep last night.

Mar 27. Clear and quite warm. Continued grading today for hoisting works. Herman Sulten in from San Carlos. Wrote to brother Charley and Harry Temple of San Carlos.

Mar 28. Clear and quite warm. Smelter closed down for want of coke. Worked at grade today and am quite tired tonight. Temperance society organized last night. I do not intend to join.

Two days later, the *Silver Belt* announced, "Rev. F. W. Downes to preach on 'Evil of Intemperance' Methodist Church—Sun—7:30 pm."[21]

By definition, "temperance" implied moderation in all aspects of life. However, with the establishment of the "temperance movement" the word took on a new meaning: abstinence. Frank's decisive declaration leaves no doubt about how he viewed the movement. To Frank, a few libations and a wager did not constitute immorality. Although his views regarding dancing, drinking, and gambling contradicted the doctrine of his church, his strong commitment to its basic teachings continued. In his self-imposed abstinence, he acknowledged that his children's welfare transcended his own pleasures.[22]

Mar 29. Clear and warm worked at grade. Signed and circulated Chas Connells petition for Treasury Ag [agent?] for Arizona and new mexico.

The following day's edition of the *Silver Belt* noted, "The coke supply at Old Dominion furnaces gave out on Wednesday, necessitating a temporary suspension of smelting. The recent heavy rains have interfered with the teaming between Wilcox and Globe." The effect on Frank was almost immediate.[23]

Mar 30. Some cloudy in morning. Was laid off tonight. Have worked twenty eight shifts this month and check due me $89.50. Have made arrangements to go to the river tomorrow with Mr. Haron and from there to the ranch. Wrote to Father and enclosed PO order for 50.00....

Mar 31. Clear nice morning. Picnic and sermon in Wheat Fields today. Left for the ranch with Mr. Haron with whom I rode to Salt River. Met Geo Shute on road to Globe for lumber. Must wait for his return home to get my horse Kit. Met Jim Head at Henrys he had just arrived from Coon Creek.

Apr 1. Jim and I went up river to Beards Flat looking for a bull of mine. Branded for Geo Shute one yearling. Henry is working on their ditch.

Apr 2. Stopped around Mr. Kentons. McCutcheon arrived. Jim and I took dinner with Mrs. Shute. Henry said he would not furnish a horse for Jim who I think will quit. Geo arrived and Jim and I will start for Coon Creek in morning.

Apr 3. Left for ranch—drove up old Rhony to milk. Found everything all OK.

Apr 4. I went over to Pringles camp to get some horse shoes. No one home. Jim went after horses, but could not find them. We both searched in after-noon but in vain. Branded one steer calf ⑄.

Apr 5. Searched again for band of horses and again in vain. Can't think where they are. Drove down Dry Creek branded:

4 heff	3 str clves	HH [Hammon]
2 "	2 "	H [Pringle]
4 "	5 "	⊕ [Middleton]

Jim went after Pringles men to come over tomorrow.

Apr 6. Pringles men Rob Anderson and Ed Tewksbury came over and we worked Salt river divide and high mesa. Branded:

3 heff	1 str calf	HH
4 heff	1str calf	⊕
23 clves		H
1 heff clf		WF
1 Str clf		XꞀ

Ed Tewksbury's outward demeanor indicated that the Pleasant Valley feud was behind him. Charges had been dropped against all adversaries, and most participants had either died or disappeared. Tom Graham had escaped to Tempe to become a well-respected farmer and family man. Just the same, he retained title to his Pleasant Valley properties with intentions of someday returning.

For the next three years, Ed Tewksbury would cover the range driving and branding cattle for Robert Pringle and George Newton. Elected constable in 1890, he became a commanding presence in Globe. Beneath his composed facade seethed continuing hatred for Tom Graham. The feeling was mutual. For all practical purposes, the vendetta had ended, but venomous anger simmered within both men.[24]

In April 1892, Globe jeweler and Tewksbury mentor George Newton mysteriously disappeared at the Salt River. Tewksbury suspected Graham and his bodyguard, Charley Duchet, of foul play. Anonymous, threatening letters postmarked Tempe supposedly incited Tewksbury's animosity. On August 2, Tewksbury and his brother-in-law, John Rhodes, ambushed Tom Graham on a dusty Tempe road. Hours later Graham died, surrounded by his wife, four-year-old daughter, and friends.

On his deathbed, Tom Graham identified his killer—Ed Tewksbury. Eyewitnesses also identified Tewksbury and implicated John Rhodes as his accomplice. Rhodes's preliminary hearing in Maricopa County erupted in an emotional drama. Graham's widow, Annie, entered the courtroom with her husband's revolver concealed in her purse under a shawl. At an opportune moment, she pressed forward within inches of the defendant, drew the weapon, and fired. As fate would have it, her shawl caught between the pin and the bullet, causing the gun to misfire. The distraught widow was quickly subdued and ushered from the disrupted proceedings.

To the consternation of Tempe residents, Rhodes's friends supplied him with an ironclad alibi, he was not charged in Graham's death. After a change of venue from Maricopa County, a Tucson jury convicted Ed Tewksbury of Tom Graham's murder. The verdict was overturned on a technicality, and a second trial ended with a deadlocked jury. Almost four years after Tom Graham's murder, a frustrated court dismissed charges. Ed Tewksbury returned to Globe, married, and served as Gila County constable.[25]

Apr 7. Worked Dry and Chalk Creek Canyons and high mesa. Branded:

1 str calf	⊕
9 str calves—10 heffs	Ⱶ
1 " "	Ⱪ [Pringle]

Apr 8. Worked head of Dry and Coon Creeks branded:

2 heffs	1 str calf	Ⱨ
1 "	1 Bull—1 Steer calf	⊕
1	heiffer Yer	Ƶ

Pringle and McCutcheon came from Globe.

Apr 9. Worked on Cherry Creek branded:

1 heiffer calf	Ⱨ
58 Calves	Ⱶ

Rained some today. Jim Head quit work for us today and starts in for Vosberg.

Apr 10. Went up and found our band of horses on range. Caught Charley to take to town. Got kicked by Henrys mare Mary on the ankle. Quite seriously. Am afraid the bone is broken or fractured. Rained some today.

Apr 11. Cloudy and threatening—Went to Salt River and returned Georges black horse. My leg is much improved but cannot get my boot on yet.

Meanwhile, the *Silver Belt* announced that "Sheriff Reynolds left for the rural districts, on Thursday, as bearer of invitations to citizens of the United States to appear in Globe on the 17th to answer touching their qualifications as grand jurors.[26]

Apr 12. Cloudy—Got my boot on this morning and rode to Globe. I am drawn on Grand Jury for 17th inst.

Apr 13. Clear and nice. Drew my check due from Old Globe Co. of 89.50. Paid Mrs. Ramsdel for board to yesterday amt $31.00. Traded to John Jones my horse Charley for a brown pony branded NA on right thigh and $25.00, he paying me 20.00 and still due $5.00. Loaned my new pony to Tom Lonergan to ride to Redmans ranch.

Apr 14. Clear and delightful. Wrote to Mr. Kelly and brother Glenn. Attended Sunday School and called on Mr. and Mrs. Fox in evening.

Apr 15. Clear and quite warm—Collected bal due from John Jones on horse trade of 5ᵗʰ and paid same out very foolishly I think. Called at Mrs.Whites this afternoon. Job Atkins and I as committee for O. O. H. paid Mrs. Anderson for bal. due for hall rent amounting to $66.65. Tom Lonergan left with Joe Redman for Redmans Ranch in mountains, will return my horse as soon as possible.

Apr. 16. Clear and warm—Judge Porter arrived this evening and court will open in the morning. Judge Campbell also came.

Apr. 17. Clear and warm. Court opened. Found indictments against John Newman for attempt to commit murder and against Ed Price for burglary. Grand jury nearly through.

Apr 18. Clear and warm. Petty [petit] jury are arriving from outside. Grand jury adjourned so I am through with court and could leave were my horse here. Attended surprise birthday for Sadie Ramsdel at Mrs. Vans this evening. Had a grand time, gave Sadie a toilet set.

Apr 19. Clear and warm. John Newman found guilty on trial today, as charged in indictment. He had no defense and only pled insanity which was too thin.

John Newman, in his deposition on April 9, testified that James E. Evans had several times threatened his life and that he believed himself in danger. Without witnesses to verify the threats, insanity became his only defense.[27]

Apr 20. Clear and warm. Ed Price found guilty today as indicted and sentenced to 1 year in Yuma. John Newman 10 years in Yuma. Court Adjourned.

On April 25, John Newman entered Yuma Territorial Prison to serve his ten-year sentence. In operation since 1875, the "hell-hole" was located on a hill in view of the Colorado and Gila rivers. It is doubtful that Newman ever noticed the scenery. He joined his fellow inmates in steel-gated cells forged from a solid rock hill. Prisoners labored in temperatures exceeding 120 degrees in the summer and were subjected to hard labor until overcome by heat prostration. During winter, a single blanket and a scant straw mattress placed on a wooden bunk afforded minimal protection from below freezing temperatures. Disobedient convicts, unshackled in the "snake den," were placed in ten-by-ten foot cells without the barest of necessities. Often fifteen inmates shared a single dank, dark cell. Solitary confinement meant communal isolation.[28]

Overcrowded conditions, poor ventilation, vermin infestation, and foul water spawned epidemics of pneumonia and tuberculosis. Many inmates arrived from other prisons, already suffering from the dread lung disease and infecting others. In the early years, "the sick were merely kept in one of the corridors running through the main cell block." Eventually, a fully stocked infirmary carved from a hillside administered treatment to the ailing.[29]

In 1887, Governor Zulick outlined a system for reforming the prison and making it self-supporting. Idle inmates fired bricks, cut wood, crushed rock, sewed clothes and farmed vegetables. A chapel, schoolroom, and small library hollowed out of a hill, also provided constructive leisure activities. John Newman survived his incarceration.[30]

Following his early release, Newman enlisted in Governor Myron McCord's First Territorial Regiment during the Spanish-American War. Returning to Globe without seeing active service, he invested his accumulated soldier's pay in mining properties, which he later sold for a profit. One Sunday, Newman accompanied developers on an inspection tour of the Inspiration Mine. As his companions surveyed the surrounding land, Newman paused, dismounted, and walked the area. Without saying a word, he rejoined the group. His fellow capitalists had discounted the property as worthless. The next morning, Newman filed thirteen claims on 260 acres the group had rejected. He called his cluster of claims the Oates-Newman Group.[31]

In 1907, he sold the properties to the Lewisohns of New York for $180,000 in cash and $330,000 of stock in the company. At the time he left Globe in 1910, Newman's real estate holdings included the Dominion and Pioneer hotels, the Miner's Hall, and several office buildings.[32]

Settling in Los Angeles, Newman saw to it that his children received the education he lacked. They attended private schools, while their father invested in oil, ranches, and real estate. Newman died in Santa Monica, California in 1928, leaving a $12 million estate to his wife and four children. Globe's illiterate immigrant, the ultimate survivor, achieved the American dream.[33]

Apr 21. Clear and warm—Bot from Mrs. R. Gill bill of provisions for ranch and sent same to the river by Tomps Naiderffer. Amt of bill $8.60. I paid on said bill $3.55 and had charged to Henry bal of $5.05. I also bought powder and shot from Bailey and Westmeyer amting to $1.50 for which I paid. Making amt for which I paid and amt Chgd. to Henry the same viz $5.05.

Apr 22. Quite warm—Nothing to do and cannot leave as my horse has not returned yet and it is so very tiresome laying around town. Geo Rogginstroh is in town.

Apr 23. Still quite warm. Geo Shute came in today and left in evening. Oh, I am so tired of loafing around town. Hyman Sultan is going to leave town next Monday for good. A party will be given him next Thursday evening at the rink. Have accepted invite for card party at Mrs. Thompsons tomorrow evening. Will take Mamie and Lizzy Kennedy.

Apr 24. Warm day—Left my jury certificate for two days time and 30 miles travel with Martin for presentation at meeting of board. Wrote to sister Dell. Tom Lonergan returned with my horse and I may either go to the ranch or San Carlos the day after tomorrow.

Apr 25. Very warm—Attended Mrs Thompsons party with Mamie and Lizzie last night. Had a pleasant time. Asked Sadie Ramsdel to go to the picnic with me on May 1st. Will go to San Carlos tomorrow.

Apr 26. Very hot day—Attended dance last night with Miss Ella White. Given as a farewell to Hyman Sultan. Had a very pleasant time. Went to San Carlos arrived at 4 P.M.

Apr 27. Hot and windy—Everything quiet at San C. Saw all the boys that are left, several are gone and many are to leave. Harry Temple and Ed Arhleger among them. Took supper with the Agency mess.

The military presence at San Carlos had been reduced after Geronimo's capture. But Frank remained friendly with the soldiers still stationed there. Supper conversation in the mess hall probably centered around the "Captain Jack decision" handed down two weeks before by the U.S. Supreme Court.

The case involved a popular Apache convicted of murder in the federal court at Globe and serving a thirty-year sentence in an Ohio penitentiary. The Indian Rights Association adopted Captain Jack's case to test the 1885 Major Crimes Act, which gave "jurisdiction to territorial courts for the prosecution of murder and six other major crimes committed by Indians on or off reservations." The association filed a writ of habeas corpus with the U. S. Supreme Court. The ruling on April 15, 1889, impacted all Apaches convicted under federal laws and incarcerated in federal prisons. It stated that the Second Federal District Court at Globe had acted outside its jurisdiction in convicting Apaches accused of capital crimes. Among others, the ruling nullified Nah-deiz-az's sentence for killing Lieutenant Mott. On May 24, Lieut. B. C. Lockwood of the 22nd Infantry, arrived at Willcox from Columbus, Ohio, with ten Indians released from the Ohio penitentiary and destined for the San Carlos reservation. Soldiers at San Carlos and Gila County residents were outraged. Legal minds began preparing to retry the Indians in territorial court.[34]

Apr 28. Hot and very windy and dusty. Rob Montgomery is on a tear and the way he is carrying on gambling and drinking he surely cannot hold his appointment long.

Frank's disgust with Montgomery's conduct was out of character. Frank couldn't help but feel frustration with the inappropriate behavior of government employees at the San Carlos agency. Similar accusations had surfaced during Captain Bullis's tenure as Indian agent.[35]

Apr 29. Windy again and very dusty. I fear the chance to sell beef here is very slim. Had a talk with Mr. Chapel—He will sell out to whoever gets a license. Montgomery I cannot get to see. McGinnis arrived from Thomas.

Apr 30. Much cooler and not much wind—Saw Mr. McGinnis cannot sell him beef. No Employment at San Carlos at present. Left for Globe arrived at 2:00 PM.

Chapter Twenty

Everything All OK

It haunted me that other western children grew up working on ranches alongside their widower fathers. Why not Frank's? I speculated how different my grandmother's life would have been had she been raised in Arizona. I remembered her piercing blue eyes offset by voluminous dark hair, her square refined jaw line, and her frail health. Throughout her life, Eva required medical attention unavailable in Arizona. I resolved in my own mind the necessity for Frank's separation from his children.

Frank and fifteen-year-old Sadie Ramsdel joined the migration of young people to the Wheatfields for a day of picnicking and games. In the shade of the cottonwoods, swings suspended from tree limbs swayed lazily with small occupants; archery and horseshoe contests entertained the gents; couples rhythmically rowed boats across the calm lake. But disturbing news interrupted the delightful outing.[1]

> May 1. Beautiful day. Started for picnic at 8 AM. A large party. We had a delightful time. Arrived home at 7 PM. Henry sent me word to come out immediately and bring ammunition to the ranch as the indians had run our man off and took possession of the ranch. Will start in the morning.

Chief Lu-pe's band of White Mountain Apaches had returned to their old haunts. For generations they had hunted and worked the land between Coon and Cherry creeks. Seventy men, women, and children overran Bob Pringle's spread and continued on to Coon Creek ranch. Frank's terrified hired hand abandoned the property, leaving the Apaches to continue their "extended drunk which was continued throughout the night after their arrival." By morning, the desperate Apaches commenced tilling the soil and planting crops. Anticipating the ranchers' armed response, Captain Bullis ordered Lieutenant Lewis Johnson from Fort Apache to intervene before bloodshed triggered an uprising.[2]

> May 2. Started for the ranch via the river. Met some of the round-up crowd driving from the river. They said the indian scare did not amount to much, called over the rodeo crowd at Beards.

> May 3. Stayed with Henry last night, and went with Geo today and helped him work his range north of the Salt River. We drove to Mrs. Medlers corral and branded. Henry's wife with Mrs. Howard Livingston and Mrs. Willet went to town today.

> May 4. Stayed with Henry last night, left for ranch arriving early. Everything all OK. Looked for horses bal of day. Found all but Kit, Dead Eye and Grey filly. Got up old Rhony to milk.

> May 5. Found Kit and Dead Eye on River. Branded Rhonys calf. Saw a calf with worms in its brand. Went up to Shutes Spring and found George and Walter there working.

> May 6. Worked from river up to correl branding nearly thirty calves.

> May 7. Worked from river again, and on returning to camp found McMillan outfit arrived.

The Indian scare was the first of several contentious moments Frank experienced that summer. In Globe, children playing with matches torched Frank's vacant house on the hill, reducing it to ashes.[3]

May 8. Moved to Redmans flat on the river. We worked down the washes to the river. Found in camp outfit from below. Got news of my house burning in town.

Seemingly undaunted by the news of his damaged house, Frank continued with the roundup—or more aptly, the hunt. At daybreak the wrangler rounded up the horses and confined them inside a rope corral. After a breakfast of strong coffee, fried beef, biscuits, and gravy, each man roped his own mount and saddled-up.

Customarily, the cowboys scattered to prearranged locations, turned around at a designated spot, and herded all cattle back to a centrally located corral. Undulating, unfenced ranges covered with mesquite thickets offered cover for a stubborn cow and her calf. More times than not, the pair needed coaxing to be driven to the enclosure. Once hemmed in, all unmarked animals were skillfully cut away from the herd, "bulldogged" to the ground, and their hide seared with a scorching iron.[4]

May 9. Moved camp to Coon Creek. Drove over all our brand which we found. Worked the breaks and Dry Creek…Vented two Ħ heiffer close to Ħ Pringle mistake in branding due to one of them being a Ҝ which brand Pringle has bot.

May 10. Worked bal of range…Crowd moved to Cherry Creek. I turned over to Jim Head two 3 year old steers in full payment for my share of his wages, one of said steers he killed while working for us.

Once the cow and calf were corralled, cutting out a calf required teamwork between cowboy and pony. Anticipating the twisting, turning motions of a frightened calf meant the difference between success and failure. With the gentle pressure of the rider's knees signaling directions, a well-trained pony could turn on a dime, keeping the gyrating calf in check. In Frank's case, his success in capturing a calf depended largely upon his skill with a lariat. His eye-hand coordination and agility, coupled with his pony's ability to become "ground-hitched" (stand firm with the reins down), guaranteed a quick tie-up. Savvy calves learned to avoid the rope once missed.[5]

As the coiled lasso snared the calf's neck or foreleg, Frank and his horse needed to react simultaneously. With the lariat attached to the saddle horn, his pony stopped short, jerking the rope taut. Jumping from his mount, Frank had to "bulldog" the calf to the ground, hobbling the forelegs with a length of rope. Once secured, the pony could slacken the taut rope. Then the branding began. Later, the calves were turned out on the range.[6]

It took five or six cowboys to brand the calf. Several flanked him, while one branded him with a searing iron. Others tended the fire and packed the various irons. The more experienced cowboys managed the herd. A knowledgeable student of the range noted "when an animal broke away a cowboy would take after it, trying to circle around it and so steer it back into the herd." By day's end the tired crew welcomed the sight of the chuck wagon, the campfire, and a good night's sleep.[7]

> May 11. Went to Pringles and borrowed harness and Veach and I hawled up and stacked the hay after which we took harness home and while there ground axe. Pendleton went to town in response to a telegram to come to Flagstaff to survey out R. R. line. Pringle drove beef steers to town.

Optimism soared when Dennis Riordan wired Alex Pendleton to come survey a new Mineral Belt route. Pendleton eventually found a way down the Mogollon Rim into the Tonto Basin without tunneling through the rock wall. Unable to abandon his dream, Colonel Eddy resurfaced to advance a new scheme, but Hinckley and Riordan rejected his terms. To avoid litigation, Hinkley agreed to binding arbitration in July 1889. Two years later, the arbitrators found no liability. Hinckley and Riordan proceeded with their plans. Riordan proposed tying in with the Sonora Railway and the Utah Central to connect central Arizona with Salt Lake City. Without financing, the project never materialized. In the end, a portion of the completed track transported Riordan's logs to his Flagstaff lumber mill. A year later, in 1890, the Santa Fe, Prescott and Phoenix Railroad bought and removed the remaining twenty-five miles of rails. Today, the only reminder of the Mineral Belt Railroad is a terminus tunnel to obscurity.[8]

> May 12. I went up to Oak springs and got my Grey filly and put her with our band of horses. Drove all down to house and secured all. My bay colt bucked saddle off.

> May 13. Turned out all horses but Henrys two mares and colts. Brought them down to him. Found Geo quite sick. Old lawyer Griff passed.

> May 14. Geo felt better and we harnessed up and came to town. Found house burned otherwise nothing new.

> May 15. Very windy—Geo and I took dry washer or gold seperator out and tried it. Dont yet know results. We will go out and try it for a few days, if we succeed I am to get miners wages.

> May 16. Went out with Geo to Gold Gulch and Mr. Allison and old Mr. Middleton along. We took out about 3.00. Yesterday about 1.00. The ground is not very rich.

> May 17. George and I worked alone and very faithfully today. We took out what we estimated at about 5.00.

> May 18. Gene Middleton came out this morning. We prospected several gulches but none of them paned out much. We took out about 1.00. I concluded that I could not get even small wages out. I came to town.

May 19. Very warm. I paid Tom Pascoe in full to date for my correll bill amting to 7.00. Paid to C. T. Martin $5.00 over charge in my bill as Road Overseer of Globe road dist, and disallowed by Board of Supervisors. Attended Sunday school + church. Geo and Mr. Middleton came in today. They did pretty well today.

May 20. Warm day. Stopped around town which is very dull and hard to put in the time. Charley wrote me that he would forward my application for an Indian Tradership at San Carlos to the Comm. of Indian Affairs today.

May 21. Very warm day. Therm. registered in the coolest place 90 deg. Spent foolishly 2.00. I find that I drew a 5.00 prize in the La [Louisiana] lottery.

May 22. I sent away to the Louisiana or New Orleans Nal Bank for collection my ticket of No. 59616 which drew 5.00 prize—for collection. Wrote to Mark A. Smith for his support in getting appointment of Indian Trader at San Carlos. Asked Judge Hackney and Alonzo Bailey to write him in my favor.

May 23. Warm day. Nothing important today. No employment yet. Called on Miss Ella White in evening.

May 24. Very warm, cool evening. Wrote to Chas Connel to write to Mr. Safely in the interest of my appointment as Indian Trader. I think he will do it. Mr. Bailey and Judge Hackney told me that they had written Mark A. Smith in my favor. Chas Fisk returned from Tonto tonight. Called on Miss Mamie Kennedy.

May 25. Saw Chas Fisk and he said he would write to his father asking his father to use his influence in my favor.

Globe banker Charles A. Fisk was well connected in the east through his politically savvy father, General Clinton Fisk. Six years earlier, San Carlos agent P. P. Wilcox had accused the younger Fisk of being part of a sinister syndicate "that pretended to purchase the coal lands on the reservation for the payment of forty dollars per head to fourteen ignorant and deceived Indian chiefs." In a letter to Secretary of the Interior H. M. Teller, General Crook endorsed Wilcox's claim. Although General Fisk's endorsement would have been impressive, it is unknown whether he supported Frank's appointment.[9]

Obviously, Frank felt the recommendation of Territorial Delegate Mark A. Smith carried great weight. The highly regarded politician mesmerized Arizonans with his statesmanship and oratory. He visited each county, attended dinners, gave speeches, and called "notable residents his dear friends." With Smith's persuasive rhetoric and colorful style, Frank felt he had an advantage. In reality, Smith's two-year non-voting term in the U. S. House of Representatives was a thankless position carrying little political clout. Because the position of Indian trader was a presidential appointment, it is doubtful that Democrat Smith's endorsement of Frank would have impressed Republican president Benjamin Harrison.[10]

May 26. Very warm. I borrowed a mule from Mr. Middleton. Got Will Spence's pony to go and hunt him. Hunted through Russell's Gulch but could not find him.

May 27. Geo Rogginstroh came in last evening. I got his horse to again hunt the mule and found him at the mouth of Russells Gulch. Will go out with Geo R in the morning.

May 28. Geo R. and I left for his ranch at Horse Shoe Bend. And on the way looked his band of horses up with a view of making a horse trade. After arriving at his house we made the trade. He to get my horse Kit and I a bay mare five years old, bald face branded Tom Curnows brand, also XT and vent. Also I branded right thigh HH. Also a two year old colt in next Aug. black with Tom Curnows brand and XT, wither vented and my brand not on yet. Agreed that Rogginstroh to cut colt and to take chances. Should he die, he to return my horse and I to him his mare.

May 29. Left for Coon Creek Ranch taking the mare along. John Cook, Geo hired man going along. John and I drove in our horses and I turned over to Geo R. my horse Kit.

May 30. Geo R., John Cook and I started out to find black colt which we did. He being at Redmans old ranch at Salt River. He was very bronco. We roped him and took him home to Coon Creek. Agreed to let him run as a stud until next fall or spring. Geo. R then castrate him and take chances on as agreed yesterday.

May 31. Went up to find our band of horses, but made a failure. Caught and branded a calf for Geo. R. Geo and John left for home. I irrigated alfalfa.

Jun 1. I went up to Oak Spring and found our horses. Drove them down to ranch and tied up Middletons mule and my mule Jack. Turned out with the band the mare and her 2 year old colt which I just got from Rogginstroh. Gathered some mulberries to take to town, and got ready to start tomorrow.

Jun 2. Started for Globe riding Mr. John Jones pony and driving Middletons two mules and my mule Jack. Caught some fish as I passed the river and put on pack. Arrived at Globe about 5:30 PM. Delivered to Gene Middleton my mule and he to pay me for same $50.00. Attended church. Subscribed $2.00 toward the church.

Jun 3. Gave Mrs Van Wagenen mulberries I brought from ranch. Sent some fish to Alonzo Bailey, Chas Taylor, Will Spense, Mrs. Ramsdel and others. Recd from W. House rent to apply on house rent 10.00. He rented my house on May 1st at $8.00 per month. Sent home $30.00. Borrowed from Wm. Brookner 5.00. Attended birthday party at Shanleys—Mollys birthday.

Jun 4. Bot from Mrs Gill for ranch and had it charged to Henry Middleton: 50 lbs flour 2.65, matches .25, lard 1.00, rice .50, coffee 1.00, sugar 1.50— total 6.90. Bot from Bailey and charged to myself: maple syrup 1.20, maple sugar .50, 25 lbs salt 1.25, beans 1.25, candles 1.50, dried fruit 1.00, yeast powder 1.20, bacon 1.00, rope .50, horse shoe nails .75, tea .50—total 9.95. Sent to Salt River by Chas Baquet to be left at Kentons, also sent blankets and Henrys pack saddle and will go down tomorrow on way to ranches. Sold today to N. H. Price my shot gun for 3000 lbs of barley hay to be delivered to me at Globe in Chas Taylor stable. A part now and a part after while.

Jun 5. Left on horseback for Salt River on way to our ranch about ten oclock arrived early in the evening. Stopped at Henrys. Will go to ranch tomorrow. Henrys cows got away with the calves and we think have gone to Coon Creek.

Jun 6. Left for Coon Creek after a horse to pack provisions on. Hunted all the afternoon and around Oak Springs. Could not find the band. Came to ranch without them. Found Geo Shutes grey horse at ranch and will take him tomorrow to the river after the pack.

Jun 7. Left for river. Sent Henry who has come over for his cows, but we cannot find them. So we drove down his white cow with four mos. calf. In afternoon I helped Henry hawl in and stack three loads of hay.

Jun 8. Left with pack for ranch, rode Geos grey and packed my pony— arrived all okay. Got up old Rhony to milk.

Jun 9. Mr. Veach our hired man and I went over to Cherry Creek to look at our wagon. He stayed and repaired it and I went after horses to hawl it home which we did in afternoon. Henry came over today. I worked with Old Kate. My new mare Kelty, which I got from Rogginstroh, had to work or break her.

Jun 10. I helped Henry drive two milk cows as far as divide on the way to Salt River. Then returned and Veach and I hawled up poles and posts for corral balance of day. Old Kate backed on us and we had a bad time.

Jun 11. The old man Veach and I hawled up posts and poles all day. Peaches are getting ripe and figs. Mulberries are nearly gone.

Jun 12. Hawled poles and posts and finished today and turned out the mares. We dug one half of post holes today.

Jun 13. I went up to Stallos ranch and borrowed Frenchys auger to bore holes for the bars to the correl. Veach went after some ash timber from which to make pins and when he returned he dug the bal of post holes.

Jun 14. We set posts and laid up part of the poles.

Jun 15. Neerly finished the correll. I left the old man to finish and went down to the river to get Henry to help me to gather up some beef steers and drive to town, but he could not leave.

Jun 16. I returned to the ranch and went on over to Rogginstrohs and he agreed to help me. I traded to John Cook old man Veachs burros for a three year old pony. John to bring pony to Coon Creek tomorrow and get burros.

Jun 17. I stayed with Rogg last night and today went to Coon Creek and correlled a couple of beef steers. Went up after horses found them at Oak Springs and drove them home. Old Kate had worms in wound—her front leg. Kept her up and Charley and Kitty to ride.

Jun 18. Gathered eight steers making ten in all and drove to river correlled at Redmans old ranch. Lost two on way down—leaving eight—4 two year olds and four yearlings. Bob Anderson, Pringles man, came over and said he had a bunch gathered and was going to drive to town tomorrow and we agreed to drive together.

Jun 19. Anderson arrived at Redmans with his bunch about nine oclock and we drove to the Wheat Fields correlling at Pringles. Rogginstroh left for home before noon or about.

Jun 20. We drove to Globe arriving early in afternoon. I think my calves will arrange 400 or over—my yearlings 265. Found in P. O. letter from Mark A. Smith to Comm. Indian Affairs in my favor. Also three letters from home. One from New Orleans enclosing $5.00 which I cashed and paid Wm. Brookner for money borrowed. Wrote to Comm. I. A. enclosing letter from Mark A. Smith.

Jun 21. Helped Gene Middleton to make a wagon shed. He has bot out Tompsons int in stage line.

The *Silver Belt* noted on June 21 that "Eugene Middleton, proprietor, informs us that he will make no change in the schedule, but that buckboards will be run daily between Globe and Riverside."[11]

Jun 22. Wrote to J. H. W. Jensen—Phoenix, also Mark A. Smith, Tombstone. Also sister Bertie and daughters Alberta and Eva and my little boy Milton. Also to brother Charley sent enclosed P.O. order for $15.60 to pay my insurance premium due July 1st '89. I borrowed from F. W. Westmeyer for above purpose $16.00 and agreed to pay same on July 10th '89. Gave Mrs. Ramsdel an order on R. Pringle for $28 in full for board to June 24 '89.

Jun 23. Started for Coon Creek with Wm. Spense and [Mr.] Shirley Neffe. Stopped at Salt River and caught a good mess of fish. Found all okay at ranch. Figs ripe, early peaches gone.

Jun 24. Mr. Veach and I went after our horses. Found them scattered among the band at Oak Springs got them together and drove them down. I kept up my unbroken three year old colt and will try and break him and ride him to town. Kept up Middletons old mule also to take in to him. Spense has been sick all day and will go back to town tomorrow. When coming down with the horses today we met Jack mule that I sold to Gene Middleton. Will have the boys take him to town.

Jun 25. Spense and Shirley left for Globe this morning. Veach and I hawled up poles for stable. Used Middletons old mule. I rode my colt around the field and he did not offer to pitch. Bob Anderson came over to borrow wagon. Will come after it tomorrow. Spence left his old pony here. I turned him out with horses.

Jun 26. We shod my colt and had a great time doing it, and in afternoon I tried to ride him but he bucked me off among the rocks and bruised me up some but I got on him again and rode him several miles. Bob Anderson came and got wagon to hawl hay.

Jun 27. We partially built shed for stable and in afternoon rode my colt to river and back—he is getting quite gentle. Bob brot our wagon home and said he was going to kill a beef and to come over and get a piece in the morning.

Jun 28. Went over to Pringles and got some meat. Finished stable and manger.

Jun 29. Went up and drove down horses. Turned out extra horses and old mule as I shall ride my colt to town tomorrow and cannot take him.

Jun 30. Went to Globe, rode my colt which went all right. Attended church in evening. Took in a few figs.

Jul 1. Globe very dull, recd letter from bro Chas and J. H. W. Jennings [Jensen]. Wrote to Jennings [sic] and recd from Ugene Middleton in payment for mule Jack and days work $42.50....

Jul 2. Wrote home to father and mother sent them check on New York, E. F. Kelner Co. for $40.00. The hottest day of the season this far 98 [degrees]. Am riding my colt everyday and he is getting quite gentle. Exchanged my check with E. F. Kilner Co for $2.50 cash and a New York check for $40.00 which I enclosed in my letter home. Called on Miss Annie Pascoe.

Jul 3. Very hot and some indications of rain. Have agreed to act as starter in the horse races tomorrow and one of the timekeepers in the steer tying contests.

At sunrise, a giant explosion of powder inaugurated Globe's Fourth of July celebration. By half-past eight, the horse races and steer tying began at the ball grounds. The stifling heat, tempered by a stiff breeze, generated thirsts satisfied by cool beer and soda water. While the San Carlos string band performed, men placed their wagers on the day's contests.[12]

As official starter of the quarter-mile race, Frank stood at the starting line across from the flagman holding the white flag. The riders trotted their horses back forty yards from the starting line, then turned them to face the starter. With a controlled gallop, they attempted to hit the starting line simultaneously. When satisfied of a fair race, Frank yelled "Go" and the flag dropped. Nervous mounts often took twenty minutes for a clean start. The two judges at the finish line started their watches with the dropped flags, and the crowd cheered on their favorites.[13]

Jul 4. Our national anniversary of national freedom. Horse races and steer tying a success. Time—throwing and tying a steer—first prize 58 seconds. Second 1:13. Amusing excercises in the afternoon and a grand ball in the afternoon or rather evening. Everything passed off well. I acted as a special Dep. Sheriff. Borrowed $1.00 from Wm. Brookner and $2.00 from D. Heron which I will pay tomorrow.

According to the *Silver Belt*, "Tom Horn won first money, in the fast time of 58 seconds. His dexterity was much admired…. Timers—A. L. Walker, W. W. Brookner, Frank Hammon…. Messrs. W. T. McNelly, E. H. Cook, Glenn Reynolds, T. A. Pascoe and James Woods composing the committee…deserve thanks for their successful management of affairs."[14]

Tom Horn's performance in Globe did not compare to the world record of forty-nine and one-half seconds he set against formidable "Arizona Charlie" Meadows in Phoenix two years later. Horn should have continued roping steers. Instead, his early exposure to brutality prepared him for a more violent profession. Known to embroider the truth, Tom Horn opened the door to speculation when he penned his autobiography. Independent sources offer conflicting viewpoints that paint a blurred picture of his life and the events preceding his demise.[15]

According to Doyce B. Nunis's *The Life of Tom Horn Revisited*, teenager Horn left his Missouri home after a row with his uncompromising father. Tom worked his way west as a railroad construction hand, livestock drover, silver miner, and stage driver. Along the way he mastered Spanish, lariats, horses, and guns. Recruited by the Overland Mail Company to drive replacement mules to Arizona, Horn found new employment with the U. S. Army at Camp Verde. He caught Al Sieber's attention in Prescott, where he was hired as a lowly "scrub-packer." During the winter of 1881-1882, Horn lived among peaceful Apaches, absorbing their language and customs. His linguistic skills proved to be a valuable asset during

General Crook's 1883 Sierra Madre expedition, as Horn and seventy-six other packers trailed the troops tracking Geronimo and his followers into Mexico. In Crook's 1885 campaign, Horn served as a scout during an unfortunate encounter with Mexican troops in which Capt. Emmet Crawford was mistakenly killed and Horn slightly wounded.[16]

In Sieber's absence, Horn took over as chief of scouts under Gen. Nelson Miles. Horn translated as Lt. Gatewood negotiated Geronimo's surrender. Tom Horn's rendition of the campaign, in which he claims responsibility for Geronimo's final surrender to Miles, clashes with reality. Although commended for his contributions, he played an insignificant role. Gen. Leonard Wood's biographer describes Horn as "a pleasant, adventurous soul with the gift of convincing himself that he was the sole hero of every episode in which he figured."[17]

Unemployed after Geronimo's extradition to Florida and the military downsize, Horn turned to his Aravapai mine and odd ranch jobs. In the late 1880s, his involvement with the Tewksburys during the Pleasant Valley feud, occasional deputy stints, and cowboy jobs provided an impressive resume for future employment. By the 1890s, Horn had moved on to work as a Denver Pinkerton agent and range detective.[18]

Holding impressive credentials and riding under an assumed name, Horn became an undercover assassin for large Wyoming cattle companies. Infiltrating the rustlers' inner circle, he systematically exterminated gang members, charging $600 per hit. He crowed, "If I undertake the job, *No cure no pay* is my mottoe." After each killing, Horn retreated to a Denver bar for an extended binge and an occasional altercation. His quiet, soft-spoken demeanor switched to garrulous bragging when inebriated. After a few whiskeys, he referred to himself as "an exterminatin' son-of-a-bitch." Well-schooled in the art of liquidation, he rightfully tooted his own horn: "I stopped cow stealing…in one summer."[19]

After a brief stint of packing mules during the Spanish American War, Horn returned to Wyoming to work as a range detective for wealthy cattlemen John Coble and Frank Bosler. Coble and Horn's relationship evolved from employer to confidant. The hired gunman mesmerized Easterner Coble and his associates with storytelling, charisma, and western ways. Horn revered aristocrat Coble's life of luxury, his ranch, and his influential contacts.[20]

At this point the tale becomes murky. Supposedly, Coble's prominent friends had hoped their feuding neighbors Kels Nickells and James Miller would exterminate each other. This would leave the quarrelers' coveted farmland available for incorporation and eliminate suspected rustling. Coble himself had argued with both men over missing cattle. Hired as a range detective, amiable Horn covertly scoped Coble's lands while cultivating the settlers' confidence. Allegedly, Horn formulated a plan to earn his pay.[21]

At dawn on July 18, 1901, Horn had his opportunity. Behind hillside rocks, he watched a familiar figure in a yellow slicker dismount from his horse to open a cattle gate. Thinking it was Kels Nickell, Horn allegedly aimed and fired two or three shots. The figure stumbled toward his house and fell facedown on the rocky road. The barefoot killer crossed the gravel to inspect his grizzly work. As he turned over the body he discovered Kels' thirteen-year-old son, Willie. He opened the boy's shirt, placed a rock under his head, and disappeared into the mist. Two weeks later, an ambusher seriously wounded Kels Nickell.[22]

Tom Horn and James Miller became prime suspects in the killing. A $1,000 dollar reward for the conviction of the boy's slayer brought easygoing U. S. Marshal Joe LeFors into the picture. He knew of Tom Horn's reputation. Working undercover, LeFors met Horn in a chance encounter and identified Horn's Achilles-heel—his braggadocio personality.[23]

LeFors's investigation focused on Tom Horn. The marshal played to Horn's weakness by pretending to offer him a contract to eliminate Montana rustlers. After an evening of drinks, the new pals walked to the marshal's office. Loose-mouthed Horn offered a drunken statement implicating himself in the boy's murder. Then he stated, "I shot the kid at three hundred yards. It was the best shot and dirtiest trick I ever done. Killing men is my specialty; I look at it as a business." A deputy, hidden behind an adjoining office door, documented Horn's confession. Arrested the next day, Horn recanted his revelation and vehemently maintained his innocence.[24]

John Coble and other stockmen hired high-powered attorneys to defend Horn. The prosecution based the purely circumstantial case around Horn's drunken confession and several questionable witnesses. Nearly a year after Willie Nickell's murder, a jury convicted Horn of the crime. After several botched jailbreak attempts, Tom Horn was hanged in Cheyenne, Wyoming on November 20, 1903.[25]

Did Tom Horn kill Willie Nickells? This "who done it" has sparked debate for the last century. Sadly, Horn's flawed character eclipsed his extraordinary talents. If Tom Horn's self-implicating statements were true, his soft-spoken, courteous demeanor disguised a sociopath personality.

<u>Jul 6</u>. Around town which is very dull. Spoke to Berry about work. No chance now. Commenced raining in evening.

<u>Jul 7</u>. Rained slowly all last night. Went to Salt River today to see Henry Middleton about selling our ranch and cattle. We agreed to sell for $11.00 for cattle and $1,000 for ranch on Coon Creek. I rode down with Robt. Schell and led my colt.

<u>Jul 8</u>. Returned to Globe today. Rode my colt back. Wrote to J. H. W. Jensen offering to sell our stock and ranches for figures as stated on opposite page. Heard that Mr. Chapel had sold out to a man from Kansas City his stock of goods at San Carlos.

The *Silver Belt* elaborated, "There is talk at San Carlos of W. W. Chapel selling out his business to Mr. Kingsbury, of Kansas City, who is reported to have received the appointment of Indian Trader."[26]

It is safe to assume that Frank's decision to sell the ranch was a consequence of Ezra Kingsbury's appointment as Indian trader. Frank should not have been surprised. As a sixty-year-old Civil War veteran and an experienced storekeeper for the western district of Missouri, Kingsbury had maintained close political ties with the Republican leadership and had clout with future president William McKinley. It appeared a judicious choice until cantankerous, outspoken Kingsbury created a colossal controversy.[27]

Kingsbury and card-playing buddy Al Sieber both disdained affable Captain Bullis. The feeling was mutual. Sieber's remarks in a September 1889 interview with the Tucson *Arizona Citizen* escalated the tension between himself and Bullis: "They are a dissatisfied people [Apaches], and will always be as long as the present conditions surround them... a number of full-blooded Mexicans... renegades from Sonora...are used by the Indians in procuring arms, whiskey, and ammunition."[28]

A year later, on November 8, 1890, Bullis closed Kingsbury's store for receiving a soldier's liquor shipment and thwarting efforts to confiscate the cargo. Kingsbury defended his position, arguing that he was away from the post on the day the illegal goods were forwarded to Globe. Sieber had watched as the illegal cargo was loaded onto the mail coach and declined to intercept the brew, asserting that he had no authority to seize it. Accepting no excuses, Bullis charged Kingsbury with violating Indian Bureau regulations regarding excessive absence from his business. Kingsbury presented his side of the story in a letter to the commissioner of Indian affairs.[29]

The Bureau investigated the incident while Kingsbury fought for reinstatement as trader. The flow of correspondence that followed exposed a troubling situation. It exposed Kingsbury as a wrathful man with a contorted view of the facts and rancorous Bullis as an unyielding officer reluctant to settle the legalistic row. The results of the investigation cleared Kingsbury of intentional wrongdoing, chastised Sieber for "stupidity," and recommended that Kingsbury be reinstated as Indian Trader.[30]

Bullis's angry response included accusations that politics had influenced the commissioner's findings. "In reference to his [Kingsbury's] general character as it has become known to me here I would say that he is an industrious card player," Bullis fumed. He also defamed Sieber, claiming the chief of scouts "was a drunkard, vulgar, profane and brutal in his treatment of the Indians, and from his position had ample opportunity to exercise his evil propensities." With that face-saving outburst, Bullis fired Sieber. The *Tombstone Prospector* reported that "Kingsbury had a pull with McKinley and it would be a breach of political etiquette to fire him.... Bullis compromised; Sieber went and Kingsbury stayed."[31]

Angry at the firing of his friend, Kingsbury leveled more serious allegations. In a tirade to the commissioner he charged that Bullis exhibited a "laxity of morality as is seldom met with." According to Kingsbury, it was common knowledge that Bullis "cohabits with his housekeeper," had refused to prosecute Frederick Dalton for molesting his housekeeper's daughter until the post surgeon had Dalton arrested, incarcerated Indians for trivial offenses in order to supply workers for his pet projects, and mismanaged the grain harvest.[32]

Kingsbury further alleged that Bullis overlooked farm instructor Benton's fla-grant insobriety and immorality in appointing him to succeed Sieber. Was this the same Jack Benton whom Frank had paid five-dollars for the Indians' road repair work? Inspector Frank C. Armstrong, in his 1889 annual report to the Bureau of Indian Affairs, indicated that all Indian labor was "done without pay."

"A great deal of work has been done here, by the Indians, within the past two years," he reported. "About fifty miles of main ditches or canals; some seven large dams on the Gila, and about 18 small dams on the San Carlos River; road-making, clearing, etc.... All this work has been done by Indians without pay except the regular rations."[33]

Who supplied information to the inspector? What happened to the Gila County funds Frank reported paying Benton on January 13, 1889? Could Kings-bury's allegations have been valid?

Not in the eyes of Inspector Armstrong who insisted "Capt. Bullis and his employes [sic] are attentive and energetic, and too much praise cannot be given them for their persistent efforts to advance and improve these people and their condition."[34]

A year after Frank left Globe, the charges and countercharges spurred another half-hearted investigation. Old cronies attested to Bullis's good character, while key witnesses were unavailable. Bullis was exonerated on minor charges and the gravest questions went unanswered. The San Carlos scandal was swept under the carpet. If Frank had remained in Globe through the summer of 1891, his testimony might have supported Sieber.[35]

> Jul 10. Recd from R. Pringle on a/c $20.00. Paid F. W. Westmeyer $16.00 money borrowed. Will go on picnic in the mountains tomorrow. Will take Sadie Ramsdel and Mamie Kennedy. Ordered rig from Pascoe.

> Jul 11. Left for mountains at 7:30 AM arrived at 10:30. Had a very enjoyable time. The air was cool and delightful arrived home at 8 oclock PM.

> Jul 12. Very warm, No mail for which I am waiting and no work yet. Oh, I am so tired of doing nothing and I don't know what I shall do. Gave J. Sultan an order on Robt. Pringle for $5.50. Called on Miss Silva Kennedy who is visiting here from Tuson.

> Jul 14. Am very tired and wish I could get to doing something. Recd a favorable reply from Mr. Jensen who will send a man up to look at our interests with a view to purchase. Leaving P [Phoenix] on 15th or 16th inst.

Although Frank never mentions receiving word from the Bureau of Indian Affairs, he must have believed the rumors that Kingsbury had been appointed Indian trader at San Carlos. Disappointed, Frank pursued a potential buyer for the ranch.

Jul 15. A splendid shower this morning. Several parties went up to the mountains today. I will drive Mrs. Van Wagenen and Mrs. Ramsdel up tomorrow and on Wednesday will go to the river....Wrote in A.M. Charley. Kinsler came in on the stage. Wrote to Cousin Wen.

At the same time, Frank contacted his cousin Wendell P. Hammon regarding business opportunities in California.

Jul 16. Recd a favorable reply from Williamson at San Carlos. Raining this morning so did not go up to the mountains today. Called on Miss Sylva Kennedy at Alon Baileys this evening. Will go to Henrys on Salt River tomorrow. My colt is getting very gentle and is going to make a nice saddle horse.

Dan Williamson had his own issues with Bullis. He resented the agent's alleged personal gain from his administrative position. Williamson claimed Bullis had made millions in Texas by using Seminole Indian Scouts to drive out Mexican settlers, then buying up their land for a few cents per acre. Although never proven, the suggestion of Bullis's misconduct followed him and affected morale at the San Carlos Agency.[36]

Jul 17. Came to Henrys on Salt River. Did not find Mr. Jensens man there and hardly expected him so soon.

Jul 18. Our party not here yet. Very hot—laid around George Shutes and ate mellons.

Jul 19. Went out with Henry for load of posts. A Mr. Patterson from Phoenix arrived from Mr. Jensen. He and I went to Coon Creek. Henry to come over in the morning.

Jul 20. Mr. Veach went down to Henrys. Patterson and I went up on upper range and drove down our horses. Henry arrived. We all rode over Dry Creek and up Coon Creek.

Jul 21. Rode around upper mesa and Dry Creek box and up Coon Creek. Sold out our cattle to Mr. Jensen through Mr. Patterson at $11.00 per head for all branded cattle in HH and ⊕ brands and ranches and range for $1,000. Cattle to be rounded up on or before Nov 1st 1889. He to pay $500 down. Went to Salt River.

Jul 22. Went to Globe Mr. Patterson and I. Henry to come up tonight. Patterson telegraphed to Phoenix for $500.

Jul 23. Got Cook to draw up contract and Mr. F. W. Westmeyer agreed to go on my or our bond. Henry arrived. Patterson and I went to smelter and mine. Patterson recd answer to telegram that draft had been sent by post, it will arrive by day after tomorrow.

Jul 24. Mr. Alonzo Bailey agreed to go on our bond with Mr. Westmeyer. It is very tedius waiting for the remittance. We managed to get the day in some way. We, Henry and I, signed the contract and bond. I got Mr. F. W. Westmeyer and Alonzo Bailey to sign bond after Henry and I. The papers are now all ready, and we only await the remittance to clinch the sale.

Jul 25. The check or draft arrived and I received and receipted for it under name of Hammon and Middleton and delivered the bond to Mr. Patterson. The contract we left in the hands of Cook, the lawyer. Patterson will leave for Phoenix tomorrow via the King [mine].

Three days later, the *Silver Belt* announced, "Frank M. Hammon and Henry Middleton have sold their cattle (between 350 and 400 head) and ranch of Coon Creek, Gila County, to J. H. W. Jensen and S. S. Patterson, of Phoenix. While the price is not to be made public, we understand it is a good one in comparison with values ruling in other parts of the Territory."[37]

After finalizing the Coon Creek sale, Patterson left for Phoenix, stating that he and Jensen intended to take possession of the ranch and livestock following the fall roundup.

Chapter Twenty-One

Beyond the Lamplight

*F*rank's role in Arizona history became my primary
focus. His real-life western adventure captivated me; Globe's lively
past intrigued me; his tragic love story tore at my heart. I saw his
diaries as compelling firsthand accounts of a remarkable period in
Arizona's past. Trying to be objective, I had disregarded my own
personal relationship to Frank. As I contemplated the last diary
written in Globe, I empathized with his distress, disappointment,
and anxiety. The authenticity of his writings underscored his most
insignificant actions.

Survival drove Frank to the strength-sapping drudgery
of the mine. Although a proud, well-educated man, Frank embraced
menial labor born of necessity. By the fall of 1889, he poignantly
communicated his despondency.

Through the years, Frank carefully preserved his four
diaries written in Globe. The small leather books survived as he traversed the western states. For whom were these diaries written? Frank
was a man of few words. Were the diaries his attempt to communi-
cate, if only with himself? Perhaps he saved them for his children, to
give them insight into a father they barely knew.

But without historical perspective, his words had little
meaning. It is probable that Alberta, Eva, and Milton felt abandoned, never completely understanding their father's absence or his

sacrifice. As she matured, Eva often referred to her father with a fond-
ness reserved for a visiting uncle.

During middle-age, my grandmother returned to her
birthplace searching for information regarding her parents. No evi-
dence of their existence remained. Eva died unaware of her mother's
background, her father's loneliness, or his shattered dreams. She never
realized the physical toll providing for his children had exacted on her
father. I finally understood the depths of Frank's love for his family.

During the summer of 1889, Frank experienced the warmest temperatures since his arrival in Arizona. The daytime thermometer hovered around 100 degrees, barely cooling to the 70s at night. Once again, he retreated to the Old Globe mine to make ends meet.[1]

Jul 26. I went to work at the Old Globe Co.s smelter wheeling charges. Deposited the check recd from Patterson with Alonzo Bailey to be credited, one half to Henry and one half to myself. Henry will leave for home in the morning. I change from the morning to the graveyard shift tomorrow.

Jul 27. Very hot and feel very sore, but got through todays shift very well. Called on Miss Annie Pascoe in evening. I dont go on shift until tomorrow night at 11 oclock.

Jul 28. Very hot. dont work today. A basket picnic comes off. . .at the wheat fields today. Attended church and Sunday School acted as teacher of the bible class. Walked home with Miss Edna Neffe. Went on shift at 11 PM.

Jul 29. Very warm last night and a hot day today. Came off shift at 7 oclock this morn. Tried to sleep until eleven AM, rested poorly. Drew from A. Bailey one $201.00 check and sent it by mail to the Bank of California to be remitted in the shape of two $100.00 money orders to me at Globe.

Jul 30. Worked last night but rested very poorly today. The heat is so intense that one cannot sleep during the day.

Jul 31. Rested fairly this morning. Wrote several letters and feel much better for work this evening.

Aug 1. I got up at 12 oclock little refreshed and also got very little sleep in evening. John Murphy—Mike Welsch and Molly Shanley left for Hot Springs, Arkansas today.

Aug 2. Sleep much broken this morning. Heat still great. Went House pd my house rent for July today. I paid bills at Herrons, McNellys and Job Atkins—total $6.00.

Aug 3. Very hot. I find the work at the smelter very hard although am getting used to it now and get along better.

Aug 4. No Church. Mr. Downs being away. Called on Miss Annie Pascoe in evening.

Aug 5. Slept until noon quite well. The nights are very hot.

Aug 6. No mail tonight and no rain either. Weather still very hot. Tonight makes the tenth night shift, four more and we will change to the 3 oclock PM shift which will be much better.

Aug 7. Recd two P. O. orders from Bank of Cal for $100.00. Each in return for check sent them. Recd letter from J. H. W. Jensen to consider my horses sold to him for $300.00.

Aug 9. Have put in another day with little sleep. Went down to smelter early and relieved Bohse one half hour early which makes up the hour he worked for me.

Aug 10. Slept well until two PM today. Tonights shift will be the last of the graveyard shift. Tomorrow I change to the 3 PM shift. Recd my check for my six days labor of last month amting to $19.50.

Aug 11. Change shifts today, going on at 3 PM. A most welcome change. Can now have night time for sleeping.

Aug 12. …Paid Chinaman for wash bill today amount $5.20. Pd. Mrs. Ramsdel my board bill to Aug 1st amting to $22.00. Recd a letter from Bertie enclosing a motto worked by my little daughter Albertie. They urge me to come home.

In spite of pressure to return home, Frank still felt the best prospects for success lay west. Glowing reports stimulated Frank's optimism for California opportunities. Nevertheless, he vacillated between his Illinois family and California fortune. Cousin Wendell proposed several ventures that Frank seriously considered.

Aug 13. Am getting tired of this hard manuel labor and wish Mr. Patterson would hasten and come to round up, so that I can get away and go home. Recd a letter from bro Charley and he too urges me to come east for good. I would be only too glad to do so, if I was sure to do as well as I can do in the west. A very heavy shower fell last night.

Aug 14. Nothing new. Weather a little cooler but still quite sultry. John Jones leaves today for the east. I wish I were all ready to go with him.

Reflecting the extreme heat and bone-breaking work, Frank's diaries resonated with discouragement. Perhaps his personal ambition began to overshadow
the desire to be near family. One by one, longtime friends were leaving Globe
for new and more productive pastures. The *Silver Belt* faithfully mentioned the
California exodus and may have influenced Frank's decision: "Col. Geo. E. White
says many from Globe are in L. A."; "J. J. Vosburgh has established stockyards
in L. A."; "E. F. Kellner makes San Diego permanent home—purchased lots on
Coronado Beach for handsome house."[2]

Aug 15. Arose this morning at 8 oclock and feeling very tired and
worn out.

Aug 17. Got my ankle hurt on shift last night and am some lame today.
Think I shall not work tonight.

Aug 18. Laid off last night. Hugh Higdon took my shift.

Aug 19. Went on shift again last night and got through all OK.

Aug 20. Worked last night as usual. No reply from Jensen yet.

Aug 21. Worked last night as usual. Nights are getting very pleasant
to sleep.

Aug 23. Paid Mrs. Annie Welsh $100.00 to apply on my note due her
of $500.00 on which the interest is paid up to date. Said $100.00 was
paid in Old Dominion check of $40.00, Gold coin $40.00, and two
greenbacks of $10.00 each— total $100.00....Worked as usual last
night. Have now in 20 shifts. Recd letter from home and [Dan] Williamson at San Carlos.

Aug 24. Tomorrow we change into the day shift—going on at 7 AM.

Aug 25. Worked today getting in 99 charges and am very tired tonight.
Attended church in the evening.

Aug 29. A hard and monotonous life a workingmans. I would not like
to think I had to follow it very long.

Aug 31. I am making expenses I think at any rate which is a consola-
tion, but I am doing no more.

Sept 1. Chas Connell arrived from Tucsan with his wife today. Recd a
letter from Jensen today and answered same. Told him I would accept
checks on the Bank of Cal in payment for cattle except about $100.
Wrote to Henry.

The *Silver Belt* also noted Connell's visit. "Mr. and Mrs Chas. T. Connell and
children, who made Globe a brief visit this week...now reside in Tucson, Mr.
Connell being in charge of a gold mine located 10 miles from the old pueblo,"
the newspaper reported.[3]

<u>Sept 2</u>. Worked as usual am getting very tired of it and am very anxious to get away.

As the summer ended, Frank became increasingly impatient and despairing. His aspirations for a prosperous cattle company had vanished. Although the ranch sold for the asking price, to Frank the sale must have represented failure. Coon Creek was the last reminder of Frank and Daisy's shared dreams. With that transaction completed, there was nothing for Frank in Globe.

<u>Sept 3</u>. I am feeling quite unwell today, but worked as usual. John Wentworth came in today from Payson, I noticed considerable change in him.

A colorful persona, Wentworth had been elected justice of the peace in 1884 and studied law under District Attorney J. D. McCabe. A number of colorful stories, many perhaps apocryphal, were told about the justice. Shortly after Wentworth's election, one of Globe's "soiled doves" charged that she had been abused by the madam of the local brothel. Arrested and arraigned, the madam entered a not-guilty plea, certain that the jurymen—many of whom were her clientele—would never convict her. She was mistaken. The jury found her guilty, and she vowed revenge. One by one, she publicly humiliated each of her jurors. For days, she pursued Justice Wentworth in and out of Globe saloons. The fleet-footed justice outsmarted her by ducking out the rear as she entered the front door. Eventually, she gave up the chase.

During his tenure, Justice Wentworth presided over 295 cases, settling each of them in his own unique way. Ultimately, the criminal element was almost eradicated, and the justice's future looked promising. Then one afternoon, Sheriff Pascoe arrested two desperadoes who pled not guilty, requiring a jury trial. Instead of granting a preliminary hearing, Wentworth, who was presumably late for a poker game, ordered the sheriff to jail them overnight.[4]

The dilapidated adobe jail was overflowing with suspects awaiting trial. Before morning, the two outlaws escaped, along with the other jailbirds. As the escapees hightailed it from town, they ignited the jail. No-nonsense federal judge W. W. Porter was irate when he arrived for the regular court session. Wentworth hastily skipped town, leaving legends behind. He settled in Payson, where he established himself as a teacher, lawyer, and saloonkeeper.[5]

In December 1887, Wentworth applied for a law license and interviewed with Judge Wright in Prescott. His reputation had preceded him. Although the board of examiners verified Wentworth's ability, they questioned his character. They recommended five months probation. At the end of his probationary period, Wentworth produced questionable letters of recommendation. Allegedly, a Payson bartender simply wrote, "Wentworth has made good at my bar and will make good at the bar of justice." The judge, a drinking man, issued the license. Eventually, Wentworth was appointed chief clerk of the Arizona Territorial Legislature. During the 1889 session, the Gila County delegation managed to annex a 1,500 square-mile parcel of Yavapai County, including Payson and Pleasant Valley, that encompassed Wentworth's land holdings.[6]

About this time, Wentworth began courting young Katharine Houston, the sister of successful Payson ranchers. Smitten by her grace and beauty, Wentworth proposed marriage. The refined young lady demanded that her happy-go-lucky suitor abstain from alcohol. Although desperately in love, he declined temperance but vowed moderation. His honesty won her heart. Perhaps this prompted Wentworth to adjust his lifestyle, as Frank noted.[7]

> Sep 6. We had a terrible hail storm and flood. It did considerable damage, flooded my rooms and damaged my carpet. The creek was higher than I have ever seen it.

> Sep 7. Another awful storm and flood doing more damage to property, am still working every day.

On Friday afternoon, the violent storm drenched the parched earth with two inches of rain in twenty minutes. The deluge cooled the scorching temperatures, but the devastating torrents rapidly filled the arroyos flowing into Pinal Creek. The turbulent waters swept away obstacles in its path as the creek overflowed its banks. Frank's lower room in Mrs. Anderson's house, located near the engorged gully, flooded and was unlivable. Saturday's storm dumped almost three inches of rain, bringing the total to six inches in two days.[8]

> Sep 8. Changed shifts, am now working on the graveyard shift, so called, and go on at 11 oclock tonight. Took Miss Edna Neffe to church.

> Sep 9. ...Paid Mrs. Anderson five months house rent to Aug. 1st '89—$15.00. Shall moove my room.

> Sep 10. Pay day for Aug. I drew my check amt. $96.00. George Shute is in town. Paid Mrs. Ramsdel my board for month of August 1889—Amt $31.00. Mooved into Mrs. Tom Pascoes house near the church. Am to pay 4.00 per mo. rent.

> Sep 11. Worked last night. Mr. Pard, Hugh Higdon will lay off for 10 days. Sent home $50.00 in PO order.

> Sep 12. I have felt very bad today, but got through with my shift all OK. I asked Mr. Aquavace to change me if he could to work below. He said he would when the other smelter started which I think will be next Monday.

> Sep 13. No news from Jensen yet. I wish he would hurry as I am anxious to get through.

> Sep 14. I don't get much sleep during the day and therefore don't feel well or hardly able to work. I sometimes have the blues and feel very bad, but soon forget them. I have so many things to be thankful for.

Frank's distinctive handwriting trails off, exhibiting an uncharacteristic sloppiness. His suppressed despair surfaced through his writings. His downcast spirits masked themselves in physical ailments. His lack of sleep, minor afflictions, and constant complaints clearly indicate despondency. Interestingly, Frank's depression surfaced only after his financial burden had been lifted.

Sep 15. Worked as usual. I think the other smelter will start tomorrow. Attended church this evening and walked home with Miss Neffe.

Sep 16. No three smelter started today. I think I have worked my last shift at charge wheeling for a while.

Sep 17. I was changed on to the clay pots last night with Larry Ryan for a pardner. I like the work much better than wheeling charges. Rain commenced falling about midnight last night and lasted until daylight.

Sep 18. It rained again last night about half the night making our work somewhat disagreeable.

Sep 19. No rain today—worked as usual. The hills are getting greener. Am disappointed that Mr. Jensen dont come to round up.

Sep 20. Col and Mrs. White returned this evening. Will change to the 3 oclock shift day after tomorrow.

Sep 23. Coke coming in slowly—Weather very beautiful. Am getting tired waiting for Jennings or Jensen.

Sep 24. No 3 smelter leaked badly and closed down indefinitely. All new hands discharged.

Sep 26. I was put back to wheeling charges yesterday and today. Laid over to tomorrow to go on as general utility man.

Sep 27. Worked as usual. Had a hard day under the crusher.

Sep 28. Worked at the dam today.

Sep 29. Worked in #3 stack taking out copper plate and am very tired.

Sep 30. Helped carpenter today build fence around wood yard.

Oct 7. I was changed to the helper of blacksmith today. Scotty in place of Higdon and Bob Broom in place of Scotty and I in Brooms. Pay day tomorrow. Recd letter from Jensen today. He and Patterson leave for Globe abt Oct 20. Wrote to him and Henry Middleton.

Oct 8. Worked in blacksmith shop. Recd pay for Sept labor $92.00. Sent home $50.00 Paid Mrs. Ramsdel for Sept board $30.00.

<u>Oct 9</u>. Worked in blacksmith shop. Got a chip of iron in my eye.

<u>Oct 10</u>. Got doctor to extract the metal from my eye. Laid off today, and have concluded to work no more....

In the beginning, Frank's inconsistencies confused me. Initially, the need to return home dominated his dealings. Once Frank had psychologically relinquished his children to his family, his goals became ambiguous. Overwhelmed by obligations and grief, his decisions fluctuated from day to day. During his last years in Globe, as he vacillated over his future, Frank formed attachments that would be difficult to sever. Globe, for better or for worse, had become home. With all job opportunities explored and exhausted, Frank finally sold his ranch, and grew impatient to move on.

Contradictions and human frailties are a part of man's existence in this changing world. Goals and choices change daily, depending upon a person's circumstances. In Frank's case, his survival instincts ultimately dictated a course of action.

Chapter Twenty-Two

STORMS OF THE SOUL

*W*indow bars and heavy doors once protected Globe citizens from the lawless; now they protect Globe's art works. I thought of Frank while wandering through the old courthouse corridors reminiscent of Apache trials, questionable justice, and resounding verdicts. He had occupied the basement office for only a few months before he was displaced by Glenn Reynolds and Jerry Ryan.

I sensed Frank's disappointment over the lost election and assessed his relationship with Glenn Reynolds. The sheriff had deputized Frank when shorthanded. Had hard feelings been put aside? I concluded that Frank remained outside the inner circle of Texas cattlemen, but had quietly gained their respect.

While Frank waited for Jensen's arrival to finalize the Coon Creek sale, preparations were underway for the opening of the Second Judicial District Court session. The overflowing jail held the Apaches released following the "Captain Jack" decision. The bitter, confused Indians believed their debt had been paid and that their freedom was permanent.

> Our jail now contains 5 Indians charged with murder, one of whom for the assassination of Lt. Mott at the agency, another for the killing of Cosper, a freighter on the Globe Road... the other three for killing of persons whose skin is as colored as their own. Four brought yesterday from Maricopa....[1]

Fanned by frequent publicity in the *Silver Belt*, a bitter fury had erupted in Globe over the Indians' pending release. Civic leaders contemplated their legal options and decided to retry the Apaches in territorial court. Gila County geared-up for new judicial proceedings.

The Apache Kid's case differed from the other cases. A Washington, D. C., investigation into Kid's court-martial had uncovered evidence of prejudice among officers serving on his jury. In addition, the judge advocate ruled that the scouts' penalty exceeded their crime. Kid and his followers were released after spending ten months in Alcatraz. In October 1888, they had arrived back at San Carlos, serenaded by the 10th Cavalry Band. As-ke-say-la-ha, Na-con-qui-say, and Margy vanished after their arrival. Bach-e-on-al (Pash-ten-tah) and Kid became reservation recluses.[2]

After a year at San Carlos, the legalities surrounding their release still confused the dishonored Apache Kid and his fellow scouts. Distrustful of the military he had once revered, Kid lived as a hermit in a box canyon on the Gila River, six miles from the agency. Without Kid's military pay, his family survived on rations. Kid alertly avoided contact with military personnel on his weekly trips for provisions. Rumors of attempted murder charges bewildered Kid. He had not attempted to kill his friend Al Sieber and had served his time for desertion.

Although he claimed otherwise, Sieber may have harbored resentment over Kid's reduced sentence. Possibly, he held Kid responsible for insubordination that resulted in Sieber's injury. Inconclusive court-martial testimony left doubt whether Kid was even armed when Sieber was shot. Weeks before the fall court session opened, Sieber persuaded Globe officials to charge Kid and his scouts with attempted murder. The three previously convicted scouts (As-ki-say-la-ha, Na-con-qui-say, and Margy) were omitted from the new arrest warrant. Singled out for trial, Kid's nightmare began.[3]

On October 14, 1889, Sheriff Glenn Reynolds wired General Miles a list of Indians scheduled for arrest, requesting the army's assistance. By evening, Miles had promised Bullis's full cooperation.[4]

Oct 21. No judge yet.

Apache Kid. AHS/TUCSON #15755.

Ultimately, Joseph H. Kibbey would try the case. Appointed by President Benjamin Harrison in 1888, Judge Kibbey's close friendship with Abraham Lincoln concerned some of Globe's residents. They anticipated liberal sentences if the Indians were convicted.[5]

Oct 22. Judge arrived this evening and court will open tomorrow.

Oct 23. I went to San Carlos with Dep. Sheriff Ryan after some indian prisoners. Called on the ladies at the school. Met Williamson and the other boys.

Frank rode with Deputy Ryan to San Carlos to bring back prisoners, but makes no mention of arresting Kid. He only describes his social contacts.

Oct 24. We left San Carlos with three prisoners and seven witnesses. Arrived at Globe all OK. Capt Johnson gave us an escort of four soldiers and an uncommisioned officer.

More than a week after Miles had notified Captain Bullis, Frank and Deputy Ryan returned with the most dangerous prisoners. The sizable escort Captain Johnson assigned to the deputies indicated the degree of danger he attached to their mission. The *Silver Belt* never mentioned Kid's incarceration in the Globe jail prior to court opening, so it is safe to assume the trio included Kid. From Frank's diary, it appears that he and Deputy Ryan rode alone to transfer the prisoners.

Jess Hayes, in his highly colored book *Apache Vengeance*, maintains that ten days before court convened, Sheriff Reynolds and Deputy Ryan left for San Carlos to collect the jailed prisoners. As the story goes, all except Kid were arrested as they claimed rations at the agency. Reynolds and Ryan devised a plan to lure Kid to the agency for a special food distribution. Hungry and unsuspecting, Kid started out, cautiously watching for soldiers.

Deputy Ryan, supposedly the only man on post unknown to Kid, rode along the trail with Reynolds a safe distance behind. After a few miles, Ryan noticed an unarmed figure riding towards him. As they converged on the narrow pathway, Kid stopped and asked the stranger for a smoke. Ryan handed over his Bull Durham. As Kid rolled his cigarette, Deputy Ryan drew his six-shooter to place the unsuspecting Indian under arrest. Wary of the military, Kid was caught off guard by the lone cowboy. Ironically, in his scouting days Kid had used the same tactic to capture fugitives. The sheriff appeared with handcuffs to secure the passive prisoner.[6]

This romanticized yarn makes a good story. However, Frank's diary casts doubt on its authenticity. One possibility may be that Hayes substituted Sheriff Reynolds for anonymous Frank. It could have been Frank hanging back, avoiding identification. After all, Kid would have remembered Frank from his early Globe days. We will never know. The military escort provided Frank's entourage indicates the high level of respect the military had for Kid's cunning. Unfortunately, Reynolds failed to heed the army's precautions.

<u>Oct 25</u>. Mr. Jensen arrived from Phoenix on the stage tonight. I like his appearance very much. Mr. Patterson will arrive in a day or two and their wagon which is on the way. Trial of the Indian who murdered lieut Mott came off tonight or today. He was convicted of murder in the first degree.

A courtroom packed with unsympathetic spectators and uniformed soldiers sought justice for Lieutenant Mott's murder. Farm boss Frank Porter, F. B. Fowler, disabled Al Sieber, and Mott's attending physician, Dr. Davis, all testified against Nan-deiz-az. Nan-deiz-az, testifying on his own behalf, was the only defense witness.[7]

Frank's interest in the trial's outcome is evident. He knew most of the participants. Lieutenant Mott had been his friend; District Attorney J. D. McCabe, his counsel; court-appointed defense attorney Ed Cook, his attorney; jury foreman George Shute, his boss; witness Frank Porter, a recent lodge inductee. Without a doubt, Frank cheered the guilty verdict.

At this point, fate interceded. Patterson, long-awaited, finally arrived from Phoenix to finalize the sale of the Coon Creek ranch. Consequently, Frank missed the rest of the Indian trials.

<u>Oct 26</u>. Patterson arrived today or rather Tex and the wagon and Patterson will come tomorrow and we will leave for Coon Creek next day.

<u>Oct 27</u>. Pat arrived today. Cap Adams and Cliff Griffin will help us.

<u>Oct 28</u>. We all left for Henrys on the river and arrived all OK.

<u>Oct 29</u>. Went to Coon Creek—Packed three horses.

On the day Frank went to Coon Creek, the unrepentant Nan-deiz-az was sentenced "to be hanged...December 27, 1889." He probably welcomed death over life in the Yuma penitentiary. He had witnessed the ghastly black lung disease that claimed his brothers. His would be the first legal execution in Gila County. Nan-deiz-az's father witnessed the bungled execution. Mistaken calculations in the rope's length caused his son to catapult upward, smashing him into the scaffolding. His crushed body was buried in Globe's cemetery, alongside Hawley and Grime.[8]

Vaulted away in the cellar of the courthouse, a conglomeration of Indians waited their turn as the court continued its agenda. Some prisoners were released for insufficient cause; others were found not guilty. Those who remained included: Apache Kid, charged with attempted murder; Say-es, Hale, and Pash-ten-tah, indicted as his accomplices; Has-cal-te, Bi-the-ja-be-tish-to-ce-an (Blue Stone), El-cahn, and Has-ten-tu-du-jay, charged with murder; and Jesus Avott, accused of embezzlement.

One by one, the Indians emerged from basement cells to appear in the jammed courtroom. Kid and his scouts were tried together. Hasty deliberations followed brief translated testimonies. With the crowd's mood, the verdict was predictable. Foreman George E. Shute announced "guilty." San Carlos blacksmith Ed Arhelger later explained: "All were promptly found guilty, which I think myself was wrong, but the sentiment was such that a good Indian was a dead Indian."[9]

<u>Oct 30</u>. Henry went back for another load of grain and provisions. I went up with the boys and got the horses and drove down a lot of cattle.

<u>Oct 31</u>. Branded up this morning 28 ⊞ and 19 ⊕.

It was Reynolds's job to deputize guards and transport the sentenced prisoners to the Yuma penitentiary. Upon arrival, Reynolds would be issued a receipt for the "expenses maintaining, feeding, clothing, and guarding the prisoners" to be reimbursed by the territory. The sheriff's office, however, was responsible for the cost of transporting the prisoners. Was Reynolds trying to cut costs by hiring on fewer deputies? Then again, fall rodeo in the Tonto Basin may have contributed to Reynolds's deputy shortage. In the event Sheriff Reynolds had solicited Frank's help, the arrival of Coon Creek's prospective new owners probably saved Frank's life. Understanding the danger in transporting Apaches, Sieber offered the sheriff an escort of scouts. Reynolds overconfidently refused. "I don't need your scouts. I can take those Indians alone with a corn-cob and a lightening-bug," he boasted. Jess Hayes's description of Reynolds as "a plain man, unsubtle and unimaginative," might explain his lack of precaution. This was his first mistake.[10]

Ultimately, Reynolds deputized fifty-six-year-old bachelor W. D. "Hunkydory" Holmes to help transfer the prisoners. An adventurous trailblazer, successful miner, and jovial poet, Holmes had enjoyed a rollicking lifestyle that possibly contributed to an undisclosed heart condition. Reynolds engaged Eugene Middleton's heavy-duty Concord stage to make the trip to Casa Grande, where the lawmen and prisoners would catch the Yuma-bound train. Middleton reluctantly agreed to drive. He had had enough exposure to Apaches.

At dawn on Friday, November 1, Eugene Middleton drove his yellow and green coach past the barren sycamore to the courthouse steps on Broad Street. One by one, the sullen prisoners were led out through the drizzling rain and loaded into the roomy vehicle. The well-armed lawmen felt secure with Kid and Hos-cal-te shackled, and the other Indian prisoners handcuffed in pairs.

Reynolds mounted his horse carrying a double-barreled shotgun; his heavy overcoat concealed a Colt-45. Holmes, openly displaying a lever-action Winchester and a six-shooter, joined the silent prisoners inside the coach. Middleton's pistol lay on the driver's seat beside him. Thus armed, the tense trio began their journey, leaving deputies Floyd Blevins and Jerry Ryan behind to guard the jail.

The contingent planned to cover forty miles the first day, before stopping overnight at the Riverside Station. The adobe stage station in Kelvin provided safe shelter, good well water, and food for weary travelers. On this night, the Apache prisoners were fed and jailed in the dining room. While the lawmen rotated between guarding and sleeping, the seated and shackled Indians catnapped through the night. Jesus Avott sat unrestrained in a chair.

Apache prisoners who killed Glenn Reynolds and "Hunkydory" Holmes en route to the Yuma Territorial Prison. ASLAPR #96-3660.

The party departed in the bitter pre-dawn cold destined for the 4:00 train at Casa Grande. At this point, Reynolds made his second mistake. For some unknown reason, he left his horse behind at the station. Now he and Holmes sat together inside the coach, facing six Apaches crammed together across from them. Jesus Avott sat jammed in the boot, and two other prisoners rode on top with Middleton. Kid and Hos-cal-te were individually hobbled and handcuffed. The rest of the Indians shared handcuffs, leaving each with one free hand.

Middleton nervously pressed his skittish horses to a full gallop. He knew his team was incapable of pulling a fully loaded coach up the Kelvin Grade, four miles ahead. Even in dry weather, passengers disembarked to lighten the load. From experience, he knew the risk of unloading prisoners to walk the steep, sandy grade. Just the same, he had confidence in Reynolds.

The landscape's savage beauty went unnoticed as the team approached rain-soaked barrancas strewn with cholla, mesquite, and cactus. The saguaro-covered ridge signaled the Kelvin Grade ahead. At the incline, Middleton stopped his team and let out his passengers in the freezing drizzle. All exited except Kid and Hos-cal-te, who were unable to walk because of their shackles. As Middleton drove his team ahead, the coach's clamor and the horses' hooves muffled sounds from behind.

Here the Sheriff made his last, deadly mistake. According to Jesus Avott's later explanation, the sheriff led the way, gripping his rifle in his gauntlet gloves, his overcoat buttoned over his revolver. One step behind followed Say-es handcuffed to El-cahn; then Has-ten-tu-du-jay chained to Blue Stone; and finally Pash-ten-tah attached to Hale. Avott walked between the pairs. Hunkydory Holmes, with his rifle cradled across his arm, brought up the rear. The stagecoach disappeared around a bend as the lawmen and prisoners slowly ascended the soggy slope.

Strategically positioning themselves, the Indians behind Reynolds inched closer to the sheriff. Simultaneously, the last pair of prisoners lagged, allowing the huffing Holmes to draw abreast. Giving a prearranged signal, Pash-ten-tah and Hale threw their blankets over the nonresistant Holmes. Literally scared to death, Holmes crumbled to the ground, felled by a heart attack. Pash-ten-tah grabbed the rifle from his quivering grasp. Simultaneously, Say-es and El-cahn jumped the startled sheriff, encasing him with their handcuffed arms as they grappled for his weapon. Reynolds firmly gripped his shotgun in his left hand, while desperately trying to unbutton his coat. Pash-ten-tah and Hale ran to where the sheriff was fighting for his life and shot him in the neck with Holmes's rifle, ending his struggle. Jesus Avott, terrified and afraid of being shot as an accomplice, ran to catch the stage seventy-five yards ahead.[11]

Middleton, who heard the shots behind him, figured Reynolds was target shooting and surged forward. He stopped when he saw Avott rounding the bend. Covering Avott with his pistol, he motioned the prisoner into the coach. Close on his heals were Pash-ten-tah and Hale. Pash-ten-tah fired, wounding the stage driver in the mouth and neck, barely missing his spinal cord. Middleton toppled from the seat, landing in a pool of rainwater, where he remained semi-conscious but temporarily paralyzed. Afraid for his life, Jesus Avott ran into the brush as rifle fire whistled around him.[12]

Pash-ten-tah and Hale then returned to where Say-es and El-cahn had stripped Holmes and Reynolds's bodies of money, watches, warm clothing, and keys. Has-ten-tu-du-jay and Blue Stone withdrew a few yards to the side of the road to watch the action. Returning to where Middleton lay feigning death, the Indians stripped him of his possessions before freeing Kid and Hos-cal-te from the stage.

As El-cahn raised a rock to crush the motionless Middleton's skull, Kid spoke in Apache and grabbed El-cahn's arm, causing the rock to drop harmlessly to the ground. Did Kid intentionally spare Middleton's life? With that, the fugitives disappeared into the white wilderness, the falling snow covering their tracks.

When it was safe, Jesus Avott emerged from the brush and approached the coach. Finding only Middleton's blood, he unsuccessfully attempted to mount one of the horses. A wrangler from a nearby ranch who noticed the stalled stage and approached to investigate, found Avott babbling in Spanish about the disquieting events. The wrangler gave Avott a gentle horse to ride for help and reported the massacre to his foreman. Governor Lewis Wolfley later granted Avott a full pardon for providing helpful testimony against the fugitive Apaches.

Middleton somehow stumbled back to the Riverside Station, where Shorty Sayler spotted the swaying driver lurching towards him. While passengers nursed Middleton, Shorty galloped on Reynolds's horse to Globe for help. At San Carlos, Dan Williamson received a disturbing telegraph reporting the massacre. The largest manhunt in Arizona history commenced.[13]

Did Frank hear of Reynolds and Holmes's deaths? If the news reached him at the ranch or during his overnight stay in Globe, he never mentioned the tragedy.

> Nov 10. Went to Globe via Horseshoe bend looking for saddle horses. Attended church in evening. Rode Jack mule.

> Nov 11. Left for ranch—rode the mule to the Wheat Fields and got Tom Pascoes old rhone and Billy Sultans to ride for which I have agreed to pay $1.00 per day for both or 50 cts per day for each. Went on to the ranch.

The November 16, 1889 *Silver Belt* announced the Coon Creek Ranch sale: "Frank Hammon, with J. H. W. Jensen, of Phoenix, is absent rounding up the Hammon & Middleton cattle, which together with the ranch on Coon Creek, have been purchased by Mr. Jensen. They are among the best cattle in the country."

Notified of the Reynolds-Holmes tragedy, Acting Sheriff Jerry Ryan led a civilian posse to scour the Riverside area for the escaped prisoners. Troops from half of Arizona's posts searched for tracks obliterated by snow. Numerous attempts to capture the fugitives failed. Governor Wolfley offered a $500 reward for their arrest and capture. During the next six months, impatient Arizonans blamed every unsolved depredation on Kid and his band. Secretly, the military offered sizable rewards for the renegades' capture—dead or alive. Apparently the tactic worked, as only one of the fugitives eluded capture or death.[14]

Kid alone remained at large, using his intelligence, endurance, skill, and resourcefulness against the army he once served. Rewards for his capture went unclaimed. Kid's tragic life became a legend; his fate a mystery. Stories of his depredations reportedly broke his mother's heart. Twice a day during her remaining years, she uttered a mournful wail into the dawn and dusk—the Apache custom of grieving the dead.[15]

As the town reeled from the tragic events of November, Frank prepared to leave Globe.

> Nov 21. Our hay gave out and we are forced to stop work. I have gathered and turned over 150 head and Henry 125 head. I also have turned

over 7 horses, and one a grey two year old filly I haven't been able to find. We went up to the mountains to pack down some shakes, but did not succeed as our pack saddles were not arranged right.

Nov 22. I went to Globe, Henry Jensen to the river. Wrote to cousin [Wendell] that I would leave for Cal. about the 1st.

Nov 24. Had papers drawn up viz. a deed of Hammon and Middleton interest in ranches and range on Coon Creek. Also bills of sale of cattle viz. for 150 head of cattle branded HH and 125 in ⊕ brand all delivered and vented, also a bill of sale from myself for 7 head of horses for $250.00—One grey filly not found yet, but we agreed Mr. Jensen and I, that when she is delivered to him or agents at Coon Creek that he will pay me $50. for her. Also my cattle in our brands HH and ⊕ delivered before May 1st '90 to be paid for at $11.00 per head at that time. Brands to be delivered to him free of costs.

Nov 25. Recd from H. W. Jensen of Phoenix, Ariz. in payment of cattle already turned over $1690. For horses already delivered $250.00 and bal on ranch $250.00—Total $2190. I paid Mrs. Welch my note and Int. $416.00 and she released the mortgage on my cattle. I pd my taxes of $75.74. Pd. Alonzo Bailey money borrowed $25.00, and bills amting to $15.90. Pd. Henry for horse shoes $2.00. Pd for making and acknowledging deed and other writing $2.75. Sent to the Bank of Cal the three checks of $500. each total $1500.00 (drawn on the bank of Cal by John Proctor—nos 141-142 and 144 and endorsed to me by J. H. W. Jensen of Phoenix, Arizona as part of above payment for ranch and stock) to be deposited to my credit.

Nov 26. Bill of Cap Adams—10 days @ 2.50—25.00. Bill of C. C. Griffen—17 days @ 1.50—25.50. 1800 lbs grain @ 1-1/2 cts—27.00. I paid Henry half of above amounts. He to pay Griffen and Adams and himself for the grain. I paid him yesterday. Patterson and Jensen left for Phoenix. Patterson paid me for my rifle $15.00. Paid Tom Pascoe for horse livery and corral bill in full to date—$13.50.

Nov 27. Paid Wm Beard for ½ of the bill for cooking for our round-up outfit $13.75. Made arrangements with Bob Anderson to gather and turn over the balance of our cattle. We to pay him $2.00 per head.

Nov 28. Thanksgiving Day—Horse races and steer tying and a dance in the evening. I attended with Miss Edna Neffe the party.

Nov 29. I attended a horse race at Miami today and won on the black horse. Spoke to Ed Cook to take charge of my house and business in Globe.

Dec 1. This day I did not attend church because I could not feel like saying good-bye to many. I feel so sad to bid them farewell. Called on Mrs. Ramsdell in the evening in place of going to church. This is my last.

Dec 2. …It seemed like leaving home. I have been at Globe for the part of eleven years and have many good friends there whom it was hard to leave. Weather cloudy and occassional drizzly rain.

There was no fanfare or going away party. Frank left Globe as he lived his life, in quiet dignity. Alone and rootless, Frank walked past the solitary sycamore and climbed aboard the waiting stage.

Chapter Twenty-Three

EVENTUALITIES

*M*ore than a century later, Frank Hammon's story
has captivated me. What relevance could his life have to mine? As
I unraveled Frank's odyssey, it jogged memories of my own youth.
I recalled my own need for adventure, desire for space, and search
for contentment. I longed for distance away from the urban sprawl
and the hustle of post-World War II Chicago. A yearning to explore,
examine, and question stirred within me. As a suburban teenager,
I too looked for answers Out West. As I perused Frank's writings,
I identified with his adventure, restive spirit, and inconsistencies.
Time spent in the Colorado Rockies had calmed my restless energy.
Although our times and challenges have sharply differed, I derive
strength from Frank's example.

<u>Dec. 3</u>. Passed on to Casa Grande. Took dinner at Florence where we met Ugene Middleton who is recovering from his wound received from the Indians....

<u>Dec. 5</u>. Passed up the beautiful San Jouquin Valley, most delightful at this season of the year. The country stretching away like a green carpet on each side of the road. Level as a floor to the snow topped mountains and dotted here and there with neat farm houses and pretty groves of old live oak trees. I enjoyed this days ride more than I ever did a day on the road before. Aboard the train and in my car were Gov. Perkins, Mr. Garrett and Frank Pixley. Rained after passing Merced.

Unable to return to Illinois during the unpredictable winter weather, Frank traveled by train to Oakland, California to visit his cousin Wendell. Nine years had passed since Wendell left Globe. His and Frank's lives had dramatically changed, but their childhood bond remained intact. Reunited, Frank and Wendell spent hours recalling years past, and considering business ventures. Ultimately, they formed a partnership to supply nursery stock to farmers throughout northern California and Nevada.

During another lonely Christmas season, the hardest winter storms of the decade threatened to shut down Frank's operation.

<u>December 24</u>. ...Christmas Eve and Oh, so lonely for me. Did no work today as I could not get out on account of the fearful storm.

<u>Jan 1, 1890.</u> ...went to Bishop got four letters from Wen and my New Year present from home in photos of my little children. How precious to me. A most beautiful and acceptable gift. God bless them and their Angel mother....

By late spring, Frank recalled his delightful train ride through the sprawling San Joaquin Valley. Using Wendell's San Francisco connections, the cousins investigated buying and subdividing cheap San Joaquin Valley ranch land. After surveying the property in Tulare County, Frank and Wendell entered into an agreement contingent on Frank successfully marketing the parcels to Chicago investors. In early May, Frank left for Chicago.

<u>May 14, 1890</u>. Arrived at Ottawa at 2:40 this morning and surprised mother while making a fire and father and all the rest as they arose from bed. I had a very happy reception and feel so much rejoiced to be home again. I drove down with father after my trunk and met sister Bertie coming home....

<u>May 15, 1890</u>. Bertie wrote to all the boys to come home and we expect them all and anticipate a happy family reunion. Oh, I am so very happy to be with my little ones again. Time flies so fast and I am so happy.... Passed the day at home with the folks and children in quiet happiness.

Frank Hammon with his children in Ottawa, Illinois, ca. 1895.
Left to right: Alberta, Milton, Frank, and Eva. AUTHOR'S COLLECTION.

Conservative Chicago investors listened attentively to Frank's stock company proposal. Leery of risky western land schemes, they politely declined to invest. Frank's brother urged him to stay and sell insurance for his firm. That summer, Frank sold Traveler's Insurance policies to Evanston, Illinois, merchants with little success. Discouraged, he jumped at earning one hundred dollars per month developing W. P. Hammon's Butte County ranch near Biggs, California. Once again, Frank's restless spirit beckoned him West.[1]

Frank's 1890 diary was his last. Other than a few infrequent letters, the subsequent years are undocumented. The remainder of Frank's life emerges through family correspondence, obituaries, and legal documents.

For the next three years, Frank planted and tended the Alexander & Hammon orchards at Biggs. His job completed, Frank returned to Illinois in time for the 1893 World Columbian Exposition in Chicago. For the next year, Frank wore the distinctive blue sackcloth uniform of the Columbian Guard and assisted the masses attending the Exposition. Outside the gates, Buffalo Bill's Wild West show celebrated the heroic Indian warrior while also exploiting him as a menace. This extravaganza counteracted the image projected by the Indian Bureau's exhibit: natives as industrious productive citizens. While the audience loved it, Frank must have wondered how Indians, lured from their reservations by the gold and glitz of a traveling "circus," could develop a work ethic.[2]

Among the corporate exhibitors at the Exposition was the California Nursery Association. Frank made valuable connections there. He was hired as superintendent of Darby Fruit Farms in Amoret, Missouri, where he laid-out, planted, and tended 800 acres of apples. During this time, Frank wrote a reflective letter to his younger brother, Glenn, expressing regret over his lost opportunities.[3]

October 23, 1895

Dear bro Glenn

Your good letter I recd yesterday and perused with pleasure. Was much pleased to learn of your full success. Intimations of which I had heard occasionally. While you are and can make the money you are, dont drop your present business viz: Stay with it as long as it lasts or until your capacity for wealth is filled, revenues will come soon enough, they do with everyone—now is your time. You are on the track and under steam with a tender supplied with fuel. Make the most of it. In later years when you have changed and present opportunities have disappeared—with money and youthful vigor gone, with the best part of ones life, the golden wand usually becomes a rotten stick and the smiles of the fickle goddess seek some more youthful and favored one. At this time one has usually attained the married state and with the added cares and heavy expenses of a growing family. If one in this the winter season of their life has not in his gaining the golden result of the sunshine and the smiles of harvest time, it fares ill with him and his. I was at one time where you now stand, making money hand over hand. I failed to realize the importance of taking advantage of fortunes favor, and saving my means for a later and more expensive and less profitable period. I can now see my error. Dear brother, you were always my favorite among my brothers and I am anxious for your success. If these lines may induce you to be a bit more careful—economical, or steadfast where success is being achieved my object will have been achieved and I can afford to take chances of being smiled at for this discourse. I am very buisy now which is a common thing with me but unusually so now—my duties are many and time at present will not allow me to enumerate them. Am getting along well and keep in good health. I will send you some papers which will

Mayme Hassig Hammon (left), Frank's second wife, with Frank's oldest daughter, Alberta (right). AUTHOR'S COLLECTION.

inform you of Amoret and surroundings and save me time. Regarding the 75.00 cant send it now. Just had my insurance to pay. Will pay it with my first money. Write occasionally and let me know your address and I will write. Have not known your address for some time. Kind regards to your pard. Aff your bro

Frank

Did you get late photo of my little folks and I?

While teaching at Rush Medical School, Glenn had entered private practice in Chicago. After ten childless years, Glenn and Emma Hammon's life was about to change. On December 27, 1895, Frank's father died of pneumonia, a complication of influenza; his mother succumbed four days later. Frank returned to his family, consumed by guilt. Glenn and Emma offered to raise his youngsters, ages twelve, eleven, and nine. Frank consented, knowing that his brother's nurturing home would provide a rich educational environment during their adolescence. Uncertain of his future, Frank knew what was best for his children. Alberta, Eva, and Milton were enrolled in Lewis Academy, fulfilling Frank and Daisy's educational dreams for their children. Frank, meanwhile, returned to Missouri.[4]

During his years in Amoret, Frank began courting Mary Augusta "Mayme" Hassig, a lovely young musician with a rich contralto voice. Assigned as supervisor of Darby's experimental farm and extensive rice fields in Port Arthur, Texas, the

*Frank Hammon
in Port Arthur,
Texas, ca. 1900.*
AUTHOR'S COLLECTION.

pair conducted a long distance romance. Frank returned to Missouri often, and April 12, 1899, Frank and twenty-two year-old Mayme were married. The family welcomed his May-December bride, only five years older than Frank's oldest daughter. They rejoiced in his marriage, grateful he had finally found the love and serenity that had eluded him since Daisy's death.[5]

Unfortunately, the happiness was short-lived. While establishing rice fields near Brownsville, Texas, for an eastern syndicate, Frank suffered a protracted chest cold. His chronic condition was diagnosed as tuberculosis, probably dormant since his Globe mining days. For the next five years, Frank struggled to regain his health.[6]

Frank and Mayme returned to Missouri to be near family. Frank's teenagers spent their vacation months in Amoret, developing a warm, loving relationship with their father. In the spring of 1906, Frank and Mayme moved to Denver, hoping the drier climate would alleviate his symptoms. Frank's handwriting in a July 8 letter home revealed more than its contents. His script, its distinctive flair gone, formed words that expressed an optimism belying his weakened state.

July 8, 1906
2749 W. 33rd Ave. Denver, Colo.

Dear Sister Bertie:

    I have received a couple of letters from you which we enjoyed very much—am glad to know you have improved your condition by moving and that you are getting along so well. We are keeping house now in Denver and like it very much. Mayme's sister is here with us now on a visit which makes it nice for us. I have improved some and am getting along quite well at present. Wen and his folks were not injured in anyway by the earthquake and I think are living at Marysville or Oroville. Their property in San Francisco was not injured seriously. Milton is getting along quite well and enjoying good health. I enclose his last letter to me. I do not know what Carl is doing.

    We enjoy your letters very much Bertie and hope you will write when you have time. Mayme joins with much love. Aff . Your Brother

Frank

Frank Malcolm Hammon died on July 30, 1906, three weeks after penning his optimistic letter. His devoted young widow accompanied his body to Chicago, where his family interred him in Graceland Cemetery. In repose, Frank was permanently reunited with his "dear ones."[7]

    The children's sisterly bond with Mayme perpetuated their father's memory. Mayme Hammon never remarried. Living in Kansas City with her sister until her death, she carefully preserved Frank's letters and diaries in their black metal box. After Mayme's death at age ninety, her niece found the box and sent Frank's few mementos to his children in Illinois.

    Three years after her father's death, Eva Hammon married Harvey T. Woodruff, conductor of "The Wake of the News" column and sports editor of the *Chicago Tribune*. Alberta married banker David Stearns. While serving in France with the 131st Infantry, American Expeditionary Forces, during World War I, Milton ingested "mustard gas." Removed to a hospital unit, he wrote home often, relating the distress that permanently disabled him. Unmarried, Milton led a simple life, loved by his sisters' families.

    Back in Globe, Francis Howell, Daisy's father, had continued corresponding with his grandchildren after his daughter's death. As they grew older, their memories faded along with his letters. Francis was briefly married to Sara Sanford the year after Frank left Globe. On November 27, 1897, sixty-six-year-old Francis wed twenty-year-old May Fowler and became the father to her two-year-old son. Two years later, Francis sold his house for $800 and moved his new family to Bisbee. He secured a night watchman position at the Copper Queen Mine. The rollicking mining town offered the aging Argonaut an easier job and excitement

Eva Hammon sunbathing on a South Haven,
Michigan, beach, ca. 1900. Author's collection.

for his young bride. However, by 1904 he was living alone in a rented room. On September 23, 1908, the Masons directed and financed his burial in Bisbee's Evergreen Cemetery. No record exists of Francis's young wife.[8]

Viewed as a hazard, Globe's "hanging tree" was removed in 1896, two years after fire had incinerated it. A monument dedicated to Gila County law enforcement commemorates the sycamore's role in the "orderly lynching" of Grime and Hawley.[9]

On December 1, 1898, the first train officially arrived in Globe from Bowie. With railroad service, Globe's fortunes rose. Mines flourished, finally able to develop and transport the vast deposits of low-grade copper ore. By the end of the nineteenth century, Globe's rail transportation brought increased commerce to accommodate its growing population. Miners arrived needing housing, and prices escalated. During this time, both Frank Hammon and Francis Howell sold their Globe properties. Eight years after Frank's departure, Globe became the vibrant town he had envisioned.[10]

While the winds of adversity had howled around him, Frank remained firmly planted. His resilient spirit was bent but not broken. In his later seasons, renewed vigor emerged. Although fate changed his course and affluence escaped him, Frank's vitality endured—a victory for the human spirit.

When I began my journey to unearth Frank's life, the road signs along the path were not obvious. Sometimes only a subtle hint, or a surprising coincidence spurred me on. As I gained confidence in my instincts, I ventured into unknown territory. Beckoned by the unexplainable, I drove Arizona highways intrigued by the state's haunting wilderness. I felt a part of it. Three of my ancestors comprise Arizona's dust. Frank's sweat built ranches and roads; his honor brought justice; his resilience brought respect; his ultimate sacrifice granted opportunity. Frank's spirit was his gift to posterity and his legacy to me. I have "arrived all OK."

Charles Milton Hammon wih the AEF in France, ca. 1918.
AUTHOR'S COLLECTION.

AFTERWORD

"Civilized" whites, guided by "Providence," felt justified extinguishing the "barbaric" Apache culture to absorb their land. In spite of his compassionate nature, sprinkled throughout Frank's writings are undercurrents of prejudice that reflect the prevailing attitudes of his time. Centuries of deceit and disregard for Indian culture still affect today's Apache. Only recently has the Bureau of Indian Affairs apologized to Native Americans for years of broken treaties and inflicted wrongs. "Never again will we attack your religions, your languages, your rituals, or any of your tribal ways. Never again will we seize your children, nor teach them to be ashamed of whom they are. Never again." As we examine our current positions, we realize we've come far, with miles to go.[1]

Restless and reckless Civil War residue sifted into Arizona, forming a society removed from eastern laws. Unification of "righteous" men compensated for an inadequate legal system. Vigilantism, a uniquely American tradition, rose to impose unwritten laws on lawbreakers. Historical legends often depict frontiersmen as either heroes or rogues. In reality, they were both. Good men often did bad deeds, and bad men did good ones. Today's newspapers are filled with horrendous accounts of crimes equal, or worse, than those of territorial times. Man continues to be inhumane to his fellow man. Arizona's existing judicial system strives to improve on its territorial legacy.

Although nothing implicates Frank in vigilante activities, undoubtedly he knew all participants and their actions. As a brave but gentle man, Frank sometimes appears at odds with his crude surroundings. Often his writings contain contradictions, making him appear indecisive. Perhaps his survival mechanism impelled him to remain neutral, for he was a survivor.

As an educated man, Frank endured one of the most dangerous and inhospitable eras in western history. With his faith intact, he undauntedly persevered following the premature death of his beloved wife. Through risky entrepreneurial endeavors and backbreaking labor, he supported his motherless children as best he could. Having few options and ignoring great risks, he bravely wore a badge during Arizona's bloodiest feud. In numerous positions of trust and authority, he served with honor, quietly gaining respect.

Crossing the trans-Mississippi West a minimum of eight times, Frank witnessed the greatest cultural and commercial expansion in our nation's history. While he observed his country evolve from a post-war depressed nation to a productive industrial society, he sought to share in its wealth—aware of fleeting fortunes.

Sweeping legends are the underpinning of modern Arizona; to deal judiciously with current issues, we must analyze the past. Many frontier tales have been enhanced by word of mouth or gleaned from inaccurate newspaper accounts. Glorified and digested as fact, they have been recreated into pulp fiction by the media and entertainment industry. Frank's writings present realism, minus enrichment.

Frank Hammon's story is Arizona's story. Although he lived an unspectacular life in an unremarkable way, his experiences represent thousands of undocumented tales depicting frontier life. Like many territorial pioneers, Frank exhibited the same gritty toughness and relentless tenacity that built the territory. Few pioneers had the time, education, or inclination to document their experiences. Frank was an exception. His writings disclose a comprehensive look at Arizona's heritage. Communicating a unique authenticity, his writings present a raw, microscopic exposé, revealing the foundation of today's Arizona.

ACKNOWLEDGMENTS

A simple family project that began a decade ago mushroomed into an extraordinary endeavor. This venture has depended upon the support of family, the kindness of friends, and the assistance of strangers. They spurred me on by giving me valued advice and encouragement, or sharing their expertise. Without their help Frank's story might have remained one of my good intentions.

Posthumously, I thank my parents for their loving guidance and valuable input. During the last difficult years of their lives, research and writing rendered solace to me, and brought hope to them. Although my husband, David, has endured my obsession for the past ten years, he remains my constant source of solid advice, unequivocal support, and unconditional love. Cathy, Joan, Danny and Amy's faith in their Mom kept me going, even when I doubted myself. Our grandchildren's interest in the "wild west" validated the importance of this work for future generations. My sisters, Carol and Mary, read my first chapters, offered a fresh perspective, then cheered me on. The gratitude I feel for my family's support is immeasurable.

One of the significant benefits of this project has been the discovery of previously unknown cousins. John and Roberta Hammon, Newman Hall, and Donald Moore have filled in some blanks, and embraced me as family. My aunt Alberta Hunsberger, her cousin Jane Minor, and recent acquaintance Lillian Sherman, provided a glimpse into the lives of another generation. I appreciate the time they shared with me musing over old memories.

Research professionals at the repositories where I spent many hours deserve a special word of praise. Their dedication and expertise simplified an otherwise overwhelming job. I thank the staffs at: the Arizona Historical Society, Tucson; the Arizona State Library, Archives, and Public Records, Phoenix; the Arizona Historical Foundation; the Arizona State University Libraries, Special Collections; the University of Arizona, Special Collections; St. Paul's Methodist Church, Globe; the Gila County Historical Society, Globe; the Phoenix Museum of History; the Arizona Room, Phoenix Public Library; the Sharlot Hall Historical Society,

Prescott; the Yuma Territorial Prison State Historic Park; the Yuba County Library, Marysville, California; the Lemuel C. Shattuck Library, Bisbee; the Newberry Library, Chicago; the Kings County Library, Hanford, California; the LDS Family History Center, Hanford, California; the Sonoma County Records Office, Santa Rosa, California; the National Archives, Washington, D. C.; the court and administrative officials of Gila, Maricopa and Yavapai counties.

In large and small ways I am indebted to several individuals: Carolyn Barnes, Jeanne Barnett, Pat Browning, Carol Dyer, Bob Dyer, Thomas Hayes, Judy Hopper, Sylvia Huntington, Jean Jacobus, Brian Keliher, Katy Macherey, and Kathy Norton. They lent valued advice, read early manuscript drafts, or became sounding boards for my scattered thoughts.

My deepest gratitude goes to Don Dedera, who mentored and challenged his "naive" friend with gentle humor. Without his expertise, wisdom, and patience my work would rest unfinished in some dusty cupboard.

Finally, I thank Bruce J. Dinges, publications director at the Arizona Historical Society, for recognizing the value of Frank's diaries, and lending his gift of insightful, sensitive, and masterful editing to my work.

NOTES

ABBREVIATIONS

ACRO   Arapahoe County Records Office, Denver

ADLAPR   Arizona Department of Library, Archives, and Public Records

AHF   Arizona Historical Foundation

AHS   Arizona Historical Society

BCRO   Bates County Records Office, Missouri

GCDCR   Gila County District Court Records

GCRO   Gila County Records Office

EU   Edinboro University, Pennsylvania

MCRO   Maricopa County Records Office

HFB   Hammon Family Bible

LDS   Church of Jesus Christ of Latter-day Saints, Family History Center, Salt Lake City, Utah

NGCG   Northern Gila County Genealogical Society

PPL   Phoenix Public Library

SCRO   Sonoma County Records Office

SC, ASUL   Special Collections, Arizona State University Libraries

SC, UAL   Special Collections, University of Arizona Library

NA   National Archives, Washington, D. C.

YCDCR   Yavapai County District Court Records

Notes to Chapter One

1. Anderson, ed., *Honor the Past...Mold the Future*, p. 29.

2. Altshuler, *Starting with Defiance*, p. 51. Eventually, nearly 5,000 Indians occupied Camp San Carlos, established May 29, 1873.

3. Woody and Schwartz, *Globe*, p. 27.

4. Edinboro University Alumni Records, Pennsylvania; Delay, *History of Yuba and Sutter Counties, California*, p. 1194.

5. Hammon family records; 1880 U.S. Census, Arizona, Pinal County, Globe. Roommates Wendell P. Hammon listed as "mine operator"; Scott Bell and Frank Hammon as "News Dealers."

6. 1880 U.S. Census, Pinal County, Miami, lists Frank Howell as farmer. Francis N. Howell, known as Frank, will be referred to as Francis in order to avoid confusion with Frank Hammon.

7. 1850 U.S. Census, El Dorado County, California, lists "Francis Howell, 18, miner."

8. Maricopa County Recorder's Office, Mine Claims, 1:316. John H. Eaton was owner of the Howard Mine at Pioneer.

9. GCRO, lot 5, block 75. The adobe house on the corner of Broad and Mesquite streets was sold to Ferdinand (also referred to as Fred) Hatch on May 2, 1883, and repossessed by F. M. Hammon on September 24, 1885.

10. *Arizona Silver Belt*, December 25, 1880.

11. Spude, "Mineral Frontiers in Transition," pp. 26-27; Dunning and Peplow, Jr., *Rocks to Riches*, p. 110; Bigando, *Globe*, p. 32.

12. Delay, *History of Yuba and Sutter Counties, California*, p. 1194.

13. *Arizona Silver Belt*, Centennial Edition, April 27, 1978.

14. Jeffrey, *Frontier Women*, pp. 118-19; Fischer, "A Profile of Women in Arizona in Frontier Days," p. 50.

15. St. Paul's Methodist Church records, Globe.

16. Ibid.

17. Butchart, "The Frontier Teacher," pp. 55, 57; Jeffrey, *Frontier Women*, pp. 88-91; Fischer, "A Profile of Women in Arizona in Frontier Days," p. 46.

18. *Arizona Silver Belt*, Centennial Edition, April 27, 1978; Robinson, *Apache Voices*, p. 177.

19. Woody and Schwartz, *Globe*, pp. 47-48.

20. Jeffrey, *Frontier Women*, pp. 121-22; *Arizona Silver Belt*, Centennial Edition, April 27, 1978.

21. Jeffrey, *Frontier Women*, p. 131; *Arizona Silver Belt*, February 19, 1881.

22. St. Paul's Methodist Church records; Gila County Marriage Certificate; Hammon Family Bible.

Notes to Chapter Two

1. 1880 U.S. Census, Sonoma County, California.

2. *Besh-Ba-Gowah*, videocassette; Bigando and Hohmann, *Besh-Ba-Gowah Archaeological Park*, pp. 3-5. Evidences of the Salado culture remain today at the Besh-Ba-Gowha Archeological Park in Globe.

3. Basso, ed., *Western Apache Raiding and Warfare*, p. 13; Bret Harte, "San Carlos Indian Reservation," pp. 7-8.

4. Bret Harte, "San Carlos Indian Reservation," pp. 4, 7; Basso, *Apache Raiding and Warfare*, pp. 15-17.

5. Bergon and Papanikolas, eds., *Looking Far West*, p. 19; Basso, *Wisdom Sits in Places*, p. 35.

6. Bergon and Papanikolas, eds., *Looking Far West*, pp. 61, 113.

7. Bret Harte, "San Carlos Indian Reservation," pp. 28-29; Basso, *Apache Raiding and Warfare*, p. 20; Roberts, *Once They Moved Like the Wind*, p. 69.

8. Thrapp, *Conquest of Apacheria*, pp. 88, 90; Basso, *Apache Raiding and Warfare*, p. 21.

9. Basso, *Apache Raiding and Warfare*, pp. 21-22; Roberts, *Once They Moved Like the Wind*, pp. 76-77.

10. Basso, *Apache Raiding and Warfare*, pp. 22-23; Bret Harte, "San Carlos Indian Reservation," p. 2; Brown, *American West*, p. 356; Altshuler, *Starting With Defiance*, p. 51. Most of the San Carlos Reservation was set aside by military orders in June 1870. President Ulysses S. Grant added the lower section on either side of the Gila River on December 14, 1872, which is recorded as the founding date.

11. Anderson, "Protestantism, Progress, and Prosperity," pp. 4, 5.

12. Bret Harte, "San Carlos Indian Reservation," p. 683; Roberts, *Once They Moved Like the Wind*, p. 155; Thrapp, *Al Sieber*, p. 246; Anderson, "Protestation, Progress, and Prosperity," p. 8.

13. Basso, *Apache Raiding and Warfare*, p. 23.

14. Bret Harte, "Strange Case of Joseph C. Tiffany," pp. 385-86.

15. Ibid, pp. 388-89.

16. Ibid., pp. 383, 401-402; Thrapp, *Conquest of Apacheria*, p. 257. As a footnote Thrapp writes, "although Tiffany was accused of sundry abuses, he was never, I believe, convicted of any misdoing...the territorial press indulged in the most outrageous calumnies upon rival newspapers, editors, and political figures as a matter of course."

17. Bret Harte, "San Carlos Indian Reservation," pp. 606-607; Roberts, *Once They Moved Like the Wind*, p. 220. State Historian Dan R. Williamson wrote in a letter to Connell's anticipated publisher on March 25, 1930: "Connell, in an unofficial capacity visited amongst the dissatisfied Indians and warned the agency authorities that trouble was brewing and very shortly thereafter the CIBICU outbreak occurred." ASLAPR.

18. Thrapp, *Al Sieber*, p. 220; Thrapp, *Conquest of Apacheria*, pp. 217-18; Collins, *Apache Nightmare*, pp. 14-16; Bergon and Papanikolas, eds., *Looking Far West*, p. 53.

19. Collins, *Apache Nightmare*, pp. 22-23, 33.

20. Ibid, pp. 33, 44, 56; Thrapp, *Al Sieber*, p. 220.

21. Collins, *Apache Nightmare*, pp. 75, 78, 95, 186.

22. Woody and Schwartz, *Globe*, p. 41. Telegraph operator G. M. "Mack" Allison arrived in Globe February 1, 1881, from California. He later served as county recorder, probate judge, and ex-officio superintendent of schools. He and Hattie Middleton were married for sixty years. Hattie is buried next to her brother, Eugene, in the Globe Cemetery.

23. Ibid, pp. 54-55.

24. Connell, "Apache, Past and Present"; Collins, *Apache Nightmare*, pp. 78-81; Woody and Schwartz, *Globe*, p. 55; de la Garza, *Apache Kid*, p. 88. Capt. Charles T. Connell served as Indian agent beginning in 1879, conducted the first census of Indians in Arizona, served as a secret agent on the Mexican border during the Spanish-American War, and in 1910 went to Los Angeles to head up the Southern California Immigration District. *Arizona Republic*, November 17, 1934.

25. Connell, "Apache, Past and Present."

26. Eugene Middleton's account, McClintock Papers.

27. Connell, "Apache, Past and Present."

28. Eugene Middleton's account, McClintock Papers.

29. Ibid.; Connell, "Apache, Past and Present."

30. Thrapp, *Al Sieber*, pp. 222-24; Woody and Schwartz, *Globe*, pp. 55-60.

31. Woody and Schwartz, *Globe*, pp. 55-60; Haak, *Copper Bottom Tales*, pp. 18-19; Thrapp, *Al Sieber*, pp. 209-210; Rose, *Prehistoric and Historic Gila County*, p. 11.

32. Woody and Schwartz, *Globe*, p. 59.

33. Ibid., p. 60. Taken from Mrs. York's remembrances.

Notes to Chapter Three

1. Enclosed with Frank's May 3, 1882 letter.

2. *Arizona Silver Belt*, Special Centennial Edition, April 27, 1978.

3. 1880 US Census, Pinal County, Globe, Arizona, lists Jacob Abraham with wife Martha and three daughters. Globe Book 1:27, GCDCR.

4. Gordon, *Great Arizona Orphan Abduction*, pp. 79, 114, 190, 201, 254, 295-96.

5. Bret Harte, "San Carlos Indian Reservation," pp. 666-68.

6. Connell, "Apache, Past and Present"; Collins, *Apache Nightmare*, pp. 207-208.

7. Connell, "Apache, Past and Present"; Bret Harte, "San Carlos Indian Reservation," p. 669. Bret Harte claims Colvig killed three members of Nan-tia-tish's band two months previously. Tis-win is a highly intoxicating brew made from soaked fermented corn.

8. Connell, "Apache, Past and Present"; Collins, *Apache Nightmare*, pp. 207-208.

9. Connell, "Apache, Past and Present"; Thrapp, *Al Sieber*, pp. 244-45. Charles T. Connell married Chesie Moore on May 20, 1882. St. Paul's Methodist Church records.

10. Connell, "Apache, Past and Present"; Thrapp, *Al Sieber*, pp. 244-46.

11. Curnow, "Journey With Tom," pp. 63-65.

12. Woody and Schwartz, *Globe*, pp. 62-63; Thrapp, *Al Sieber*, p. 247.

13. Bret Harte, "Strange Case of Joseph C. Tiffany," p. 388; Connell, "Apache, Past and Present."

14. Thrapp, *Al Sieber*, p. 247; Thrapp, *Conquest of Appacheria*, p. 255; Connell, "Apache, Past and Present"; Woody and Schwartz, *Globe*, p. 64; Bret Harte, "San Carlos Indian Reservation," p. 671. Although Crook received his orders on July 13, he did not assume command until September 3, 1882.

Notes to Chapter Four

1. Hayes, *Boots and Bullets*, pp. 19-30.

2. Ibid., pp. 121-24.

3. Ibid., p. 19.

4. Hietter, "Popular Justice Run Amok," p. 8.

5. Hayes, *Boots and Bullets*, p. 39.

6. Ibid., p. 28; Hietter, "Popular Justice Run Amok," pp. 8-9.

7. Hayes, *Boots and Bullets*, pp. 29-30.

8. Ibid., p. 38; Hietter, "Popular Justice Run Amok," p. 9.

9. Woody and Schwartz, *Globe*, pp. 71-73. Daniel Boone Lacy was supposedly the grandson of frontiersman Daniel Boone.

10. Hietter, "Popular Justice Run Amok," pp. 8-9. Taken from Charles Clark, "Episode of a Pay Roll Robbery," in *Silver Belt* January 22, 1924. Clark, who lived in Globe, recorded the confessions of Grime and Hawley and participated in the lynching.

11. Woody and Schwartz, *Globe*, p. 73; Hietter, "Popular Justice Run Amok," pp. 11-12.

12. Hayes, *Boots and Bullets*, p. 40.

13. Cicero Grime was sentenced to twenty-one years in the Yuma Penitentiary. He feigned insanity and was sent to a Stockton, California, asylum from which he escaped and reportedly joined his family in Oregon. Spude, "Shadow Catchers," p. 238. In the fall of 1882, J. C. Burge replaced Cicero Grime as photographer. Burge traveled the circuit from Phoenix to Florence,

Pinal City, Silver King, and Globe, photographing balls, picnics, and main streets, as well as courthouses, sawmills, mines, and San Carlos Reservation Indians.

14. On May 2, 1883, F. M. Hammon sold to Ferdinand Hatch, Lot 13, blk. 73, for $3,000. In 1885, Hammon won a lawsuit against F. Hatch for non-payment. GCRO. Woody and Schwartz, *Globe*, p. 75.

15. Woody and Schwartz, *Globe*, pp. 75-76.

16. Ibid., pp. 76-78; *Arizona Gazette*, August 28, 1882.

17. Hietter, "Popular Justice Run Amok," pp. 3-4.

18. Hietter, "Lawyers, Guns and Money," p. 32; Utley, *High Noon in Lincoln*, pp. 172-73; Moses, *Lynching and Vigilantism in the United States*, p. 14; Hietter, "Popular Justice Run Amok," p. 4; Brown, *Strain of Violence*, pp. 59, 152. Brown quotes prominent Baltimore attorney O. F. Hershey, writing in 1900. See also, Burrows, *Vigilante!*, pp. 38-39. The expression "Lynch Law" was coined after Colonel Charles (William or Robert) Lynch printed a manifesto of moral rationalization for vigilante acts against outlaws in 1780 Bedford, Virginia. His statement laid the groundwork for the vigilante movement in the United States.

19. Hietter, "Popular Justice Run Amok," pp. 6, 10-12.

20. On October 9, 1882, L. Robinson deeded to F. M. Hammon a lot on the corner of Cedar and Sutherland Streets. GCRO.

Notes to Chapter Five

1. Alberta Estelle Hammon was born January 7, 1883. HFB.

2. Myrick, *Railroads of Arizona*, vol. 2, p. 834; Bigando, *Globe*, pp. 37-38.

3. *Silver Belt*, April 28, 1883, copy in Woody papers. Trennert, "A Vision of Grandeur," pp. 340-42; Myrick, *Railroads of Arizona*, vol. 2, p. 834.

4. Trennert, "A Vision of Grandeur," p. 353.

5. Ibid., pp. 342-44, 353; Myrick, *Railroads of Arizona*, vol. 2, p. 832.

6. Grantors Book 1:573, GCRO. William Henry Middleton and Ora Howard were married June 10, 1883. St. Paul's Methodist Church Records.

7. *Silver Belt*, January 5, 1884.

8. Ibid., June 7, 1884.

9. Ibid., June 16, 28, 1884.

10. Eva Pauline Hammon, the author's grandmother, was born on September 10, 1884.

11. Dedera, *A Little War of Our Own*, pp. 37-38.

12. Woody and Schwartz, *Globe*, p. 109; Forrest, *Arizona's Dark and Bloody Ground*, p. 41.

13. Dedera, *A Little War of Our Own*, p. 52.

14. Zachariae, *Pleasant Valley Days*, pp. 17-19; Woody and Schwartz, *Globe*, p. 116.

15. Dedera, *A Little War of Our Own*, pp. 53, 55.

16. *Arizona Weekly Democrat*, January 26, 1883, quoted in Woody and Schwartz, *Globe*, pp. 116-19.

17. *Phoenix Herald*, January 20, 1883, quoted in Dedera, *A Little War of Our Own*, pp. 63-64.

18. Dedera, *A Little War of Our Own*, pp. 63-64.

19. Ibid., pp. 63-75. Dedera discovered the document in the Superior Court archives, Prescott.

20. Ibid., p. 176.

21. Ibid., p. 80.

22. Ibid., pp. 79-80.

23. Woody and Schwartz, *Globe,* pp. 121-22; Dedera, *A Little War of Our Own,* pp. 81-84.

24. Quoted from a copy of Andy Cooper's letter given to author, April 3, 2003, by Lillian Buckley Sherman, the granddaughter of John Black Blevins.

25. F. M. Hammon brand, recorded February 23, 1885, Book of Brands, GCRO.

Notes to Chapter Six

1. Jeffrey, *Frontier Women,* p. 73.

2. Jeffrey, *Frontier Women,* p. 86; Curnow, "Journey with Tom," p. 41.

3. Fischer, "A Profile of Women in Arizona," p. 47; Zachariae, *Pleasant Valley Days,* pp. 12-13.

4. Jeffrey, *Frontier Women,* p. 86; Fischer, "A Profile of Women in Arizona," pp. 45, 51. Quote from Robert H. Forbes "The Penningtons," pp. 38-39.

5. Recollections of Alberta E. Hammon Stearns as told to her daughter Jane Stearns Minor; Clardy interview with Jane Minor, August 1997; Curnow, "Journey with Tom," p. 83.

6. GCDCR. No reason was given for the dismissal.

7. Hatfield, *Chasing Shadows,* p. 53; Thrapp, *Conquest of Apacheria,* p. 267; Faulk, *Arizona,* p. 140.

8. Thrapp, *Conquest of Apacheria,* p. 250; Faulk, *Arizona,* pp. 136, 140. Crook received his assignment in July, but did not assume command until September 1882.

9. Thrapp, *Conquest of Apacheria,* pp. 256, 261; Debo, *Geronimo,* p. 172.

10. Thrapp, *Conquest of Apacheria,* pp. 261-62.

11. Thrapp, *Al Sieber,* p. 269; Roberts, *Once They Moved Like the Wind,* pp. 224-27; Faulk, *Arizona,* p. 140.

12. Thrapp, *Al Sieber,* pp. 270-71; Roberts, *Once They Moved Like the Wind,* p. 227; Debo, *Geronimo,* pp. 175, 178; Bourke, *An Apache Campaign in the Sierra Madre,* pp. 57-58.

13. Thrapp, *Conquest of Apacheria,* pp. 286-89; Debo, *Geronimo,* pp. 256-63.

14. Debo, *Geronimo,* p. 197; Thrapp, *Al Sieber,* p. 286.

15. Thrapp, *Conquest of Apacheria,* pp. 310, 312-13.

16. Debo, *Geronimo,* pp. 34-37; Barrett, *Geronimo,* pp. 118-20; Thrapp, *Conquest of Apacheria,* pp. 314-18. The actual date of Geronimo's family's massacre is unclear. Betzinez claims it was 1850.

17. Simms, *Great Western Indian Fights,* p. 259; Thrapp, *Conquest of Apacheria,* p. 364.

18. Miles, *Serving the Republic,* p. 221; Turcheneske, "Arizona Press and Geronimo's Surrender," p. 135. Crook resigned on April 1, 1886, and Miles assumed command on April 12.

19. Miles, *Serving the Republic,* pp. 222-24; Thrapp, *Conquest of Apacheria,* pp. 350-51; DeMontravel, *A Hero to His Fighting Men,* p. 161.

20. Opler, "A Chiricahua Apache's Account of the Geronimo Campaign," p. 76; Debo, *Geronimo,* pp. 282-83.

21. DeMontravel, *A Hero to His Fighting Men,* p. 174; Thrapp, *Conquest of Apacheria,* pp. 350, 352, 355-65; Anderson, *Honor The Past...Mold The Future,* p. 14. The Chiricahua families at San Carlos had been sent from Arizona to Florida on August 29, 1886. Geronimo surrendered to Miles on September 3, 1886.

22. Turcheneske, "Arizona Press and Geronimo's Surrender," p. 140.

23. Opler, "A Chiricahua's Account of the Geronimo Campaign," p. 86; Debo, *Geronimo*, p. 343.

24. Sonnichsen, "From Savage to Saint," p. 31; Robinson, *Apache Voices*, p. 56.

Notes to Chapter Seven

1. The original use of the word "rustle" did not have a criminal connotation. A rustler was a hard-working cowboy who was paid a gratuity for finding and branding a maverick calf. The expression became synonymous with the urban slang word "hustle." Tinkle and Maxwell, eds., *Cowboy Reader*. Foreclosure of Mortgage, F. M. Hammon vs. F. Hatch, September 16, 1885, "indebted...in the sum of two thousand dollars." On September 29, 1885, Ferdinand Hatch paid F. M. Hammon $500 and deeded him lot 5, block 75. Book 2, No. 238, GCRO.

2. Frank M. Hammon was born August 13, 1855. HFB.

3. HFB.

4. Daniel Hammon attended Kingsville Academy near Ashtabula, Ohio. Newman Hall Papers. Newman Hall is a descendant of Thomas Hammon(d). Victor Orin was born on January 20, 1867. The sixth child, Forest Waters, was born on March 13, 1864, to forty-two-year-old Adeline. HFB.

5. HFB.

6. Marcus and Charles Hammon were Daniel Hammon's brothers.

7. Many families during this generation dropped the final "d" from their names.

8. HFB; Newman Hall Papers.

9. HFB; Newman Hall Papers. John Landon's son, Alfred M. Landon, was the presidential candidate soundly defeated by Franklin D. Roosevelt in 1936. Taken from Frank M. Hammon obituary, Amoret, Missouri, newspaper, undated.

10. Curnow "Journey with Tom," pp. 99-100.

11. Ibid.; Spude, "Mineral Frontiers in Transition," p. 30; Bigando, *Globe*, p. 41. The Old Dominion Mine temporarily shut down in May 1885 and reopened in December 1885.

Notes to Chapter Eight

1. Daisy's letter is to Frank's sister, Dell Strawbridge, of Sunbright, Tennessee.

2. Trimble, *Arizona*, p. 212; Luckingham, *Phoenix*, pp. 20-22; *Silver Belt*, January 8, 1881.

3. Trimble, *Arizona*, pp. 213-14; *Arizona Gazette*, May 9, 1882; *Silver Belt*, July 20, December 24, 1882.

4. Luckingham, *Phoenix*, p. 28.

5. Murphy, "W. J. Murphy and the Arizona Canal Company," p. 2; Myrick, *Railrods of Arizona*, vol. 2, p. 495.

6. *Phoenix Herald*, May 13, 1885. Simm's initials are misprinted. The swimming baths were on the present site of the Chase Bank parking lot.

7. Wendell P. Hammon's mother, Harriet Cooper Hammon, died on April 14, 1886. HFP.

8. Frank M. Hammon 1886 diary. Frank Luke, Sr., Maricopa County Supervisor and State Tax Commissioner, was father of Frank Luke, Jr., the first Army flier in World War I to receive the Congressional Medal of Honor. Luke Air Force Base west of Phoenix bears his name.

9. Charles "Milton" M. Hammon was born on June 6, 1886. HFB.

10. Alberta E. Hammon Stearn's recollections, as told to her daughter Jane Stearns Minor. Interview with author, August 1997.

11. Born on March 1, 1863, Daisy was twenty-three-years old at the time of her death.

12. Frank M. Hammon 1886 diary; Jane Minor interview.

13. Beebe, *Central Pacific & The Southern Pacific Railroads*, pp. 322, 615; Jane Minor interview.

14. Jane Minor interview.

15. Frank Hammon to his parents, October 12, 1885.

Notes to Chapter Nine

1. Peterson, "Cash Up or No Go," p. 206; Trennert, "A Different Perspective," pp. 352-53.

2. Wilson B. Ferguson died before February 23, 1887, from unknown causes. Maricopa County, Probate Court Records, ADLAPR. Today, the route is known as the Apache Trail.

3. George Roggenstroh, an Englishman, lived on the Salt River. His name has many varied spellings, including Rogginstrogh and Rockinstraw.

4. Frank continued making payments on the swimming baths through the summer of 1887.

5. J. J. Vosburgh, a thirty-seven-year-old New Yorker, was the Wells-Fargo agent in Globe. George Newton purchased the Middleton ranch for his brother-in-law, George Wilson, following the Indian raids of 1881 and 1882.

6. Hayes, *Sheriff Thompson's Day*, p. 163.

7. Ibid., p. 164.

8. Ibid., p. 166. Governor John N. Irwin pardoned Thomas on June 15, 1892.

9. Bob Samuels married Al Rose's widow, Elizabeth, after her husband was killed by the vigilantes during the Pleasant Valley feud.

10. Bloody Tanks Wash, west of Globe, was the scene of an Indian massacre by King Woolsey in the 1860s.

11. *Silver Belt*, December 25, 1886.

Notes to Chapter Ten

1. *Silver Belt*, March 19, 1887.

2. Ibid., January 29, 1887.

3. Goff, *George W. P. Hunt*, pp. 9-12, 25; Dedera to author, September 17, 1997; Dedera, *A Little War of Our Own*, p. 257.

4. The Carlisle Indian School buildings were donated by the military to the Department of Interior in the late 1870s, and used as an educational facility for Indian boys. Jim Thorpe was a noted alumnus.

5. de la Garza, *Apache Kid*, pp. 71-72.

6. Hayes, *Apache Vengeance*, pp. 12-13; Altshuler, *Cavalry Yellow and Infantry Blue*, p. 240. Frank Porter was the freighter who rode for help following the Wells-Fargo robbery five years before.

7. Thrapp, *Al Sieber*, p. 319.

8. Altshuler, *Cavalry Yellow and Infantry Blue*, p. 240. Mott was buried in Rockville, Madison County, N. Y. Three years later, West Point classmates and regimental officers erected a plaque in his honor at Fort Leavenworth.

9. Ibid., pp. 240-41; de la Garza, *Apache Kid*, p. 72. Yuma prison was designated a territorial penitentiary. All federal prisoners were sent to Columbus, Ohio, or Menard, Illinois.

10. *Phoenix Weekly Herald*, March 17, 1887, quoted in Beatty, "The Tunnel," p. 177.

11. Trennert, *Mineral Belt Railroad*, pp. 344-45, 348; Dedera, *Arizona's Mogollon Rim*, p. 63.

12. Trennert, *Mineral Belt Railroad*, pp. 348, 351-52; Beatty, "The Tunnel," p. 177; Haak, *Copper Bottom Tales*, pp. 47-48; Bigando, *Globe*, p. 38. The railroad arrived on February 19, 1899, after thirty-six failed attempts to bring a line to Globe.

13. *Silver Belt*, April 16, 1887.

14. Wharfield, "Apache Kid and the Record," p. 38; de la Garza, *Apache Kid*, pp. 3-4. Wharfield was an army officer with the Tenth Cavalry in 1917. While posted at Fort Apache, Wharfield heard many of the old Apache scouts' stories. Thrapp, *Al Sieber*, p. 325, states that "The published accounts are all based on scraps of evidence, much speculation, and interviews with individuals long after the affair was over."

15. de la Garza, *Apache Kid*, p. 7; Wharfield, "Apache Kid and the Record," p. 38; Thrapp, *Al Sieber*, pp. 323-24.

16. de la Garza, *Apache Kid*, p. 27. Following his duty as commanding officer at San Carlos, Captain Pierce served as agent for the Sioux at Pine Ridge, South Dakota. *Silver Belt*, January 10, 1891. On October 22, 1896, Pierce fell from a balcony at the San Francisco Presidio and died from injury complications. *Silver Belt*, November 19, 1896.

17. Wharfield, "Apache Kid and the Record," pp. 39-40. At one time federal law permitted this custom under certain circumstances.

18. Arhelger "questionnaire," p. 7, Woody Papers.

19. de la Garza, *Apache Kid*, p. 30; Arhelger "questionnaire," p. 8.

20. Wharfield, "Apache Kid and the Record," p. 40; de la Garza, *Apache Kid*, p. 31. There is some confusion over whether Kid's father, or grandfather, was murdered.

21. de la Garza, *Apache Kid*, p. 31.

22. *Arizona Star*, June 7, 1887, quoted in Thrapp, *Al Sieber*, pp. 327-28.

23. de la Garza, *Apache Kid*, pp. 35-36; Williamson, "Apache Kid," pp. 30-31.

24. de la Garza, *Apache Kid*, pp. 36-37.

25. Williamson, "Apache Kid," pp. 30-31.

26. Thrapp, *Al Sieber*, p. 333; de la Garza, *Apache Kid*, p. 55.

27. Thrapp, *Al Sieber*, p. 333.

Notes to Chapter Eleven

1. Luckingham, *Phoenix*, p. 125; Myrick, *Railroads of Arizona*, vol. 2, pp. 494, 501. The school today is Arizona State University.

2. Sheridan, *Arizona*, p. 122.

3. Myrick, *Railroads of Arizona*, vol. 2, pp. 498-501; Powell, "Phoenix," p. 298; Trimble, *Arizona*, p. 204.

4. "O. W. Stubbs killed himself yesterday in an alley back of Fuqua's corral. Deceased was a native of Maine, from which he went as a colonist to…Mexico with H. M. Chase who arrived with him in Phoenix Tuesday morning last." *Phoenix Herald*, May 12, 1887.

5. 1880 U.S. Census, Sonoma County, Santa Rosa, California.

6. Miller, "Recollections of the Life of Minnie Kathryn Miller." Veronda, *History of Sonoma County*, p. 644. Daisy's father, Francis Howell, became the first postmaster of Fulton Crossroads in 1874.

7. Somers B. Fulton's name is listed in the back of Frank Hammon's 1887 diary, under correspondence received.

8. Unidentified newsclipping, McClintock Papers.

9. Anderson, *Arizona Legends and Lore*, p. 149.

10. Dedera, *A Little War of Our Own*, p. 35. Frank lists Albert Fulton's letter in the back of his diary, under correspondence received – July 12, 1887.

11. Dedera, *Arizona's Mogollon Rim*, p. 45; Deed Book 64, pp. 303-304, SCRO.

12. Undated newsclipping, McClintock Papers.

13. Myrick, *Railroads of Arizona*, vol. 2, p. 502.

14. Ibid., p. 503; Luckingham, *Phoenix*, p. 30; Trimble, *Arizona: A Cavalcade*, p. 189.

15. Deal, "That Town Ditch Again," *Arizona Republican*, April 1924. The old town ditch was eliminated in the 1920s.

16. *Phoenix Herald*, July 12, 1887.

17. Thrapp, *Encyclopedia of Frontier Biography*, vol. 1, p. 461.

18. Dedera, *A Little War of Our Own*, pp. 176, 278. Although J. W. Ellison served as a CSA soldier, there is no evidence that he was a Confederate colonel.

19. Ibid., p.176. The Apple ranch was located on what is today known as Ellison Creek. The Q Brand eventually was moved to the bigger range east of Pleasant Valley.

20. Dedera, *A Little War of Our Own*, p. 177.

Notes to Chapter Twelve

1. Woody and Schwartz, *Globe*, p. 129.

2. Ibid., pp. 129-31; Dedera, *A Little War of Our Own*, pp. 108-111.

3. Dedera, *A Little War of Our Own*, pp. 108-111.

4. Ibid., pp. 115-16; Woody and Schwartz, *Globe*, p. 124.

5. Woody and Schwartz, *Globe*, p. 124.

6. George Wilson was brother-in-law to George Newton and brother to Alice Wilson Newton. George Newton became Wilson's guardian following his parents' deaths. In time Wilson owned much of Pleasant Valley, including the Ellison Q ranch. He became a prominent Globe banker before his death in 1930. George Wilson and his wife, Betty, are buried in the Globe Cemetery.

7. Dedera, *A Little War of Our Own*, pp. 121-24. It has been suggested that the Daggses supplied the Tewksburys with the sophisticated weaponry.

8. Ibid., p. 126.

9. Criminal Cases, 1886-1887, microfilm, YCDCR.

10. Leslie Gregory, "Arizona's Haunted Walls of Silence," quoted in Hanchett, *Arizona's Graham-Tewksbury Feud*, p. 58.

11. Dedera, *A Little War of Our Own*, p. 131-32; Carlson, "James D. Houck: The Sheep King of Cave Creek," p. 47; Woody and Schwartz, *Globe*, p. 137.

12. Dedera, *A Little War of Our Own*, pp. 133-34; Hanchett, *Arizona's Graham-Tewksbury Feud*, p. 60. Forrest, *Arizona's Dark and Bloody Ground*, p. 93, states, "[Billy] did not know why the Tewksburys wanted to kill him."

13. Dedera, *A Little War of Our Own*, p. 135; Hanchett, *Arizona's Graham-Tewksbury Feud*, pp. 61-63.

14. Dedera, *A Little War of Our Own*, p. 135.

15. McKinney, "Reminiscences," p. 202.

16. Dedera, *A Little War of Our Own*, p. 142.

17. Ibid., pp. 145-46.

18. Ibid.; Ball, *Desert Lawmen*, p. 195; Woody and Schwartz, *Globe*, pp. 144-50.

19. *Apache County Critic*, September 10, 1887.

20. Ball, *Desert Lawmen*, pp. 195-96.

21. Thrapp, *Encyclopedia of Frontier Biography*, vol. 3, pp. 675-76. Dedera, *A Little War of Our Own*, p. 256, quotes Earle R. Forrest: "[Horn was] Known to have been associated with the Tewksburys, but his part in the vendetta has never been clearly established," Lillian Buckley Sherman Papers. Blevins's granddaughter, Lillian Buckley Sherman, retains a copy of the pardon dated October 24, 1888. Five-year-old Lillian survived the automobile accident that killed her grandfather, John B. Blevins, on May 23, 1929.

22. Sheridan, *Arizona*, p. 63; Dedera, *A Little War of Our Own*, pp. 156, 184; W. T. Sherman to W. W. Belknap, January 7, 1870, quoted in Ogle, *Federal Control of the Western Apaches*, p. 73. "The best advice I can offer is to notify all settlers and miners to get out of Arizona and then withdraw the troops and leave the country to the tribes as a perpetual Indian territory where they can plunder and kill each other to their hearts content," Sherman added.

Notes to Chapter Thirteen

1. Dedera, *A Little War of Our Own*, p. 158; Woody and Schwartz, *Globe*, p. 134. William Mulvenon, born in Massachusetts in 1851, worked as a miner, liveryman, bartender, and deputy sheriff and served two terms in the territorial legislature. Ball, *Desert Lawmen*, p. 241. Governor Zulick possibly considered sending in Fort Verde troops to end the feud. Zulick obviously had full confidence in Sheriffs Mulvenon and Owens's abilities to control the feudists.

2. Forrest, *Arizona's Dark and Bloody Ground*, pp. 140-42; Dedera, *A Little War of Our Own*, p. 162.

3. Dedera, *A Little War of Our Own*, pp. 162-63, 277 n.; Forrest, *Arizona's Dark and Bloody Ground*, pp. 142-43. Ellenwood may have been riding with Billy Graham when the young man was shot. His name is also spelled: Ellingwood, Ellinwood, and Underwood.

4. *Silver Belt*, September 24, 1887. Jim Anderson took Henry Hayse to see his Birds Nest Copper Mine adjoining the Globe mine. As he descended the ladder, Anderson lost his grip and fell sixty-five feet to the bottom of the shaft.

5. Dedera, *A Little War of Our Own*, p. 163.

6. McKinney, "Reminiscences," pp. 200-201; Dedera, *A Little War of Our Own*, p. 166.

7. *Silver Belt*, September 24, 1887.

8. Hayes, *Boots and Bullets*, p. 61.

9. Ibid., p. 62.

10. Burrows, *Vigilante*, p. 19; Brown, *Strain of Violence*, pp. 156-57. Clara Woody interview with Robert Voris and Dale S. King (1957), typescript, pp. 67-70, Woody Papers; Dedera, *A Little War of Our Own*, p. 184.

11. Dedera, *A Little War of Our Own*, p. 186.

12. Ibid., Voris and King interview, pp. 67-70. Accounts conflict over how Al Rose died. Earle Forrest, *Arizona's Dark and Bloody Ground*, p. 177, maintains he was shot.

13. Dedera, *A Little War of Our Own*, pp. 186, 188, 279 n.; Voris and King interview, p. 67. Some historians question the accuracy of Voris's statements.

14. Brown, *Strain of Violence*, pp. 93, 97; Ball, *Desert Lawmen*, p. 242; Burrows, *Vigilante*, p. 20.

Notes to Chapter Fourteen

1. *Silver Belt*, October 6, 29, 1887; Ball, *Desert Lawmen*, p. 345.

2. Maricopa County Records, Certificates of marriage, 1871-1960.

3. *Silver Belt*, November 5, 1887.

4. Ball, *Desert Lawmen*, pp. 7, 24, 26-27, 30.

5. Haak, *Copper Bottom Tales*, p. 61. As Globe's postmaster (1880-1885), Willis E. Spence's name appeared below the date within the postmark. Spence, who was suspected of torching the post office before turning it over to his successor, Edward O. Kennedy, served several months in jail before settling with postal officials.

6. Ball, *Desert Lawmen*, p. 21.

7. *Silver Belt*, November 14, 1887.

8. Prassel, *The Western Peace Officer*, p. 92; Ball, *Desert Lawmen*, pp. 108, 110, 119-21.

9. Anderson and Anderson, *Honor the Past*, p. 3; *Silver Belt*, December 3, 1887.

10. *Silver Belt*, December 3, 1887; Myrick, *Railroads of Arizona*, vol. 1, p. 835; Bigando, *Globe*, pp. 41, 48. The Old Dominion Mine Company was incorporated on January 28, 1888.

11. Myrick, *Railroads of Arizona*, vol. 1, p. 504.

12. Ball, *Desert Lawmen*, pp. 111-13.

13. Francisco Arellana was arrested by Frank Hammon on December 28, 1887, for breaking and entering, and "removing" forty dollars worth of possessions. GCDCR.

14. Forrest, *Arizona's Dark and Bloody Ground*, pp. 143, 338; *Silver Belt*, January 14, 1888, quoted in Woody and Schwartz, *Globe*, p. 249.

15. Banks, "The Pistol-Packing Red Poet McNeil," pp. 35-37.

16. Ball, *Desert Lawmen*, pp. 6-7, 42-43.

17. Adolph Solomon may have been related to Isador E. Solomon, businessman, banker, and founder of Solomonville, Arizona.

18. The Old Dominion Mine remained open under the ownership of William Keyser.

19. San Carlos farm boss Frank Porter had recovered from the wounds inflicted by Nah-deiz-az the previous spring.

20. Ball, *Desert Lawmen*, pp. 2, 3, 7. Following the 1846 Kearny Code, Arizona Territory set sheriff's fees for services rendered, established a two-year term, and required bonds for the sheriff and tax collector's positions. The county would provide office space and a $200 annual salary, plus a percentage of fees collected.

21. Bergon and Papanikolas, eds., *Looking Far West*, pp. 12-13.

22. Typescript, Woody Papers.

23. Ibid.

24. On June 4, 1889, legal proceedings were dismissed against Ellenwood, Louis Parker, Thomas Graham, Miguel Apodaca, William Bonner, William Gould, and Thomas Carrington. Criminal cases 21 and 22, YCDCR.

Notes to Chapter Fifteen

1. Initially, the telegraph connected Arizona's military outposts, but the heliograph proved more effective in the field. Private enterprise gradually took over, extending wires between counties. This enabled rapid exchange of information. Instead of relying on erratic mail deliveries, lawmen collaborated against criminals through the network of wires. Rue, "Pesh-Bi-Yalti Speaks White Man's Talking Wire In Arizona," pp. 256-57.

2. Ball, *Desert Lawmen*, p. 351; Lauer, *Tales of Arizona Territory*, pp. 97-98.

3. Lauer, *Tales of Arizona Territory*, pp. 106-108. Taken from Rice biographical file.

4. GCDCR.

5. Various spellings are used: Alviso, Arviso, Arvisu.

6. Ball, *Desert Lawmen*, pp. 66, 351; Swearengin, *Good Men, Bad Men, Law Men*, pp. 137-52.

7. Lauer, *Tales of Arizona Territory*, pp. 90-91.

8. Ball, *Desert Lawmen*, p. 66.

9. Trimble, *Arizona: A Panoramic History*, p. 292.

10. Lauer, *Tales of Arizona Territory*, pp. 92, 95; Ball, *Desert Lawmen*, p. 66; Trimble, *Arizona: A Panoramic History*, pp. 292-93; Rice biographical file.

11. Haak, *Copper Bottom Tales*, p. 42.

12. Ibid., pp. 41-42.

13. Woody and Schwartz, *Globe*, p. 189. The Gila Valley, Globe and Northern Railway arrived on December 1, 1898.

14. GCDCR.

Notes to Chapter Sixteen

1. *Silver Belt*, March 7, 1888.

2. Record Book 1, p. 109, file film 69.43, GCDCR.

3. Dr. Trippel returned to become superintendent of the Buffalo Mine.

4. LDS Ancestral File shows no relationship between Henry and the Hugh Blevins family.

5. Ball, *Desert Lawmen*, pp. 207-208; Prassel, *Western Peace Officer*, p. 248.

6. GCDCR.

7. Arrest warrant of Thomas Burns, March 24, 1888, Record Book 1, file film 69.43, GCDCR. There were four men in the Blevins family: father Hugh Thomas Vance Blevins; sons Cyrus Hugh, Hugh T., and Floyd. The most likely victim was Hugh Blevins, Sr. LDS.

8. GCDCR.

9. Unpublished typescript, Woody Collection; LDS; Hayes, *Sheriff Thompson's Day*, p. 43.

10. GCDCR.

11. *Silver Belt*, March 24, 1888.

12. Ibid.

13. Baeza, "The Lynching of Stott, Scott, and Wilson," pp. 34-37.

14. Dedera, *A Little War of Our Own*, pp. 188-89. Taken from Woody Papers.

15. Morris (or Maurice) Belnap. Possibly a Tewksbury sympathizer.

16. Although Frank indicates "last night," the attempted break-in occurred at 2:00 A.M. on April 13.

17. Ball, *Desert Lawmen*, p. 138.

18. Ibid.; Record Book 1, p. 46, film 69.43, GCDCR. "Dismissed" is handwritten in the records book.

19. Hayes, *Apache Vengeance*, pp. 31-33; Matthews, *Interwoven*, p. 162.

20. Dedera, *A Little War of Our Own*, pp. 166-67, 185-86.

21. Matthews, *Interwoven*, p. 162.

22. Ellison, *Cowboys Under the Mogollon Rim*, p. 9. "Slim" Ellison was named for his father Perle's idol, Glenn Reynolds.

23. Records Book 1, file film 69.43, GCDCR. Frank did not know McDonald previously, as he refers to him as "The man Arkansaw."

24. Ball, *Desert Lawmen*, pp. 138-39.

25. Records Book 1, file film 69.43, GCDCR. George Shute died in 1926, and is buried with his wife, Ella, in the Globe Cemetery.

26. Criminal Cases 256, 257, Maricopa County Superior Court Records, ADLAPR.

27. GCDCR. The Gila County board of supervisors was indicted for "Neglect of Official Duties." The offense included "construction of two certain Bridges across Pinal Creek...an expenditure exceeding two hundred dollars without first having given public notice."

28. *Silver Belt*, April 28, 1888.

29. Sam Bullock killed Ferdinand Hatch in a classic shootout over an election bet about 1886. Bullock was acquitted. Rose, *Prehistoric and Historic Gila County*, p. 20; Curnow, "Journey with Tom," pp. 71-72.

30. Criminal Cases 256, 257, Maricopa County Superior Court Records, ADLAPR; GCDCR; Hayes, *Boots and Bullets*, p. 84. On November 11, 1894, Blevins began his incarceration in Yuma Territorial Prison. Yuma Territorial Prison Records, ADLAPR.

31. Dedera, *A Little War of Our Own*, p. 256.

Notes to Chapter Seventeen

1. The *Silver Belt* issues are: March 31, 1888 through June 9, 1888; October 20, 1888 through January 26, 1889; October 26, 1889 through December 1889.

2. Unidentified newspaper articles, 1922 and April 1, 1931, McClintock Papers. Shute, "Pleasant Valley War, Revised," *Arizona Cattlelog*, April 1956, quoted in Dedera, *A Little War of Our Own*, p. 193. Gila County Superior Court Judge George W. Shute, son of George E. Shute, sat on the bench between 1912 and 1918. In 1931, Judge Shute was found guilty of concealing assets in voluntary bankruptcy proceedings and was disbarred from legal practice.

3. Ball, *Desert Lawmen*, pp. 247-48, 253.

4. Ibid., p. 209.

5. Unidentified newspaper article, May 5, 1888, McClintock Papers.

6. Ibid.

7. McKinney, "Reminiscences," p. 203. In 1892, John Rhodes appeared in a Phoenix courtroom for a preliminary hearing in the murder of Tom Graham.

8. *Phoenix Herald*, May 28, 1888.

9. *Silver Belt*, June 23, 1888.

10. Ball, *Desert Lawmen*, pp. 188-89; Prassel, *The Western Peace Officer*, p. 111.

11. *Silver Belt*, July 14, 1888.

12. William Croft Barnes, "The Pleasant Valley War of 1887," *Arizona Historical Review* (January 1932), quoted in Woody and Schwartz, *Globe*, p. 250 n.

13. *Silver Belt*, August 25, 1888, quoted in Dedera, *A Little War of Our Own*, pp. 189-90.

14. Osmer D. Flake, "Some Reminiscences of the Pleasant Valley War and Causes That Led Up to It," ed. Levi S. Udall, typescript, ASLAPR, quoted in Woody and Schwartz, *Globe*, p. 171. As a youth, O. D. Flake joined posses during the feud.

15. Dedera, *A Little War of Our Own*, p. 193.

16. Ibid., pp. 193-94; Baeza, "The Lynching of Stott, Scott, and Wilson," p. 36.

17. Baeza, "The Lynching of Stott, Scott, and Wilson," p. 36.

18. Barnes, *Apaches and Longhorns*, p. 154.

19. Dedera, *A Little War of Our Own*, pp. 194-96.

20. Baeza, "The Lynching of Stott, Scott, and Wilson," p. 36; *Journal-Miner* quoted in Dedera, *A Little War of Our Own*, p. 196.

21. McKinney, "Reminiscences," p. 203; Dedera, *A Little War of Our Own*, pp. 196-99.

22. Woody and Schwartz, *Globe*, p. 172.

23. Dedera, *A Little War of Our Own*, p. 202; Forrest, *Arizona's Dark and Bloody Ground*, pp. 124-25; Voris typescript, Woody Papers; Burrows, *Vigilante*, p. 20; Gordon, *The Great Arizona Orphan Abduction*, p. 258.

24. Brown, *Strain of Violence*, pp. 123, 157.

25. Hietter, "Lawyers, Guns, and Money," pp. 327-28, 342.

26. *Silver Belt*, August 11, 1888.

27. Ibid., August 18, 1888.

Notes to Chapter Eighteen

1. Unpublished typescript, Woody Collection; Ball, *Desert Lawmen*, p. 306. Benjamin Pascoe ended his own life on May 20, 1900, in Safford.

2. Records Book 1, file film 69.43, GCDCR.

3. Curnow, "Journey with Tom," p. 123.

4. Gordon, *The Great Arizona Orphan Abduction*, p. 260.

5. Ball, *Desert Lawmen*, p. 346. Beginning in 1870, territorial voters elected sheriffs to two-year terms in November. Their terms began January 1.

6. John Lapham Bullis joined the 126th New York Volunteer Infantry during the Civil War and saw action at Gettysburg. He served as San Carlos Reservation agent from June 1888 to 1891. Bullis's controversial firing of Al Sieber prompted unproven accusations of graft against the agent.

7. Thrapp, *Al Sieber*, p. 364; Thrapp, *Encyclopedia of Frontier Biography*, vol. 1, p. 189.

8. Benton taught the Indians farming methods. Thrapp, *Al Sieber*, pp. 369-70.

9. *Silver Belt*, January 26, 1889.

10. Hayes, *Apache Vengeance*, p. 33.

11. *Silver Belt*, January 26, 1889, notes that "Messrs. Thompson and Middleton, mail carriers on the Florence and Globe route, have been contending against great odds since the storm of last week."

12. Thrapp, *Al Sieber*, p. 359; Hayes, *Apache Vengeance*, pp. 27-29; de la Garza, *Apache Kid*, p. 73.

13. Hayes, *Apache Vengeance*, pp. 27-29.

14. *Silver Belt*, February 9, 1889.

15. Ibid., notes: "On motion it was ordered that the Sheriff be hereby authorized to employ all persons confined in the County jail…in working on the public works…or let out such prisoners at some labor….On motion the account of F. M. Hammon, Overseer of Globe Road District, was accepted."

16. The grand jury brought indictments; the petit jury was the trial jury.

Notes to Chapter Nineteen

1. March 9, 1889, diary entry; Gordon, *The Great Arizona Orphan Abduction*, pp. 211-12.

2. Young, *Western Mining*, p. 178; Gordon, *The Great Arizona Orphan Abduction*, p. 212.

3. Lingenfelter, *The Hardrock Miners*, pp. 23-24.

4. *Merck Manual*, 16th Edition.

5. Young, *Western Mining*, pp. 152, 302.

6. Ibid., p. 191; Gordon, *The Great Arizona Orphan Abduction*, p. 213.

7. Young, *Western Mining*, p. 191; Gordon, *The Great Arizona Orphan Abduction*, p. 213.

8. Young, *Western Mining*, p. 189; Lingenfelter, *The Hardrock Miners*, p. 25.

9. Young, *Western Mining*, p. 180.

10. Lingenfelter, *The Hardrock Miners*, p. 23.

11. Curnow, "Journey With Tom," p. 112.

12. Haak, *Copper Bottom Tales*, p. 27.

13. Ibid., p. 28; Hayes, *Sheriff Thompson's Day*, pp. 49-51; Curnow, "Journey With Tom," p. 111.

14. *Silver Belt*, March 9, 1889; Curnow, "Journey With Tom," pp. 112-13.

15. *Silver Belt*, March 9, 1889; GCDCR.

16. *Silver Belt*, March 16, 1889.

17. Hanchett, *The Graham-Tewksbury Feud*, pp. 76, 130.

18. Lamar, *The Far Southwest*, p. 434; Goff, *George W. P. Hunt*, pp. 11-12; Woody and Schwartz, *Globe*, p. 207.

19. *Silver Belt*, March 16, 1889. Dan Williamson served as San Carlos quartermaster clerk and telegraph operator until 1894. He was elected sheriff of Gila County in 1896. Williamson served as county treasurer in 1907 and as state historian in 1929. McClintock, *History of Arizona*, vol. 3, p. 600.

20. *Silver Belt*, April 6, 1889.

21. Ibid., March 30, 1889.

22. As a precursor to Prohibition, the movement resulted in the ratification of the 18th Amendment in 1919.

23. *Silver Belt*, March 30, 1889.

24. ADLAPR.

25. Ibid; Dedera, *A Little War of Our Own*, pp. 230-31, 250, 285 n. Ed Tewksbury married Braulia Lopez on March 12, 1897, and had several children. He died of "quick consumption" on April 4, 1904.

26. *Silver Belt*, April 20, 1889.

27. GCDCR.

28. Yuma Territorial Prison Records, ADLPR; Hietter, "Lawyers, Guns, and Money," p. 117; Faulk, *Arizona*, pp. 179-80; Hubbard, "Life in the Arizona Territorial Prison," p. 320; de la Garza, *The Apache Kid*, pp. 89-90. From July 1, 1876 to September 15, 1909, Yuma Territorial Prison housed 3,069 prisoners, including twenty-nine women. One hundred eleven prisoners died while incarcerated, most from tuberculosis. Twenty-six escaped, but only two from inside the walls.

29. Hubbard, "Life in the Arizona Territorial Prison," pp. 325-28.

30. Ibid., pp. 328-29.

31. Haak, *Copper Bottom Tales*, p. 29.

32. Ibid., pp. 29-30.

33. Ibid., p. 30.

34. Hietter, "Lawyers, Guns, and Money," pp. 109-110; Thrapp, *Al Sieber*, pp. 333-34; Hayes, *Apache Vengeance*, p. 40; *Silver Belt*, May 25, 1889.

35. Could Rob Montgomery be the same individual Dan Thrapp lists in his *Encyclopedia of Frontier Biography*? Thrapp states that Robert Hugh Montgomery arrived in Arizona in early 1872 and saw action in Captain Julius Wilmont Mason's fight at Muchas Cañones. "He [Montgomery] was brevetted Major for his Arizona work . . . [and] became Major of the 10th Cavalry March 8, 1891." Montgomery retired April 8, 1892, and died September 19, 1905, in Washington, D.C. Thrapp, *Encyclopedia of Frontier Biography*, vol. 2, pp. 1002-1003; Heitman, *Historical Register and Dictionary of the United States Army*, vol. 1, pp. 720-21; Thrapp, *Al Sieber*, p. 100 n.; Altshuler, *Cavalry Yellow and Infantry Blue*, p. 235.

Notes to Chapter Twenty

1. Gila County School Census, 1882-1907, NGCG.

2. *Silver Belt*, May 4, 1889.

3. Ibid.

4. Culley, *Cattle, Horses and Men of the Western Range*, pp. 188-89; Brown, *The American West*, pp. 59-62.

5. Culley, *Cattle, Horses and Men of the Western Range*, p. 190; Brown, *The American West*, p. 62.

6. Culley, *Cattle, Horses and Men of the Western Range*, p. 192; Brown, *The American West*, p. 62.

7. Culley, *Cattle, Horses and Men of the Western Range*, pp. 189-90, 193.

8. Trennert, "A Vision of Grandeur," pp. 350-53; Woody and Swartz, *Globe*, p. 192.

9. Thrapp, *Al Sieber*, p. 371 n.

10. Fazio, "Marcus Aurelius Smith," pp. 26-27. Kentuckian Smith became a Cochise County attorney, U. S. territorial delegate, and U.S. senator who championed Arizona statehood and water reclamation projects.

11. *Silver Belt*, June 22, 1889.

12. Ibid., July 6, 1889.

13. Ringgold, *Frontier Days in the Southwest*, pp. 41-42.

14. *Silver Belt*, July 6, 1889.

15. Monaghan, *Tom Horn*, p. 112; Nunis, *The Life of Tom Horn Revisited*, p. 50; Thrapp, *Encyclopedia of Frontier Biography*, vol. 2, p. 675.

16. Nunis, *The Life of Tom Horn Revisited*, pp. 11-13.

17. Ibid., pp. 28, 31, 36; Hagedorn, *Leonard Wood*, vol. 1, p. 85; Faulk, *The Geronimo Campaign*, p. 198; Davis, *The Truth About Geronimo*, p. 196; Thrapp, *Encyclopedia of Frontier Biography*, vol. 2, pp. 675-76.

18. Nunis, *The Life of Tom Horn Revisited*, pp. 49-53; Carlson, *Tom Horn*, pp. 36, 40-41.

19. Ball, ed., "'No Cure, No Pay', A Tom Horn Letter," p. 202; Thrapp, *Encyclopedia of Frontier Biography*, vol. 2, pp. 675-76; Monaghan, *Tom Horn*, p. 17.

20. Nunis, *The Life of Tom Horn Revisited*, pp. 58-59; Carlson, *Tom Horn*, p. 87; Monaghan, *Tom Horn*, p. 192. Horn served as U. S. Army packmaster in Santiago, Cuba, contracted yellow fever, and was honorably discharged in September 1898.

21. Monaghan, *Tom Horn*, p. 192.

22. Ibid., pp. 193, 195-96, 198; Krakel, *The Saga of Tom Horn*, pp. 17-18; Carlson, *Tom Horn*, pp. 20, 143-45; Nunis, *The Life of Tom Horn Revisited*, pp. 59, 61-62; Thrapp, *Encyclopedia of Frontier Biography*, vol. 2, p. 676.

23. Monaghan, *Tom Horn*, p. 198.

24. Ibid., p. 208; Nunis, *The Life of Tom Horn Revisited*, pp. 66-67.

25. Nunis, *The Life of Tom Horn Revisited*, pp. 74-79, 88. While in prison, Horn wrote a book of vindication, *Life of Tom Horn, Government Scout and Interpreter, Written by Himself*. Controversy abounds over the book's inaccuracies, exaggerations, and disputed authorship.

26. *Silver Belt,* July 6, 1889.

27. Thrapp, *Al Sieber*, pp. 365, 368.

28. Ibid., p. 361.

29. Ibid., p. 365.

30. Ibid., p. 367.

31. Ibid., p. 368

32. Ibid., p. 370.

33. "Synopsis of Report of Inspector Frank G. Armstrong, San Carlos Agency, Arizona (Bullis, Agent) August 6, 1889," M-234, RG 75, NA.

34. Ibid., pp. 369-70.

35. Thrapp, *Al Sieber*, pp. 372-73.

36. Ibid., p. 364.

37. *Silver Belt,* July 28, 1889.

Notes to Chapter Twenty-One

1. *Silver Belt,* August 17, 1889.

2. Ibid.

3. Ibid., September 7, 1889.

4. Hayes, *Boots and Bullets*, pp. 54-55; Ball, *Desert Lawmen*, p. 42.

5. Hayes, *Boots and Bullets*, pp. 54-55.

6. Ibid., p. 68.

7. Ibid., p. 79. Katherine Houston and John W. Wentworth, married October 1, 1890, moved to Globe in 1904 where he became probate judge and clerk of the Board of Supervisors. After statehood, he was elected clerk of the Superior Court, a position he held until age eighty-eight.

8. *Silver Belt,* September 7, 28, 1889.

Notes to Chapter Twenty-Two

1. *Silver Belt*, September 28, 1889.

2. Arhelger Papers, p. 9, Woody Collection; de la Garza, *Apache Kid*, pp. 63-65.

3. Thrapp, *Al Sieber*, p. 334; de la Garza, *Apache Kid*, p. 81; Hayes, *Apache Vengeance*, p. 46. Dan Williamson claimed Sieber had no animosity towards Kid.

4. Thrapp, *Al Sieber*, pp. 334-35; de la Garza, *Apache Kid*, pp. 74-75.

5. de la Garza, *Apache Kid*, p. 80. Joseph H. Kibbey, appointed by President Benjamin Harrison, later served as Arizona's territorial governor, 1905-1909.

6. Hayes, *Apache Vengeance*, pp. 48-51.

7. Ibid., pp. 59-60; Thrapp, *Al Sieber*, pp. 335-37.

8. GCDCR; de la Garza, *Apache Kid*, pp. 105-107.

9. de la Garza, *Apache Kid*, pp. 82-83; Arhelger Papers, Woody Collection. "At various points [in Arizona history] minorities were indeed treated differently—and unfairly—when compared to white defendants....Arizona's court and prison records suggest that minorities fared far better...than most scholars have acknowledged." Hietter, "Lawyers, Guns and Money," p. 417.

10. Hollister, "Organization and Administration of the Sheriff's Office in Arizona," p. 14; de la Garza, *Apache Kid*, p. 180; Hayes, *Apache Vengeance*, p. 67. Forrest, *Lone War Trail of Apache Kid*, p. 46, explains that Tom Horn was scheduled to assist Reynolds, but instead entered a Phoenix calf-roping contest. "The boys at Globe had bet their shirts and saddles on Tom Horn," so Reynolds excused him.

11. Middleton typescript, McClintock Papers; de la Garza, *Apache Kid*, p. 94; Hayes, *Apache Vengeance*, pp. 93-95.

12. *Silver Belt*, November 23, 1889. Jesus Avott's version of the shooting differed from that of Hos-cal-te.

13. Salyer, uncle of Jess Hayes's brother-in law, was undoubtedly Hayes's source of information. Gustie Reynolds, beside herself with grief, turned over her property to Ed Cook to sell and returned to Albany, Texas, with her four small children. In May 1890, Mexican rurales found Reynolds's watch and gun on a dead elderly Apache. Ed Cook returned the items to Reynolds's angry wife, who reportedly threatened a lawsuit against Gila County for failing to provide a suitable escort to accompany her husband.

14. Robinson, *Apache Voices*, p. 81; de la Garza, *Apache Kid*, p. 104. On July 4, 1890, newlywed Sheriff Jerry Ryan drowned as he unsuccessfully attempted to rescue Mary Frush from a capsized canoe on Pascoe Lake.

15. Williamson, "The Apache Kid," pp. 14-15, 31.

Notes to Chapter Twenty-Three

1. In 1902, Wendell P. Hammon developed a citrus ranch on the Feather River near Oroville. While digging a well, his Chinese workers discovered gold flecks deposited in silt. Wendell Hammon combined the ordinary sluice-box and common river dredge to produce the first successful bucket-elevator dredge. Mining journals were filled with stories of the incredible invention. Hammon expanded his holdings, making him the largest dredge operator in the nation. McGie, *History of Butte County*, p. 155. He was posthumously inducted into the Alaska Mining Hall of Fame in July 2001.

2. Moses, *Wild West Shows and the Images of American Indians*, p. 131.

3. Gilbert, *Perfect Cities*, p. 112; Frank Hammon obituary, undated newspaper, Amoret, Missouri.

4. HFB. Lewis Academy was later known as the Armour Institute, and then Illinois Institute of Technology.

5. Frank Hammon obituary; marriage license, Bates County Records, Missouri.

6. Jones, *Health-Seekers in the Southwest*, p. 160, observes that "overworked, undernourished, and debilitated factory workers and miners were easy prey for the silent working parasitic germ."

7. Death certificate, ACRO.

8. Warranty Deed, June 23, 1899, GCRO; U.S. Census, Cochise County, Arizona, 1900; *Bisbee-Douglas City Directory*, 1904, BMHM. Obituaries in *Bisbee Daily Review*, September 24, 1908, and *Bisbee Evening Miner*, September 23, 1908, mention no family attending the funeral, which was arranged and financed by the Bisbee Masons. Dugan Mortuary Records, Bisbee.

9. Engraved marker on Broad Street, Globe.

10. Woody and Swartz, *Globe*, p. 189. Frank Hammon sold his adobe house at Broad and Mesquite streets on May 19, 1897. His lot on the hill was sold on May 18, 1899. GCRO.

Notes to Afterword

1. "Head of BIA grants apology to Native Americans," *Hanford* (California) *Sentinel*, September 9, 2000.

Bibliography

Primary Sources

Archival Material

Arizona Department of Library, Archives and Public Records, Phoenix (ADLAPR)

Arizona Territorial Prison Records, 1875-1914. RG 85, file film No. 23.1.1, November 11, 1894.

Charles T. Connell. Biographical, Vertical file.

Gila County

    Gila County Great Registers, 1882, 1888. RG 103, file film, 51.12.2.

    Gila County Roster of Officials 1881-1899. Works Progress Administration (WPA), file film, 51.27.1.

    Gila County Records. RG 103, Appointments, Box 1.

Maricopa County

    Maricopa County Superior Court, Probate Records. RG 107, Case No. 98, February 23, 1887.

    Maricopa County Superior Court. *Territory of Arizona vs. Thomas Burns and Henry Blevins.* RG 107, Case Nos. 256, 257, file film No. 4, April 19, 1888.

Yavapai County

    Yavapai County Justice Court. *Territory of Arizona vs. Louis Parker, Thomas Graham, Miguel Apodaca, William Bonner, Joseph Ellenwood, William Gould, and Thomas Carrington.* RG 113, Case No. 20, December 3, 1888.

    _____. *Territory of Arizona vs. James Tewksbury, Ed. Tewksbury, Joseph Boyer, James Roberts, George Newton, Jacob Lauffer, George Wagner.* RG 113, Case Nos. 21, 22, December 3, 1888.

Arizona Historical Society, Tucson (AHS)

    Manuscript Collections

      Curnow, Alice. Papers.

      Hazelton, Drusilla. Papers

      Rice, Michael M. Papers.

      Smith, Marcus Aurelius. Papers.

      Williamson, Dan R. Papers.

      Woody, Clara T. Collection, boxes 6-8, 16.

Oral History Collection
  Clara Woody and Dale Stuart King interview with Robert Voris in 1957.
Photograph Collections
  Buehman Collection.
  Charles Morgan Wood Collection.
  Will C. Barnes Collection.
  Camillus S. Fly Collection.

Arizona State University, Tempe
  Arizona Historical Foundation (AHF)
    Hunt, George W. P. Collection.
  Special Collections (SC, ASUL)
    Barnes, Will C. Collection.
    Ellison, Glenn R. "Slim." Collection.
    Duette Ellison Hunt autograph book, Arizona Collection.

University of Arizona Library, Special Collections, Tucson (SC, UAL)
  Shute, George. Papers.
  Tewksbury, Edwin. Papers.

Arapahoe County Records Office, Denver (ACRO)
  Department of Vital Records

Bates County Records Office, Missouri (BCRO)
  Marriage Records

Bisbee Mining and Historical Museum
  Bisbee-Douglas City Directory, 1904.

Church of Jesus Christ of Latter-day Saints, Family History Center, Salt Lake City (LDS)
  Hugh Thomas Vance Blevins Ancestral File, 1KMK-864.

Edinboro University, Erie County, Pennsylvania (EU)
  Alumni Records, 1871-1877.

Gila County District Court Records, Globe (GCDCR)
  Territory of Arizona vs. Frank M. Hammon. Book 1, file film 69.43, p. 27, May 10, 1882.
  F. M. Hammon vs. F. Hatch. Case No. 243, September 16, 1885.
  Territory of Arizona vs. John Thomas. Book 1, file film 69.43, September 28, 1885.
  Territory of Arizona vs. John H. Eaton. Book 1, file film 69.43, December 13, 1887.
  Territory of Arizona vs. Francisco Arellana. Book 1, file film 69.43, December 28, 1887.
  Territory of Arizona vs. Rafael Arviso. Book 1, file film 69.43, February 28, 1888.
  Territory of Arizona vs. W. R. McDonald. Book 1, file film 69.43, March 11, 1888.
  Territory of Arizona vs. Thomas Burns and Henry Blevins. Book 1, file film 69.43,
    April 1888.
  Territory of Arizona vs. Pearlie [Perle] *Ellison.* Book 1, file film 69.43, p. 45,
    April 13, 1888.
  Territory of Arizona vs. Glenn Reynolds. Book 1, file film 69.43, p. 46, April 13, 1888.
  Territory of Arizona vs. Cyrus Blevins. Book 1, file film 69.43, p. 47, April 16, 1888; October
    24, 1889.
  Territory of Arizona vs. Alfred Kinney, Joseph Redman, and Louis Sultan. Book 1, file film
    69.43, April 20, 1888.
  Territory of Arizona vs. John Newman. Book 1, file film 69.43, March 8, 1889.

Territory of Arizona vs. Has-tui-tu-jay, Captain Jack, El-cahn, Te-te-che-le, and Lah-ca-hor. Book 1, file film 69.43, October 1889.

Territory of Arizona vs. Kid, Hale, Say-es, and Pash-ten-tah. Book 1, file film 69.43, October 1889.

Territory of Arizona vs. Nan-deiz-az. Book 1, file film 69.43, October 1889.

Territory of Arizona vs. Jesus Avott. Book 1, file film 69.43, October 1889.

Gila County Records Office, Globe (GCRO)

Book of Brands.

Gila County Real Estate Grantee and Grantor Books 1-10.

Gila County Mine Register.

Maricopa County Records Office (MCRO)

Certificates of Marriage, 1871-1960.

Wills and Estates, 1877-1948.

Mine Claims

Newberry Library, Chicago

Everett D. Graff Collection

Livestock Sanitary Board of Arizona. *Territorial Book of Brands and Marks: Cattle, Horses, Sheep, and Horses.* Phoenix: Press Arizona Republican, 1898.

Edward E. Ayer Collection

Northern Gila County Genealogical Society, Payson (NGCG)

Gila County School Census, 1882-1907.

Phoenix Public Library (PPL)

McClintock, James H. Papers.

Sherman, Lillian Buckley. Papers, Hanford, California

Andy Cooper (Blevins) letters, August 19, 1886, April 17, 1887.

Martin J. Blevins (Mart) letters, February 20, 1887, May 26, June 20, 1887.

Albert Charles Blevins (Charlie) letter, June 21, 1887.

Petition for Pardon of John Black Blevins signed by Governor C. Meyer Zulick, October 24, 1888.

Sonoma County Genealogical Society, California

Sonoma County Marriages, 1847-1902.

Sonoma County Records Office, Santa Rosa, California (SCRO)

Index and Abstracts of Wills, 1850-1900.

Real Estate Abstracts, Books 48-76.

St. Paul's Methodist Church, Globe (SP)

"St. Paul's Methodist Church History," unpublished typescript.

Record of Marriages.

Yavapai County District Court Records, Prescott (YCDCR)

Territory of Arizona vs. George Wilson. File film 1886-1887. August 15, 1887.

Territory of Arizona vs. Louis Parker, Thomas Graham, Miguel Apodaca, William Bonner, Joseph Ellenwood, William Gould, and Thomas Carrington. File film 1886-1887, Criminal Cases No. 21, 22. June 4, 1889.

Yuba County Library, Marysville, California (YCL)

Hammon, Wendell P. Collection.

National Archives, Washington, D. C. (NA)
Record Group 75
Bureau of Indian Affairs. "Synopsis of Report of Inspector Frank G. Armstrong, San Carlos Agency, Arizona, (Bullis, Agent) August 6, 1889." Microfilm #M-234.

GOVERNMENT DOCUMENTS
Heitman, Francis B. *Historical Register and Dictionary of the United States Army, From Its Organization, September 29, 1789, to March 2, 1903.* 2 vols. Washington D. C.: Government Printing Office, 1903. Reprint 1994.

U.S. Bureau of the Census
1850 El Dorado County, California.
1880 Pinal County, Globe, Miami, Arizona.
1860, 1870, 1880, 1890 (reconstructed) Sonoma County, California.
1900 Cochise County, Arizona.

PERSONAL COMMUNICATIONS AND INTERVIEWS
Alberta W. Hunsberger, Evanston, Illinois, August 1997.
Jane Stearns Minor, Evanston, Illinois, August 1997.
Lillian Buckley Sherman, Hanford, California, April 2003.
Julia Hammon Woodruff Snead, Palm City, Florida, April 1998.
John H. Hammon, Berry Creek, California, August 18, 2000.

PERSONAL DOCUMENTS AND CORRESPONDENCE
Hammon Family Bible.
Hammon Family Papers.
Frank M. Hammon diaries, 1886-1890.
Frank M. Hammon letters, 1882-1906.
Daisy Howell Hammon letters, 1882-1886.
Adeline Fisher Hammon diaries, 1865-1868.
Newman A. Hall Papers.
Don Dedera letter, September 17, 1997.

PRIMARY SOURCES

UNPUBLISHED
Curnow, Alice. "The Journey With Tom or Law Beyond the Pinals," typescript, Arizona Historical Society, 1940.
Flake, Osmer D. "Some Reminiscences of the Pleasant Valley War and Causes That Led Up to It," typescript edited by Levi S. Udall, Arizona Archives, Library and Public Records, 1958.
Hazelton, Drusilla. "The Tonto Basin's Early Settlers," Arizona Historical Society, 1977.
Miller, Minnie Kathryn. "Recollections of The Life of Minnie Kathryn Miller," typescript, Sonoma County Library, 1975.

ARTICLES
Barnes, Will C. "The Pleasant Valley War of 1887. Part 2." *Arizona Historical* Review. 4 (January, 1932): 23-40.
Connell, Charles T. "The Apache, Past and Present." *Tucson Citizen*, February 6-July 31, 1921.

Forbes, Robert H. "The Penningtons, Pioneers of Early Arizona." *Arizona Archeological and Historical Society* (1919): 31.

McKinney, Joe T. "Reminiscenses." *Arizona Historical Review* 5 (1932): 198-204.

Murphy, Merwin L. "W. J. Murphy and the Arizona Canal Company." *Journal of Arizona History* 23 (Summer 1982): 139-70.

Shute, George W. "Pleasant Valley War, Revised." *Arizona Cattlelog* (April 1956).

Williamson, Dan R. "The Apache Kid: Red Renegade of the West." *Arizona Highways* 15 (May, 1939): 14-15, 30-31.

BOOKS

Barnes, Will C. *Apaches and Longhorns: The Reminiscences of Will C. Barnes.* Los Angeles: Ward Ritchie Press, 1941; reprint, 1982.

Barrett, S. M., ed. *Geronimo, His Own Story.* New York: E. P. Dutton & Company, 1970.

Bourke, John G. *An Apache Campaign in the Sierra Madre.* New York: Charles Scribner's Sons, 1886; new ed., 1958.

Davis, Britton. *The Truth about Geronimo.* New Haven: Yale University Press, 1929.

Ellison, Glenn R. "Slim." *Cowboys Under the Mogollon Rim.* Tucson: University of Arizona Press, 1968.

Horn, Tom. *Life of Tom Horn, Government Scout and Interpreter, Written by Himself, Together with His Letters and Statement by His Friends: A Vindication.* Denver: The Louthan Book Company, 1904; reprint, Norman: University of Oklahoma Press, 1964.

Matthews, Sallie Reynolds. *Interwoven: A Pioneer Chronicle.* College Station: Texas A&M University Press, 1936.

Mazzanovich, Anton. *Trailing Geronimo.* Los Angeles: Stanley J. Wilson Publisher, 1926.

McClintock, James H. *Arizona: Prehistoric, Aboriginal, Pioneer, Modern.* 3 vols. Chicago: The S. J. Clarke Publishing Co., 1916.

Miles, Nelson A. *Serving the Republic: Memoirs of the Civil and Military Life of Nelson A. Miles.* New York: Harper & Brothers Publishers, 1911.

Munro-Frazer, J. P. *History of Sonoma County.* San Francisco: Alley, Bowen & Co., 1880.

Ringgold, Fannie Parks, *Frontier Days in the Southwest.* San Antonio: The Naylor Co., 1952.

Rose, Dan. *Prehistoric and Historic Gila County, Arizona.* Globe: self-published, 1935.

Summerhayes, Martha. *Vanished Arizona: Recollections of the Army Life of a New England Woman.* Reprint, Lincoln: University of Nebraska Press, 1979.

NEWSPAPERS

Arizona Citizen (Tucson)

Apache County Critic

Arizona Gazette (Phoenix)

Arizona Republican (Phoenix)

Arizona Sentinel (Yuma)

Arizona Silver Belt (Globe)

Arizona Star (Tucson)

Arizona Weekly Democrat (Prescott)

Bisbee Daily Review

Bisbee Evening Miner

Chicago Daily News

Hanford Sentinel (California)

Phoenix Weekly Herald

Prescott Journal-Miner

San Francisco Exchange
Tombstone Epitaph
Tombstone Daily Prospector

SECONDARY SOURCES

UNPUBLISHED

Bret Harte, John. "The San Carlos Indian Reservation 1872-1886: An Administrative History." 2 vols. Ph.d. dissertation, University of Arizona, 1972.

Hietter, Paul Thomas. "Lawyers, Guns and Money: The Evolution of Crime and Criminal Justice in Arizona Territory." Ph.d dissertation, Arizona State University, 1999.

_____. "Popular Justice Run Amok: The Globe Lynchings of 1882." Paper presented at the Arizona History Convention, Prescott, April 1999.

Hollister, Charles A. "The Organization and Administration of the Sheriff Office in Arizona." Masters Thesis, University of Arizona, 1946.

ARTICLES

Anderson, Douglas Firth. "Protestantism, Progress, and Prosperity: John P. Clum and 'Civilizing' the U. S. Southwest, 1871-1886." *Western Historical Quarterly*, 33 (Autumn 2002): 315-35.

Ball, Larry D. "No Cure, No Pay." *Journal of Arizona History* 8 (Autumn 1967): 200-202.

Banks, Leo W. "The Pistol-Packing Red Poet McNeil." *Arizona Highways* 76 (October 2000): 34-37.

Baeza, Jo. "The Lynching of Stott, Scott, and Wilson." *Arizona Highways* 75 (October 1999): 34-37.

Beatty, William B. "The Tunnel: A Fragment of Railroad History in Arizona Territory." *Arizona and the West* 1 (Summer 1959): 174-77.

Brandes, Ray. " A Guide to the History of U. S. Army Installations in Arizona 1849-1886." *Arizona and the West* 1 (Spring 1959): 62-67.

Bret Harte, John. "The Strange Case of Joseph C. Tiffany: Indian Agent in Disgrace." *Journal of Arizona History* 16 (Winter 1975): 383-404.

Brinckerhoff, Sidney B. "Frontier Soldiers in Arizona: Graphic Arts on the Arizona Frontier." *Journal of Arizona History* 12 (Autumn 1971): 168.

Butchart, Ronald E. "The Frontier Teacher: Arizona, 1875-1925." *Journal of the West* 16 (July 1977): 54-65.

Carlson, Frances C. "James D. Houck: The Sheep King of Cave Creek." *Journal of Arizona History* 21 (Spring 1980): 43-47.

Deal, Ralph. "That Town Ditch Again." *Arizona Republic*, April 13, 1924.

Egerton, Kearney. "The Big Holbrook Gunfight." *Arizona Republic*, February 17, 1987.

Fazio, Steven A. "Marcus Aurelius Smith: Arizona Delegate and Senator." *Arizona and the West* 12 (Spring 1970): 23-62.

Fischer, Christiane. "A Profile of Women in Arizona in Frontier Days." *Journal of the West* 16 (July 1977): 42-53.

Gregory, Leslie. "Arizona's Haunted Walls of Silence." *Arizona Highways* (October 1947) 34-35.

Hubbard, Paul G. "Life in the Arizona Territorial Prison, 1876-1910." *Arizona and the West* 1 (Winter 1959): 317-30.

Mawn, Geoffrey P. "Selection of the Phoenix Townsite." *Arizona and the West* 19 (Autumn 1977): 212-19.

Opler, Morris E. "A Chiricahua Apache's Account of the Geronimo Campaign of 1886." *Journal of Arizona History* 27 (Spring 1986): 71-90.

Peterson, Thomas H., Jr. "Cash Up or No Go: The Stagecoach Era in Arizona." *Journal of Arizona History* 14 (Autumn 1973): 205-207.

Powell, Lawrence. "Phoenix." *Journal of Arizona History* 18 (Autumn 1977): 295-98.

Rue, Norman L. "Pesh-Bi-Yalti Speaks White Man's Talking Wire In Arizona." *Journal of Arizona History* 12 (Winter 1971): 229-57.

Schmidt, Mrs. Kurt. "Commodore Perry Owens." *Journal of Arizona History* 1 (Autumn 1960): 6-8.

Simms, D. Harper. "The Apache Scouts Who Won A War." *Great Western Indian Fights.* New York: Doubleday & Company, 1960.

Sonnichsen, C. L. " From Savage to Saint: A New Image for Geronimo." *Journal of Arizona History* 27 (Spring 1986): 5-34.

Spude, Robert L. "Mineral Frontiers in Transition: Copper Mining in Arizona 1880-1885." *New Mexico Historical Review* 51 (January 1976): 19-34.

_____. "Shadow Catchers: A Portrait of Arizona's Pioneer Photographers, 1863-1893." *Journal of Arizona History* 30 (Autumn 1989): 238-40.

Trennert, Robert A. "A Vision of Grandeur: The Arizona Mineral Belt Railroad." *Arizona and the West* 12 (Winter 1970): 339-54.

_____. "A Different Perspective: Victorian Travelers in Arizona, 1860-1900." *Journal of Arizona History* 29 (Winter 1988): 349-68.

Turcheneske, John A., Jr. "The Arizona Press and Geronimo's Surrender." *Journal of Arizona History* 14 (Summer 1973): 133-47.

Wharfield, H. B. "Apache Kid and the Record." *Journal of Arizona History* 6 (Spring 1975): 37-46.

Willson, Roscoe G. "Long-Haired Sheriff Was No Bluffer." *Arizona Sheriff* (September-October 1962): 10.

BOOKS

Altshuler, Constance Wynn. *Starting With Defiance: Nineteenth Century Arizona Military Posts.* Tucson: Arizona Historical Society, 1983.

_____. *Cavalry Yellow and Infantry Blue: Army Officers in Arizona Between 1851 and 1886.* Tucson: Arizona Historical Society, 1991.

Anderson, Dorothy Daniels. *Arizona Legends and Lore.* Phoenix: Golden West Publishers, 1991.

Anderson, Guy and Donna, eds. *Honor the Past...Mold the Future.* Globe: Gila Centennials, 1976.

Ball, Larry D. *Desert Lawmen: The High Sheriffs of New Mexico and Arizona 1846-1912.* Albuquerque: University of New Mexico Press, 1992.

Basso, Keith H. *Wisdom Sits in Places.* Albuquerque: University of New Mexico Press, 1996.

_____. *The Cibecue Apache.* New York: Holt, Rinehart and Winston, 1970.

_____. *Western Apache Raiding and Warfare.* Tucson: University of Arizona Press, 1971.

Beebe, Lucius. *The Central Pacific & Southern Pacific Railroads.* Berkley, Calif.: Howell-North Books, 1963.

Bergon, Frank, and Zeese Papanikolas, eds. *Looking Far West: The Search for the American West in History, Myth, and Literature.* New York: New American Library, 1978.

Bigando, Robert. *Globe, Arizona: The Life and Times of A Western Mining Town.* Globe: Mountain Spirit Press, 1989.

_____. and John W. Hohmann. *Besh-Ba-Gowah Archaeological Park: Interpretive Guide,* Globe: City of Globe, 1987.

Brandes, Ray. *Frontier Military Posts of Arizona.* Globe: Dale Stuart King, 1960.

Brewer, William H. *Up and Down California*. New Haven: Yale University Press, 1930.

Brown, Dee. *The American West*. New York: Simon & Schuster, 1994.

Brown, Richard Maxwell. *Strain of Violence*. New York: Oxford University Press, 1975.

Burrows, William E. *Vigilante!* New York: Harcourt Brace Jovanovich, 1976.

Carlson, Chip. *Tom Horn, Blood on the Moon: Dark History of the Murderous Cattle Detective*. Cheyenne, Wyo.: High Plains Press, 2001.

Collins, Charles. *Apache Nightmare: The Battle At Cibecue Creek*. Norman: University of Oklahoma Press, 1999.

Culley, John H. *Cattle, Horses and Men of the Western Range*. Tucson: University of Arizona Press, 1967.

Debo, Angie. *Geronimo: The Man, His Time, His Place*. Norman: University of Oklahoma Press, 1976.

Dedera, Don. *A Little War of Our Own: The Pleasant Valley Feud Revisited*. Flagstaff: Northland Press, 1988.

_____. *Arizona's Mogollon Rim: Travel Guide to Payson and Beyond*. Phoenix: *Arizona Highways* and U. S. Forest Service, 1992.

de la Garza, Phyllis. *The Apache Kid*. Tucson: Westernlore Press, 1995.

Delay, Peter J. *History of Yuba and Sutter Counties, California*. Los Angeles: Historic Record Co., 1924.

DeMontravel, Peter R. *A Hero to His Fighting Men: Nelson A. Miles, 1839-1925*. Kent, Ohio: Kent State University Press, 1998.

Dillard, Gary. *Bisbee's Fabulous Queen*. Bisbee: Frontera House Press, 1998.

Dunning, Charles H. and Edward H. Peplow, Jr. *Rocks to Riches: The Story of American Mining...Past, Present and Future*. Phoenix: Southwest Publishing Co., 1959.

Faulk, Odie B. *Arizona: A Short History*. Norman: University of Oklahoma Press, 1970.

_____. *The Geronimo Campaign*. New York: Oxford University Press, 1993.

Forrest, Earle R. *Arizona's Dark and Bloody Ground*. Caldwell, Idaho: The Caxton Printers, 1936; revised and expanded, 1952; reprint, Tucson: University of Arizona Press, 1984.

_____ and Edwin B. Hill. *Lone War Trail of Apache Kid*. Pasadena, Calif.: Trail's End Publishing Co., 1949.

Gilbert, James. *Perfect Cities: Chicago's Utopias of 1893*. Chicago: University of Chicago Press, 1991.

Goff, John S. *George W. P. Hunt and His Arizona*. Pasadena, Calif.: Socio-Technical Publications, 1973.

Goodwin, Grenville. *Western Apache Raiding and Warfare*. Keith H. Basso, ed. Tucson: University of Arizona Press, 1971.

Gordon, Linda. *The Great Arizona Orphan Abduction*. Cambridge: Harvard University Press, 1999.

Greever, William S. *The Bonanza West: The Story of the Western Mining Rushes, 1848-1900*. Norman: University of Oklahoma Press, 1963.

Haak, W. A. *Copper Bottom Tales: Historic Sketches from Gila County*. Globe: Gila County Historical Society, 1991.

Hagedorn, Hermann. *Leonard Wood: A Biography*. New York: Harper & Brothers, 1931.

Hanchett, Leland J., Jr. *Arizona's Graham-Tewksbury Feud*. Phoenix: Pine Rim Publishing, 1994.

_____. *Black Mesa*. Phoenix: Pine Rim Publishing, 1996.

_____. *The Crooked Trail to Holbrook: An Arizona Cattle Trail*. Phoenix: Arrowhead Press, 1993.

Hatfield, Shelley Bowen. *Chasing Shadows: Indians Along the United States-Mexico Border, 1876-1911*. Albuquerque: University of New Mexico Press, 1998.

Hayes, Jess G. *Apache Vengeance.* Albuquerque: University of New Mexico Press, 1954.

_____. *Boots and Bullets: The Life and Times of John W. Wentworth.* Tucson: University of Arizona Press, 1967.

_____. *Sheriff Thompson's Day.* Tucson: University of Arizona Press, 1968.

Horan, James D. *The Great American West.* New York: Crown Publishers, 1959.

Jeffrey, Julie Roy. *Frontier Women: The Trans-Mississippi West, 1840-1880.* New York: Hill and Wang, 1979.

Jones, Billy M. *Health-Seekers in the Southwest, 1817-1900.* Norman: University of Oklahoma Press, 1967.

King, Jean Beach. *Arizona Charlie.* Phoenix: Heritage Publishers, 1988.

Krakel, Dean F. *The Saga of Tom Horn: The Story of a Cattlemen's War.* Lincoln: University of Nebraska Press, 1954.

Kuykendall, Ivan Lee. *Ghost Riders of the Mogollon.* San Antonio: The Naylor Company, 1954.

Lamar, Howard Roberts. *The Far Southwest, 1846-1912: A Territorial History.* Alburquerque: University of New Mexico Press, 2000.

LaFarge, Oliver. *A Pictorial History of the American Indian.* New York: Crown Publishers, 1956.

Lauer, Charles, D. *Tales of Arizona.* Phoenix: Golden West Publishers, 1990.

Lingenfelter, Richard E. *The Hardrock Miners: A History of the Mining Labor Movement in the American West 1863-1893.* Berkley: University of California Press, 1974.

Lowe, Sam. *The Old West Highway, Where History Still Lives.* Globe: Old West Highway Committee, 1996.

Luckingham, Bradford. *Phoenix: The History of a Southwestern Metropolis.* Tucson: University of Arizona Press, 1989.

McGie, Joseph F. *History of Butte County.* Oroville, Calif.: Butte County Office of Education, 1956.

McNamee, Gregory. *Gila: The Life and Death of an American River.* New York: Orion Books, 1994.

Martin, Douglas D. *An Arizona Chronology: The Territorial Years 1846-1912.* Tucson: University of Arizona Press, 1963.

Miller, Joseph. *Arizona, The Grand Canyon State: A State Guide.* New York: Hastings House, 1940.

Monaghan, Jay. *Tom Horn: Last of the Bad Men.* Reprint, Lincoln: University of Nebraska Press, 1997.

Moses, L. G. *Wild West Shows and the Images of American Indians, 1883-1933.* Albuquerque: University of New Mexico Press, 1996.

Moses, Norton H. *Lynching and Vigilantism in the United States: An Annotated Bibliography.* Westport, Conn.: Greenwood Press, 1997.

Myrick, David F. *Railroads of Arizona.* Vols. 1-2. San Diego: Howell-North Books, 1980.

Nunis, Doyce B., Jr. *The Life of Tom Horn Revisited.* San Marino, Calif.: Los Angeles Corral of the Westerners, 1992.

Ogle, Ralph Hedrick. *Federal Control of the Western Apaches, 1848-1886.* Albuquerque: University of New Mexico Press, 1970.

Prassel, Frank Richard. *The Western Peace Officer: A Legacy of Law and Order.* Norman: University of Oklahoma Press, 1972.

Roberts, David. *Once They Moved Like the Wind: Cochise, Geronimo, and the Apache Wars.* New York: Simon & Schuster, 1994.

Robinson, Sherry. *Apache Voices: Their Stories of Survival as Told to Eve Ball.* Albuquerque: University of New Mexico Press, 2000.

Sheridan, Thomas E. *Arizona: A History.* Tucson: University of Arizona Press, 1996.

Swearingen, John A. *Good Men, Bad Men, Lawmen and A Few Rowdy Ladies.* Florence, Arizona: self-published, 1991.

Tinkle, Lon and Allen Maxwell, eds. *The Cowboy Reader: The American Cowboy's Life On The Range.* New York: Longmans, Green & Co., 1959.

Thrapp, Dan L. *The Conquest of Apacheria.* Norman: University of Oklahoma Press, 1967.

_____. *Al Sieber: Chief of Scouts.* Norman: University of Oklahoma Press, 1964.

_____. *Encyclopedia of Frontier Biography.* 4 vols. Glendale, Calif.: Arthur H. Clark, 1988.

Trimble, Marshall. *Arizona: A Panoramic History of a Frontier State.* Garden City, New York: Doubleday & Company, 1977.

_____. *Arizona: A Cavalcade of History.* Tucson: Treasure Chest Publications, 1989.

Veronda, Charmaine Burdell, ed. *History of Sonoma County.* Repub. Petaluma (Calif.): 1973.

Woody, Clara T. and Milton L. Schwartz. *Globe, Arizona.* Tucson: Arizona Historical Society, 1977.

Wyllys, Rufus Kay. *Arizona: History of a Frontier State.* Phoenix: Hobson and Herr, 1950.

Young, Otis E, Jr. *Western Mining.* Norman: University of Oklahoma Press, 1970.

Zachariae, Barbara. *Pleasant Valley Days.* Young: Pleasant Valley Historical Society, 1993.

REFERENCE WORKS

Warriner, Gray, prod., *Besh-Ba-Gowah.* Globe: Camera One, 1996. Videocassette.

Merck Manual, 16th Edition, Rahway, N.J.: Merck Research Laboratory, 1992.

INDEX

Howell, Francis N. (Daisy's dad), 68; after death of Daisy Hammon, 251-253; life in Globe, 7, 11, 89, 91-92; photograph of, 91; and Pleasant Valley War, 44

Howell, May Fowler, 251-252

Howell, Sara Sanford, 251

Howet, Mr., 184

Hughes, Miss, 199

Hunsaker, D. N., 90

Hunt, George W. P., 92, 198-199

Hunt, Helen "Duette" Ellison, 92

Hunter, David, 31

Hyndmen, Jeremiah, 161

Ice Works (Phoenix), 69

Idaho, 146

Illinois, 60, 64, 71, 75, 90, 95, 104; federal prisoners sent to, 267 n9; Frank Hammon's family in, 227, 251; Frank Hammon returns to, 173, 246-247

Illinois Institute of Technology. See Lewis Academy

Indian Rights Association, 207

Ingalls, Mr., 155

Insane Asylum (Phoenix), 69, 74

Inspiration Mine, 206

Iowa, 46

Irwin, John N, 266 n8

Isabell Sharp vs. W. H. Duryea, 147

Jackson, Mr., 194

Jacobs, John, 47,

Jacobs, Wash, 168,

Jacobs, William, 114, 117, 199

James (Graham County deputy sheriff), 144

Jeffrey, Julie Roy, 11

Jensen, J. F. W., 216-217, 220, 222-224, 227-228, 230-231, 237, 241-242

J. J. Pfister & Company, 103

Joe Chinaman, 84

Johnson, Capt., 236

Johnson, Carter, 99

Johnson, David, 144

Johnson, Lewis, 210

Jones, John, 37, 204-205, 214, 227

Jordan, Frank, 154

Joseph Redman et al. vs. J. H. Eaton, 144

Juh (Chiricahua Apache), 23

Julliard Park (Santa Rosa, California), 15

Jun H, 147

Jun H vs. Robert Shell, 147

Kansas, 100, 158

Kansas City, Missouri, 220, 251,

Kayihtah (Apache Indian scout), 58

Kellner, E. F., 228; photograph of, 197

Kelly, Mr., 204

Kelner, E. T., 194

Kelner Company, 192, 195

Kelvin, 238

Kelvin Grade, 239-240

Kennedy, Edward O., 270 n5

Kennedy, Mrs. John, 9

Kennedy, Lizzie, 206-207

Kennedy, Mamie, 181, 185, 189, 192, 206-207, 213, 222

Kennedy, Sylva, 222-223

Kennedy, Tonnie, 9

Kenney, Augusta "Gussie." See Hammon, Augusta "Gussie" Kenney

Kenton, Mr., 93, 202

Kenton Ranch, 115, 120, 215

Kenyon, Charles H., 161

Keyser, R. Brent, 134

Keyser, William, 134, 270 n18

Kibbey, Joseph H., 145, 236, 277 n5

Killingly, Connecticut, 64

King Mine, 145, 147

Kingsberry, Judge, 139

Kingsbury, Ezra, 220-222

Kingsville Academy, 265 n4

The Arizona Historical Society, 2006